The Art of M&A Financing and Refinancing

Other books by Lajoux

The Art of M&A Integration
The Art of M&A, with Stanley Foster Reed

Other books by Weston (as author or coauthor)

The Role of Mergers in the Growth of Large Firms
Public Policy Toward Mergers
Financial Theory and Corporate Policy
Mergers, Restructuring, and Corporate Control

The Art of M&A Financing and Refinancing

A Guide to Sources and Instruments for External Growth

Alexandra Reed Lajoux

J. Fred Weston

With a Foreword by Alex Sheshunoff

McGraw-Hill

New York San Francisco Washington, D.C. Auckland Bogotá
Caracas Lisbon London Madrid Mexico City Milan
Montreal New Delhi San Juan Singapore
Sydney Tokyo Toronto

Library of Congress Cataloging-in-Publication Data

Lajoux, Alexandra Reed.
    The art of M&A financing and refinancing: sources and instruments
for growth / by Alexandra Reed Lajoux and J. Fred Weston.
        p.   cm.
    ISBN 0-07-038303-0
    1. Consolidation and merger of corporations--Finance.   I. Weston,
J. Fred (John Fred), 1916- .   II. Title.   III. Title: Art of M&A
financing and refinancing.   IV. Title: Art of M and A financing and
refinancing.
    HG4028.M4L35   1999
    658.15—dc21   99-18008
                                                                        CIP

McGraw-Hill

*A Division of The **McGraw·Hill** Companies*

    2 3 4 5 6 7 8 9 0 DOC/DOC   0 3 2 1 0

ISBN 0-07-038303-0

The sponsoring editor for this book was *Kelli Christiansen,* the editing supervisor was *John M. Morriss,* and the production supervisor was *Tina Cameron.* It was set in Palatino by *Judy Brown.*

Printed and bound by R. R. Donnelley & Sons Company.

CONTENTS

PART ONE

Prerequisites 1

Chapter 1

Basic Definitions and Data 3

Introduction. Definitions of Key Terms. Basic Data. Key Instruments. Key Sources. Concluding Comments. Endnotes.

Chapter 2

Assessing Financing Needs 17

Introduction. Basic Principles. Danger Zones. Targeting the Amount of Financing Needed. Estimating the Amount of Financing Possible. Selecting the Most Appropriate Type of Financing (Debt versus Equity). Concluding Comments. Appendix 2–A: Tools. Endnotes.

Chapter 3

Regulatory, Tax, and Accounting Issues in Structuring Deal Financing 47

Introduction. General Regulatory and Tax Considerations. Choice of Entity. Distinguishing between Debt and Equity. Tax Considerations in Structuring Debt. Capital Gains versus Ordinary Income. Structuring an Installment Sale. Cost Basis versus Carryover Basis. Accounting Considerations. Concluding Comments. Endnotes.

PART TWO

A Closer Look at Instruments   91

Chapter 4

Dynamics of Debt-Based Financing   93

Introduction. Debt Fundamentals. Types of Debt. Using Notes
and Bonds to Pay for Acquisitions. Using Multiple Layers of Debt.
Sale/Leasebacks. Tax-Exempt Bonds. Junk Bond Basics. Concluding
Comments. Endnotes.

Chapter 5

Dynamics of Equity-Based Financing   125

Introduction. Equity Fundamentals. Private Equity Offerings.
Public Equity Offerings. Using Stock to Pay for a Transaction.
Beyond IPOs—Equity-Based Fund-Raising Strategies. Concluding
Comments. Endnotes.

Chapter 6

Dynamics of "Hybrid" Financing   147

Introduction. The Hybrids. Mezzanine Financing. Registration
Rights. Seller Takeback Financing. Concluding Comments.
Endnotes.

PART THREE

A Closer Look at Sources   167

Chapter 7

Working with Debt Sources   169

Introduction. Overview of Lenders. Commercial Banks. Bank
Lending. Approaching a Source of Debt Financing: The Bank Book
and Commitment Letter. Insurance Company Financing. Special
Considerations in Junk Bond Lending. Concluding Comments.
Endnotes.

Endorsements for Lajoux and Weston's *The Art of M&A Financing and Refinancing*

"Wondering how to finance or refinance your urge to merge or divest? Studying Drs. Lajoux and Weston's clear and effective Q&A treatment of this complex subject will show you how to greatly enhance the value of your future transactions."

> David I. Goldenberg, Ph.D.
> Chief Economist and Vice President, Operations
> The R.O.I. Group

"Readers of this guidance will never lament, 'If only we had known!' Authors Lajoux and Weston take a step-by-step approach to effective financial management—from making to closing the deal. Written in easy-to-access Q&A format, this valuable resource is chock full of merger/acquisition definitions, explanations, role clarifications, and global implications. The work brings clarity to the entire M&A financial process and accuracy to deal-value analysis and expectations. It should definitely be a prerequisite to M&A involvement."

> Trish W. Harris
> Manager, Marketing & Public Relations
> The Institute for Internal Auditors
> International Headquarters

"As was its predecessor in the series, the book is a comprehensive and very useful reference for a wide array of transaction finance questions. It will be a valuable addition to our firm's library and an essential guide for investment bankers, corporate development officers, and others."

> Michael Syracuse
> Managing Partner
> Hamilton Capital Partners, LLC

"This book is a dream for anyone interested in learning about acquisitions and the rigors of financing them. It is the most complete and understandable handbook written on the subject, containing a thorough descriptive analysis of all available financing options along with practical tips for approaching various lenders in order to consummate a successful acquisition. I highly recommend it!"

> Nelson E. Timken, Esq.
> J.N. Capital, Inc.
> Corporate Finance Consultants

On the Power of
Financial Ideas

Alex Sheshunoff
President
Alex Sheshunoff Management Services, Inc.
Austin, Texas

As I pondered themes for this foreword to *The Art of M&A Financing and Refinancing* by Alexandra R. Lajoux and J. Fred Weston, one phrase continually came to mind: *the power of ideas.* Bored already? Eager to get on to the facts and figures, names and places, that can help you obtain funds for your next deal? Just fasten your seat belt. Anyone who doubts the power and importance of financing *concepts,* pure and simple, should consider the modern parable of the "The Miner's Headlamp." Here's how I tell it:

THE MINER'S HEADLAMP

Every morning, as soon as he boarded the 5:30 A.M. bus from Cherry Hill, New Jersey, into New York City to report to work, the young researcher began the same routine: Strapping a miner's headlamp to his forehead, he would read a few more pages of W. Braddock Hickman's research on low-grade bonds. The junior executive, fresh out of Wharton Business School's Class of '70, saw great potential in Hickman's study, which showed that over time, lower-grade bonds can outperform higher-grade bonds. Yes, low-grade bonds had more than their share of crashing failures, but they also had many huge successes—resulting in a net gain over time to most investors. Could the young man's small investment banking firm capitalize on this paradox? As the bus rumbled through the narrow streets of Manhattan, the studious passenger dreamed of glory . . . .

The young man, of course, was Michael Milken, and the investment banking firm was Drexel Harriman Ripley, later renamed Drexel Burnham Lambert. Much ink has spilled to tell their tragic story—notably Connie Bruck's account, *The Predators' Ball* (New York: Penguin Books, 1989), which features (in her more eloquent words) the scene above. The bus ride readings, as Bruck and others have chronicled, would develop into a thriving "junk bond" empire, which Milken and company virtually ruled for the next decade and a half—before they crashed. History was harsh: Found guilty of violating various laws and rules, Drexel Burnham went bankrupt, and Milken went to jail.

This lesson may seem to be a dreary way to introduce readers to a book on M&A financing and refinancing, but for those of steely nerves it is the only way. The tale of the miner's headlamp does include some measure of tragedy, to be sure: The junk bond "era" and Milken himself remain clouded in enormous controversy. But in my view, this story is an inspiring symbol of the power of *financial ideas to create and reform economic markets.*

Whatever one thinks of the Drexel legacy, whatever one thinks of Michael Milken, the fact remains that Milken's early studies of Hickman built the foundation of what today is a thriving and valuable financial market. In the early 1970s, when Milken was taking those bus rides into the city from Jersey, there was no significant market for low-grade debt. Over time, this market has grown. Right now, the value of investment funds holding junk bond issues (both corporate and noncorporate), exceeds $100 billion. In 1980, U.S. corporations issued a total of $1.4 billion in high-yield debt. By the end of the decade, in 1989, the annual total was $25.3 billion—for a cumulative total of $153.7 billion for that decade. Junk bond growth has continued, despite a slump in the early 1990s. As of January 1, 1999, the decade's total of all corporate high-yield debt underwritings stands at $261.4 billion, with $35.5 billion underwritten in 1998 alone.

This is only a small part of the financial picture—junk bond debt is typically less than 10 percent of all corporate debt issued. Nonetheless, it has played—and continues to play—an important role in our free enterprise economy.

ON TRAPEZAI

The story of the miner's headlamp does not stand alone as evidence of the power of financial ideas. In fact, we can find such proof millennia ago, thanks to the work of historians such as Edward E. Cohen. A prominent Philadelphia banker and philanthropist, Cohen has one true passion: the history of banking. He spent over a decade trying to disprove those who said bankers of ancient Greece were mere pawnbrokers. The result is a splendid book entitled *Athenian Economy and Society: A Banking Perspective* (Princeton: Princeton University Press, 1992).

In this book, Cohen shows that the banks, or *trapezai,* of Athens in the fourth century B.C. worked through a largely invisible economy to generate "risk-laden revenues through other people's money." Far from merely ex-changing coins, these early banks developed lending and deposit taking as ac-tivities separate from commerce—and they did this in a largely "invisible" economy that extended well down the social hierarchy. Whereas the public law of the time accorded power and rights only to free males, the private econ-omy of this era enabled broader participation by including wives and slaves. This expanded entree helped Athenians of that era meet the needs of "eco-nomic reality." In doing so, says Cohen, bankers "transformed them-selves—and their society."

JOINT STOCK COMPANIES

Ancient Greece had no monopoly on financial genius. Every generation sees financial innovations—many of them transformative. Consider the first lim-ited liability corporations, called *joint stock companies,* that arose in six-teenth-century Europe. These companies, the precursors of the modern cor-poration (although not bearing that name) brought a new idea to the world of business: the concept of limited financial liability. Joint stock companies brought something new and valuable to the world of commerce *by limiting the risk of each investment to the amount invested,* and no more.

This was a distinct improvement over partnerships and regulated com-panies, the main alternatives available to entrepreneurs prior to the rise of joint stock companies. Looking back on the development of joint stock compa-nies a century after their emergence, Adam Smith recognized their historic im-portance. In his *Inquiry Into the Nature and Causes of the Wealth of Nations,* pub-lished in 1776, Smith noted that the joint stock form was ideal for industries requiring large amounts of capital, such as banking, insurance, and transpor-tation. It is no coincidence that these three sectors would grow substantially after the introduction of joint stock companies.

RISKS AND BENEFITS OF FINANCING INNOVATION

These early innovations, like the junk bond era, were baptized in failure, be-ginning with the Athenians. In the very last section of his last chapter, after a long encomium to the genius of these early Greek bankers, Ed Cohen ad-dresses the crucial and unavoidable subject of bank failures. Insolvencies, says Cohen, were "pervasive" in this golden age, which featured several "spectacular" failures. For example, the treasurers of Athens, who oversaw money that was donated to a temple devoted to the goddess Athena, had di-verted some of this money to *trapezai* in the hopes that it could grow through investment. They planned to replace the principal amount later and pocket the difference. The scheme was discovered, though, so to hide the evidence, someone torched the buildings. The treasurers went to prison.

The limited risk of joint stock companies also led to many early abuses, which Adam Smith chronicles in *Wealth of Nations*. The most famous of these is the South Sea Company. This early joint stock company quickly amassed huge amounts of capital—"thirty-three millions, eight hundred thousand pounds," recorded Smith faithfully in the style of his day—yet it wound up, through "folly, negligence, and profusion" at the end of its life with a net loss amounting to "upwards of two hundred and thirty-seven thousand pounds." (Mind you, these are in *eighteenth-century dollars*.) Accounting for inflation over the past two centuries, the sums are staggering.

Considering the burning temple of Athens and the sunk fortunes of the South Sea Company, combined with the ignoble end of Drexel Burnham, still so fresh in memory, it is clear that new ideas in financing are not without their downside.

Sometimes good financial concepts can go wrong when misapplied—capitalism, for one. This was the premise of global investor George Soros's book *The Crisis of Global Capitalism* (New York: Harper Collins, 1998) and his iconoclastic essay "The Capitalist Threat," published in the February 1997 issue of *Atlantic Monthly*. Even the corporate form can lead to unintentional destruction, as noted by shareholder activist Robert A. G. Monks in a thoughtful book entitled *The Emperor's Nightingale: Restoring the Integrity of the Corporation* (Oxford: Capstone, 1998).

In my view, however, the benefits of financial innovation outweigh the risks.

SUSTAINED APPLICATION

All financial innovations, including the three briefly mentioned here, are prone to difficult beginnings. They start out boldly as a creative person runs with an idea and charms others into coming along. But then, inevitably, the hero or heroine meets disaster. There's an old expression that says you can always tell an entrepreneur—"He's the one with an arrow in his back." (The same fate, of course, befalls female entrepreneurs!) Without these pioneers, however, ideas would remain locked up in books—like the obscure tome Milken clutched on his early bus rides. That's not where ideas belong.

Nor do ideas belong only with the bold. At some point in the life of every idea, the community must support the idea and enable it to become a part of daily life. This has happened to banking, which has become and will always remain a treasure of the public trust. Corporations, too, have become a necessary aspect of free economies everywhere. And high-risk finance has become indispensable to the growth of economies, and will become ever more so. Finally, all these legacies in financing have echoed in the realm of *re*financing, where they find applications "downstream."

A BETTER WORLD

Without such innovations in financing, we would surely be in a state of brutish nature. Ideas of democracy, human dignity, and expanding opportunity are combined inexorably with ideas of the free flow of capital, safeguarded by communities.

Without the lender there to mediate between public rules and private realities, ancient Greece might never have generated its ideas of democracy for future generations around the globe.

Without the joint stock companies of seventeenth-century Europe, the colonization of the New World would have occurred much more slowly and with different—and perhaps less desirable—results. Perhaps even more dramatically, early corporations freed society from the limitations of its social hierarchy. Early corporations, by creating liquid wealth beyond mere paper and metal money, freed society from the confines of primogeniture, which decreed that only one heir—the oldest son if possible—would inherit all a family's wealth. It is hard to split up a farm, but one can parcel out stock. The rise of the corporation and the new freedom from tangible assets increased opportunities for the deal maker—arising often from classes of society with little more than intelligence and drive to their names.

Finally, junk bonds have helped great numbers of companies obtain the financing and refinancing they have needed for growth. Compaq Computers, Harley Davidson, and MCI have all benefited from junk bond financing at crucial points in their journey toward stable growth. Moreover, the influence of junk bond financing continues. Along with other innovations in M&A financing, it has helped accelerate a *financial services revolution* of tremendous importance.

THE FINANCIAL SERVICES REVOLUTION

I would like to conclude this panegyric on financial ideas by talking a little about the famed "financial services revolution." What exactly is it? Many have used this phrase in many different ways, but in my own view there are two sides to the coin: the destruction of old distinctions based on turf, and the rise of new distinctions based on a quest for financial services excellence. For those who cherish a particular turf, geographic or otherwise, the destructive force of this revolution has caused no little anguish. But no one can doubt the benefits of what has come in its wake.

Consider the relatively new ability of bank holding companies to own securities brokerage operations. Established securities firms resisted this change, but today it is widely agreed that this type of "one-stop shopping," discussed in Part Four of this book, provides a valuable service for customers. Conversely, consider the new ability of nondepository institutions (such as commercial finance companies) to offer traditional bank services, such as loans. Clearly, the financial services revolution has changed our financial world forever.

I do not make this statement lightly. Nearly three decades ago, I cast my lot with commercial banks and have remained committed to this sector ever since. Since the early 1970s, I have devoted a substantial part of my professional time and energy to improving bank financial performance, to refining methods for bank valuations, and to advising banks involved in mergers. In my opinion, nothing else in finance compares with an institution that safekeeps deposits. Such an institution has real financial capital—not merely relationships (although these are important too).

COMPLEX ECONOMY

Yet today, undeniably, the commercial banking sector exists within a much more complex economic world. Twenty years ago, my efforts were concentrated solely in the banking sector, and for good reason—it dominated the field. As Lajoux and Weston point out in this book, in 1950 commercial banks held over half (52 percent) of all intermediary assets. Accompanied only by life insurance companies and savings and loan companies, which also had a sizable shares of the market (22 percent and 14 percent accordingly), commercial banks stood almost alone as major holders of the nation's funds. Other types of financial institutions controlled 4 percent each or less.

Today, as the authors rightly point out, the wealth of financial intermediaries is far more evenly distributed, thanks in part to deregulation.

Banks still maintain an impressive lead as holders of over one quarter (26 percent) of all financial assets in the $18 trillion intermediary market—far more than any other type of institution. Other big holders include, in descending order of magnitude, private pension funds (17 percent), mutual funds (13 percent), life insurance companies (12 percent), and public pension funds (10 percent). Other intermediaries include savings institutions (6 percent), finance companies (5 percent), non-life insurance companies (5 percent), money market funds (5 percent), and credit unions (2 percent), as the authors note.

Facilitating the creation and movement of this wealth has been another type of financial institution, the investment bank, which acts as a vital link between savings (in effect, commercial bank deposits) and investment.

M&A: A KEY DRIVER

In all this, one of the key drivers of the financial services revolution has been the phenomenal growth of M&A as a strategic activity, thanks in part to the work of financial intermediaries—including commercial and investment banks and securities brokerage firms.

Worldwide, according to Securities Data Publishing, the total number of completed deals (worth $5 million and up) in 1998 was 16,919—an all-time high. Most of these were deals involving U.S. companies (domestic, inbound, or outbound) for a total of 9,140—a historic level. The other deals outside the United States totaled 7,770—again the highest ever recorded. And so far, based on the hundreds of transactions completed and pending as we go to press, it looks as though 1999 is yet another blockbuster year in M&A.

- Narrowing our focus to *financial services,* what do we see? In 1998, there were 1,346 deals involving U.S. companies, worth $442.2 billion, making this the highest-ranking area by both number of deals and dollar volume. Commercial banks were particularly active, with 255 deals worth $285 billion. Of the top 10 deals of 1998, six involved banks. The largest merger of 1998 was the union of two diversified financial services companies—one from the insurance field, the other from the banking sector.

CITIGROUP AS SYMBOL

In 1998, Travelers combined with Citibank for over $72.6 billion—at that time, the biggest merger of all times. (It has recently been superseded by the pending $76 billion merger of Mobil and Exxon.) The new institution has almost $700 billion in assets and more than 3,200 offices in 100 countries. It couples Citicorp's strong consumer and commercial banking franchise with Travelers' insurance operations and the investment banking/asset management operations of Travelers' unit Salomon Smith Barney. Smith Barney has been a dominant player in obtaining M&A financing. In 1998 it earned $225.5 million in fees, making it the fourth most active investment bank in M&A financing. Citicorp, which had been the second largest bank in the United States behind Chase Manhattan Corp. with $311 billion in assets, is a leader in consumer and corporate banking. It ranks as the world's largest issuer of credit cards, with approximately 60 million cards.

Let us pause to reflect on this development: the merger of financial services companies formerly in *five separate areas* of the financial world—commercial banking, credit cards, insurance, investment banking, and stock brokerage. If Citigroup succeeds in managing and (to some extent) integrating this portfolio of services, it will come to exemplify the best of the financial services revolution—a revolution that can be traced to myriad financial innovations before its time, and that will succeed thanks to many innovations—and applications—to come.

CHANGING THE WORLD

Without a doubt, there is power in ideas. But there are two more stages that must occur after an idea is conceived. First, there must be a period of testing—as bold entrepreneurs run through the streets, yes, suffering the slings and arrows of outrageous fortune, but persisting nonetheless. Then there must be a period of sustained application, ideally in a community or public setting. Some fortunate entrepreneurs can find their rewards in this important, and lasting, phase.

As companies live through this ongoing financial services revolution, they must be daring, yet cautious. The fact is that no company can rely on a single source of capital any more. Every company needs to develop strong ties with the Main Street of commercial banking as well as the Wall Street of investment banking, and everything in between. Before capital markets slowed down in the fall of 1998, everyone was talking about the shift in U.S. borrowing from credit markets to capital markets. Commercial loans were out; commercial paper was in. In my view, companies must be prepared to use both venues—and others—as they finance and refinance to suit their changing needs. Even if a company finances with one source, it might refinance with another, different source. For example, a firm might do an initial public offering (IPO), but then need a loan to support the newly public company.

Truly, M&A financing and refinancing can be a path to progress—starting today, as you read the ideas in this book and dream up your own. You can trust the authors to guide you well. Lajoux has spent 20 years as a successful editor and writer of practical books and articles for business managers. Weston, an unparalleled authority in the field of finance, has never seen an idea he could not express simply or apply realistically. Together they have created a book that is worth your study. So strap on that headlamp and get ready for the ride! May it be long and prosperous.

Business? It's quite simple. It's other people's money.

Alexandre Dumas the Younger, *La Question d'Argent,* 1857

In early 1999, as we go to press with *The Art of M&A Financing and Refinancing,* two topics rivet the business world: *mergers and money.* Mergers are the talk of towns and cities as megamergers punctuate a steady stream of smaller transactions, provoking new questions about the proper scope and scale of enterprises and the nature of competition. Meanwhile, money is a hot topic getting hotter, as upheavals in global currency markets, volatility in equity markets, and a recent dramatic cut in U.S. interest rates have combined to perch the commercial world on the edge of its collective trading seat, wondering what will happen next.

Each of these topics has grown so great in importance and so complex in substance that no single book can comfortably contain both of them. We know, because each of us has experienced the growth of a book devoted to one of these topics. Alexandra Lajoux is the coauthor (with Stanley Foster Reed) of *The Art of M&A: A Merger/Acquisition/Buyout Guide,* now a 1,000-page book in its third edition (1999), with a spin-off volume by Lajoux on postmerger integration. J. Fred Weston is the coauthor (with Thomas Copeland) of *Managerial Finance,* a 1,200-page, two-volume tome now heading toward its tenth edition (1999) and supported by Weston's additional books and articles on the topic.

To present a book on M&A financing and refinancing—in essence a book about *both* mergers and money—we obviously need to exercise restraint. Rather than exploring both of these topics in depth, we have opted here for a narrower approach—focusing on the vital *intersection* of these two economic phenomena. The *only* aspect of mergers treated here in depth is the financial aspect, and conversely, the *only* aspect of managerial finance treated here in depth is the merger area. This narrow focus—combined with the question-and-answer format that has become a hallmark of the McGraw-Hill "Art of M&A" book series—can benefit busy deal managers in need of quick, concise guidance in this complex area.

As managers or owners of a business, or as advisers to a business, we must first pose questions of a broad strategic nature: Should the firm move forward in a particular direction, and if so, should this be through acquisition? If the choice is acquisition, pricing will be an important concern: Can the company get the deal at the best possible price, and can it afford to pay this price? Each of these subjects merits a separate book, and many such books have been written.

Our concern in this book lies elsewhere, in an often neglected area of deal *financing:* Can the company pay for the deal out of its own funds, or should it seek outside funding? And if it seeks outside funding, should this be in the form of debt, equity, or some combination of the two? How can a company approach different kinds of sources? In a transaction involving multiple instruments, how can the company plan ahead to ensure the best positive impact on the company's future operations? In a transaction involving multiple sources, how can the company and its creditors ensure that their competing interests are served? What impact will the particular financial instruments used in the deal have on the company's operations? How can the company ensure effective ongoing relationships with the sources of the financing? When and how must a company go "back to the well" via refinancing? And how does all this work in transnational deals? These are the broad concerns treated in this book.

These are important matters. If business means using "other people's money," it also means giving those people something back for that money, and making something extra for ourselves in the process. This is the true art of M&A financing and refinancing—an art that can be mastered only by asking and answering many questions. The questions framed within this book are only the beginning. The truly important questions are the ones that lie beyond, in *your* dynamic world of deal making. Go to it!

Alexandra R. Lajoux
J. Fred Weston
April 1999

ACKNOWLEDGMENTS

Creating a good book requires teamwork. Like M&A financing itself, nothing of quality can happen without outside help. This book would not be possible without collaboration—not only between the two authors, but also between the authors and the many talented individuals who helped shape and inform this work.

The authors gratefully acknowledge the keen editorial insights of McGraw-Hill editor Kelli Christiansen and the entire McGraw-Hill team, including copy editor Louise Marinis, typesetter Judy Brown, proofreader Robert Saigh, indexer Kay Schlembach, and last but never least the incomparable John Morriss, editorial supervisor. As always, many thanks to publisher Jeffrey Krames for supporting the "Art of M&A" series.

Alexandra Lajoux is especially grateful to Mary Graham and Braulio Agnese for their highly competent work in support of this endeavor. Fred Weston wishes to thank Marilyn McElroy, Brian Johnson, and Juan A. Siu for their invaluable support. Both authors are indebted to the financing practitioners and scholars they consulted for this book, duly credited in the appropriate places.

PART ONE

Prerequisites

Financing is one of the most important functions of any company. The sources of funds a company finds, the way it invests those funds, and the way it delivers returns to shareholders all give a company vitality and ensure its longevity.

Vision gives a company its eyes, and entrepreneurship its heart, but cash is what gives any company the force of life. As managers obtain, spend, and return money again and again over time, they create a kind of lifeblood for the company.

M&A financing plays an important part in this vital process. By raising funds and investing them in new business ventures through mergers, acquisitions, and buyouts, companies can revive failing enterprises and ensure the continued success of dynamic ones.

So what exactly is M&A financing? What types and sources of financing are there? Chapter 1 guides readers in these basics. Chapter 2 offers guidance on how to assess financing needs and approach financing sources. Chapter 3 wraps up this introductory section with some heavily technical—but arguably necessary—information about the tax and accounting aspects of financing a merger, acquisition, or buyout.

Basic Definitions and Data

Someone's got to . . . set the door in its frame.

Wislawa Szymborska, "The End and The Beginning," 1993

INTRODUCTION

The worlds of mergers and money intersect in the topics of *M&A financing* and *refinancing*. In this opening chapter, we define these key financing terms, introduce readers to key financing sources (including lenders, underwriters, and backers), and define some of the key instruments of financing. In the closing section, we discuss current financing trends and identify some general strategic issues.

DEFINITIONS OF KEY TERMS

What is financing?

Most broadly, financing is money—obtained from any source, and used for any purpose. A business gets financing from either internal or external sources. Internal financing is money generated by the sale of goods and/or services, sometimes with additional funds generated by loaning or investing that money elsewhere. Today, over two thirds of all the money used by U.S. companies is internally generated in this sense. The other source of financing—and the focus of this book—is external. This is money obtained from outside sources with the understanding that the money will be repaid under agreed-upon conditions. Table 1–1 summarizes both sources.

Internal financing generally has advantages over external financing. It imposes less of a tax burden, and requires less monitoring by financing sources.

TABLE 1-1

Sources of Funds for Business Corporations, 1950–1997 (Billions of Dollars)

Year	Total	Internal		External Securities and Mortgage		Loans and Short-Term Paper		Other*	
		Amount	Percent	Amount	Percent	Amount	Percent	Amount	Percent
1950	42	18	42	4	10	4	10	16	38
1960	48	36	75	8	16	4	8	1	2
1970	102	62	60	26	26	8	8	4	4
1980	324	200	62	30	10	40	12	54	16
1985	458	352	76	–3	0	54	12	54	12
1989	512	380	74	–45	–10	80	16	98	20
1997	1,015	695	68	87	9	94	9	139	14

*Consists of tax liabilities, trade debt, and direct foreign investment in the United States.

Source: President's Council of Economic Advisers, *Economic Report of the President* (Washington, D.C.: Government Printing Office, 1991); *Economic Indicators*, February 1998.

Percentages are rounded to the nearest integer, so not all rows add up to 100.

Yet external financing does play an important role—especially when investment requirements are high in relation to profitability levels.

One type of external financing is the loan—an agreement in which an individual or entity obtains money from another individual or entity with an understanding that the money, called *principal*, will be repaid within a certain time period, along with perhaps an additional amount, called *interest*, that compensates the provider of the money for the temporary loss of the money, and for the risk that it may not be repaid. This type of financing is referred to as *debt*. Nearly 10 percent of the money coming into companies today is generated by debt.

Another type of financing is the stock sale—the sale of a portion or share of a business in return for certain rights to the holder of the sale. These rights are usually expressed in a shareholder agreement and protected by law. This type of financing is referred to as *equity*. Nearly 10 percent of the funds used by business corporations comes from this source.

Finally, some financing is *hybrid* in nature, combining some debt elements and some equity elements. One of the challenges in U.S. tax law, which treats debt and equity differently, is to determine the exact nature of an instrument to see whether it is debt or equity. One type of hybrid financing is *mezzanine* debt, also called *second-tier* debt. Mezzanine debt is unsecured subordinated debt, where the lender also receives some rights to acquire equity.[1] It provides an additional layer of (debt-based) financing between a company's equity and its senior debt (which, as we will discuss in later chapters, is debt that gets paid back first). Although mezzanine financing is relatively rare, it is used in all kinds of highly leveraged transactions (or HLTs, another subject we will discuss in later chapters).

Most financing, of course, is more complex than the examples given here. The participants in the financing may be multiple entities, not just one. Furthermore, organizations may use several types of financing. Nonetheless, it is always useful to bear in mind the fundamental natures of debt versus equity when seeking to finance or refinance a venture. As we shall see throughout this book, these two sources have very different dynamics and consequences in the growth of any enterprise.

What are "M&A financing" and "M&A refinancing"?

M&A financing is money obtained by one company to buy or join another in a merger, acquisition, or buyout.[2] M&A refinancing, generally speaking, is a change in one or more terms of an agreement signed to finance such a transaction. (In the case of bonds or preferred stock, refinancing has a special meaning—namely, the effective "call" of the issuance, thus effectively ending the agreement.)

BASIC DATA

How much money is involved in M&A in comparison with other economic activities?

Every year in the United States, hundreds of billions of dollars are exchanged as a result of acquisitions. In 1998, the amount was a record-breaking $1.3 trillion, according to Securities Data Publishing in Newark, New Jersey, the publisher of *Mergers & Acquisitions Journal* and other M&A sources.[3] About 77 percent of this money financed deals between U.S. companies, 9 percent financed outbound deals (U.S. acquisitions of non-U.S. firms), and 15 percent financed inbound deals (non-U.S. acquisitions of U.S. firms). (U.S. transborder deals have been increasing steadily over the past 15 years, despite fluctuating exchange rates.)

The trillion-plus volume of M&A activity, in terms of sheer size, rivals the very wealth base of the corporate economy. Although it is dwarfed by our gross national product, which is greater than $8 trillion, it is in fact about the same size as our true corporate wealth base: Corporate profits for 1997, with inventory valuation and capital consumption adjustments, were $817.9 billion, according to the *Economic Report of the President, 1999* (Table B90, p. 431).

How much new money do U.S. banks loan annually to finance M&A activities?

We can get a good idea of new lending for M&A from Securities Data Publishing, which collects regular statistics on all syndicated loans made by U.S. banks.[4] Syndicated loans, as explained more fully in Chapter 4, are loans made by groups of commercial banks. Of the $1.1 trillion in 1997 loans, $172.4 billion financed acquisitions (277 packages in all), $13.1 billion financed leveraged buyouts (49 packages), $859 million was offered in bridging loans (9 packages), and $384 million supported management buyouts (4 packages). This adds up to $186.7 billion in loans devoted to some type of M&A in 1997.[5]

What does this mean in terms of M&A leverage: What percentage of a typical cash deal is borrowed, on average?

To estimate M&A leverage, let's compare the $186.7 billion figure for U.S. syndicated loans in 1997 with U.S. M&A activity for 1997, which totaled $791.3 billion worth of M&A deals. Furthermore, let's look at mode of payment. Of these transactions, 51 percent were financed with cash, over 32 percent with stock, and under 17 percent with a combination of stock and cash. Assuming that the combination deals were divided fairly equally between stock and cash, this means 59 percent of deal dollars came from cash and about 41 percent were generated from equity. In dollar terms for that year, that gives us $466.9 billion in U.S. deals financed entirely or partly by cash,[6] and $324.4 billion in U.S. deals financed entirely or partly by stock, with some overlap.[7]

Comparing the amount of syndicated loans devoted to M&A ($186.7 billion) with the amount of deals done wholly or partly in cash ($466.9 billion), it seems reasonable to suggest that 40 percent of the cash funding used by companies in 1997 may have been borrowed—more or less.[8] We say more or less because some M&A loan funding comes from individual banks, rather than syndicates (which would suggest a higher percentage), and some of the syndicated lending by banks is for deals that do not involve U.S. companies (which would suggest a lower percentage). Individual banks are more likely than syndicates to fund smaller deals—that is, deals where the purchase price suggests that the selling company is small.

We should also note that in 1997, as in most years, smaller transactions were more likely to be funded in cash, and larger transactions in equity. In 1997, 54 percent of transactions involving companies worth between $5 million and $10 million were funded in cash, 29 percent in stock, and 17 percent in a combination. By contrast, 45 percent of transactions valued at $100 million or more were funded in cash, 35 percent in stock, and under 20 percent in a combination.

How are acquirers paying for companies currently?

There seems to be overall a higher bias toward cash, with smaller companies leading the trend as usual. In 1998, 54 percent of *all* transactions were paid for in cash, 34 percent in stock, and 12 percent in both—a more cash-heavy mix than the 1997 totals cited earlier. As in past years, smaller deals were most likely to be funded at least partly in cash, and larger deals were most likely to be funded at least partly in stock. Of transactions valued between $5 million and $10 million, 58 percent were paid in cash, 27 percent in stock, and 17 percent in a combination of cash and stock. By contrast, of transactions valued at $100 million or more, 48 percent were paid for in cash, 42 percent in stock, and under 10 percent in a combination of the two. Coauthor Weston's ongoing research on transactions involving companies valued at $1 billion and up shows that over 90 percent of these deals are financed entirely in stock.

What percentage of M&A deals involve small companies?

The majority. In fact, although the average size of a transaction in 1997 was $213.5 million, the median size was $36 million. This means that half of the transactions were valued at under $36 million, and half at over $36 million. In 1998, the average shot up to $325.5 million, but the median remained low—$40.7 million.

How much money is loaned annually to help companies refinance existing acquisition debt?

It is hard to track refinancing numbers in general, but we do know from Securities Data Publishing that U.S. banks in 1997 loaned $107.4 billion through syndicates to help companies refinance existing debt (including no doubt some debt that was incurred indirectly as a result of acquisitions). In addition, U.S. banks loaned $1.6 billion through syndicates for the sole purpose of helping four companies refinance debt that was incurred directly from acquisitions.

KEY INSTRUMENTS

What are the main types of debt financing?

Debt financing covers a wide range. The borrower or issuer of debt can choose from among term loans, revolving credits, private and public debt offerings, sale/leaseback notes, bankers acceptances, commercial paper, and various types of bonds. Bonds may be sold via underwriters to institutional investors such as insurance companies, pension funds, and mutual funds. Most bonds receive a rating from bond rating agencies—from Triple A (AAA) to Triple B (BBB) or below. In large debt markets, including international debt markets, there are loan syndicates. We explore these instruments more fully in Chapter 4. In 1998, U.S. corporations issued $1.7 trillion in debt, according to Securities Data Publishing. Current outstanding corporate debt in the U.S. is $3.6 trillion, according to the Federal Reserve.

What are the main types of equity financing?

Equity financing includes private and public stock offerings of preferred or common stock. The issuance of stock opens up other opportunities for equity-based financing. Stock may be repurchased (called a *buyback*), spun off into a separate company (called a *spin-off*), or sold to employees through employee stock ownership plans (ESOPs). In 1998, reports Securities Data, U.S. corporations issued $152.4 billion in equity, including initial public offerings (IPOs). We discuss these instruments in Chapter 5.

What about hybrid financing?

Hybrid instruments include *convertibles, exchangeables, preferred stock*, and *warrants*. Convertible debt issues currently make up about 4 percent of all debt issues. Preferred stock makes up about one quarter of all stock issues. We cover hybrid instruments in Chapter 6.

What are the basic characteristics of equity versus debt?

One of the fundamental aspects of financing—and the tax codes of many countries—is the distinction between debt and equity.

Pure debt is an unconditional obligation to repay principal and interest, has a fixed maturity date, and is not convertible to or attached to any other instrument. Neither the principal nor the interest owed by the debt instrument is contingent on profits or other factors. In short, it is a financial instrument without any equity features.

Pure equity, by contrast, is ownership of shares in a corporation. Its value is realized through exchange (by buying low and selling high). In a liquidation situation, equity is what is left of a company after all debts (liabilities) have been paid. In this sense, it represents a claim on assets. This is expressed in the balance sheet, where assets equal liabilities plus equity (hence equity equals assets minus liabilities). In short, pure equity is a financial instrument without any debt features.

KEY SOURCES

What are the key sources for M&A financing and refinancing?

One key source is operating companies themselves, which may fund their own transactions (using existing cash or selling assets to generate it)[9] or may fund the transactions of others through financing subsidiaries, such as General Electric's GE Capital. Another key source is vendors, which often provide liberal credit terms in exchange for a share in profits or ownership. These sources are obviously close at hand—somewhat like finding gold buried in your own back yard. Truly external financing can be obtained from the following basic list of 10 types of firms.[10]

- Asset-based lenders (such as factors, which loan against or buy accounts receivable, and leasing companies, which can buy and lease back equipment)
- Commercial banks (depository institutions)
- Commercial finance companies (nonbank banks for businesses)
- Insurance companies (via their investment divisions)
- Investment banks (via their investment divisions—sometimes combined with a stock brokerage firm)
- Investment companies or funds (which back buyouts)
- Merchant banks (which arrange financing)
- Private buyout investment firms (which back buyouts)
- Small business investment corporations (SBICs) formed under the auspices of the Small Business Administration (SBA) in the United States (or other government-sponsored lending programs)
- Venture capital firms (which back growth in general)

These sources are discussed more thoroughly in Chapters 7 through 9.

How common is each type of financing?

It depends on the size of the firm and its growth stage.

Newly formed companies have little or no internal financing, yet they are not large enough to attract most of these types of lenders or backers. Such companies use personal credit or savings, loans from individuals, trade credit, and government agencies (such as SBICs). In any event, unless a new company has been formed for the specific purpose of being a pass-through entity to use in a merger or acquisition (see Chapter 3), it is unlikely to be seeking financing to buy another company.

High-growth companies tend to use a combination of internal financing and trade credit, commercial bank loans, and venture capital investments. Because of their accumulating assets, they may be candidates for asset-based lenders and commercial finance companies as well. Here, too, M&A financing is relatively rare.

Maturing companies may use any of the above; in addition, they use the equity markets (hence, investment and merchant banks) along with money markets and capital markets generally (see Chapter 13). If they are growing via acquisitions, they will derive debt capital from commercial banks and insurance companies, and equity capital from investment banks and merchant banks.

Mature companies also may use any of the above, but they are most likely to use a combination of internal financing, their own shares, and loans from syndicates that include both banks (commercial, investment, and merchant) and insurance companies.

Looking at all small firms, what would a typical breakdown of financing sources be?

In a 1997 survey, the Arthur Andersen Enterprise Group and National Small Business United (AA/NSBU) asked small firms to name all their financing sources. Here is what they said, in order of frequency. (Numbers add up to more than 100 because many respondents used more than one source.)

- Commercial bank, nonmortgage-based: 38 percent
- Commercial finance/credit card company: 34 percent
- Asset-based lenders: 24 percent (asset-based collateral: 4 percent; leasing: 16 percent accounts; receivable: 4 percent)
- Vendor credit: 20 percent
- Private business loans: 16 percent
- Personal or home equity loans: 16 percent
- Private buyout investment firm/private placement of stock: 4 percent
- SBICs or other Small Business Administration-guaranteed financing sources: 4 percent
- Venture capital firm: 2 percent
- Investment banks/brokerage firms (for initial public offerings): 1 percent[11]

Nearly one third (30 percent) used no external financing.

Roughly what percentage of all this external financing (from the various sources put together) goes to finance acquisitions?

Only about 3 percent (again, relying on the AA/NSBU 1997 survey).

Can a company obtain financing online?

Yes. Scores of financing brokers are now online, either under their own name or as part of broader M&A networks. Here is a partial list of M&A networks (which you can access by typing www. before each listing):[12]

- bizbuysell.com (general M&A site aimed at business brokerage)
- bizlist.com (links to firms that offer services to companies wishing to sell; also has list of "professional corporate buyers")
- cbex.com (info exchange on middle market M&A opportunities and financing, including bulletin board)
- firstlist.com (national listing of acquisition, merger, financing, joint venture, and licensing opportunities)
- hazlewoods.co.uk/malinks.html (links to other M&A networks worldwide)
- madaily.com (reports on merger and acquisition activity)
- maol.com (free database used to post companies for sale)
- masource.org (directory of members of the International Business Brokers Association representing M&A intermediaries for the middle market and indexed by state and region)
- mergercentral.com (an M&A research resource under construction)
- mergernetwork.com (discussion groups and M&A classifieds including buyers, sellers, and advisers)
- mergers.net (annotated directory of international firms specializing in M&A, organized by country)
- onelist.com (has subscription bulletin board called "cgi/consolidations" for technical M&A discussions; free buy/sell listings for companies over $1 million in revenues)
- nvst.com (links to professionals, publications, and associations such as the Association for Corporate Growth and the International Mergers and Acquisitions Professionals).
- worldm-anetwork.com (M&A classified, including buyers and sellers, organized by industry)

Some sites specialize in industries. For example:

- fourleaf.com (acquisitions, alliances, and investments in Internet-related businesses)

Other sites specialize in countries or regions. For example:

- innostar.com (for deals and financing in China)
- niemi.no (for deals and financing in the Netherlands, Norway, and the United Kingdom—particularly in energy)

Also, some links focus exclusively on financing. For example:

- bbean.com (financing bulletin board, typically featuring detailed requests for real estate funding)
- datamerge.com (worldwide funding sources of debt and equity capital)
- snlnet.com (information on and links to the financial services industry)

The financing sources data bank at DataMerge (datamerge.com) is particularly ambitious. It profiles over 10,000 alternative financing sources for such diverse ventures as commercial real estate construction and acquisition, small business loans, factoring and accounts receivable financing, initial public offerings, private placements, venture capital, equipment leasing, and, last but not least, mergers and acquisitions.

Approximately 21,000 business owners, consultants, and commercial real estate professionals use the DataMerge data bank (as of early 1999) to locate funding for projects that do not qualify for traditional bank financing. According to DataMerge's founder, Spencer Kluesner, companies that borrow through this Internet site include high-risk or out-of-the-ordinary ventures and companies lacking collateral or credit. Many also use the program to find lenders that can provide the most favorable financing terms. The DataMerge search software pinpoints a company's "most likely" funding sources, often locating sources of capital previously unknown to the user because they are located outside a particular city or state.[13]

CONCLUDING COMMENTS

Clearly, the field of M&A financing and refinancing abounds with opportunity. The growth of M&A activity, combined with the increasing competition of vendors for M&A financing customers, makes it both a financing "seller's" and a financing "buyer's" market, with high-quality participants on both sides. The growth of Internet-based sources for M&A financing offers new risks and opportunities. The bottom line: Business is still very much a matter of "other people's money"—and today there is more of it than ever. So let's now find out how to obtain and repay this money, starting with the questions covered in our next chapter: How much financing is needed? What kind of financing is appropriate?

ENDNOTES

1. This definition of mezzanine financing is based in part on a discussion by Douglas L. Batey, an attorney with the law firm of Stoel Rives, in "Hidden Costs and Benefits of Mezzanine Level Financing." An Internet posting of Mr. Batey's discussion states that the discussion is copyrighted by the NorthWest Venture Group (e-mail: acquisitions_northwest@convene.com).

2. It may also be applied to joint ventures, but throughout this book, we have focused only on mergers, acquisitions, and buyouts, so we will keep this definition narrow.

3. In 1999, the trend continues. In January alone, 15 M&A pairs announced transactions worth over $1 billion each—notably the $76 billion Exxon-Mobile deal—according to the March/April 1999 "Almanac" issue of *Mergers & Acquisitions*. For more information about the "Almanac" issue, contact Barbara Martin, Securities Data Publishing, 1290 Avenue of the Americas, 36th Floor, New York, New York 10104.

4. 1998 was an even bigger year for M&A financing. Of the over $806 billion loaned in the first 11 months of 1998, approximately one quarter, or $195 billion, was devoted to acquisition financing worldwide for 301 transactions—or an average of $648 million per transaction. Clearly, these loans tend to involve large transactions and include lending beyond purchase price. In addition, U.S. banks in the first 11 months of 1998 loaned out $8.8 billion for 16 bridge loans (an average of $548 per loan package), $7.2 billion for 23 leveraged buyouts (an average of $315 million per package), and $45 million for one management buyout (a relatively small package).

5. Also, another $39.6 billion in 1997 loan dollars financed "future" acquisitions (156 packages).

6. Cash, we should note, can be from companies' treasuries (which in larger companies runs in the billions), may be borrowed, or promised. Factoring in promises, the cash figure may be lower, since in some deals "cash" may be in the form of notes—whether straight debt or a promise to pay on contingency of good performance.

7. Note also that smaller companies are more likely to pay with cash, and larger companies are more likely to pay with stock. Furthermore, larger companies are more likely to disclose their means of payment. Therefore, cash-funded M&A was probably higher than 59 percent in 1997—or in any given year.

8. Another way to estimate M&A leverage is to rely on our knowledge that historically about 9 percent of all cash coming into a company is borrowed and assume that this is true of deals as well as companies. That calculation, however, would give us a figure of only $42 billion in borrowed funds for M&A in 1997 (9 percent of the $466.9 billion in cash-based deals)—a number that is clearly too low to square with the syndicated loan figures.

9. A good example is Imperial Chemical, which raised most of the $8 billion it used to buy Unilever's specialty chemicals unit in 1997 by selling all or part of several subsidiaries. Source: "Imperial to Buy a Uniliver Specialty Chemical Unit for $8 Billion," *The New York Times,* May 8, 1997, p. D5.

10. This list is based on the categories used by Securities Data Publishing in its annual *Directory of Buyout Financing Sources* (New York, 1999). Subcategories and hybrids of these 10 basic types include: asset-based lending company, nonbank commercial lender, conduit for receivables securitization, debt/equity sourcing company, equipment leasing and finance company, intermediary for private investors, employee stock ownership plan (ESOP) financing, investment manager, investment/money management firm, intermediary, M&A intermediary, manager of corporate development programs, manager of third-party minority stakes, mezzanine firm, LBO/equity fund (same as private buyout), mezzanine investor, seed money investor, turnaround specialist, and venture leasing firm.

11. The survey did not specify the exact source of help for IPOs, but we can assume that the underwriting was done by these traditional sources.

12. This list was originally compiled by Alexandra Lajoux for publication in *The Art of M&A: A Merger/Acquisition/Buyout Guide,* 3rd ed. (New York: McGraw-Hill, 1999), pp. 37ff, a book coauthored by Lajoux with Stanley Foster Reed. It has been expanded for this discussion. Although these sites (which Lajoux and/or Weston have accessed) appear to be useful and accurate, their mention here does not constitute endorsement.

13. This is based on information provided by DataMerge on its Web site: datamerge.com. The program appears to be useful, but our description of it does not constitute an endorsement, since we have no direct experience with DataMerge or its Web site.

C H A P T E R   2

Assessing Financing Needs

When the well's dry, we know the worth of water.

Benjamin Franklin, *Poor Richard's Almanac,* January 1746

INTRODUCTION

Just as the decision to grow through merger or acquisition requires considerable planning, so, too, does the decision to finance an M&A transaction. If the transaction is in cash, and the funds for the transaction are borrowed, will the borrower be able to pay the funds back? If the transaction is financed through stock, what impact will this have on shareholders before and after the transaction? These and other important financial questions face managers and financiers alike as they approach any M&A deal.

In this chapter, we will begin by discussing some basic principles of finance, including rate of return, present value, and future value as well as debt and equity "danger zones." These basic concepts will prove useful as we explore how to target the amount of financing needed, how to estimate the amount of financing possible, and how to select the most appropriate type of financing (debt, equity, or hybrid).

BASIC PRINCIPLES

How can I interest another company in financing a proposed M&A transaction?

As the promoter of a transaction (whether as a principal of the deal or an adviser to it), you should have a good idea of what the combined revenues, net income, and market share of the two companies will be, as well as their prospects for growth in all these areas. Be wary, though, of getting carried away with isolated numbers. They all need to be converted into a dynamic formula: the return that lenders or equity investors can expect to get from your proposed transaction.

How do lenders or equity investors determine the rate of return they want?

Providers of capital have different needs and expectations. Those who provide debt capital as lenders have a relatively low tolerance for risk and generally low expectations of returns. Those who provide equity capital as investors look for higher returns and have a higher tolerance for risk. The language common to both groups is the language of discounted cash flow. All capital providers and their clients need to know how to discount cash flow, which means knowing two things: the likely future value of the money they invest today, and the present value of the money they are likely to receive in the future.

What is the rate of return calculation, and how does it differ from determining future value and present value?

The following small-scale, simplified example will compare rate of return, future value, and present value. Most of the calculations should be familiar exercises to the readers of this book. To see illustrations, refer to the financial "tools" at the back of this chapter. This example is addressed to potential sources of funds—including lenders, investors, and backers—but it can also be instructive to those who seek such funds.

Suppose you have the opportunity to provide $1,000 today to support a transaction that can return $1,210 in one year. The applicable market rate of interest is 10 percent. You can analyze the decision using the rate of return, future value, and present value concepts. This example assumes simple interest, and an equivalent riskiness between the potential market investment and the transactional investment.

Under the *rate of return* method, you would simply note that the market rate promises a return of 10 percent, while the transactional investment offers a return of 21 percent.

Under *future value* analysis, you could decide not to support the transaction, but instead invest the $1,000 somewhere else at the market interest rate of 10 percent. At the end of the year, you would have: $1,000 (1 + 0.10) = $1,100.

This gives you two numbers to compare: the $1,210 promised by the deal versus the $1,100 your could get elsewhere.

Alternatively, you could use the concept of *present value* to compare the two investments. Present value tells you what a future sum or sums would be worth to you if you had those funds today. It is obtained by discounting the future sum or sums back to the starting point, which is the present. Thus, finding present values (or *discounting*, as it is commonly called) is simply the reverse of finding the future value. You can calculate the present value by multiplying the future value by $1/(1 + r)$—where r is the market rate—or alternatively dividing by $1 + r$. This also gives you two numbers to compare: a present value of $1,100 for the transactional investment discounting back from the future versus $1,000 "in hand" today.

Comparing the future and present value numbers for the two investments, you can see that the relationships are equivalent. In both cases, the transactional investment is superior to the market investment by a factor of 10 percent. This equivalence should not be surprising. Mathematically, present value factors are reciprocals of future value factors.

If future value and present value calculations are so closely correlated, why use present value at all?

The present value calculation is of greater relevance to lenders and investors because it can help them choose from among different transactional investments *now* in a fluid, negotiation-based situation. Here is another small-scale example, this time using multiple years and, therefore, compound interest.

Suppose you are offered the alternative of receiving either $1,610.50 from a transaction at the end of five years or x dollars today. Having no current need for the money, you could deposit the x dollars in a financial institution paying 10 percent interest; the 10 percent is your opportunity cost. How small must x be to induce you to accept the promise of $1,610.50 in five years?

You know that the future value factor of $1,000 invested at a 10 percent interest rate compounding over five years is $1,610.50. (See Tool 2–1.) Alternatively, you could use a table showing the present value interest factor as a function of interest rates to find a multiplier, which in this case would be 0.6209. (See Tool 2–2.) Again, the future value factor would be $1,610.50.

Simply divide this factor into $1,610.50 to find a present value of $1,000. Thus, if x is less than 1,000, you would prefer $1,610.50 after five years. If x equals $1,000, you would be indifferent, and if x is greater than $1,000, you would choose x now. Over time, the transactional investment would be better than the market rate investment. (See Tool 2–3.)

The examples so far involve lump sums. What about payments or repayments over time?

Financial economists have developed formulas to determine the future and present values of such payments, which are called *annuities*. These formulas can be applied to both *ordinary annuities,* which are paid at the end of the period like mortgage payments, and to *annuities due,* which are paid in advance like lease payments. In most M&A transactions, payments are beginning of the period, so the most useful tool will be a knowledge of annuities due.

In the following examples, we will illustrate the time lines first for the *future value* of an ordinary annuity and for an annuity due, and then for the *present value* of each of these instruments.

A typical *future value* question might be framed as follows: Suppose you anticipate receiving three payments of $1,000 a year for three years—a three-year annuity. If you do receive such an annuity and then invest each annual payment to earn 10 percent interest, what will be the future value at the end of three years? The future value of the ordinary annuity will be $3,310, whereas the future value of the annuity due is $3,641. (See Tool 2–4.)

This same question can be posed as a *present value* question, with a twist, as follows: Suppose you anticipate receiving payments of $1,000 per year from a transaction for three years. The applicable discount rate is 10 percent. What amount should you be willing to loan or invest for that kind of return? If the annuities are received at the end of each year (ordinary annuities), the present value of the payments is $2,486.85. If the annuities are received at the end of each year (annuities due), then the present value of the payments would be $2,735.54. These two amounts represent the maximum you should be willing to invest if you want at least to break even on the investment. (See Tool 2–5.)

Cash flow from M&A transactions is often uneven. How can the present value of uneven cash flows be determined?

It can be calculated using a simple present value formula. (See Tool 2–6.)

M&A transaction cash flow usually has no end point. How can the present value of such cash flows be calculated?

Financial economists have a method for calculating the present value of these payments, which are called *perpetuities.* The future value of a perpetuity is infinite, since the number of periodic payments is infinite. The present value of a perpetuity made in constant payments is the periodic flow divided by the discount factor. This equation will work even if the market rate of interest changes.

Assume that initially the annuity is $120 and the rate of interest is 10 percent. The present value is calculated as $120 divided by 0.10, or $1,200. If the rate of interest falls to 8 percent, the present value would rise to $1,500. Thus, the present value is very sensitive to the size of the discount factor. This is also generally true for investments even if they do not have infinite lives, but the impact is greatest for a perpetuity.

So far we have seen some simple models for rate of return, present value, future value, annuities, and perpetuities. What are some other basic financial concepts that must be mastered to make (or persuade someone to make) an investment decision?

Other basic concepts include amortization and semiannual and other compounding periods. We discuss these and other dynamics of debt instruments in Chapter 4.

DANGER ZONES

What are some of the risks in debt financing?

First and foremost is the risk of *not borrowing enough cash* to finance the transaction. Borrowers tend to underestimate their needs. They think that growing sales and profitability will throw off enough cash for future financing needs. In fact, firms that are increasing in size need more outside funds than firms that are shrinking in size, and this is true even when the high-growth firms are highly profitable.

It seems counterintuitive that it would be risky to refrain from borrowing. What evidence do you have for this assertion?

Growing, profitable firms may need to borrow money from time to time in order to reduce value-destroying volatility in a key ratio: *return on capital employed* (ROCE). In a recent study of 100 companies within process industries, Mercer Management Consulting found that the greatest increase in market value was realized by those companies that achieved revenue and profit growth while maintaining low volatility in ROCE. For example, between 1987 and 1995, the compound annual growth rate in market value in the chemical industry for profitable growers with low ROCE volatility was 13 percent, while the growth rate for similar firms with high ROCE volatility was 9 percent. Companies with high volatility in ROCE spent money when they had it and refrained from spending money when they did not have it, thus following their business cycles.

"Less successful companies," says Mercer, "tend to follow a 'herd' mentality and are more likely to invest when they have cash on hand." By contrast, more successful firms invest even when they do not have cash on hand—that is, they obtain external financing. "Those firms that actively manage, rather than accept, cyclicality are the ones that will survive and increase shareholder value through the tough times ahead."[1]

In summary, needing outside capital is not a sign of weakness; in fact, it can be a sign of strength. True, borrowers that *repeatedly* ask for more in multiple, unexpected refinancings can develop a poor reputation among sources. But this is not because they asked for the money. Rather, it is because these chronic borrowers show an inability to assess the amount of money they require to support future growth.

Isn't there also a risk of borrowing too much cash?

There is some risk, of course. As in personal financing, a business should never borrow more than it can reasonably pay back. But nothing says that all the cash the firm borrows must be spent immediately. If the cash is excessive, and is not spent (or, if the loan is structured as a revolving line of credit), it can be returned to the lender. Also, remember that in a typical leveraged deal, as the buyer pays back the loan, the company's debt-to-equity ratio decreases. It is not set in stone. The problem is in borrowing an amount of cash that causes the firm to become overleveraged, and may force it to default on its loan covenants, making it vulnerable to the charge of fraudulent conveyance. This powerful litigating tool of "burned" lenders and shareholders can target anyone and everyone involved with an overleveraged transaction, with or without fraudulent intent, even third parties.

All these risks—overleverage, covenant defaults, and fraudulent conveyance—are discussed in depth in Chapter 4. Suffice it to say here that overleverage is not a vague concept. There is a technical definition for it. By regulatory definition, with certain exceptions, highly leveraged loans are finance transactions in which the borrower would end with a debt-to-equity ratio of 75 percent or higher. These *highly leveraged transactions* (HLTs) must be identified as such in bank disclosure documents. Regulators also encourage banks and bank regulators to discourage HLTs, and they have published complete guidelines for this purpose. In addition, Internal Revenue Code Sections 163 and 279 disallow an interest deduction for certain types of debt.[2]

What are the main risks in equity-based financing?

There are two—volatility and dilution. Volatility means changes in stock price values, in terms of both individual stocks and the market as a whole. Some volatility is normal, but excessive volatility can make planning difficult. If the market as a whole drops during the preparation of an initial public offering (IPO) of stock, then sources of funding can dry up suddenly—as occurred in 1998, one of the worst years ever for IPOs.

    Dilution occurs when issuing new shares reduces the value of existing shares. For an explanation of dilution, see Chapter 10.

This discussion so far has talked about financing risks, but what about pricing risks? Isn't overpaying a risk, no matter what the source of financing?

Certainly. No matter how soundly a deal is financed, price matters greatly because it increases the amount of money a buyer must come up with, whether internally or externally. If a buyer turns to external sources, a high price can force the buyer to take on too much debt or to sell too much equity, thus incurring the risks mentioned above (e.g., overleverage and dilution).

What does "paying too much" for a company really mean and what harm does it do?

Paying too much means paying more than a company is worth. Of course, the real worth of a company—whether separately or as part of a future combination with synergies—cannot be determined with absolute certainty; different approaches will yield different answers. Nonetheless, each company, and each potential merger, has a certain reasonable range of values, both considered separately and considered in combination. Paying a price above this range is overpaying, which always has negative consequences.

    First of all, there is an opportunity cost for the overpaid funds. After all, this is not a numbers game. The bidder is using real-life economic resources to acquire a company. If the company uses cash or issues more debt, paying too much means forgoing other (potentially more productive) uses of these funds. If stock is used for payment, it is not just a matter of redistribution: The stock could have been sold for cash, and the cash could have been used for other purposes.

Second, overpayment harms the acquiring company's shareholders. This fact is particularly clear in any case involving payment with stock. A simple example will help convey the point.

Company A (the acquirer) has a current market value of $40 (it is understood that all the numbers are in millions). Company B (the company to be acquired) has a current market value of $40. The sum of their values as independent firms is therefore $80. Assume that their synergy as a combined company (AB) will increase the value to $100. If B is valued at $50, the sellers of B shares receive a 25 percent premium. Also, the synergies are split equally between the two companies.

If A pays $60 for B, however, B shareholders will own 60 percent of the combined company. *None of the synergy gains will be received by A's shareholders.* Also note that the shareholders of B company will have 1.5 shares in the new company for every 1.0 share held by the shareholders of the acquiring company.

The situation is even worse if A pays more than $60 for B. Assume A pays $70 for B. Since the combined company AB has a value of $100, the value of A company's shares must decline to $30. The consequences are terrible. The shares of the acquiring company will decline in value by $10, or 25 percent. Furthermore, A shareholders will own only 30 percent of the combined company; for every one share that they own, B shareholders will own 2.3 shares.

So don't forget, even if a company is bought with shares of stock, paying too much will seriously injure the shareholders of the acquiring firm.

TARGETING THE AMOUNT OF FINANCING NEEDED

How can a company determine the amount of financing it needs?

To determine the amount of financing needed to buy another company, three questions will be paramount.

First, *what it will it cost to acquire the business,* including:

- the purchase price of the stock or assets of the acquired company (offset by the cash in the company and the cash that can be generated from asset sales)
- any existing debt that must be assumed, paid off, or refinanced at closing

- administrative and/or tax costs of the acquisition
- fees paid to professionals (accountants, appraisers, investment bankers, lawyers, etc.)

Second, *what it will cost to run the business* after it is acquired, including:

- immediate working capital needs of the acquired company (bills due now!)
- postacquisition payments stemming from settlement of litigation (if such exposure was discovered when the acquirer was conducting a "due diligence" review of the candidate seller to assess postacquisition risk)
- severance and early retirement pay (offset over the long term by compensation savings)

Third, *what will it cost to improve and/or expand the business* after it is acquired, including:

- capital investments for future growth (new plants, research and development, etc.)
- marketing costs

These three costs—for acquisition, maintenance, and improvement—are universal costs in any investment. To use a simple analogy, suppose you were going to buy a fixer-upper house (leaky roof and all) for a bargain price. Would you borrow only the purchase price and related fees? Or would you also borrow funds to keep the electricity going—and to buy a new roof?

Insiders understand these issues, but the further down the list we go, the more need there is for external expertise. Investment bankers and other outside advisers may be better than internal managers in estimating how much it will or should cost to acquire a particular company).

Beyond the need to pay for, run, and improve the business, what other factors should a buyer consider when seeking capital?

A prime consideration is the cost of capital. If money is cheap—because of either low interest rates or high stock market values—a company should attempt to raise more than it needs. As mentioned earlier, it can always give the money back, either through early repayment (being careful to keep prepayment penalties out of its contracts with lenders) or through a stock buyback.

ESTIMATING THE AMOUNT OF FINANCING POSSIBLE

Just because a company *wants* to borrow or raise a certain amount of capital doesn't mean it *can.* How can a buyer estimate the amount of money it can borrow?

Much depends on the value of the company being acquired. Obviously, the money will be in proportion to size and value, with larger amounts being possible for the purchase of a large company of high value than for the purchase of a small company of low value. This observation only scratches the surface of the question, however. The art of valuation is extremely complex, with many different methods used to assess the value of a company.

How much a lender is willing to lend, or an underwriter is willing to underwrite, will depend on what method that source of capital is using to value the company being acquired—not to mention the value of the company doing the acquiring.

On your first point, assessing the value of a company to be acquired, what are the basic methods of valuation?

There is a long list. In fact, one valuation expert (John Lewis, publisher of *Valuation Issues* newsletter) has identified 17 techniques used by institutional investors to assess the value of a publicly held company. However, when it comes to all companies, private as well as public, the following list is a good beginning.[3]

1. The Replacement Value Method.   The replacement value method is the simplest but the most tedious of the valuation processes. Given a particular company or company unit, the buyer sets out to discover the cash costs to create from scratch an exact duplicate of the company in all its perspectives. Valuation includes both hard and soft assets. Hard assets include land, buildings and machinery, inventories, and so forth. Soft assets include the costs of recruitment and training of people, the creation of markets and protective devices such as copyrights and trademarks, the development of a customer base, and so on. This estimate is compared with the asking price for the company or is used as the basis for an offer and the subsequent negotiation. Properly done, it is the best of the valuation methods because it asks and answers the simple question "What will it cost the buyer to duplicate the company right now?" without the complications of factoring in past or future accounting-based earnings that may or may not represent reality.

Such a formal estimate of replacement value can be used in internal negotiations within the buying company, since it serves to support the argument that it is often cheaper to buy than to build.

One major advantage in the replacement value approach is that professional appraisal firms are highly skilled in generating the basic numbers. These numbers will usually stand up in court should there be a challenge. Its disadvantage is in getting enough accurate information about the company and its industry to generate the costs to create a valid duplicate.

In an acquisition, the buyer will not have to compete with the seller. With a replacement value calculation for de novo entry, continued competition must be factored in. The replacement value method seems to give a potential buyer a negotiating edge over a seller. Computing out replacement value can also be a factor in fulfilling due diligence requirements.

2. The Investment, or Average Rate of Return, Method.   The investment, or average rate of return, method has been the most common approach to valuing acquisitions. It is an accounting-based method that compares the projected average return with the projected average investment in the project. The projected average required return is sometimes called a *hurdle rate,* which is most often the buyer's cost of capital. This, as mentioned above, is modified at will to reflect entry risk, since the rate will be lowered for businesses with which the buyer is more familiar.

In practice, in the M&A field, this valuation analysis begins with the up-front sum to be paid for the company or, in an installment purchase, for the down payment. This figure is modified through the years as additional capital is invested or capital is recovered. It is especially useful if an installment purchase is to be made, or when major assets are to be sold off or acquired. Its advantage is in its simplicity. Its usual disadvantage is in its failure to properly take into account the time value of money.

3. The Payback Method.   Payback is one of the time-honored methods used for the evaluation of an acquisition. Borrowed from the capital budgeting area, it has been and is still used for the purchase of major machine tools and other capital items. In the payback method, the corporate powers-that-be arbitrarily decide that their capital investments should be recovered or "paid back" in some set period of time. Typically, the purchaser of a large computer-controlled machine tool or a bank of such machines must pay back its purchase price—including the costs of freight, installation, operator training, and so on—in three to five years, or the investment will not be made. Risk factors of technological obsolescence, downturns in sales, labor strikes, and other catastrophes are all taken into account by shortening the payback period, while projected positive events will lengthen it.

Payback is a simple method that can be understood by people who are not trained in finance, and it is easy to incorporate in simple budgeting and marketing programs. For many years it was used (and still is) for the purchase of competitors in the service industries. As with the investment method, its advantage is in its simplicity; its disadvantage is that it does not properly take into account the time value of money. It is recommended for use only in the simplest of transactions where the operating parameters are well known and are easily budgeted and controlled.

4. The Internal Rate of Return (IRR) Method. For many years, larger companies that had access to sophisticated technology and qualified accounting staff used the IRR method to value investments, and some still do. In this method, the object is to discover what discount rate is needed to make the present value of the future cash flows of an investment equal the cost of the investment. When the net present values of cash outflows and cash inflows equal zero, the rate of discount being used is the IRR. To be acceptable, it must equal or exceed the hurdle rate.

The IRR method, unless fully understood by the analyst, is not very useful for M&A financing. First, mathematically, there are always at least two solutions to an IRR calculation and sometimes, when several income reversals are projected, many more. Second, the calculations take time even on the fastest computers, since they are done by a long series of successive approximations. Third, varying the inputs in performing sensitivity analyses to produce the net present value (NPV), compared with the discounted cash flow (DCF) method, can be time-consuming. Also, human computational errors may occur and get compounded. Finally, even without errors, results can be misleading and are not easily defended in court. The IRR method of valuation is "old hat" and is not recommended. On the other hand, it is still used by some lenders, so deal makers should understand it.

5. The Market Value Method. The market value method, used primarily for the acquisition of publicly traded companies, requires a search for "comparables" in the publicly traded markets. It assumes that the public markets are "efficient"—that is, all the information about the comparables is available to buyers and sellers and is being used to set the prices for their securities.[4] Still used today, and required by the due diligence process in the case of the purchase of controlling interests in publicly traded companies, the market value method uses the published price/earnings (or P/E) multiples of publicly traded comparable companies to establish a price or a range of prices.

In many cases, the problem of comparability is difficult to solve. There are simply no truly comparable companies anywhere, and the valuator then must average the figures for a group of close comparables. For some sellers it is a dangerous method, since an experienced buyer can cherry-pick the comparables. There are also other flaws. In past markets, many stocks were undervalued by the public, and it was not unusual for a buyer to pay a 50 percent premium over the publicly traded stock price *after* a DCF or other analytical method indicated that a premium price was in order. In those cases, it was assumed that the market was truly "inefficient."

Accounting variables are also important here. For instance, the prices and P/E ratios of several dozen property/casualty (P/C) insurance companies can be averaged, and the resulting number used to negotiate a purchase price. But insurance accounting is not uniform from company to company, and historically accurate numbers are difficult to come by, since they were never kept product by product. Allocating the surpluses to the product lines that produced them is a near impossibility, and figuring the incremental costs of fixed and working capital to add $1 of premium inflow on a product-by-product valuation is nearly impossible. The only way to price out a purchase of a P/C company properly is by direct examination of the risks that the particular insurer faces product by product, and when this is run against projected revenues and totaled, it will generally yield an entirely different number than that derived by averaging the P/E multiples of a group of "comparable" insurance companies.

Although the differences are dramatic in the insurance industry, lack of accounting standards and their consistent application makes historical earnings figures difficult to rely on in many industries. But many investors still rely on the "efficient market theory," which says that the investing public sees through the accounting facade and properly values most securities, even when attempts have been made to manipulate prices in anticipation of a sale. The market value method remained the method of choice in the M&A area until the advent of the discounted cash flow (DCF) method, described below, which has largely displaced it. (For due diligence purposes, acquirers must still review market values of comparables based on P/Es and explain differences between the numbers and the DCF/NPV values.)

6. The Comparable Net Worth to Market Value Method.   Net worth is not a good measure of the present value of anything unless it's all in cash and can be immediately withdrawn, which is never the case. In most cases, only lip service has been paid to the requirements for consistency, uniformity, and comparability in generating operating figures that have produced earned surpluses. Thus, a net worth progression is difficult to use as a proxy for predicting future profits. Where and when the surpluses arose is of great importance in understanding past performance in order to predict future performance.

A better approach to use is the *comparable net worth to market value method.*[5] It is usually employed in unfriendly situations such as "squeezeouts," where a majority control group is squeezing out the minority holders; information on future sales and profits is not made available to the challenging minority stockholders, and the courts usually sustain the majority stockholders' contention that to release such information would aid competitors. (Such information would also be needed to do a proper DCF/NPV valuation.)

In this method of valuation, 5 to 10 comparable publicly traded companies are identified. Their accounting practices are carefully analyzed and various adjustments, especially to accounting treatments of inventories, cash, and receivables, are made to increase the comparability, and any excesses (or shortages) of cash, cash equivalents, and other nonworking assets are computed. The resulting adjusted net worths are then compared with the price at which their stocks are being traded.

The method's major advantage is that it uses only publicly available information in computing values. Its disadvantage is that it requires a great deal of sophistication to remake the balance sheets, and in some cases the operating statements, of the sample group of public companies to make them comparable to the company being valued.

7. The Discounted Cash Flow (DCF) Method.   The DCF method is a recommended way to value a going company. Any company is worth the NPV of its future earnings stream taken out to infinity and discounted at some rate that approximates the risk. In its simplest form, the DCF process proceeds as follows:

> Step 1. Set aside the value of all assets—current and fixed—not used in the business to produce the estimated future earnings stream that is to be discounted.
>
> Step 2. Estimate future sales year by year over a preselected time span.
>
> Step 3. Estimate the gross margins year by year, including depreciation expenses.
>
> Step 4. Estimate earnings before interest and taxes (EBIT) year by year.
>
> Step 5. Subtract interest and estimated taxes year by year.

Step 6. Compute and subtract the average marginal incremental working capital costs required to put on each additional dollar of sales year by year (do the reverse for any downsizing).

Step 7. Compute and subtract the average marginal incremental fixed capital costs of putting on each additional dollar of sales year by year (reverse for any major asset sales).

Step 8. Add back depreciation (reverse for recaptures).

Step 9. Compute the residual value of the company after the end of the horizon period by capitalizing the last year's projected earnings at the reciprocal of the selected discount rate.

Step 10. Discount all values (including residual value) to present value, using a risk-adjusted cost of capital for the discount rate.

Step 11. Add back all set-aside values (step 1) for current and fixed assets not used to produce revenues. The total is the NPV value of the business.

An excellent variation on the DCF approach is cash flow return on investment (CFROI). This approach, which is used by Holt Value Associates in Chicago, Illinois, focuses more on the productivity of assets, using project finance logic, among other tools.[6]

So much for figuring out how much a company is worth. As you mentioned, though, a buyer needs to obtain capital to maintain and improve or expand operations. How can these future needs be assessed?

There are two main ways to assess future needs. Financial economists refer to these activities as "forecasting financial statements"—seeing what financial needs and opportunities lie ahead. The first method is called *percent of sales;* the second, *regression analysis.*[7] Both results should be adjusted using subjective judgment, as explained below.

What is the percent of sales method for predicting future financing needs?

This method basically says that the volume of a firm's sales is a good predictor of the amount the firm should invest in assets. Sales forecasts are, therefore, the first step in forecasting financial requirements.

The percent of sales method begins by expressing each individual balance sheet item as a percentage of sales. As an example, consider the Moore Company, whose sales are running at $500,000 per year, the limit of its capacity; its after-tax profit margin on sales is 4 percent. During 1998, the company earned $20,000 after taxes and paid $10,000 in dividends.

How much additional financing will be needed if sales expand to $800,000 during 1999 after the merger or buyout? To determine this amount, we will use the percent of sales method.

First, isolate the balance sheet items that can be expected to vary directly with sales. In the case of Moore Company, this step applies to each category of assets—a higher level of sales necessitates more cash for transactions, more receivables, higher inventory levels, and additional fixed plant capacity. On the liability side, accounts payable as well as accruals may be expected to increase as sales do. Retained earnings will go up as long as the company is profitable and does not pay out 100 percent of earnings, but the percentage increase is not constant. In addition, common stock will not necessarily increase proportionately with an increase in sales.

The items that can be expected to vary directly with sales are calculated as a percentage of sales (see Table 2–1). For every $1.00 increase in sales, assets

---

T A B L E   2–1

The Moore Company Balance Sheet as of December 31, 1998 (Percent of Sales)

Assets (%)		Liabilities (%)	
Cash	2	Accounts payable	10
Receivables	17	Accrued taxes and wages	5
Inventories	20	Mortgage bonds*	—
Fixed assets (net)	30	Common stock*	—
		Retained earnings*	—
Total assets	69	Total liabilities and net worth	15
Assets as percent of sales		69	
Less: Spontaneous increase in liabilities		(15)	
Percent of each additional dollar of sales that			
must be financed		54	

*Not applicablo.

must increase by $0.69; this $0.69 must be financed in some manner—preferably before the acquisition, to avoid the need for refinancing.

Accounts payable will increase proportionately with sales, as will accruals; these two items will supply $0.15 of new funds for each $1.00 increase in
sales. Subtracting the 15 percent for proportionately generated funds from the
69 percent funds requirements leaves 54 percent. Thus, for each $1.00 increase
in sales, the Moore Company must obtain $0.54 of financing, either from inter-
nally generated funds or from external sources.

Moore's sales are expected to increase from $500,000 to $800,000, or by
$300,000. Applying the 54 percent developed in the table to the expected in-
crease in sales leads to the conclusion that $162,000 will be needed. (All these
amounts should be adjusted for inflation.)

In all of this, how can managers forecast future sales (the increase, in this case, from $500,000 to $800,000)?

The best way is to take both a top-down and a bottom-up approach.

In the top-down approach, senior managers and staff at the corporate
level will forecast the future world economy, the future national economy, future sales volumes in the industries where the firm sells products, and the
company's future market share of those industries. This last figure can be used
as a top-down sales forecast.

In the bottom-up approach, each segment of the firm can analyze trends
in sales patterns, taking into account the effect of future advertising and marketing campaigns. These can be turned into sales forecasts, which in turn can
be aggregated for the firm as a whole.

We now have two sales forecasts, one macroeconomic, one microeconomic. Dialogue between the management teams responsible for the two forecasts can result in a consensus forecast for sales.

How can a buyer determine what portion of the new money must be met by retained earnings and what portion must come from external financing?

Some of the money must be met by retained earnings. Moore Company's total
revenues during 2000 will be $800,000. If the company earns 4 percent after
taxes on this volume, profits will amount to $32,000. Assuming that the 50 per-
cent dividend payout ratio is maintained, dividends will be $16,000, and
$16,000 will be retained. Subtracting the retained earnings from the $162,000

that was needed leaves a figure of $146,000—the amount of funds that must be obtained by borrowing or by selling new common stock.

So much for the percent of sales method for assessing future financing needs. What about the regression method?

Regression analysis is a more general method for forecasting financing requirements, among other things. In statistics, regression is the relationship between the mean value of a random variable and the corresponding values of one or more other variables. This approach is more sensitive than a "percentage of" approach, because it does not automatically assume that the line that best fits the data goes through the origin (fixed as point 0 in an x/y axis). Instead, it allows us to find the relationship that best fits the data.

Three concepts are necessary: the *mean*, the *variance*, and the *standard deviation*. The mean is the sum divided by the number of observations—the average value. The variance is a measure of the dispersion from the average value. (It is the squared deviations from the mean divided by the number of observations less one.) The standard deviation is the square root of the variance. Using these three basic numbers, the buyer or financier can make a series of calculations and plot their results in a "scatter diagram" that shows correlations. This diagram can show the precise closeness of various relationships. Rather than using a simple percentage, it reveals a more dynamic series of relationships.

To be effective, both the percent of sales and the regression approaches rely to some extent on stability—the notion that the relationships of the past will repeat themselves in the future. In seeking M&A financing, however, as in any financial activity, managers know that this is not necessarily so. Therefore, the participants in M&A financing should adjust the relationships using subjective judgment.

How can the percent of sales or regression method be adjusted using subjective judgment?

The most common adjustment is the *subjective probability distribution*. This represents the alternative possible future outlooks for the company—good, average, or bad. These are then adjusted for probability. Then, using these forecasts, managers may adjust the findings of their percent of sales or regression correlations.

SELECTING THE MOST APPROPRIATE TYPE OF FINANCING (DEBT VERSUS EQUITY)

If a company is considering the acquisition of another company, should it always try to use its own existing cash if possible, or should it try to find new cash by taking out a loan, issuing stock, or taking on a backer?

Most financial decisions involve risk/return trade-offs, and financing an M&A deal is no exception. The company should first assess how well it balances risk and reward through its current financial structure, and then decide whether it wants to maintain that balance after the merger, or change it in one direction or the other.

An increase in the cash position of a firm reduces risk, but since cash is not an earning asset, converting other assets to cash also reduces profitability. Conversely, the use of additional debt raises the rate of return, or profitability, on stockholder net worth, but more debt means more risk. Another factor to consider is the impact of issuing new stock: Will this cause dilution, and if so, will it harm relations with shareholders (including employee shareholders)?

Managers should weigh all these issues when deciding on the levels of debt and equity in the firm. The good deal maker seeks to strike the balance between risk and profitability that will maximize stockholder wealth.

What is heavy leverage, and is it good or bad for a business?

The jury is still out, and the evidence is mixed.[8] The conventional business wisdom that looked with alarm at the prospect of imposing large amounts of debt upon a company was challenged in the mid- to late 1980s, when underpriced companies could be bought with borrowed money that was to be paid off by selling assets and pumping up cash flows. But by the decade's end, the old antileverage school seemed to be vindicated when the inevitable failures came.

forces point to the successes and say that having a large amount of debt on the balance sheet provides "survival" incentive for managers to perform efficiently. Management, say these leverage boosters, will focus on making the core business profitable, minimizing the use of capital, and maximizing cash flow, rather than on building personal empires. With the burden of debt comes an advantage: a real outside check on the leveraged buyer's economic analysis.

The antileverage philosophers would disagree. Heavy debt servicing competes against operating excellence as dollars once marked for needed research and development or plant and equipment go to interest payments, often with dire consequences for the acquired company and eventually its community. This was the dominant view of the nearly 50 witnesses testifying in Senate and House hearings on leveraged buyouts (LBOs) and mergers held in January and February 1989, and it has been echoed ever since.[9]

Both sides agree, however, on one point: If the buyer plans to impose heavy financial leverage on a company, the buyer must be sure that the company can bear the interest and paydown burdens and must minimize operating risks. LBOs are *not* recommended for those who feel uncomfortable with substantial amounts of financial exposure for their companies. (We are not even contemplating here the personal exposure of individual buyers through guarantees, which presents an even higher level of risk.)

If the acquired company does not do well, bankruptcy and charges of fraudulent conveyance may follow. On the other hand, the higher the percentage of equity acquired in a deal, the higher the return on equity if the acquired company does well. For more on leveraged buyouts, see Chapter 9.

What kinds of businesses lend themselves to financial leverage—and thus to debt-based financing?

Look for businesses that generate cash flow on a steady basis. High growth potential is not necessarily a prerequisite; more probably, suitable candidates will show only moderate growth and will be easier to buy.

Leveraged buyout candidates should be on the opposite end of the spectrum from venture capital operations, which tend to be predominantly equity financed. Producers of basic products or services in stable markets are the best candidates for a leveraged transaction. Start-ups and highly cyclical companies should be avoided. So should companies whose success is highly dependent on forces beyond the control of management. Oil and gas deals that depend on fuel prices are thus not suitable for highly leveraged deals, in contrast to oil pipeline or trucking companies, which receive a steady, stable payment for transportation charges and do not speculate on oil prices.

Trucking companies, by the way, are good candidates for "leveraged buildups," a series of small acquisitions in an industry that contains many sole proprietorships (a "fragmented" industry, as the jargon goes). Other industries good for leveraged buildups include cable TV, financial services, publishing, radio, and resort properties.

In any industry, stable management offers an important element of reassurance. A team that works well together and has been through several business cycles can provide the stable, conservative projections necessary to evaluate whether the debt can be paid off.

What are the first steps in structuring a highly leveraged deal?

The art of structuring a debt financing involves allocating the revenues and assets of the acquired company to lenders in a manner that does the following:

- Maximizes the amount loaned by the most senior and highly secured and, thus, lowest interest rate lenders
- Leaves sufficient cash flow to support, if needed, a layer of subordinated, higher interest rate "mezzanine" debt, as well as any seller takeback financing
- Provides for adequate working capital and is consistent with seasonal variations and foreseeable one-time bulges or dips in cash flow
- Permits the separate leveraging of distinct assets that can be more advantageously set aside for specialized lenders, such as sale/leasebacks of office buildings or manufacturing facilities
- Accommodates both good news and bad—that is, permits debt prepayment without penalty if revenues are sufficient and permits nonpayment and nonenforcement of subordinated debt if revenues are insufficient
- Avoids and, where necessary, resolves conflicts between lenders

Customarily, these results are achieved through layering of debt, discussed in great detail in Chapter 7.

How can a buyer minimize borrowing in a leveraged transaction?

A buyer's first thought in financial planning should be a very simple one: The less I have to lay out at closing, the less I have to borrow. (At the same time, as mentioned above, the buyer should be careful to establish enough credit, in terms of both a term loan and a line of credit, for future needs.)

How can the buyer minimize the purchase price?

A buyer need not offer the highest price in order to gain the contract. It should also offer the seller noncash incentives for the deal, such as the following:

- "We can close faster."
- "We have a good track record in obtaining financing for and closing similar transactions."
- "We can offer a substantial deposit on signing the acquisition agreement."
- "We can retain you, offer you stock, and add value to your company."

Close relations with and incentives for management are likely to be an important part of the financial plan; management may be receiving shares in the company, favorable employment contracts, profit-sharing plans, and the like. If so, managers will want to know about postmerger plans. If the seller is interested in ensuring that the departing management is well treated, these arrangements may favorably dispose a seller toward a particular buyer.

One of the most delicate questions of buying (or buying out) a company is whether to obtain a lower price by assuming substantially greater risks or to accept significant defects in the candidate. Such risks or defects can loom very large in the eyes of the acquisition lenders, and the timing of negotiations does not always permit risks to be checked out with a lender before signing the contract. Here is a cardinal rule: Negotiate and sign *fast* when the price is right. Some of the most spectacularly successful deals have been achieved when a buyer has been able to discern that management and a lender could live with something the seller thought was a major problem primarily because it had stymied other deals.

Another way to lower the purchase price is to buy only some of the assets or divisions of a company.

When planning postdeal sell-offs, how easy is it for an acquirer to pick and choose among acquired assets?

It is desirable—but often difficult—for a buyer to be selective about what it acquires. The seller may be packaging some dogs together with some strong operations; therefore, the buyer should consider "gaming" the offer out from the seller's point of view and making a counterproposal. Crucial for such selection is knowing the seller's business better than it does—not impossible if the seller is a large conglomerate of which the unit is a small part, and management is the buyer or is already on the buyer's side. This happened, for example, when AT&T Capital Corp. management joined with GRS Holding Co. Ltd. and Babcock & Brown Inc. to buy the financial services company from AT&T for $2.6 billion in 1996.[10] The offer of sale may include several businesses, some of which are easier to finance than others, or assets used in part by each of several business operations. The buyer may have a choice, for example, between buying a building or a computer system or merely renting it.

Sometimes a deal can be changed to the buyer's advantage after the main price and other negotiations have been completed. The seller may then be receptive to either including or excluding what appear to be minor ancillary facilities as a last step to signing. To encourage the seller, the buyer may guarantee the resale price of unwanted assets or share any losses realized on their disposal. Taking or not taking these "minor" assets may become the key to cash flow in the critical first two years after the buyout.

Can a buyer always finance all or part of a transaction through partial divestments or spin-offs?

Not necessarily. Divestment is possible only when the business acquired consists of separate components or has excess real estate or other assets. The buyer must balance financial and operational considerations; there should always be a good business reason for the divestment. Consider selling off those portions of the business that are separable from the part you are most interested in. As indicated earlier, not all businesses generate the cash flow or have the stability necessary for highly leveraged transactions, yet many cash-rich buyers are available for such businesses. A solid domestic smokestack business with valuable assets, itself highly suitable for leveraged financing, may have a subsidiary with foreign manufacturing and distribution operations, a separate retail division, and a large timberland holding—all candidates for divestiture. The foreign operations are accessible to a whole new set of possible buyers, the retail division would function better as part of another company's nationwide chain, and the timberland does not generate cash flow.

Many buyout transactions are undertaken in order to divest assets at a profit. These transactions are better called restructurings or breakups. For example, the acquisition of Beatrice Foods by Kohlberg Kravis Roberts resulted in the disbanding of its senior management and the sale of most of its assets. This is an entirely different kind of transaction from a management buyout (MBO), where the core business is highly leveraged, but preserved, and management takes an ownership interest and stays on as a team.[11]

There is a question of timing here; it is not advisable to start beating the bushes for a purchaser for a unit until you have a signed contract for the purchase of the parent company as a whole. The timeliness of the closing can be crucial. It is not uncommon to have an escrow closing of the divestiture in advance of the closing to minimize the risk of last-minute holdups. Even if the deal does not close simultaneously with the main acquisition, the presence of the divestiture agreement of such "presold assets" may make possible a bridge loan to be taken out at the closing.

Where can a buyer find cash in a company?

Cash can be found on the balance sheet, as well as in more unusual places. Does the acquired company have a lawsuit pending against a third party that can be settled quickly and profitably? Does it have excess funded reserves? Is its employee benefit plan overfunded, and if so, can the plan be terminated or restructured? Can its pension plan acquire any of the company assets? Typically, pension plans can invest a portion of their assets in real estate of a diversified nature, including real estate acquired from the company. Has the company been acquiring marketable stock or debt of unrelated companies? Does it have a valuable art collection that can be cashed in at the next Sotheby's auction?

Keep track of changes in the company's cash position between signing the acquisition agreement and closing. The terms of the acquisition agreement can ensure either that the buyer retains cash at the closing or that all cash goes to the seller. Don't forget: Identify and take into account the cash and cash equivalents held by the acquired company. You need not borrow the dollar you spend to buy cash.

CONCLUDING COMMENTS

When senior managers engage in strategic planning, they consider what they want to do and how they want to do it, often relegating the decision of how they will pay for it to financial professionals within and outside the company. But financing requires strategic vision as well, as this chapter has shown. In the following chapters, we will show how to turn this vision into reality, starting with the highly detailed work of tax and accounting considerations.

A P P E N D I X   2–A

TOOLS

T O O L 2–1

Interest Factors as a Function of Interest Rates

	$FVIF_{r,n} = (1 + r)^n$			
Period (n)	0%	5%	10%	15%
1	1.0000	1.0500	1.1000	1.1500
2	1.0000	1.1025	1.2100	1.3225
3	1.0000	1.1576	1.3310	1.5209
4	1.0000	1.2155	1.4641	1.7490
5	1.0000	1.2763	1.6105	2.0114
6	1.0000	1.3401	1.7716	2.3131
7	1.0000	1.4071	1.9487	2.6600
8	1.0000	1.4775	2.1436	3.0590
9	1.0000	1.5513	2.3579	3.5179
10	1.0000	1.6289	2.5937	4.0456

T O O L 2–2

Present Value Interest Factors as a Function of Interest Rates

	$PVIF_{r,n} = \dfrac{1}{(1+r)^n} = \left(\dfrac{1}{1+r}\right)^n$			
Period (n)	0%	5%	10%	15%
1	1.0000	.9524	.9091	.8696
2	1.0000	.9070	.8264	.7561
3	1.0000	.8638	.7513	.6575
4	1.0000	.8227	.6830	.5718
5	1.0000	.7835	.6209	.4972
6	1.0000	.7462	.5645	.4323
7	1.0000	.7107	.5132	.3759
8	1.0000	.6768	.4665	.3269
9	1.0000	.6446	.4241	.2843
10	1.0000	.6139	.3855	.2472

T O O L 2–3

Time Line Portrayal of Investments

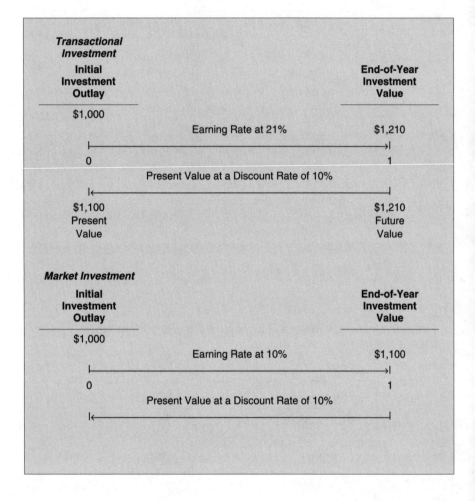

Transactional
Investment

Initial   **End-of-Year**
Investment   **Investment**
Outlay   **Value**

$1,000

                          Earning Rate at 21% $1,210

                          0   1

                   Present Value at a Discount Rate of 10%

$1,100 $1,210
Present   Future
Value   Value

Market Investment

Initial   **End-of-Year**
Investment   **Investment**
Outlay   **Value**

$1,000

                          Earning Rate at 10% $1,100

                          0   1

                   Present Value at a Discount Rate of 10%

T O O L   2–4

Time Lines for the Future Value of an Annuity at 10 Percent

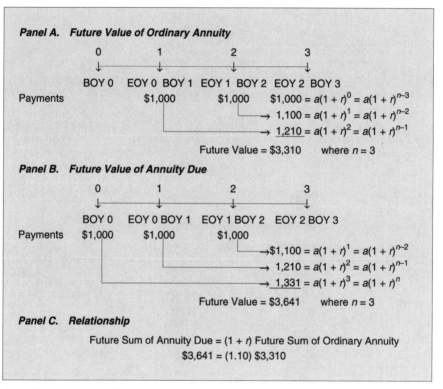

Panel A.   Future Value of Ordinary Annuity

| 0 | 1 | 2 | 3 |

BOY 0   EOY 0 BOY 1   EOY 1 BOY 2   EOY 2 BOY 3

Payments $1,000 $1,000 $1,000 $= a(1 + r)^0 = a(1 + r)^{n-3}$
$\longrightarrow 1{,}100 = a(1 + r)^1 = a(1 + r)^{n-2}$
$\longrightarrow \underline{1{,}210} = a(1 + r)^2 = a(1 + r)^{n-1}$

Future Value = $3,310   where $n = 3$

Panel B.   Future Value of Annuity Due

| 0 | 1 | 2 | 3 |

BOY 0   EOY 0 BOY 1   EOY 1 BOY 2   EOY 2 BOY 3

Payments $1,000 $1,000 $1,000
$\longrightarrow \$1{,}100 = a(1 + r)^1 = a(1 + r)^{n-2}$
$\longrightarrow 1{,}210 = a(1 + r)^2 = a(1 + r)^{n-1}$
$\longrightarrow \underline{1{,}331} = a(1 + r)^3 = a(1 + r)^n$

Future Value = $3,641   where $n = 3$

Panel C.   Relationship

Future Sum of Annuity Due = $(1 + r)$ Future Sum of Ordinary Annuity
$3,641 = (1.10) $3,310

Note: BOY = beginning of year; EOY = end of year.

T O O L 2–5

Time Lines for the Present Value of an Annuity at 10 Percent

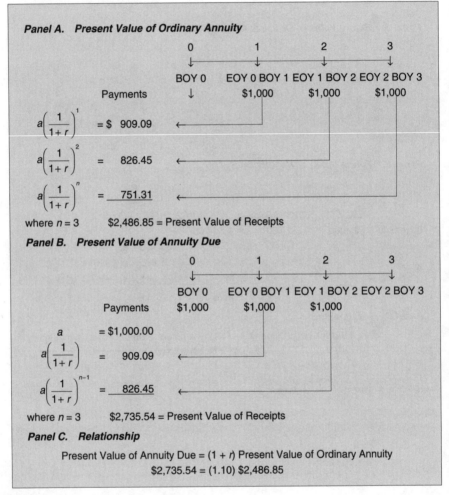

Panel A.   Present Value of Ordinary Annuity

		0	1	2	3
		BOY 0	EOY 0 BOY 1	EOY 1 BOY 2	EOY 2 BOY 3
Payments			$1,000	$1,000	$1,000

$$a\left(\frac{1}{1+r}\right)^{1} = \$\ 909.09$$

$$a\left(\frac{1}{1+r}\right)^{2} = \ 826.45$$

$$a\left(\frac{1}{1+r}\right)^{n} = \underline{\ 751.31}$$

where $n = 3$ $2,486.85 = Present Value of Receipts

Panel B.   Present Value of Annuity Due

		0	1	2	3
		BOY 0	EOY 0 BOY 1	EOY 1 BOY 2	EOY 2 BOY 3
Payments		$1,000	$1,000	$1,000	

$$a = \$1,000.00$$

$$a\left(\frac{1}{1+r}\right) = \ 909.09$$

$$a\left(\frac{1}{1+r}\right)^{n-1} = \underline{\ 826.45}$$

where $n = 3$ $2,735.54 = Present Value of Receipts

Panel C.   Relationship

Present Value of Annuity Due = $(1 + r)$ Present Value of Ordinary Annuity
$2,735.54 = (1.10) $2,486.85

Note: BOY = beginning of year; EOY = end of year.

T O O L 2–6

Time Line for the Present Value of an Annuity for Unequal Inflows

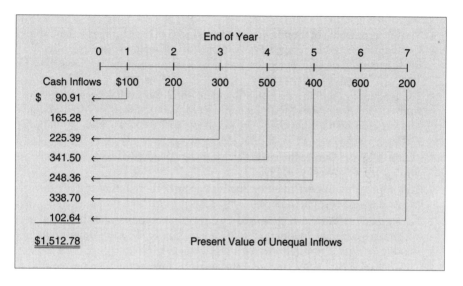

	End of Year							
	0	1	2	3	4	5	6	7
Cash Inflows		$100	200	300	500	400	600	200

$ 90.91 ←
165.28 ←
225.39 ←
341.50 ←
248.36 ←
338.70 ←
102.64 ←

$1,512.78   Present Value of Unequal Inflows

E N D N O T E S

1. "Executives Can Manage Amid Business Volatility to Drive Greater Shareholder Returns," Mercer Management Consulting press release, September 3, 1997.

2. The 75 percent rule of thumb was first introduced in the 12-page "Examining Circular on Highly Leveraged Transactions," distributed by the Controller of the Currency to its key personnel (Executive Communication 245, December 14, 1988). For more on Code Sections 163 and 279, see Chapter 4.

3. The language describing the valuation methods in this list has been adapted from Stanley Foster Reed and Alexandra Reed Lajoux, *The Art of M&A: A Merger/Acquisition/Buyout Guide*, 3rd ed. (New York: McGraw-Hill, 1999), pp. 91ff.

4. "Luck or Logic? Debate Rages on Over 'Efficient-Market' Theory," *The Wall Street Journal*, November 4, 1993.

5. This approach was developed by Stanley Foster Reed, coauthor of *The Art of M&A: A Merger*, op. cit. (note 3).

6. For a guide to CFROI, which is used by both corporations and institutional investors, see Bartley J. Madden, *CFROI Valuation: A Total System Approach to Valuing the Firm* (Oxford: Butterworth Heineman, 1999).

7. The following discussion of financial statements forecasting is summarized from a much more detailed discussion, including mathematical formulas, from J. Fred Weston and Thomas E. Copeland, *Managerial Finance*, 9th ed. (Los Angeles: Academic Press, 1998), pp. 260–277.

8. This answer has been adapted from *The Art of M&A*, op. cit. (note 3) pp. 142ff.

9. See the March 1989 issue of *Director's Monthly*, which was devoted entirely to these hearings.

10. This, incidentally, was one of the 20 largest leveraged buyouts of all times, and one of only four such large LBOs to result from a divestiture (most large LBOs are going-private transactions for an entire company). See "20 Largest LBOs in History," *Mergers & Acquisitions*, November/December 1998, p. 44.

11. The benefits of traditional buyouts were structural: large interest deductions, aggressive writeups, and accelerated depreciation of asset values. But a new breed of buyout practice is emerging in which the principals of a buyout fund add operational and technical value to what they acquire. This is the approach of Glenmount Management, LLC, according to principal Robert Forbes, interviewed April 8, 1999, by coauthor Lajoux.

C H A P T E R   3

Regulatory, Tax, and Accounting Issues in Structuring Deal Financing

The elegant simplicity of the three percents.

William Scott, Lord Stowell
From Campbell, *Lives of the Lord Chancellors,* 1857

INTRODUCTION

The interplay of financing and structure is like the old chicken and egg riddle: Which comes first? Some would say that clearly the first phase in any transaction must be the financing: You have to obtain funds for a deal before you can structure it. Others would say the opposite: Unless you have (even if only on the back of an envelope) an actual merger, acquisition, or buyout structure to fund, no money will be forthcoming.

For those who have neither a deal at hand nor the financing for it, it may seem an impossible task to begin. The entwinement of financing and structure can seem like the old Catch 22 about becoming a member of Actors Equity. To join the union, you have to have been in a show, but to be hired for a show, you have to be in the union.

How, then, to structure a deal without financing? Or conversely, how to finance a deal that has not yet been structured? Clearly, both financing and structuring are necessary and important, and both must come in quick succession. Fortunately, all it takes is a beginning. One will bring the other. The more you know about financing, the more you will know about structuring; and the more you know about structuring, the more you will know about financing. Knowledge, in turn, can hasten opportunities—deals for the right companies at the right time.

This chapter focuses on a place where financing and structure meet: tax planning. Although tax savings should never drive a transaction, they can give a nudge in either direction to a deal that is on the fence between a go and a no-go. This happens more often than not in the world of M&A, where every reward seems to have a corresponding risk. Mastering the fundamentals (and key details) of tax and accounting can help deal makers maximize their rewards and minimize their risks.[1]

GENERAL REGULATORY AND TAX CONSIDERATIONS

What are the principal goals of tax planning for a merger, acquisition, or divestiture?

From the purchaser's point of view, the principal goal of tax planning is to minimize, on a present value basis, the total tax costs of not only acquiring but also operating and even selling the acquired corporation or its assets. In addition, effective tax planning provides various safeguards to protect the parties from the risks of potential changes in circumstance or the tax laws. Moreover, the purchaser should attempt to minimize the tax costs of the transaction to the seller in order to gain advantage as a bidder.

From the seller's point of view, the principal goal of tax planning is to maximize, on a present value basis, the after-tax proceeds from the sale of the acquired corporation or its assets. This tax planning includes, among other things, deciding how to structure the transaction, developing techniques to provide tax benefits to a potential buyer at little or no tax cost to the seller, and structuring the receipt of tax-deferred consideration from the buyer.

Are the tax planning goals of the buyer generally consistent with those of the seller?

No. More often than not, the most advantageous tax plan for the buyer is the least advantageous plan for the seller. For example, the tax benefit of a high basis in the assets of the acquired corporation may be available to the purchaser only at a significant tax cost to the seller. But buyers rarely if ever pursue tax benefits at the seller's expense, because the immediate and prospective tax costs of a transaction are likely to affect the price. Generally, the parties will structure the transaction to minimize their aggregate tax costs and allocate the tax burden between them through an adjustment in price.

What is the role of state and federal securities laws in acquisition structuring and financing?

State securities laws tend to have their greatest impact when the company being acquired is publicly held. But these laws also affect the structure of corporate acquisitions of private companies. When a buyer issues consideration other than cash—say, notes, stock, and/or warrants—or when the merger agreement provides that the stockholders of the acquired company will receive noncash payment in exchange for their stock, the noncash consideration will almost certainly be classifiable as a security for regulatory purposes.

When the sellers receive securities in connection with a merger or a sale of assets requiring approval of the acquired company's stockholders (because securities will be distributed to them), Rule 145 under the Securities Act of 1933 provides that the transaction is an offer to sell the securities. If the offer constitutes a "public offering," the transaction may not take place unless there is a registration statement that has been declared effective under the Securities Act. These rules would apply, for example,

- When a buyer uses a reverse merger and when the sold company survives as a subsidiary of the buyer, and the selling stockholders get notes or preferred stock or warrants of the sold company or of the buyer (if the buyer is a corporation)
- When the buyer sets up a corporation that buys the stock of a company in exchange for cash and notes or other securities of the corporation[2]

What role do state and local taxes play in structuring mergers and acquisitions?

State and local taxes generally play a secondary role in planning M&As. First, most state income tax systems are based largely on the federal system, particularly in terms of what is taxable, to whom, when, and in what amount. Second, when the company being acquired operates in a number of states, it can be inordinately difficult to assess the interaction of the various state tax systems. On the other hand, tax planners cannot afford to ignore a transaction's state tax consequences. Although a detailed discussion of state income tax consequences deserves a book of its own, several extremely important state tax issues will be mentioned throughout the following discussion.

First and foremost, there are income taxes. These vary from state to state and may affect companies located outside the state.[3]

Beyond income taxes, there are numerous taxes imposed by states and localities that may affect an acquisition. Although these rarely amount to structural prohibitions or incentives, they often increase costs. For example, when real estate is being transferred, there will often be unavoidable real property gain, transfer, or deed recordation taxes. Perhaps the most notorious of the real property gain and transfer taxes worth mentioning specifically are those imposed by New York State and New York City, respectively, upon certain sales of real estate and of controlling interests in entities holding real estate.

Purchases of assets may not be exempt from a state's sales tax. Many states offer exemptions, but this should not be taken for granted. Check it out.

Certain types of state and local taxes not directly associated with an acquisition can be significantly affected by an acquisition or by the particular structure of the acquisition. For example, a state's real property and personal property taxes are based upon an assessment of the value of the property owned by a taxpayer. Often, a transfer of ownership of the property will trigger a reassessment of the value of the property.

Are takeover expenses tax-deductible?

Sometimes no, sometimes yes, as two 1992 cases illustrate. In 1992, the Supreme Court decided a case involving the deduction or capitalization of expenses incurred by a company (National Starch) in connection with a friendly takeover by another company (Indopco). The expenses included investment banking fees, legal fees, and other acquisition-related expenses. The high court affirmed the decision of the U.S. Court of Appeals for the Third Circuit in holding that the expenses do not qualify as current deductions, since deductions are exceptions to the norm of capitalization, and they are allowed only if there is clear provision for them in the tax code. The burden of proof is on the taxpayer to show its right to the current deduction, and this burden was not met in the *National Starch* case.

The Court specifically rejected the taxpayer's interpretation of a previous Supreme Court decision that the expenditure had to be capitalized only if it created or enhanced a separate or distinct asset. An important factor in determining whether the appropriate tax treatment is immediate deduction or capitalization of the expenditures is the taxpayer's expectation of benefits beyond the year in which the expenditures are incurred. The Court found that those future benefits did in fact exist and, consequently, that capitalization was appropriate.

On the other hand, in a 1992 Bankruptcy Court case involving the unsuccessful effort by Federated Department Stores and Allied Stores to prevent being taken over by Campeau, fees paid by Federated and Allied to potential "white knights" (Edward DeBartolo and Macy's) were held to be deductible. Testimony elicited at the hearing indicated that such fees are ordinary and customary provisions demanded by potential white knights to compensate them for all the cost and expenses they have incurred in a hostile takeover situation.

The Bankruptcy Court in *Federated* had little difficulty distinguishing this case from *National Starch.* It pointed out that both the courts and the Internal Revenue Service had historically allowed deductions for costs related to abandoned business transactions. The Bankruptcy Court noted that in this case, unlike *National Starch,* the merger expenditures of the abandoned white knight conferred no possible benefits in the corporations taken over, since the outcome resulted in the exact opposite of any possible long-term future benefit.

Does the Internal Revenue Service (IRS) play a direct role in business acquisitions?

Generally speaking, no. Unlike certain transactions regulated by federal agencies such as the Federal Communications Commission and the Federal Trade Commission, advance approval from the IRS is not required before consummating an acquisition, divestiture, or reorganization. Ordinarily, the IRS will not have occasion to review a transaction unless and until an agent audits the tax return of one of the participants.

An important and often useful exception to this rule is that the parties to a transaction can often obtain a private letter ruling issued by the National Office of the IRS. Such a ruling states the agency's position with respect to the issues raised and is generally binding upon the IRS. Requesting such a ruling is a serious business and should never be undertaken without expert legal help.

CHOICE OF ENTITY

What types of entities may operate the business of an acquired company?

Four types of entities may be used to acquire and operate a company: (1) C corporations, (2) S corporations, (3) partnerships, either general or limited, and (4) the limited liability company (LLC). The LLC is a relatively new kind of hybrid entity authorized in 1988 by the IRS. It offers the legal insulation of a corporation and the preferred tax treatment of a limited partnership. All 50 states now have passed legislation permitting such entities.[4]

What are the primary differences among the four types of business entities?

A regular, or C, corporation is a separate taxpaying entity. Therefore, its earnings are taxed to the corporation when earned and again to its shareholders upon distribution. Partnerships, S corporations, and LLCs (with some exceptions in state laws), in contrast, are generally not separate taxpaying entities.

The earnings of partnerships and S corporations are taxed directly to the partners or shareholders, whether or not these earnings are distributed or otherwise made available to them. Moreover, partnerships and S corporations may generally distribute their earnings to the equity owners free of tax. Because S corporations and partnerships are generally exempt from tax, but pass the tax liability with respect to such earnings directly through to their owners, these entities are commonly referred to as *pass-through entities*.

What is a C corporation?

A C corporation is defined in the Internal Revenue Code as any corporation that is not an S corporation. The term *C corporation* as used in this chapter, however, excludes corporations granted special tax status under the Code, such as life insurance corporations, regulated investment companies (mutual funds), or corporations qualifying as real estate investment trusts (REITs).

What is an S corporation?

An S corporation is simply a regular corporation that meets certain requirements and elects to be taxed under Subchapter S of the Code. Originally called a *small business corporation,* the S corporation was designed to permit a small, closely held business to be conducted in corporate form, while continuing to be taxed generally as if operated as a partnership or an aggregation of individuals. As it happens, the eligibility requirements under Subchapter S, keyed to the criterion of simplicity, impose no limitation on the actual size of the business enterprise.

Briefly, an S corporation may not (1) have more than 75 shareholders, (2) have as a shareholder any person (other than an estate and a very limited class of trust) who is not an individual, (3) have a nonresident alien as a shareholder, (4) have more than one class of stock, (5) be a member of an affiliated group with other corporations, or (6) be a bank, thrift, insurance company, or certain other types of business entities.

It should be noted that not all states recognize the S corporation. For those that do not, the corporation pays state income taxes as if it were a C corporation. For those states that do recognize S corporations, both resident and nonresident shareholders of the state where the corporation does business must file returns and pay taxes to that state. In such cases, a shareholder's state of residence will usually (but not always) provide a credit against its own tax.

What is a partnership for tax purposes?

Except under rare circumstances, a partnership for tax purposes must be a bona fide general or limited partnership under applicable state law.

How are LLC mergers treated?

Under most state laws, an LLC may merge with or into a stock corporation, limited partnership, business trust, or another LLC. All members of the LLC must approve the merger unless their charter provides otherwise. Filing of articles and the effective date operate the same as for corporate mergers.[5]

What is the most tax-efficient structure to acquire or operate a company?

If practicable, not even a single level of corporate tax should be paid on income generated by a company. For this reason, a pass-through entity owned by individuals (as discussed below) should be the structure wherever possible. With respect to an acquisition of assets by individuals, this means that the acquisition vehicle would be either a partnership (presumably limited) or an S corporation. In the case of a stock acquisition by individuals, the acquired company generally should be operated as an S corporation.

When the buyer is a C corporation, the acquired business, whether bought through an asset or stock purchase, should be operated as a division of the buyer or through a separate company included in the buyer's consolidated return. In either case, the income of the business will be subject to only one level of corporate tax prior to dividend distributions from the buyer to its shareholders.

Under what circumstances may a consolidated return be filed?

In order for two or more corporations to file a consolidated return, they must constitute an "affiliated group" for tax purposes. Although subject to numerous qualifications and complications, an affiliated group is essentially a chain of corporations in which a common parent owns at least 80 percent of the voting power and at least 80 percent of the value of the stock of the other members of the group. In the case of the parent's ownership of at least one first-tier subsidiary, this 80 percent stock ownership must be direct; as to all other members of the group, the 80 percent ownership may be through combined holdings of other members of the corporate group.

Nonvoting preferred stock that does not share in corporate growth and that does not have a significant discounted issue price relative to its liquidation value—so-called pure preferred—is not taken into account as stock for purposes of the affiliation rules. Thus, ordinarily, a parent may file a consolidated return with a subsidiary in which it owns at least 80 percent of the common stock, even though one or more series of pure preferred stock may be held by third parties.

When should an S corporation be considered?

Typically, an S corporation should be considered when the acquired firm is, or can become, a freestanding domestic operating corporation owned by 75 or fewer U.S. individual shareholders. Because the S corporation requirements are designed to ensure that such entities will have relatively simple structures, they are not inherently user-friendly vehicles for larger, complex operations. Nevertheless, because there is no limit on the size of the business that may be conducted in an S corporation, it is often possible to plan around obstacles to qualification under Subchapter S and to use this favorable tax entity.

When should a partnership be considered?

The partnership is an alternative to the S corporation, with several notable advantages. First, it is always available without restriction as to the structure or composition of the acquired company's ownership; therefore, it can be used when the S corporation is unavailable for technical reasons. In addition, the partnership is unique in enabling the partners to receive distributions of loan proceeds free of tax. Finally, if the acquired company is expected to generate tax losses, a partnership is better suited than an S corporation to pass these losses through to the owners. The last two advantages result from the fact that partners, unlike S corporation shareholders, may generally include financial liabilities of the partnership in their basis in the partnership.

Can equity in an S corporation be offered to corporate investors?

As we have said, a corporation will be disqualified under Subchapter S if it either has more than one class of stock or has any shareholder that is a corporation, partnership, or other nonqualifying entity. In a world where lenders and institutional investors are increasingly insistent upon receiving some kind of equity kicker in addition to a more conventional, albeit generous, fixed return, it is necessary to adapt the S corporation to equity participation by nonindividuals. This can be accomplished through the issuance of warrants, other options, or convertible debt. These must be carefully constructed to avoid the appearance or reality of de facto corporate equity holders.

There are, in fact, numerous tax issues that are unique to the financing of partnership operations, many of which directly affect the partners in the partnership rather than the lenders. These concerns relate to the determination of the partners' basis in the partnership as well as to the allocation and use of deductions. Careful tax planning, in light of the partners' objectives, should be able to mitigate these concerns. One such concern arises when tax planners seek to ensure that the particular form of the indebtedness of a limited partnership allows the limited partners to allocate their pro rata share of basis attributable to such debt. This will often involve simply making sure that the loan documents say that the lender will not have recourse to the assets of the general partner, but only to the assets of the limited partnership itself. If the loan is guaranteed by any partner, or is made by a party related to a partner in the partnership, special problems could arise.

What is the main difference between a partnership and an S corporation as far as their pass-through status goes?

The partnership is a more complete pass-through entity. With respect to issuance of stock or debt, the S corporation is treated in exactly the same way as a C corporation: Such events are not taxable transactions to it. Likewise, no taxable event is recognized to an S corporation when its warrants are issued or exercised. In contrast, most transactions undertaken by a partnership are viewed for tax purposes as if they were undertaken by the partners themselves. If the partnership is treated solely as an entity apart from its partners, the business arrangement will be undermined. Thus, the issuance and exercise of a warrant to buy a stated percentage of the outstanding stock of a corporation becomes a far more complex transaction to structure when it involves an interest in a partnership.

DISTINGUISHING BETWEEN DEBT AND EQUITY

Is the tax treatment different for debt versus equity?

Yes. Debt interest is deductible for tax purposes. However, dividends paid on common stock are not deductible in calculating income for tax purposes.

How does the double tax on corporate earnings work?

The Code sets forth a dual system of taxation with respect to the earnings of corporations. Under this system, a corporation is taxed as a separate entity, unaffected by the tax characteristics of its shareholders. The corporation's shareholders are subject to tax on their income from the corporation, if and when corporate earnings are distributed to them in any form.

What are the practical consequences of the dual system of corporate taxation?

The primary consequence of the dual system of taxation is that corporate earnings are generally taxed twice—first at the corporate level and again at the shareholder level. The shareholder-level tax may be deferred but not eliminated when the corporation retains its earnings rather than paying them out in dividends. The shareholders will pay a second level of tax when they sell their interests in the corporation.

How can leverage reduce the effects of double taxation?

A leveraged company's capital structure is tilted toward debt instead of equity. Leverage reduces or eliminates the negative effect of double taxation of corporations in two ways. First, unlike dividend payments to shareholders, which are generally taxable,[6] debt repayments to lenders are not generally taxable to the recipient. Second, in most cases, interest payments are tax-deductible to the corporation making them. [7]

It is very important to remember, however, that the IRS may take the position that a purported debt is actually equity, thus eliminating the benefit of leverage.

The tax law distinguishes between debt and equity. How exactly do the statutes define these two terms?

U.S. federal tax law offers no specific, objective criteria to determine whether a given instrument should be treated as debt or equity. State tax law, which generally applies federal criteria, offers more exemptions than rules. The debt/equity characterization issue has produced an abundance of tax litigation, with a resulting body of case law in which there are very few common principles. The judicial response in defining debt and equity has much in common with its response in defining obscenity under the First Amendment: judges may not be able to define it, but they know it when they see it.

In 1969, Congress enacted Section 385 of the Code authorizing the IRS to issue regulations regarding the debt/equity distinction. Eleven years later, the IRS promulgated the first version of the Section 385 regulations. These regulations were rewritten twice and were finally withdrawn in 1983. Since the failure of the Section 385 approach, tax advisers have dealt with the issue by consulting a number of resources, including the defunct Section 385 regulations, court cases, and IRS rulings. They look for the criteria that are most often and prominently cited, the fact patterns that are most commonly associated with recharacterization, and the arrangements that have received the most acquiescent treatment by the IRS. Finally, they keep track of what most other tax advisers—through blind faith or otherwise—are recommending.

What does the debt/equity issue boil down to, then?

A few useful generalizations can be made. Virtually all the litigation and activity by the IRS has been in the recharacterization of purported debt as equity, and not the other way around. Therefore, it is quite safe to say that recharacterization is not a problem when dealing with a purported equity instrument.

In examining a purported debt instrument, the courts look for objective indicia that the parties intended a true debtor-creditor relationship. In particular, they have placed great weight on whether the instrument represents an unconditional promise to pay a certain sum at a definite time. Other significant factors that are considered include whether the loan was made by shareholders of the borrower, the borrower's debt-to-equity ratio, whether the loan is subordinated to third-party creditors, and whether it has a market rate of interest.

How can a seller reduce tax costs, which in turn may permit a lower acquisition price for the buyer?

The simplest way to reduce the seller's tax bill is to postpone the recognition of gain. This may be accomplished in a tax-free or partially tax-free acquisition or via the installment sale route. These subjects are discussed below.

TAX CONSIDERATIONS IN STRUCTURING DEBT

What tax issues should be analyzed in structuring straight debt financing?

Straight debt is an unconditional obligation to repay principal and interest, has a fixed maturity date not too far removed, is not convertible, and has no attached warrants, options, or stock. A straight debt instrument ordinarily does not include interest that is contingent on profits or other factors, but it may provide for a variable interest rate. It will not have a principal that is subject to contingencies. In short, as stated earlier, straight debt is an instrument without significant equity features.

Straight debt instruments are generally classified as debt for tax purposes. Accrued interest on a straight debt instrument is deductible by the borrower and taxable to the lender. As a practical matter, the only tax issue in straight debt financing is the computation of the accrued interest.

The Code and proposed regulations contain an extremely complex set of comprehensive rules regarding interest accruals. These rules generally require that interest must accrue whether or not a payment of interest is made. Thus, interest may be taxed, or deducted, before or after interest is paid.

What about debt issued to third-party investors?

Until the IRS signals a newly aggressive stance, the view of most tax advisers is that debt issued to third-party investors for cash is not likely to be recharacterized as equity, even though the debt may be subordinated to senior debt, convertible into common stock, or part of a capital structure involving a high ratio of debt to equity. This will at least be true when the instrument contains the common indicia of indebtedness—that is, a certain maturity date that is neither unduly remote nor contingent, a reasonable interest rate, and creditor's rights upon default. Note, however, that even if the above criteria are met, the IRS is likely to argue for equity characterization if the conversion features of the instrument are such as to make it economically inevitable from inception that the instrument will be converted into stock. This was the case regarding certain adjustable rate convertible notes that were issued in the early 1980s.

What are the tax consequences if debt with equity features is recharacterized as equity?

The tax consequences of recharacterization of purported debt into equity may be quite severe.

First, interest payments with respect to recharacterized debt will be treated not as interest but as distributions to a shareholder and, therefore, will not be deductible. Repayment of debt principal is tax-free to the debt holder, but if treated as a redemption of stock, it may be taxed as a dividend.[8]

Second, the recharacterization may destroy the pass-through status of the issuer.[9] When debt is recharacterized as equity, it is ordinarily expected to be treated as a kind of preferred stock. Because an S corporation may not have two classes of stock, a recharacterization of debt into equity can create a second class of stock invalidating the S election and causing a corporate-level tax. If the issuer is a member of a consolidated group, the recharacterized debt will most likely be treated as preferred stock that is not "pure preferred" stock. As such, the company may be disaffiliated from the consolidated group if, after the newly recharacterized stock is accounted for, the members of the consolidated group own less than 80 percent of the company's stock.[10]

Third, a recharacterization of debt into equity may completely change the structure of the deal. For example, the recharacterization may invalidate an election to have a stock transaction treated as an asset acquisition under Section 338 of the Code. This Code section allows certain stock transactions to be treated as asset acquisitions under certain conditions. For a valid Section 338 election, the buyer and the acquired company must be affiliated at the time of the election. If the recharacterization of a purported debt into equity disaffiliates the two companies, the election is invalid. In the case of purchase money notes, the conversion of debt into stock consideration may convert a taxable acquisition into a tax-free reorganization.

Finally, a recharacterization of debt held by foreign investors may be an especially difficult event. (For more on this subject, see Chapter 14.)

What if the acquired company's operations are to be held in an affiliated group of corporations filing a consolidated federal income tax return? How is postacquisition debt treated then?

In such a case, the acquisition debt will often be issued by the parent. Therefore, for federal income tax purposes, the group is treated as a single taxpayer, in which the parent's interest deductions offset the operating income of the subsidiaries. But from the point of view of the various states in which the subsidiaries do business, there is no consolidation with the parent; therefore, the parent's interest payments, even though funded by cash flow from the subsidiary, will not reduce the subsidiary's state income tax liability.

In such cases, deal planners should consider, when feasible, passing the parent's interest deductions directly down to the subsidiaries by having them assume portions of the parent's indebtedness directly, or indirectly via bona fide intercorporate indebtedness owed to the parent by the respective subsidiaries. The parent must exercise great care to avoid adverse tax treatment under federal law—or under state law (in its own state of residency)—as a result of such restructuring.

Is interest paid on debt tax-deductible?

Not entirely. Section 279 of the Code disallows interest deductions in excess of $5 million a year on debt that is used to finance an acquisition, to the extent that the company's interest deductions are attributable to "corporate acquisition indebtedness." Because its effects are direct and harsh, Section 279 must be considered in evaluating any debt instrument used in connection with a corporate acquisition, or a refunding of such a debt instrument.

Corporate acquisition indebtedness is a type of debt incurred by a corporation to acquire either stock in another corporation or at least two thirds of the assets of another corporation. To avoid being characterized as Section 279 debt, this debt must meet certain specific subordination tests and must not be convertible into stock or issued as part of an investment unit. The issuing corporation must have a low debt-to-equity ratio as specifically set forth in the statute and regulations.

Section 279 is difficult to bypass. For this reason, corporate counsel to issuers, lenders, and underwriters must be sure that tax counsel is consulted as to even seemingly minor changes in acquisition structure or financing.

From a tax standpoint, when might preferred stock be more advantageous than subordinated debt?

When an issuer does not need additional interest deductions (for example, when it expects to generate or otherwise have available net operating losses), it may have no tax reasons to use debt, and preferred stock may be a sensible alternative.

The most common tax reason for using preferred stock over debt is to enable an acquisition to qualify as a tax-free reorganization. As discussed earlier, shareholders can obtain tax-free treatment on the receipt of nonvoting, redeemable preferred stock, and such stock will qualify in satisfying the continuity of interest requirement.

More generally, preferred stock can be used to provide tax-free treatment to an acquired company's shareholders, while still effectively converting their interest to that of a passive investor or lender. Although preferred stock dividends are not deductible to the issuer, the corporate holder may exclude from its taxable income at least 70 percent of the dividends received, called the *dividends-received deduction* (DRD).[11]

What is the most typical form for a leveraged buyout?

The buyer usually creates an acquisition corporation solely for the purpose of merging with another company. Usually the acquisition corporation does a reverse merger into the target. If the buyer wants a holding company structure—that is, wants the acquired company to be a subsidiary of a holding company—it forms a holding company with an acquisition corporation subsidiary. After the merger, the holding company owns all the stock of the acquired company, and the buyer owns all the stock of the holding company.

When do lenders prefer lending to a holding company, and how does this work?

Lenders, especially senior lenders, may have this preference when the real value of the company lies in a sale of the business as a going concern rather than in a piecemeal transaction. This is true when the business depends upon a valuable license, or when there are relatively few assets producing substantial earnings. The target may own a number of operating subsidiaries and may wish to keep litigation or other potential liabilities of each subsidiary separated. With separate subsidiaries, an extraordinary loss by one subsidiary generally won't taint the operations of the others.

In such cases, the senior lender may prefer to have a transaction structured in a holding company arrangement. In such a structure, the senior lender lends to a corporation (the holding company) that acquires the stock of the target. The senior lender obtains a senior security interest in the stock of the target, and if there are loan defaults the lender can foreclose and sell the stock to pay off the debt. For this structure to succeed, all the layers of financing must be made at the holding company level.

In addition, the senior lender in a holding company structure will often ask for a secured guarantee from the seller, notwithstanding the fraudulent conveyance risks. Junior lenders often ask for a backup guarantee in such a case. This adds a layer of complexity to the intercreditor negotiations and to the structure of financing and refinancing.

CAPITAL GAINS VERSUS ORDINARY INCOME

Is the distinction between capital gains and ordinary income still relevant in tax planning?

Yes. In recent tax bills, Congress retained the myriad rules and complexities in the Internal Revenue Code pertaining to capital gains and losses. The Taxpayer Relief Act of 1997 preserved corporate tax rates. These are still 34 percent for businesses with taxable income of up to $10 million and 35 percent for larger companies (plus a surtax on taxable income above $15 million). Capital gains may still be taxable at 28 percent, with exceptions in both directions.[12]

More important for tax planning is that the Code retains various limitations on the use of capital losses to offset ordinary income. So merger, acquisition, or buyout planners must still pay attention to the characterization of income or loss as capital or ordinary.

What is the significance of the relationship between corporate and individual tax rates?

Corporations can be used to accumulate profits when the tax rate on the income of corporations is less than the tax rate on the income of individuals. (Offsetting this benefit is the double tax on corporate earnings—paid once by the company and then by the stockholders receiving the company's dividends.) Conversely, noncorporate pass-through entities can be used to store profits when the tax rate on the income of corporations is greater than the tax rate on the income of individuals.

How does capital gains tax fit in?

A shareholder's tax on the sale or liquidation of his or her interest in the corporation is determined at preferential capital gains rates.

STRUCTURING AN INSTALLMENT SALE

Earlier, we discussed installment loans. What about installment sales? What are they and how can they help in financing a merger, acquisition, or buyout?

An installment sale is a disposition of property (by a person who is not a "dealer" in such property) in which at least one payment is to be received after the close of the taxable year in which the sale occurs. Basically, an installment sale is a sale or exchange for a promissory note or other debt instrument of the buyer. In the case of an installment sale, the gain on the sale is recognized, pro rata, whenever principal payments on the note are received, or if earlier, upon a disposition of the installment obligation. For example, if A sells property to B for a note with a principal amount of $100 and A's basis in the property was $60, A realizes a gain of $40. Since the ratio of the gain recognized ($40) to the total amount realized ($100) is 40, this percentage of each principal payment received by A will be treated as taxable gain. The other $60 will be treated as a nontaxable return of capital.

Installment treatment is available only with respect to a debt obligation of the buyer itself, as opposed to even a related third-party issuer. An obligation of the buyer will not qualify if it is payable on demand or, generally, if it is in registered form and/or designed to be publicly traded. Note, however, that an installment obligation may be guaranteed by a third party and may even be secured by a standby letter of credit. In contrast, installment obligations secured by cash or cash equivalents, such as certificates of deposit or U.S. Treasury instruments, do not qualify.

What kinds of transactions are eligible for installment sale treatment?

The installment method is generally available for sales of any property other than installment obligations held by a seller and other than inventory and property sold by dealers in the subject property. Subject to certain exceptions, installment treatment is generally available to a shareholder who sells his or her stock or to a corporation or other entity that sells its assets. Installment treatment is not available for sales of stock or securities that are traded on an established securities market.

COST BASIS VERSUS CARRYOVER BASIS

In addition to the choice of entity, what major structural issue should be considered?

From a tax standpoint, probably the most important issue is whether the buyer should seek to obtain a cost basis or a carryover basis in the assets of the company being acquired. Because of the potential for obtaining either of these results regardless of whether assets or stock is actually acquired, the determinations of the tax goal and the actual structure may initially be made on a separate basis. These considerations should be made in the light of Code Sections 338 (defined earlier), 304, and 351. (Remembering Lord Stowell's opening language in this chapter, these three sections might be called the "elegant 300s.")

What are the mechanics of achieving a cost or carryover basis?

In a taxable acquisition, carryover basis can be achieved only through a stock acquisition. For federal tax purposes, however, stock may be acquired in two ways: through a direct purchase of seller's stock and through a reverse cash merger.

As indicated earlier, a cost basis can be achieved by purchasing either assets or stock from the seller. As in the case of a stock purchase, the tax law permits an asset purchase to be effected through a direct purchase of the seller's assets, and through a forward cash merger. In the context of a stock acquisition, a cost basis can be achieved by making an election under Section 338 of the Code. Section 338, as mentioned briefly earlier, allows certain stock transactions to be treated as asset acquisitions under certain conditions.

Is it possible to obtain a cost basis in some of the assets of an acquired company and a carryover basis in other assets?

Some acquirers have wanted to pick and choose their tax treatment, seeking a cost basis for some assets and a carryover basis for others. Congress and the IRS want to prevent this, so Section 338 of the Code provides that when a buyer makes a qualified stock purchase of more than one corporation affiliated with the company being acquired ("affiliate"), it may not make a Section 338 election with respect to one of those corporations without automatically making a Section 338 election with respect to all of them. This rule is commonly called the *stock consistency rule* under Section 338.

What is Section 304 of the Code?

Section 304 of the Code was enacted many years ago to address a tax avoidance technique involving the sale of stock in one related corporation to another related corporation, in which a common shareholder could withdraw cash or property from his or her corporations while retaining undiminished ownership. The classic case involves individual A, who owns all the stock of corporations X and Y and who sells some or all of the X stock to Y for cash. In such a case, Section 304 recharacterizes the transaction and treats it as a dividend from Y accompanied by a nontaxable contribution of X stock to Y, instead of merely a sale of X stock that would qualify as capital gain.

The reach of Section 304 goes far beyond this example, however. It encompasses any situation in which there is direct or indirect "control" by the selling shareholders of the stock of both the acquiring corporation and the corporation being acquired. Control is defined here as 50 percent of the voting power or 50 percent of the value of a corporation's stock (including pure preferred). Control of the buyer acquired in the transaction itself is included.

Section 304 transactions became popular during the leveraged buyout era of the late 1980s. When a company is acquired in a leveraged buyout, and the value of the common stock of both the acquired company and the newly formed purchasing corporation, on a book value basis, is fairly negligible, even a relatively small amount of preferred stock in the purchasing corporation issued to the seller may cause its ownership of the buyer to exceed the 50 percent mark in terms of value. In such a case, Section 304 would come into play.

How may preferred stock be issued to the seller without falling under Section 304?

One way of avoiding these problems is to issue the seller a subordinated debenture or other long-term debt instrument rather than stock. In such a case, unless the debt has peculiar features involving a high risk of recharacterization as equity, Section 304 and the 80 percent affiliation problems can be clearly avoided.

When financing for a transaction requires that the seller receive equity rather than debt, an alternative approach may be in order. In such a case, it may be worthwhile to seek out a third-party preferred stock investor, whose interest could be superior to that of the seller. By thus increasing the amount of stock value not held by the seller, this approach avoids Section 304. Here is where Section 351 comes in.

What is Section 351 of the Code?

Section 351 of the Code is designed to provide nonrecognition treatment to one or more persons who transfer property (including cash) to a corporation in exchange for substantially all the corporation's stock. When the purchasing corporation is a newly formed entity, there is some risk that everyone who receives stock in the entity in connection with transactions that were firmly contemplated at the time of its incorporation will be treated as a transferor receiving nonrecognition treatment under Section 351.

The facts in this regard can vary significantly. On the one hand, when a group of investors forms a corporation to negotiate for and ultimately acquire another corporation, and the purchasing corporation has been fully capitalized prior to negotiations with the management and shareholders of the company being acquired, any stock ultimately received by the shareholders should probably not be treated in connection with the initial incorporation of the purchaser. On the other hand, when a group of individuals contemplating an acquisition negotiates with the shareholders of the company being acquired prior to the incorporation or even the capitalization of the acquiring corporation, there is a very high risk that stock in the purchaser ultimately issued to the selling shareholders will be treated under Section 351.

As is the case with Section 304, when more than 20 percent of the stock of the acquired company is received, or is treated as received, by the purchasing corporation in a Section 351 transaction, the qualified stock purchase under Section 338 will fail.

After a Section 338 acquisition, must the purchaser retain the acquired company as a subsidiary?

The purchasing corporation is permitted to liquidate the company in a tax-free liquidation as soon after the qualified stock purchase as it wishes. Such a liquidation may be effected by way of a statutory merger.

How are purchase price allocations made for tax purposes?

Although businesses are usually bought and sold on a lump-sum basis, for tax purposes each such transaction is broken down into a purchase and sale of the individual assets, both tangible and intangible. There is no specific requirement under the tax laws that a buyer and seller allocate the lump-sum purchase price in the same manner. Because each party is inclined to take positions most favorable to it, allocation issues have been litigated by the IRS fairly often over the years. At the same time, the courts and, to a lesser extent, the IRS have tended to defer to allocations of purchase price agreed upon in writing between a buyer and seller in an arm's-length transaction.

Are there any rules governing the allocation of purchase price?

Yes. If the seller transfers assets constituting a business and determines its basis as the consideration (e.g., purchase price) paid for the assets, then this transfer is considered a Section 1060(c) "applicable asset" acquisition. Both buyer and seller in such a transaction must use the "residual method" to allocate the purchase price received in determining the buyer's basis or the seller's gain or loss. This method, which is also used for a stock purchase, requires that the price of the assets acquired be reduced by cash and cashlike items; the balance must be allocated to tangible assets, followed by intangibles, and finally by goodwill and going-concern value. IRS regulations state that both buyer and seller are bound by the allocations set forth in the acquisition agreement.

What about amortization of intangibles following an acquisition?

Until the passage of the Omnibus Reconciliation Act of 1993 (OBRA 1993), acquirers found it impossible to amortize intangibles at anything close to their economic obsolescence. Under arbitrary standards set forth in Accounting Principles Board Opinion No. 17 (APB 17), a 40-year maximum was placed on amortization of goodwill. Although some write-offs were mandated at shorter periods, the burden was on the company to justify shorter periods not explicitly covered by the mandates. The 1993 tax law proposed a new Code section (Section 197) that sets a uniform standard of 15 years for amortization of intangibles in connection with taxable transactions.[13]

Exceptions to the 15-year rule include the following: ·

- Land
- Financial interests
- Certain computer software
- Certain interests or rights acquired separately
- Interests under leases and debt instruments
- Sports franchises
- Mortgage services
- Transaction costs

These intangibles are treated with either longer periods (e.g., land) or shorter periods (e.g., computer software). All other forms of goodwill and other intangibles are amortizable at 15 years (with certain restrictions meant to discourage purchase of intangibles-rich companies for tax reasons). Note also that the statute's protective language prevented acquisition of intangibles-rich companies for mere tax avoidance purposes.[14]

In general, Code Section 197 benefits acquirers of companies that have intangibles with a long life that normally would have to be amortized over a longer period. In general, businesses like to write off intangibles as quickly as possible, since this creates cash in hand from tax savings and rids the company of a drag on profits—so the 15-year rule is a great improvement over the old 40-year standard.

Another benefit of the law is that now all of an acquired company's stepped-up asset basis—such as depreciation, amortization, and cost of goods sold (with some exceptions as mentioned above)—can generate tax deductions.[15]

ACCOUNTING CONSIDERATIONS

What are the principal authoritative accounting pronouncements covering M&A accounting?

The principal authoritative accounting pronouncement covering the subject of accounting for mergers and acquisitions (business combinations) is Accounting Principles Board Opinion No. 16, "Accounting for Business Combinations" (APB 16). Since its issuance in 1970, APB 16 has been the subject of formal interpretations by the Securities and Exchange Commission (SEC), the American Institute of Certified Public Accountants (AICPA), the Financial Accounting Standards Board (FASB), and the Emerging Issues Task Force (EITF) of the FASB.

What are the accepted methods of accounting for business combinations and how do they differ?

Two acceptable methods of accounting for business combinations are described in APB 16: the purchase method and the pooling of interests method. In April 1999, the FASB voted to abolish pooling accounting and declared its intention to revise the rules for purchase accounting. These changes, however, if finalized, will probably not go into effect before January 1, 2001. Under current rules, the purchase method accounts for a business combination as the acquisition of one company by another. The purchase price and costs of the acquisition are allocated to all the identified assets acquired and liabilities assumed, based on their fair values. If the purchase price exceeds the fair value of the purchased company's net assets, the excess is recorded as goodwill. Earnings or losses of the purchased company are included in the acquiring company's financial statements from the closing date of the acquisition.

The pooling of interests method accounts for a business combination as a uniting of ownership interests of two companies by the exchange of voting equity securities. No acquisition is recognized because the combination is accomplished without disbursing resources of the constituents. In pooling accounting, the assets, liabilities, and retained earnings of each company are carried forward at their previous carrying amounts. Operating results of both companies are combined for all periods prior to the closing date.

Are these methods alternatives in accounting for the same business combination?

No. In APB 16, the Accounting Principles Board concluded that both the purchase method and the pooling of interests method are acceptable in accounting for business combinations, but not as alternatives in accounting for the same business combination. The structure of the business combination transaction (more fully described below) dictates which accounting method must be used. Also described below are the potential advantages and disadvantages of using each.

What are the advantages of using the pooling of interests method?

- Pooling of interests accounting is often preferred if the focus subsequent to the transaction is on the income statement. Income statements for periods subsequent to a pooling of interests are not burdened with additional depreciation, goodwill amortization, and other charges attributable to a purchase price in excess of book value. The higher reportable future income that usually results from application of pooling versus purchase accounting may be of added importance if the objective is a future sale of stock where the sales price is expected to be based on a multiple of reported earnings.
- There are no uncertainties or issues regarding purchase price determination and valuation.
- Prior years' financial statements are restated to reflect the business combination; thus, financial statement year-to-year comparability is not lost.

When must the pooling of interests method be used to account for a business combination?

If a business combination meets 12 specific criteria outlined in APB 16, it must be accounted for as a pooling of interests. These criteria are broadly classified as pertaining to (1) the attributes of the combining companies, (2) the manner in which the companies are combined, and (3) the absence of planned transactions. All 12 criteria must be met if pooling accounting is to be used. If any one criterion is not met, the purchase method of accounting must be used. Pooling criteria include attributes of the combining companies:

- Neither company can be a subsidiary or division of another company within two years before the plan of combination is initiated.
- Each of the combining companies must be independent of the other combining companies: Intercorporate investments in a combining company cannot exceed 10 percent of outstanding voting common stock.

A business corporation wherein these conditions are met indicates that independent ownership interests are combined entirely to continue previously separate corporations. This avoids combinations of selected assets, operations, or ownership interests that are more like purchases than sharings of risks and rights.

Pooling criteria also include the manner in which the companies are combined:

- The combination must be effected in a single transaction or completed in accordance with a specific plan within one year of the plan's initiation.

- A corporation must offer and issue only common stock with rights identical to those of the majority of its outstanding voting common stock (the class of stock with voting control) in exchange for substantially all the voting common stock interest of the other company at the date that the plan of combination is consummated ("substantially all" means a minimum of 90 percent).

- None of the combining companies may change the equity interest of the voting common stock in contemplation of the combination, either within two years before initiation of the plan of combination or during the time between the initiation and consummation of the combination. Changes in contemplation of the combination may include distributions to stockholders, additional issuances, exchanges, and retirements of securities.

- If either of the combining companies has acquired shares of the other's voting common stock (treasury stock), this must be for a purpose other than business combination, and no combining company may acquire more than a normal number of shares between the initiation date and the consummation date. Treasury stock acquired for purposes other than business combinations includes shares for stock option and compensation plans and other recurring distributions, provided a systematic pattern of reacquisitions is established at least two years before the plan of combination is initiated.

- The ratio of the interest of an individual common stockholder to that of other common stockholders in a combining company must remain the same as a result of the exchange of stock to effect the combination.

- The voting rights to which the common stock owners in the resulting combined company are entitled must be exercisable by the

stockholders; the stockholders may be neither deprived of nor restricted in exercising those rights for any period. The issued shares
may not be transferred, for example, to a voting trust.

- The combination must be resolved at the consummation date, and
  no provisions of the plan relating to the issue of securities or other
  conditions may be pending. This precludes the contingent issuance
  of additional shares.[16]

- The combined company may not intend or plan to dispose of a significant portion of the assets of the combining companies within
  two years after combination, other than disposals in the ordinary
  course of business of the formerly separate companies or disposals
  in elimination of duplicate facilities or excess capacity.

- The combined company may not enter into other financial arrangements for the benefit of the former stockholders of a combining
  company—such as the guarantee of loans secured by stock issued in
  the combination—that in effect negate the exchange of equity securities.

- The combined company may not agree directly or indirectly to retire or acquire all or part of the common stock issued to effect the
  combination.

- The SEC staff generally requires that, in order to qualify for pooling
  accounting, the combining company must be an operating entity
  with "significant operations" (that is, something other than nominal). In one case, the SEC stated that a company with little operating
  activity, but with a substantial asset base (principally natural resource assets whose book values were significantly below fair market values), could not be party to a pooling of interests. The concept
  is that, in order to qualify for pooling accounting, there must be a
  combination of operating businesses. The SEC has not defined "little
  operating activity"; this must be determined on a case-by-case basis.

What are some reasons that preclude a business combination from being accounted for as a pooling of interests?

There are literally hundreds of reasons that preclude a business combination
from being accounted for as a pooling of interests. Here are some of the more
common ones:

- Sale of significant assets by the combining companies, either prior to consummation of the business combination or subsequent to the business combination. Dispositions occurring within three months prior to the business combination are presumed to be in contemplation of the pooling (and, accordingly, violate the pooling rules). Dispositions between three and six months prior to the business combination are also presumed to be in contemplation of the pooling if a company cannot substantiate that they were not. Between six months and two years prior to consummation, a disposition is presumed not to be in contemplation of the pooling if a company will represent that fact. The measure of "significance" for this purpose has generally been construed to be the same as that used for a reportable segment in the FASB's FAS 14, "Financial Reporting for Segments of a Business Enterprise," that is, 10 percent of operating profits, assets, or sales.

- Combination with a new company formed by spinning off a subsidiary, or a new company formed to acquire the spun-off subsidiary. Although it is generally understood that the acquisition of a company through a leveraged buyout will not qualify for pooling accounting, the autonomy criterion may also prevent the acquired business from subsequently qualifying for pooling accounting. For example, if the leveraged buyout group's investment vehicle is one of several subsidiaries of a leveraged buyout fund or holding company, an acquired business would fail to satisfy the autonomy criterion. If, however, the leveraged buyout is structured so that the acquired company is not controlled by another operating entity—that is, it is not a subsidiary following the leveraged buyout—it can qualify for pooling of interests accounting after two years, provided that all the other criteria are met.

- Acquisitions of "material amounts" of treasury shares in relation to the planned combination. Treasury shares are material if they exceed 10 percent of the shares to be issued in the business combination.

- A contingency arrangement that is based on earnings levels, book values, or stock market prices subsequent to the consummation date. A contingency arrangement that relates to conditions existing at the consummation date, however, would not preclude pooling accounting—for example, an escrow related to tax returns not yet examined by the IRS.

Does the existence of a standstill agreement preclude a business combination from being accounted for as a pooling of interests?

The FASB's Emerging Issues Task Force (EITF) has addressed this issue in connection with standstill agreements that prohibit a more-than-10-percent shareholder from acquiring additional shares for a specified period. The EITF reached a consensus that pooling accounting would not be precluded if the standstill agreement was not made in contemplation of the combination and was with a less-than-majority shareholder. A standstill agreement made in contemplation of a particular business combination with a more-than-10-percent shareholder, however, would preclude pooling accounting. Under a standstill agreement with a 10-percent-or-less shareholder made in contemplation of the combination, pooling accounting would also be precluded if that shareholder and other dissenters aggregated more than 10 percent of the shares issued in the combination.

Does the granting or exercise of a lockup option preclude pooling accounting for a subsequent merger between the parties?

Lockup arrangements take many forms, but most have the same basic structure: an agreement that Company A will acquire all or a specific part of Company B, and that Company A will realize an economic gain if another company buys Company B or the specified part of Company B.

A lockup structured as an option agreement does not preclude pooling accounting, provided that no consideration is issued or received for the option and the option is not exercised. If the lockup is structured as a sale of stock, pooling accounting becomes more questionable.

What happens to the financial statements when a buyer is required to account for a business combination using the pooling of interests method?

In a pooling, the carrying amounts of the assets and liabilities of the constituent companies remain unchanged. The carrying amounts of assets and liabilities of the separate companies are added together to become the assets and liabilities of the combined corporation.

At what date should a buyer that applies the pooling of interests method report combined results?

A buyer that applies the pooling of interests method of accounting for a combination should report results of operations for the fiscal period in which the combination occurs as though the companies had been combined as of the beginning of the period. Results of operations for that fiscal period thus comprise those of the separate companies combined from the beginning of the period to the date the combination is consummated and those of the combined operations from that date to the end of the period. Previously issued financial statements are restated as though the companies had always been combined.

What accounting is required for expenses related to a pooling?

All costs incurred to effect a pooling transaction should be recognized as expenses of the combined corporation in determining net income. Such expenses include SEC filing fees; investment banking fees; legal, accounting, and consultant fees; and costs incurred in combining and integrating the operations of the previously separate companies, including implementation of efficiencies.

What are the advantages of the purchase method?

- Purchase accounting is often preferred if the acquirer's focus after the transaction will be on the balance sheet. Assets and liabilities are recognized at their fair values instead of at the acquired company's historical costs. Thus, the postcombination balance sheet appears healthier under purchase accounting than under pooling accounting. This may be of added importance if the postcombination balance sheet is a key factor in a lender's decision to finance the acquisition.
- No restatements of prior years' financial statements are required, so sales and earnings trends may show an improvement.

What are the disadvantages of the purchase method?

- Accounting income is exposed to the write-off of additional depreciation, goodwill amortization, and other charges that may adversely affect earnings trends.
- Uncertainties regarding purchase price determination and valuation exist.

- Prior years' financial statements are not restated and, therefore, are not comparable.

When must the purchase method be used to account for a business combination?

The purchase method of accounting must be used for any business combination that does not meet all the conditions for pooling of interests treatment.

How is purchase price recorded under the purchase method?

The purchase method follows principles normally applicable under historical cost accounting to recording acquisitions of assets and issuances of stock. The general principles to apply the historical cost basis of accounting to an acquisition depend on the nature of the transaction:

- If the company is acquired by exchanging cash or other assets, purchase price is the amount of cash disbursed or fair value of other assets distributed.
- If the company is acquired by incurring liabilities, purchase price is the present value of the amounts to be paid.
- If the company is acquired by issuing shares of stock, the value assigned to the stock is the fair value of the consideration received. As a practical matter, in most business combinations it is easier to value the stock exchanged, and this is normally done for convenience.

Cash paid, liabilities incurred, and securities issued constitute the major portion of the purchase price of most acquisitions. Numerous other items, however, must be considered for inclusion in the purchase price. Here are some of them:

- Direct expenses, such as finder's and directly related professional fees (legal, investment banking, accounting, appraisal, and environmental consulting)
- Premium or discount on a debt security issued or assumed, with the imputed liability adjusted to present value on the basis of current interest rates, if stated rates differ significantly from current market rates
- A negotiated adjustment to the purchase price related to assumption of a contingent liability such as a lawsuit or tax examination

Under the purchase method, how should the buyer's cost be allocated to the assets acquired and liabilities assumed?

Under APB 16, the buyer's cost is allocated to individual assets and liabilities at their fair market values at the time of acquisition. Independent appraisals may be used in determining the fair value of some assets and liabilities. Subsequent sales of assets may also provide evidence of values.

The following are general guidelines for assigning amounts to individual assets acquired and liabilities assumed:

- Present value, determined at appropriate current interest rates, of receivables (net of estimated allowances for uncollectibility and collection costs, if necessary); accounts and notes payable, long-term debt, and other claims payable; and other liabilities, such as warranty, vacation pay, deferred compensation, unfavorable leases, contracts and commitments, and plant closing expenses incident to the acquisition
- Current replacement cost of raw materials inventories and plant and equipment, adjusted to remaining economic lives
- Net realizable value of marketable securities and property and equipment to be sold or to be used temporarily
- Appraised value of identifiable intangibles and other assets
- Finished goods and merchandise at estimated selling prices less the sum of (1) the cost of disposal and (2) a reasonable profit allowance for the selling effort of the acquiring corporation
- Work-in-process inventory at estimated selling prices of finished goods less the sum of (1) the cost to complete, (2) the cost of disposal, and (3) a reasonable profit allowance for the completing and selling effort of the acquiring corporation on the basis of profit for similar finished goods

Previously recorded goodwill of the acquired company is not recognized in the purchase price allocation. If the acquired company sponsors a single-employer defined benefit pension plan, the assignment of the purchase price to the individual assets acquired and liabilities assumed shall include a liability for the projected benefit obligation in excess of plan assets, or an asset for plan assets in excess of the projected benefit obligation.

The following example illustrates the above principles. Assume that Corporation A acquires Corporation B in a business combination accounted for as a purchase on September 30, 1998. The purchase price is $750,000 cash and 50,000 shares of Corporation A common stock. Transaction costs are $200,000 (unrelated to stock issuance).

The historical carrying amounts and fair values of Corporation B's assets and liabilities on September 30, 1998, are as shown in Table 3–1. The computation of the total purchase price of Corporation B, assuming that the fair value of the common stock issued by Corporation A on September 30, 1998, was $20 per share, is given in Table 3–2. The computation of purchase price, assuming the fair value of Corporation A common stock on September 30, 1998, was $30 per share, is shown in Table 3–3. In both transactions, the purchase price was computed as cash of $750,000, out-of-pocket costs of $200,000, and assumed liabilities of $1,180,000, plus 50,000 shares of stock. If the stock is valued at $20 per share, the asset value is $50,000 more than the purchase price of $3,130,000. If the stock is valued at $30 per share, the asset value is $450,000 less than the purchase price (additional goodwill).

T A B L E 3–1

Corporation B Balance Sheet, September 30, 1998

	Carrying Amount	Fair Value
	(in thousands)	
Assets		
Cash	$100	$100
Accounts receivable, net	300	300
Inventories	600	680
Short-term prepayments	120	100
Land	500	650
Other plant assets, net	1,000	1,250
Patent	80	100
Total assets	$2,700	$3,180
Liabilities and Stockholder Equity		
Current liabilities	$700	$700
Long-term debt	500	480
Capital stock, $5 par	600	
Paid-in capital in excess of par	400	
Retained earnings	500	
Net assets acquired	_____	2,000
Total liabilities and stockholder equity	$2,700	$3,180

T A B L E 3–2

Purchase Price Allocation Based on $20 Per Share

	Fair Value	Purchase Price Allocation
	(in thousands)	
Cash	$100	$100
Accounts receivable, net	300	300
Inventories	680	680
Short-term prepayments	100	100
Land	650	634*
Other plant assets, net	1,250	1,219*
Patent	100	97*
Total assets	$3,180	$3,130

*Discount ($50) was allocated pro rata to noncurrent assets.

T A B L E 3–3

Purchase Price Allocation Based on $30 Per Share

	Fair Value	Purchase Price Allocation
	(in thousands)	
Cash	$100	$100
Accounts receivable, net	300	300
Inventories	680	680
Short-term prepayments	100	100
Land	650	650
Other plant assets, net	1,250	1,250
Patent		
Goodwill	100	550
Total assets	$3,180	$3,630

How should the difference in the value of the acquired net assets versus cost be accounted for? Suppose this is negative?

If the sum of the market or appraised values of identifiable assets acquired less liabilities assumed exceeds the cost of the acquired company, the values otherwise assignable to noncurrent assets acquired (except long-term investments and marketable securities) should be reduced by a proportionate amount of the excess to determine the assigned values. If the values of noncurrent assets are reduced to zero, then a deferred credit is recorded on the buyer's balance sheet for the excess of the aggregate assigned value of identifiable assets over cost (sometimes called "negative goodwill") of an acquired company. Negative goodwill is considered a deferred credit rather than an intangible (such as "positive goodwill"), and it should not be netted against positive goodwill when reporting those amounts in the financial statements. Negative goodwill is amortized systematically as an increase in reported income. The list of factors discussed above for amortizing goodwill should be considered in determining the amortization period for negative goodwill.

How are the differences between the market or appraised values of specific assets and liabilities and the income tax bases of those assets accounted for?

The FASB's FAS 96, "Accounting for Income Taxes," requires, as a general rule, that a deferred tax liability or asset be recognized for the tax consequences of differences between the assigned fair values and the tax bases of assets and liabilities recognized in a business combination. A deferred tax liability or asset is not recognized for a difference between the assigned amount and the tax basis of goodwill, unallocated "negative" goodwill, and leveraged leases. FAS 96 contains complexities that could affect the accounting for business combinations. The facts and circumstances of each transaction need to be evaluated.

How much time does a buyer have to complete the accounting under the purchase method?

The *allocation period,* during which the buyer identifies and values the assets acquired and the liabilities assumed, ends when the acquiring enterprise is no longer waiting for information that it has arranged to obtain and that is known to be available or obtainable. Although the time required varies with circumstances, the allocation period should usually not exceed one year from the consummation of a business combination. The existence of a preacquisition contingency for which an asset, a liability, or an impairment of an asset cannot be estimated does not, of itself, extend the allocation period.

What are preacquisition contingencies, and how should they be considered in the allocation of purchase price?

A contingency is an existing condition, situation, or set of circumstances involving uncertainty as to possible gain or loss to an enterprise that will ultimately be resolved when one or more future events occur or fail to occur. A preacquisition contingency is a contingency of the acquired enterprise that is in existence before consummation of a business combination; it can be a contingent asset, a contingent liability, or a contingent impairment of an asset. Examples of preacquisition contingencies include pending or threatened litigation, obligations relating to product warranties and product defects, and actual or possible claims or assessments. These include income tax examinations, assessments by environmental agencies, guarantees of indebtedness of others, and impairment of the carrying amount of productive assets used in the business.

A preacquisition contingency is included in the allocation of purchase price according to an amount determined as follows:

- If the fair value of the preacquisition contingency can be determined during the allocation period, that preacquisition contingency is included in the allocation of purchase price based on that fair value.
- If the fair value *cannot* be determined during the allocation period, that preacquisition contingency shall be included in the allocation of the purchase price only if information available prior to the end of the allocation period indicates that it is probable that a contingent asset existed, a contingent liability had been incurred, or an existing asset might be impaired at the consummation of the business combination. Implicit in this condition is that it must be probable that one or more future events will occur confirming the contingency, and that the amount of the asset or liability can be reasonably estimated.

Contingencies that arise from the acquisition and that did not exist prior to the acquisition are the buyer's contingencies rather than preacquisition contingencies of the acquired company.

At what date should a buyer that has applied the purchase method report combined results?

The acquisition date of a company ordinarily is the date assets are received and other assets are given or securities are issued. The reported income of the buyer includes operations of the acquired company beginning with the date of acquisition. In a purchase business combination, there is no restatement of prior period financial statements. In certain situations, however, the acquisition date may be "as of" a date earlier than the closing date. These include, for example, situations in which the parties intend to fix a determinable price as of a specified date other than the closing date or to develop a formula whereby changes in earnings or market price between the specified date and the closing date will be considered in the final purchase price. To use a date earlier than the closing date in including the results of operations of the target, the following conditions must be met:

- The parties must reach a firm purchase agreement that includes specifying the date of acquisition other than the closing date. Effective control of the acquired company (including the risks and rewards of ownership) transfers to the acquiring company as of the specified date.
- The time period between the specified date and the closing date must be relatively short.

What are typical forms of contingent consideration in an acquisition, and how should such consideration be included in determining the cost of an acquired company?

A business combination may provide for the issuance of stock or the transfer of cash or other consideration contingent on specified transactions or events in the future. Agreements often provide that a portion of the consideration be placed in escrow and distributed or returned when the specified event has occurred. In general, to the extent that the contingent consideration can be determined at the time of the acquisition, such amount shall be included in determining the cost of the acquired company.

As is often the case, however, the amount of the contingent consideration may not be known at the time of the acquisition. As an example, additional consideration may be contingent on maintaining or achieving specified earnings levels in the future. When the contingency is resolved or resolution is probable and additional consideration is payable, the acquiring company records the current fair value of the consideration paid as an additional cost of the acquired company. This subsequent recognition of additional cost requires an adjustment to the initial amounts recorded at the date of acquisition. Generally, the amount of goodwill is adjusted for the amount of additional consideration paid.

What accounting is required for expenses related to a purchase?

Direct acquisition costs incurred by an acquiring company effecting a business combination accounted for under the purchase method are included as part of the purchase price. Direct acquisition costs incurred by an acquired company, or its major or controlling shareholders, should generally not be included as part of the cost of the acquired company. Acquisition costs incurred by the acquired company are presumed to be taken into account indirectly by the acquiring company in setting the purchase price. If, however, the acquiring company agrees to reimburse the acquired company's major or controlling shareholders for acquisition costs incurred by them, these costs should be included as part of the purchase price of the acquired company. Direct acquisition costs include fees paid to investment bankers, legal fees, accounting fees, appraisal fees, and other consulting fees.

Fees paid to an investment banker in connection with a business combination accounted for as a purchase when the investment banker is also providing interim financing or debt underwriting services must be allocated between direct costs of the acquisition and debt issue costs.

What are the disclosure requirements for business combinations?

The disclosures required for a business combination accounted for by either the purchase or pooling of interests method are governed by APB 16, as amended, and the rules and regulations of the SEC.

For a *purchase* business combination, the following disclosures are required in the notes to the financial statements of both public and nonpublic enterprises:

- Name and a brief description of the acquired enterprise
- Method of accounting for the combination—that is, the purchase method

- Period for which results of operations of the acquired enterprise are included in the income statement of the acquiring enterprise
- Cost of the acquired enterprise and, if applicable, the number of shares of stock issued or issuable and the amount assigned to the issued and issuable shares
- Description of the plan for amortization of acquired goodwill, the amortization method, and the amortization period
- Contingent payments, options, or commitments specified in the acquisition agreement and their proposed accounting treatment

In addition, notes to the financial statements of the acquiring enterprise for the period in which a purchase business combination occurs should include as supplemental information the following pro forma information (public companies only):

- Results of operations for the current period as though the enterprises had combined at the beginning of the period
- Results of operations for the immediately preceding period as though the enterprises had combined at the beginning of that period, if comparative financial statements are presented

The supplemental pro forma information should, at a minimum, disclose revenue, income before extraordinary items, net income, and earnings per share. To present pro forma information, income taxes, interest expense, preferred stock dividends, depreciation, and amortization of assets, including goodwill, should be adjusted to their accounting bases recognized in recording the combination. Pro forma presentation of results of operations of periods prior to the combination transaction should be limited to the immediately preceding period.

For a *pooling* of interests, the following disclosures are required in the notes to the financial statements:

- Name and brief description of the enterprises combined, except an enterprise whose name is carried forward to the combined enterprise.
- Method of accounting for the combination—that is, the pooling of interests method.
- Description and number of shares of stock issued in the business combination.
- Details of the results of operations of the previously separate enterprises for the period before the combination is consummated that are included in the current combined net income. The details should

include revenue, extraordinary items, net income, other changes in stockholder equity, and amount of and manner of accounting for intercompany transactions.

- Description of the nature of adjustments to the net assets of the combined enterprises to adopt the same accounting practices and of the effects of the changes on net income previously reported by the separate enterprises and now presented in comparative financial statements.
- Details of an increase or decrease in retained earnings attributable to a change in the fiscal year of a combining enterprise. The details should include revenue, expenses, extraordinary items, net income, and other changes in stockholder equity for the period excluded from the reported results of operations.
- Reconciliation of revenue and earnings previously reported by the enterprise that issues the stock to effect the combination with the combined amounts currently presented in financial statements and summaries. The new enterprise formed to effect a combination may instead disclose the earnings of the separate enterprises that constitute combined earnings for prior periods.

In addition, the notes to the financial statements should disclose details of the effects of a pooling business combination that were consummated before the financial statements are issued, but that are either incomplete as of the date of the financial statements or initiated after that date. The details should include revenue, net income, earnings per share, and the effects of expected changes in accounting methods as if the combination had been consummated at the date of the financial statements.

What is pro forma financial information?

Pro forma financial information reflects the impact on historical financial statements of a particular business combination and its financing as if the transaction had been consummated at an earlier date. Pro forma information ordinarily includes (1) a description of the transaction, the entities involved, and the periods for which the pro forma information is presented, and (2) a columnar presentation of historical condensed balance sheet and income statements, pro forma adjustments, and pro forma results.

Pro forma adjustments to the income statement are computed assuming that the transaction was consummated at the beginning of the fiscal year and include adjustments that give effect to events that are (1) directly attributable to the transaction, (2) expected to have a continuing impact on the registrant, and (3) factually supportable.

How should the fair value or carrying amount of preferred stock issued in business combinations be determined?

The distinctive attributes of preferred stock make some preferred issues similar to debt securities, whereas others are more similar to common stock, with many variations between the extremes. Determining the appropriate carrying value to assign to preferred stock issued in a business combination will be affected by its characteristics.

Even though the principle of recording the fair value of consideration received for stock issued applies to all equity securities, preferred as well as common, the carrying value of preferred securities may be determined in practice on the same basis as debt securities. For example, the carrying value of a nonvoting, nonconvertible preferred stock that lacks characteristics of common stock may be determined by comparing the specified dividend and redemption terms with similar terms and market risks for debt securities.

What is pushdown accounting?

Pushdown accounting refers to the establishment of a new accounting and reporting basis in a company's separate financial statements, resulting from the purchase and substantial change of ownership of its outstanding voting equity securities. The buyer's purchase price is "pushed down" to the acquired company and used to restate the carrying value of its assets and liabilities. For example, if all a company's voting equity securities are purchased, the assets and liabilities of the company must be restated using fair market values so that the excess of the restated amounts of the assets over the restated amounts of the liabilities equals the buyer's purchase price.

In what circumstances should pushdown accounting be applied?

The SEC requires pushdown accounting for acquired corporations that are substantially or wholly owned. The SEC states that when the form of ownership is within the control of the buyer, the basis of accounting for purchased assets and liabilities should be the same regardless of whether the entity continues to exist or is merged into the buyer.

The SEC recognizes, however, that the existence of outstanding public debt, preferred stock, or a significant minority interest in a subsidiary might affect the buyer's ability to control the form of ownership. As a result, the SEC, although encouraging its use, generally does not insist on the application of pushdown accounting in these circumstances. Pushdown accounting is optional for the separate financial statements of a nonpublic company.

CONCLUDING COMMENTS

In the previous pages, you have taken a tour of the landmarks in M&A tax and accounting. It may seem excessive to spend so many pages on the nuances of the U.S. tax code, especially since so many members of the 106th Congress (January 1999 to December 2000) came in vowing to scrap the tax code entirely. In our experience, however, major regulatory changes often happen very slowly. The guidance we have given in this chapter should be generally useful for at least another few years—the least amount of time it will take the new Congress to pass major tax legislation (if any).

This said, however, *always* check with your attorneys and accountants. When it comes to M&A financing, the angels, as well as their diabolical opposites, are in the details—those elegant "3 percents" (or 28 percents or 51 percents, as the tax or accounting case may be). These details, moreover, are subject to change through rule making at any time. Keeping up with those changes—both domestically and internationally (as seen in the last chapter of this book)—is one of the many roles of M&A maestros and their advisers.

ENDNOTES

1. For more on the tax aspects of M&A, an excellent source is Martin D. Ginsberg and Jack S. Levin, *Mergers, Acquisitions, and Buyouts: A Transactional Analysis of the Governing Tax, Legal, and Accounting Considerations*, 3 vols. (New York: Aspen Law and Business, 1998), which we often consult whenever we want authoritative guidance on M&A taxation. Another source, written more for a managerial audience, is Chapter 5 of Stanley Foster Reed and Alexandra Reed Lajoux, *The Art of M&A: A Merger/Acquisition/Buyout Guide*, 3rd ed. (New York: McGraw-Hill, 1999). Weston and Lajoux (coauthor of the second book mentioned) wish to acknowledge both of these books as sources used in the preparation of this chapter. We also acknowledge the founding genius of the many partners and associates of Lane and Edson, P.C., who lent their considerable expertise in tax law and other legal matters to the first edition of *The Art of M&A*, published exactly 10 years ago, in 1989.

2. Rule 145 of the Securities Act of 1933, concerning "Reclassification of Securities, Mergers, Consolidations and Acquisition of Assets," defines transactions within the rule as including "an 'offer,' 'offer to sell,' 'offer for sale,' or 'sale.'" These fall under the rule when "there is submitted for the vote or consent of such security-holders a plan or agreement pursuant to which such holders are

required to elect, on the basis of what is in substance a new investment deci-sion, whether to accept a new or different security in exchange for their existing security." *Securities Act Rules, Volume 1, Rules 100 through 236: General Rules and Regulations under the Securities Act of 1933,* September 15, 1998 (New York: Bowne & Co., 1998), p. 30.

3. One of the laws limiting the reach of state income taxes was broadened in early 1992 when the U.S. Supreme Court declared a "de minimis" exception to a 1959 law establishing a federal limitation on state income taxes. This exception, set forth in *Wisconsin Department of Revenue v. William Wrigley, Jr., Co.,* found that certain activities were "not entirely ancillary to requests for purchases" and, therefore, not exempt from state income tax. See "U.S. Supreme Court Clarifies Federal Limitation on State Income Taxes," *Deloitte & Touche Review,* July 27, 1992, pp. 5–6.

4. Incidentally, C and S corporations are part of a larger system. In all, considering the various permutations of its provisions, Section 368 ultimately sets forth more than a dozen different varieties of acquisition reorganizations. The most commonly used forms of reorganizations are the A, B, C, and D reorganiza-tions. (Others are F and G reorganizations, and various hybrids.)

   ▪ An *A reorganization* (named after its alphabetic place in Section 368) is very simply a "statutory merger or consolidation." This type of reorganization has other, more complex names—such as a *reorganization not solely for voting stock* as distinct from a B reorganization, which *is* solely for voting stock (see be-low). It is also referred to as a *tax-free forward merger,* as opposed to the tax-able forward merger and taxable reverse merger forms discussed earlier (there is no tax-free reverse merger).

   ▪ A *B reorganization* is a stock-for-stock exchange in which one company buys the stock of another company using only ("solely") its own stock.

   ▪ A *C reorganization* is a transaction in which one company buys the assets of another company using only its own stock.

   ▪ A *D reorganization* is a transaction in which a company transfers its assets down into a subsidiary.

5. Based on a client memo from the law firm of Whitford, Taylor & Preston.

6. Shareholders may not have to pay taxes on their dividends if they hold their stock for a certain period of time. This "dividends received deduction" is avail-able to shareholders who have held the stock (and been at economic risk from it) for more than 45 days—or more than 90 in some cases (such as preferred stock). The Taxpayer Relief Act of 1997, in Section 1015, preserved this deduc-tion but made it more stringent by setting forth some more complex buy/sell time frame requirements and by stipulating that the dividends-received deduc-tion will be available only to shareholders who meet the holding period re-quirement with respect to each dividend received.

7. Under current law, an issuer of debt can deduct the interest that it pays, but an issuer of equity may not deduct the dividend payments it makes. The inter-

est/dividend distinction became somewhat complicated after the Taxpayer Relief Act of 1997, which stated that no deduction will be allowed for interest on an instrument that is payable in stock of the issuer or a related party. This raises the issue of treatment of convertible debt, but Kenneth R. Goldberg of Jones, Day, Reavis & Pogue (New York) assures clients that "it is not anticipated that the new rule will apply to convertible debt if the conversion price is significantly higher than the price of the issuer's stock at the time the debt is issued." See: "1997 Tax Reform: Summaries of Selected Provisions Affecting Corporations, Other Entities, and Business Executives," August 1997, p. 31.

8. A corporate distribution means an actual or constructive transfer of cash or other property (with certain exceptions) by a corporation to a shareholder acting in the capacity of a shareholder. For tax purposes, a transfer of property to a shareholder acting in the capacity of an employee or lender, for example, is not a corporate distribution.

9. Pass-through entities are structures that permit a single—rather than double—tax. The three types of pass-through entities are: (1) a partnership, both general and limited, (2) an S corporation, and (3) a C corporation that files a consolidated income tax return with its corporate "parent." The earnings of all C corporations are subject to double tax, but the consolidated return provisions generally permit the earnings of subsidiary members of the consolidated return group to be taxed to the ultimate parent only. The earnings of an S corporation, with certain exceptions, are subject to taxation only at the shareholder level. The earnings of a partnership are also subject to a single tax, but only to the extent that such earnings are allocated to noncorporate partners (unless the partner is an S corporation). Partnership earnings that are allocated to corporate partners are subject to double taxation, just as though the income were earned directly by the corporations.

10. A recharacterization of debt into equity raises a somewhat different concern in the case of the debt of a partnership. Debts of a limited partnership for which no general or limited partner is personally liable (nonrecourse debts) increase the basis of the limited partners in the partnership. A recharacterization will not convert a partnership into a taxpaying entity. Rather, the lender will become a partner, and the entire amount of the recharacterized debt will be allocated to increase the lender's basis. Other partners' bases will shrink, causing them to encounter unexpected tax results. For example, cash distributions in excess of their recharacterized bases will produce income, and, if the partnership generates a taxable loss, some or all of the loss may have to be allocated to the lender-partner.

11. The Clinton Administration's fiscal year 1999 budget released February 3, 1998, proposed to deny the deduction for nonqualified preferred stock, but this proposal did not get enacted into final law. See: Ginsberg and Levin, op. cit. (note 1), vol. 2, ch. 13, p. 355.

12. Gain from the sale of assets may be taxed at 8, 10, 14, 15, 18, 20, 25, 28, 31, 36, or 39.6 percent, depending on the holding period, date sold, type of asset, and amount of other income.

13. Except for transactions closed before July 25, 1991, OBRA 1993's treatment of intangibles rendered moot (at least for now) a 1991 Supreme Court decision that broadened the definition of intangibles to include goodwill. In *Newark Morning Ledger Co. v. United States,* the Supreme Court said that if the value of an acquired asset can be measured and will diminish over time, this value can be depreciated over time. Assets covered under the *Newark* decision were various types of customer lists, including insurance renewal lists, drugstore prescription files, cleaning service accounts, publication subscriber lists, and "any other identifiable asset the value of which obviously depends on the continued and voluntary patronage of customers." These will now all fall under OBRA's 15-year, 100 percent treatment, since none were excepted.

14. OBRA 1993, Section 13261, reads in part at Subsection F (9) as follows: "The term 'amortizable Section 197 intangibles' shall not include any Section 197 intangibles . . . for which depreciation or amortization would not have been allowable but for this section . . . and which is acquired by the taxpayer after the date of the enactment of this section under certain conditions." Further, Section 197 treatment will not apply to an intangible "acquired by the taxpayer . . . to recognize gain on the disposition of the intangible and to pay a tax on such a gain" under certain conditions.

15. The source of this paragraph is Ginsberg and Levin, op. cit. (note 1), vol. 1, ch. 1, p. 11.

16. The essence of a pooling of interests, or "pooling," is that separate shareholder interests lose their identity and all share mutually in the combined rights and risks of the combined entity. Mutual sharing is incompatible with alterations of relative voting rights, preferential claims to profits or assets for some shareholder groups, preservation of minority shareholder groups, acquisitions of common stock for assets or debt, and acquisitions of stock for the purpose of exchanging it. These conditions prohibit the inclusion in the negotiations, either explicitly or by intent, of certain types of transactions after consummation of the transaction. These are prohibited because they are inconsistent with the concept of combining entire shareholder interests. For information on purchase versus pooling in the global context, see Chapter 15.

PART TWO

A Closer Look
at Instruments

If an M&A maven fell asleep in the year 1979, and slept for 20 years, what would this modern-day Rip Van Winkle notice upon awakening in the year 1999? Surely it would be the proliferation of *new instruments for debt, equity, and combinations thereof.* But like Rip, the maven would be wise to search first for his old neighborhood, just to see if it is still there. The good news is that when it comes to homesteads, little has changed. The M&A expert can still rely on the three major financial statements when analyzing the financing needs of any company or group of companies: the balance sheet, the income statement, and the statement of cash flows.

The balance sheet essentially reveals two things. On its lefthand side, it shows how much investment the company has needed to make in assets in order to generate its sales. On its righthand side, it shows how the company has obtained the funds to finance those assets. The income statement essentially shows how much in hard cash these necessary assets have cost the firm, and how much cash it has left over to make further investments. The statement of cash flows, which is derived from the balance sheet and the income statements, shows the rate and volume at which this cash moves through the firm.

The experienced analyst of any proposed merger transaction can look at these three statements from each of the combining companies and can assess their financial potential going forward as a combined company.

This, however, will be *just the beginning of the maven's work.* Today, given the enormous complexity of the financing used to support M&A activity, it is also necessary to understand the individual dynamics of the *financial instru-*

ments used to pay for the deal. These instruments may be classified as debt, equity, or a hybrid combination of the two. These three subjects will be our focus in the next three chapters.

Dynamics of Debt-Based Financing

The human species, according to the best theory I can form of it, is composed of two distinct races: the men who borrow, and the men who lend.

Charles Lamb, *Essays of Elia,* 1823

INTRODUCTION

Debt-based financing is as old as time and viewed with just as much mistrust. Biblical writers warn against it: "The borrower is servant to the lender" (Proverbs). Similar warnings are found in virtually all the world's religions—notably Islam, which forbids lenders to charge interest.

Yet many successful economies have been built on borrowed capital. Most of the nations in the Americas possess economies that can be traced to an investment some European made in a voyage across the Atlantic. In the corporate world, the examples are no less impressive. The great pillars of industry—from American Express to Zurich Insurance—have grown thanks in part to borrowed capital, some of it to support acquisitions.

Gone are the days when a company could and would borrow lavishly beyond its means, while greedy bankers stood by to foreclose. This classic tale may have drawn crowds in the early days of American melodrama, but it is largely absent from the stage of life today. Instead, we see a tremendous variety and creativity in the types of debt used—and a sound prudence in how that debt is secured.

This chapter is basically organized into three parts: loans, notes and bonds, and leases.

In the loan section, we will begin by defining debt and discussing interest rates. Then we will explain different types of debt, including term loans, revolving credits, and private and public debt offerings.

In the bond part, we will discuss notes and bonds, including commercial paper, notes, mortgage financing, and collateral trust and equipment trust mechanisms. We will also review debentures, focusing on subordinated debentures. In addition, we will cover the subject of bond ratings (from AAA to "junk") and bonds sold in private placements.

In closing, we will delve into the sometimes arcane world of asset-based financing—particularly financing via sale/leaseback.

Later on in this book, we will continue the story of debt-based financing, guiding readers on debtlike hybrid instruments (Chapter 6) and on approaching lenders (Chapter 8) and backers (Chapter 9). We will also explore how to manage multiple sources of debt and/or equity capital (Chapter 10). At the end of the book (Chapters 13 through 15) we cover international debt and equity financing. For now, we will delve into the basics.

DEBT FUNDAMENTALS

What exactly is debt, and how is its value realized?

As mentioned in Chapter 3, debt is a promise (in most cases an unconditional one) to pay a certain sum at a definite time. The promise is made in the form of an agreement, also called (in multilender deals) a *facility*. To raise capital via debt, a company can do two basic things: It can take out a loan from a commercial lender or other creditor, or it can sell a bond or note. In both cases, interest is charged. Therefore, one of the fundamental concepts deal makers need to master in understanding debt-based financing is interest rates.

What interest rates might be charged in a loan or offered in a bond or note?

The interest rate for a typical loan—for example, a standard term loan—may be determined by the *bank prime rate*, the lender's *cost of funds*, the *federal funds rate*, and/or the London Interbank Offered Rate (LIBOR).

What is the bank prime rate and how does it work?

Contrary to popular belief, the prime rate (also called *base rate*) is not a fixed, lowest number that all banks charge at any given time. Rather, the prime or base rate is whatever the lending bank from time to time says it is. This in turn may be determined by the bank's cost of funds, which, as mentioned, is another determinant of lending rates. Typically, a bank will charge 1.5 to 2 percent over prime rate. The going prime rate as of March 1999 was 7.5 percent, with predictions of similar rates in the months ahead. (Readers of this book, scheduled for release in June 1999, can judge the accuracy of these predictions, reported as we go to press in April.)[1]

How does the lender determine its cost of funds?

The lender's cost of funds is the dollar cost of interest paid or accrued either on funds acquired from various sources within a bank or on borrowed funds acquired from other banks. These funds include not only regular time deposits, but also funds obtained through the Federal Reserve Banking System.[2] They also include so-called Eurodollar deposits, which are U.S. dollars deposited in non-U.S. banks.

What is the federal funds rate?

The federal funds rate is the rate banks charge each other in the so-called interbank or federal funds market for purchases of excess reserve balances. These are balances that exceed bank reserve requirements set by the central banking authority—the Federal Reserve System in the United States. The rates are set overnight each day.

   Rates are typically based on the weighted average of rates on overnight federal funds transactions with members of the Federal Reserve System arranged by federal funds brokers, as published by the Federal Reserve Bank of New York. Or they may be an average of quotes from a specified number of federal funds brokers of recognized standing selected by the bank.

What is LIBOR?

LIBOR, as mentioned earlier, is the acronym for the London Interbank Offered Rate. LIBOR, which is sometimes referred to as a Eurodollar rate, is typically calculated as the rate the lender would have realized on deposits in dollars with a "first-class" bank in the London interbank market. For further discussion of LIBOR, see Chapter 14.

Do banks ever make loans on the basis of more than one interest rate?

Yes. A loan agreement may permit the borrower to switch back and forth between prime and another rate. Common alternatives include LIBOR and the federal funds effective rate, both described above. Also, some loan agreements use one rate—for example, LIBOR—plus a floating spread based on some other indicator.

A recent borrowing by the "new" Marriott International illustrates this practice. The new Marriott is the spin-off of the lodging and senior living portions of the company formerly named Marriott International, now renamed Sodexho Marriott Services, Inc. Just after this spin-off, which occurred on March 27, 1998, Marriott entered a $1.5 billion multicurrency revolving credit agreement to permit borrowing. The facility had a term of five years, and an interest rate calculated as LIBOR plus a spread based on the Marriott's public debt rating. Marriott will also pay a fee based on its public debt rating. This line of credit has helped Marriott continue its long-established pattern of growth through acquisitions. In August 1998, for example, Marriott bought Armenia Hotel in Yerevan, Armenia, for $30 million.

How do banks determine the premium they will charge above a particular reference rate?

The amount of the premium charged by the bank above the reference rate will depend on which reference rate is used, and the present and anticipated differentials between the bank's own "prime" and the alternative third-party reference rate or rates. Premiums are generally about 100 basis points greater for LIBOR rate loans than they are for prime rate loans. This is largely, but not completely, offset by the fact that LIBOR is usually a lower rate than prime; the net effect of selecting LIBOR is probably to increase rates about 25 to 50 basis points. LIBOR is more responsive to interest rate changes and will move more quickly. A change in prime represents a significant political decision for a bank, and thus changes in prime come less frequently and in bigger steps.

How do interest-based loans work, generally speaking?

A regular interest loan is one that charges interest according to a stated rate of interest and the lender's method of charging interest. If the interest is paid at the maturity of the loan, the stated rate of interest is the effective rate of interest. For example, on a $20,000 loan for one year at 10 percent, the interest is $2,000.

If the bank discounts the loan by deducting the interest in advance, the effective rate of interest increases. On the $20,000 loan for one year at 10 percent, the discount is $2,000, and the borrower obtains the use of only $18,000. The effective rate of interest is 11.1 percent (versus 10 percent on a "regular" loan).

The regular and discounted interest loans above are both characterized by repayment of the loan principal at maturity. Under the installment method, principal payments are made periodically (for example, monthly) over the term of the loan: On a one-year loan, the borrower has the full amount of the money only during the first month and by the last month has already paid back eleven twelfths of the loan. Thus, the effective rate (i.e., the annual percentage rate, or APR) of interest on an installment loan is significantly higher than the stated rate.

Could you give an example of a recent Federal Reserve action with respect to interest rates?

On September 29, 1998, policy makers at the Federal Reserve System (Fed) cut the federal funds rate by one quarter of a percent—to 5.25 percent from 5.5 percent. This was the first time it had done so in almost three years (since January 1996). The Fed left its discount rate, which it charges on its own loans, unchanged at 5 percent. Within days, the drop caused a lowering of the prime rate and other interest rates. Since that time, the Fed has lowered interest rates several more times.

When federal funds rates drop, what impact does this have on bank lending?

It encourages lending, because banks can get their funds more cheaply. (On the other hand, worldwide, a series of U.S. rate cuts would make dollar-denominated securities less tempting for global investors.)

TYPES OF DEBT

What typical types of debt might be combined in a company?

Corporate borrowers often use more than one type of debt. A typical capital structure might include a secured *term loan,* a secured revolving *line of credit* from a bank, and an *installment loan.* In rare instances, a *bank guarantee* (also spelled *guaranty)* may facilitate a transaction. A company might also have equipment leases or a *sale/leaseback arrangement.* Furthermore, these may be combined with conventional equity (common and preferred stock) as well as mezzanine debt.[3] (See Chapter 6.)

Term loans, lines of credit, installment loans, and bank guarantees are discussed in this chapter. Other topics are discussed later (equity-based financing in Chapter 5, and lease-based and hybrid financing in Chapter 6).

Any of these types of debt may be used to finance growth through mergers and acquisitions.

What is a term loan?

A term loan is a loan made for a fixed term greater than one year and less than 15 years—usually for a period of one to five years. It is the most common kind of intermediate-term financing arranged by commercial banks. Term loans may be secured or unsecured.

Most term loans are repayable on an amortized basis. The purpose of amortization, of course, is to have the loan repaid gradually over its life rather than fall due all at once. This protects both the lender and the borrower against the possibility that the borrower will not make adequate provisions for retirement of the loan during its life.

How does a line of credit work?

A line of credit is a formal or informal understanding between a commercial bank and a borrower concerning the maximum loan balance the bank will allow the borrower. For example, a bank loan officer may indicate to a financial manager that the bank regards the firm as "good" for up to $80,000 for the forthcoming year. After this, the manager may sign a promissory note for $15,000 for 90 days, thereby "taking down" $15,000 of the total line of $80,000 in credit. The amount is credited to the firm's checking account at the bank. At maturity, the checking account is charged for the amount of the loan. Interest may be deducted in advance or may be paid at maturity. Before repayment of the $15,000, the firm may borrow additional amounts up to the total of $80,000. The borrower may be required to pay a fraction of a percent per year (typically one quarter to one half) for the unused line of credit.

One famous example is the $500 million in lines of credit that Chrysler Corporation took out two decades ago in the aftermath of the Penn Central bankruptcy.[4] During that time, banks would not back commercial paper, because they feared default. The bank syndicate that made the loan formally committed to lend Chrysler the funds if they were needed. Chrysler, in turn, paid commitment fees of approximately one quarter of 1 percent of the unused balance of the commitments to compensate the banks for making the funds available.

Both term loans and lines of credit may be offered by individual banks, or by syndicates formed for the purpose of the particular financing. As mentioned in Chapter 1, U.S. banks are involved in over $1 trillion in syndicated loans annually.

How common are installment loans and how do they work?

The installment method of interest calculation is made on most consumer loans (for example, car loans) and is often used for business loans under $15,000. It is rarely applied to business loans over that threshold amount.

Installment loans can be arranged in two ways. In an *add-on* installment loan, net loan proceeds are the same as the face amount of the loan, but interest is added on to the loan principal to calculate the monthly installments. In a *discounted* installment loan, interest is subtracted from the principal to obtain the net loan proceeds while the installments are based on the full face value of the loan. The add-on installment loan results in higher monthly payments, but a lower effective interest rate; the discounted installment loan results in lower monthly payments, but a higher effective interest rate.

In both cases, the interest is calculated on the original amount of the loan, not on the amount actually outstanding (the declining balance), and this causes the effective interest rate to be almost double the stated rate. If the banker requires a compensating balance, this can increase the effective interest rate also.

How does a bank guarantee work?

Like any guarantee, the bank guarantee is a three-part agreement in which one party (the guarantor) promises to fulfill the obligation of another party (the borrower) owing a debt to a third party (the creditor). Having a bank "back" a loan in this matter can help a borrower make a stronger case.[5]

What exactly is a compensating balance?

Banks typically require that a regular borrower maintain an average checking account balance equal to 15 or 20 percent of the outstanding loan. These balances, commonly called compensating balances, are a method of raising the effective interest rate. For example, if a firm needs $80,000 to pay off outstanding obligations, but must maintain a 20 percent compensating balance, it must borrow $100,000 in order to obtain the required $80,000. If the stated interest rate is 5 percent, the effective cost is actually 6.25 percent ($5,000 divided by $80,000). These *loan* compensating balances are in addition to any *service* compensating balances that the firm's bank may require.

What is a bridge loan?

A bridge loan is immediate short-term financing for an acquisition in exchange for the right to replace that financing later with a junk bond issue. As such, it is a common form of deal debt refinancing. (For more details, see Chapter 12.)

What is mezzanine debt?

Mezzanine debt, also called second-tier debt, is unsecured subordinated debt that allows the lender to receive some rights to acquire equity.[6] (For more about this hybrid instrument, see Chapter 6.) Unlike secured debt, mezzanine debt does not rely on collateral.

What is collateral?

Collateral is something of value that a borrower promises to preserve for a lender's use.

Anything that can be valued can be used as collateral. Typically, collateral is a "hard asset," such as real estate, but it need not be. In fact, four types of collateral are recognized by the Uniform Commercial Code:

- Trade goods (hard assets)
- Paper (negotiable instruments and title goods)
- Intangibles
- Business proceeds (cash)

Commercial banks require collateral on over half (60 percent) of the dollars they lend, and this occurs in nearly all (90 percent) of the term loans they make. The most common kinds of collateral requested by banks are stocks, bonds, machinery, and equipment. Insurance companies require collateral in less than a third (30 percent) of the loans they make. Their preferred collateral in longer-term loans is real estate. It is commonly estimated that half of all money loaned in the United States is based on some type of collateral.[7]

Of course, the lenders do not lend an amount equal to the entire value of the collateral. They usually lend some percentage—the riskier the asset, the lower the percentage. (For more details, see Chapter 7.)

Can a business be collateral, and if so under what circumstances?

Yes, a business can be collateral. Its value is typically its liquidation value. This is the amount of money that could be raised if the assets of the company were sold and all debts paid. Obviously, the valuation of balance sheet items—assets and liabilities—is key to this process.

Bankruptcy law has developed liquidation valuation to a fine art in recent years. In *BFP v. Resolution Trust Corp.* (1994), the U.S. Supreme Court gave valuable guidance in this area. The court said that the "price in fact" received at a noncollusive foreclosure sale is "reasonably equivalent value" for the purposes of the U.S. Bankruptcy Code "so long as all the requirements of the state's foreclosure law have been complied with." This decision overturned previous court rulings that that allowed bankruptcy trustees to challenge prices received in noncollusive foreclosures.[8]

What is asset-based financing?

Asset-based financing is a financial arrangement based in an asset. One form of asset-based financing is leasing, particularly the leasing of equipment. (For more on leasing, see the end of this chapter.) Asset-based lending occurs when a loan is secured by balance sheet assets—such as business inventory or accounts receivable. Some companies pledge their accounts receivable as collateral and draw against a line of credit that is less than the full amount of the receivables. The interest charged is generally above prime rate.

What is securitization?

Securitization is the conversion of assets into securities for sale to investors.

What is securitized credit?

Securitized credit is the conversion of a bank loan into marketable securities for sale to investors. After selling the loans, banks can use the proceeds to make more loans.

What is factoring?

Factoring is a type of short-term financing obtained from the outright sale of accounts receivable to a third party, known as a factor. The sale to a factor is usually nonrecourse—that is, the factor pays the creditor for the accounts receivable, and takes its chances on getting repaid, having no recourse if the bills are uncollectible. Factors may be independent companies specializing in this type of financing, or they may be subsidiaries of other companies, such as banks. For example, Capital Factors Holding, Inc., one of the nation's largest factoring companies, is a subsidiary of Union Planters Bank of Florida, a wholly owned subsidiary of Union Planters Corporation, a bank holding company.

USING NOTES AND BONDS TO PAY FOR ACQUISITIONS

What is a note?

A note is legal evidence of indebtedness—for example, commercial paper.

What is commercial paper?

Commercial paper is a set of very short-term (usually six months or less) notes, or paper, issued by a company. Such notes tend to bear a low interest rate. Commercial notes are sold to large corporations and institutions. Maturities are between 2 and 270 days—most commonly 30 days. They need to be highly secure and, thus, are usually backed by a takeout commitment from the senior lender. Some 25 percent of all commercial paper is backed by a bank holding company (as an obligation of the bank holding company or nonbank subsidiary, but not the bank itself).[9]

In leveraged buyouts, commercial paper is often considered to be critical and can be thought of as part of the revolving credit financing. Sales of commercial paper are usually transacted under securities registration requirements stipulating that the proceeds be used for working capital. Commercial paper is rated by debt rating agencies, and generally is backed by a line of credit.

How have notes, including commercial paper, been used to finance mergers?

Notes can be used to finance mergers in two basic ways. First, the notes themselves may be a mode of payment. As mentioned in Chapter 1, sellers may pay buyers in the form of stock or cash—and some of the cash may be promised (via notes) in the future. Second, notes may be sold before or after to the merger in order to gain cash for the merger.

What is a bond?

A bond is an interest-bearing (or discounted) certificate that shows indebtedness of the issuer. Over its relatively long life (with a maturity of five years or more), a bond pays a fixed rate of interest, which is why it is often referred to as a fixed income security. There is a public market for bonds, facilitated by the existence of bond rating agencies—for example, Duff & Phelps, Fitch Investor

Services, Moody's Investor Services, and Standard & Poor's. These agencies give ratings ranging from AAA, AA, and A on down to C (the lowest given by Moody's) or D (the lowest given by Standard & Poor's). Bonds may be combined with other instruments to become *convertible* or *exchangeable*. (See Chapter 6.)

How have bonds been used in financing mergers?

Like notes, bonds may be sold to gain cash for mergers. Interestingly, investment banker J. P. Morgan, one of the first merger maestros in American history, helped railroads survive a difficult period in their history by using a special type of bond-base financing repaid through cash flow. In some cases, the bond financing facilitated mergers.[10]

What are the basic rights of a bondholder in a corporation, and who grants them?

The rights of bondholders are set forth in the bondholder's indenture, which spells out terms and conditions for issuing the bond, including:

- Legal obligations of the bond issuer
- Powers of the bond trustee
- Form of bond issued for sale
- Interest to be paid
- Maturity date
- Call provisions
- Protective covenants (if any)
- Collateral pledged
- Repayment or redemption schedule (including sinking fund, if any)

What is a sinking fund?

A sinking fund is money accumulated in a custodial account to retire debt instruments according to a predetermined schedule, independent of any pricing changes in the secondary market (where the bonds may be bought and sold).

What is a bond trustee?

A bond trustee is the individual who (or entity that) has the responsibility for ensuring that interest payments are made to registered bondholders. All bonds must have a trustee, according to the Trust Indenture Act of 1939.

Specifically, the Trust Indenture Act requires that for each debt issue there will be a trustee who must protect public debt holders in the event of a default on the debt. This law also spells out some of the provisions that must be in bond indentures, including a promise that trustees will notify holders within 90 days if the issuer defaults on a payment.[11]

Why do bonds have to have trustees?

Unlike stock issues, which do not require trustees, a bond issue is due rather than discretionary. (In fact, there may be prepayment rights that accelerate payments due.) Also, bonds have default provisions, which can force acceleration of payments.[12]

What is a public debt offering?

A public debt offering is the sale or offer to sell debt (in the form of notes or bonds) to the general public. Offerings are usually carried out by a syndicate according to the terms and conditions of an underwriting agreement. A public debt offering may be an initial offering, or it may be a secondary distribution of a previously issued debt securities.

How does a private debt offering work?

A private debt offering, also called a *private placement* or a *direct placement*, is the sale of an entire issue of securities (which may be debt or equity securities) to a small group of investors. The placements are called "private" because they are exempt from the regulations that cover larger or "public" offerings. We cover this subject in greater detail in later chapters.

You mentioned earlier in this book that deductibility of interest payments makes debt financing attractive to many acquirers. If a company issues notes to buy another company, can it deduct the interest it pays on those notes as an acquisition expense?

In many cases, no. Under normal circumstances the interest paid on debt issued through notes can be deducted as an ordinary business expense. But the Internal Revenue Service is leery of debt issued to support an acquisition. Corporate-issued debt may be considered "tainted" if issued before, during, or shortly after an acquisition, as shown in Internal Revenue Code Section 163(l), enacted in 1997, and Code Section 279, enacted in 1969 but still in force.

What does Code Section 163(l) say about deductions for interest expense?

Code Section 163 (l) permanently disallows any deduction for interest paid or accrued (including an original issue discount) on a "disqualified debt instrument." Deductions will be disallowed if the debt has *all* of the following attributes:

- The debt is issued by a corporation.
- The debt is payable in, or by reference to the value of, equity.
- The equity used to pay for or provide value to the debt is equity of the issuer or a person related to the issuer.
- The debt is issued after June 8, 1997, with exceptions for some issuances pending at that time.

Other parts of this Code section disallow interest deductions for individual shareholders. Each of these seemingly simple attributes has nuances that are subject to interpretation. As always, qualified tax counsel must be consulted to determine applicability.

What does Code Section 279 say about deductions for interest expense?

Under Code Section 279, a 30-year-old provision that tax experts have called "peculiar and arbitrary,"[13] deductions for acquisition interest *may* be disallowed if the debt has *all* of the following characteristics:

- The debt is issued to provide consideration for the acquisition of stock in another corporation, or at least two thirds of another corporation's assets (by value, excluding cash, but including the stock of subsidiaries). This includes debt issued directly in exchange for the acquired company's stock or assets, debt issued to raise the money necessary to buy the company's stock or assets, and debt issued to replace the working capital spent to acquire the company.
- The debt is subordinated to "trade creditors" generally or is "expressly subordinated" to "any substantial amount" of other unsecured debt—generally 5 percent or more of the face amount of the indebtedness issued in the acquisition, whether before or after the transaction.
- The debt is convertible "directly or indirectly" into the stock of the issuer or is part of an "investment unit" that includes an option to purchase stock of the issuer. One such "investment unit" is nonconvertible debt sold in conjunction with convertible preferred stock or warrants.
- On the last day of the debtor's tax year to which the debt is issued, the debtor's debt to equity ratio exceeds two to one, or the debtor's

average earnings for the past three years do not exceed three times the annual interest to be paid or incurred.

Deductibility will be disallowed in most cases if in addition to the above characteristics, the interest exceeds $5 million less interest paid or incurred during the year on debt that was issued to provide consideration directly or indirectly for an acquisition (as described in the first item above).

Code Section 279 may seem narrow in scope, but beware. It is cumulative in effect, applying to debt incurred in multiple acquisitions. Code Section 279 *may* apply in refinancing, but it depends on the circumstances. We will return to this point in Chapter 12 on refinancing.

There are several ways to structure a transaction so that Section 279 is not triggered. These include use of common stock, subordination of debt to secured debt only, use of a holding company, and use of redemption. Acquirers are urged to consult tax specialists to consider these possibilities.

USING MULTIPLE LAYERS OF DEBT

What are the typical layers of debt that might appear in a complex loan?

Although sometimes only one secured lender is needed (or in the case of a very simple business with strong cash flow, only a single unsecured lender), multiple tiers of lenders are normally necessary for large transactions. In later chapters (especially Chapters 10 and 11), we will talk about some of the challenges of dealing with multiple instruments and multiple sources. Right here, we will discuss a specific subset of that issue, and that is using multiple layers of debt—which usually means multiple lenders.

A complex transaction funded by debt (e.g., a multilender leveraged buyout) may include several or all of the following layers of debt, in rough order of seniority:

- *Senior revolving debt,* secured by a first lien on current assets (inventory and accounts receivable), a first or second lien on fixed assets (property, plant, and equipment, or PPE), liens on intangibles, and perhaps a pledge of stock of the acquired company or its subsidiaries. This debt typically provides a part of the acquisition financing and working capital, including letter of credit financing, and is generally provided by commercial banks or similar institutional lenders. It is often referred to as "commercial paper."[14]

- *Senior term debt,* secured by a first lien on fixed assets, a first or second lien on current assets, and liens on intangibles and stock of the company and subsidiaries, to provide acquisition financing. Some-times—but not very frequently—this debt is subordinated to the se-nior revolving debt. It is normally provided by commercial banks in conjunction with senior revolving debt, or by similar commercial lenders or insurance companies.

- *Senior subordinated debt,* known as mezzanine debt (or in its less se-cure manifestations, junk bonds), unsecured or secured by junior liens on the assets securing the senior debt, used for acquisition fi-nancing. It is mainly placed by investment bankers, the principal purchasers being insurance companies, pension and investment funds, and financial institutions. (The terms *senior, junior,* and *mez-zanine* are related in debt financing. They refer to the order of repay-ment in the event of a default on the loan. Junior means that in the event of default, the lender will be repaid after another party; senior means the lender will be paid before another party. Mezzanine is re-served for the lender in the middle.)

- *Sale/or other special financing arrangements* for specific facilities or equipment. These arrangements may range from installment pur-chases of office copiers or long-term computer lease/purchases to sales of the acquired company's real estate to an independent in-vestment partnership, which then "net leases" such real estate back to the acquired company. The main sources of these arrangements are commercial finance companies. (See Chapter 6.)

- *Seller's subordinated note,* secured or unsecured, perhaps convertible to stock.

- *Seller's preferred stock,* perhaps exchangeable for a subordinated note, usually appearing as an alternative to the previous item.

- *Preferred or common stock sold to an independent third party,* perhaps to a leveraged buyout investment fund or to one of the lenders.

- *Common stock sold to the buyer* or its principals, key managers, and employees.

- *Warrants or options* to acquire common stock granted to any of the parties providing financing or to the seller. These instruments do not provide financing directly but offer inducements to other financ-ing participants.

Some of these instruments are pure debt and will be discussed below. Others involve equity or mixtures of debt and equity, so they are covered in Chapters 5 or 6. For now, let us take a quick look at all of them in tandem to as-sess financing options.

How are the amounts of the different layers of debt determined?

The initial decision is, of course, the lender's. The lender for each layer of the financing will indicate to the buyer a range or approximation of the amount it is prepared to lend. The lender's decision (or, if there are several lenders, each lender's decision) will be based largely on amount, interest rate, and payback period, but also on ability to perform. A basic objective is to maximize senior debt, which bears the lowest interest rate. At the same time, senior debt requires relatively favorable coverage ratios; therefore, there will be cash flow left over after senior debt is serviced to support junk bonds or other mezzanine debt. After mezzanine debt is covered, something should still remain to persuade the seller that the takeback financing has a reasonable chance of payment.

The process is not exact. As mentioned earlier, each lender evaluates cash flow and assets differently, and uses a different formula for setting the loan amount. The term lender may be willing to lend $10 million more if the revolving lender lends $8 million less, but the buyer may be reluctant to explore that possibility for fear that the term lender had not previously focused on the exact amount being loaned by the revolving lender, and a second review by the term lender's credit committee could result in a decision not to make the loan at all.

When resources and time permit, the best course of action for a buyer is probably to obtain bids from several lenders on each layer, and then to select, at the moment when lenders' commitment letters are about to be signed, the optimum combination and present it to each approved lender as a fait accompli, burning no bridges to the unsuccessful lenders until the package has been accepted by all the intended players. In this way, commitments can be entered into with the optimum combination of lenders. The competitive nature of the process will discourage objections by the lender fortunate enough to be selected. In addition, lenders tend to leave to the later stages of the closing a full investigation of the other lenders' terms, by which time they may be less likely to rethink the terms of their loan.

How does a senior lender decide how much to lend in an acquisition?

A number of considerations are key to a bank's lending decision:

- Liquidation value of the collateral
- Credibility of the borrower's financial projections
- Whether the borrower's projections show enough cash flow to service the debt (including junior debt)

- Whether proposed asset liquidations are likely to take place in time and in sufficient amount to amortize the term debt (or reduce the revolver commitment)
- Potential company profitability and industry prospects
- Amount of junior debt (and capacity of the junior creditor to assist the borrower with additional funds in a workout scenario)
- Amount of equity

When should the senior lender in a transaction enter the picture?

The senior lender should be brought into the transaction as early as possible. Therefore, buyers should present their planned deal to lenders as soon as they have gathered basic information. Many lenders are reluctant to review a proposed transaction unless they already have a formal or informal agreement to be involved in it. Thus, the presentation is quickly followed by a commitment letter.

The senior lender's loan will usually represent the single largest portion of the cash to be raised for the transaction. If the senior lender is not willing to finance, the deal cannot be done. For that reason, the buyer must be sure to make a correct judgment about the financeability of the transaction before incurring the considerable expense of negotiating an acquisition agreement.

What form does senior debt take?

Typically, senior debt is part term loan and part revolving loan, with the term loan used to finance the purchase price, and the revolving loan used to provide working capital (although a portion of the revolving loan is often used to finance the purchase price as well). Usually, senior debt is provided by banks or their affiliates.

What is demand lending?

It is becoming more and more common for senior debt to be provided by banks in a demand format quite different from traditional local bank financing, which relied primarily on the personal guarantees of the business owner, had a fixed term and limited covenants, and kept its nose out of the borrower's business. By contrast, demand lending gives the initial impression to a borrower of being intrusive and one-sided: The bank may have the right to call the loan at any time, make revolving loan advances only at its discretion, require all business receipts to be applied immediately to repayment, and have a bristling array of protective covenants that require bank consent for almost any action not in the ordinary course of business. The appropriate trade-offs for these provisions are absence of personal guarantees and a willingness to lend relatively large amounts.

Because this style of lending is unfamiliar to many borrowers and lenders, the logic of the trade-offs may not be observed: The bank may require a demand loan and guarantees as well, or the borrower may seek a high loan limit but refuse to consider demand repayment. The borrower and bank need to clearly understand their relationship from the start. To achieve mutual success, they must be prepared for a close relationship based on cooperation and mutual dependency.

Can lenders be arbitrary about when they call a loan?

No. A borrower can take considerable comfort in the principle of "commercial reasonableness" that binds lenders and should, thus, understand that many of the rights the bank obtains on paper cannot be exercised in practice. A number of cases have held that if a bank makes a loan on terms that give it extensive power over a company's financial affairs, it cannot use that power arbitrarily and may in fact be liable for consequential damages if the company is put out of business or otherwise damaged because of an unreasonable refusal to lend.[15] For more on the subject of refinancing, see Chapter 12.

What guidelines do banks use to judge the quality of a loan made in a leveraged transaction?

Banks follow guidelines issued by bank regulators, adding, of course, their own experience. As mentioned earlier (in Chapter 2), highly leveraged loans are finance transactions in which the borrower would end with a debt-to-equity ratio of 75 percent or higher. These highly leveraged transactions (HLTs) must be identified as such in bank disclosure documents. Regulators also encourage banks and bank regulators to discourage other HLTs, and they have published complete guidelines for this purpose.

What are the relative advantages of subordinated debt and preferred stock?

Because preferred stock (discussed more fully in Chapter 5) has the advantage of increasing the equity line on the balance sheet, it helps protect the highly leveraged company from insolvency and, thus, is more attractive to senior and junk bond lenders. Remember that an insolvent corporation cannot transfer its property to anyone else without receiving full consideration. To do otherwise would be to defraud its creditors—that is, to deprive them of access to its assets. Thus, if solvency is an issue, the seller and lenders may feel more comfortable in including some preferred stock on the balance sheet.

Subordinated debt offers considerable advantages to the seller, however. Payments are due whether or not there are corporate earnings, unless otherwise restricted by subordination provisions. Negotiators may have been told to sever the seller's connection with the company. Taking back a note bespeaks a greater degree of separation and greater apparent certainty that the amounts due will be paid. The seller may intend to sell the paper it takes back and can get more for a note than it could get for preferred stock. The seller may be able to obtain security interests in the acquired company's assets, junior of course to the liens of the acquisition lenders, but no such security interest accompanies preferred stock.

From the buyer's point of view, a note has the major advantage of generating deductible interest payments rather than nondeductible dividends unless of course it is subject to the Section 163 (l) and Section 279 restrictions mentioned earlier at note 10. Preferred stock has the important disadvantage of preventing a buyer from electing pass-through tax status as an S corporation. For both reasons, be sure that if a note does emerge, it is not subject to reclassification as equity by the Internal Revenue Service. Seller preferred stock can also have other adverse tax consequences.[16]

Absent unusual circumstances, if the buyer can persuade the senior and junk bond lenders to accept a seller's subordinated note rather than preferred stock, the seller should have no objections. If not, the lenders and seller may accept preferred stock convertible into a note at buyer's option once the company achieves a certain net worth or cash flow level. As a last resort, the buyer may persuade the seller, six months or a year after closing when debt has been somewhat reduced, to convert the preferred stock into a note. For more on convertible instruments, see Chapter 6.

SALE/LEASEBACKS

What are sale/leasebacks, and what are the pros and cons of using them?

A sale/leaseback involves the sale of the seller's real estate or equipment to a third party, which then leases the real estate or equipment back to the company.[17] In essence, a company takes out a mortgage on a property in the form of a sale/leaseback. The ownership remains with the original entity, yet the

lender is taking a lien on the assets of the surviving company as collateral on
the loan. This type of financing is ideal for leveraged buyouts, in which companies are often looking for ways to replace expensive unsecured debt or equity debt with less expensive secured debt as a means of raising cash or controlling capital debt structure.

A sale/leaseback may be structured as an installment contract, an operating lease, or a finance lease. These distinctions have important tax and accounting ramifications.[18] When a leaseback is structured as a *finance* lease,
which is considered a type of *capital* lease under U.S. accounting rules, the acquirer as lessee can make a case as owner of the asset for tax and accounting
purposes. The lending source (lessor) generally retains title and takes a perfected first security interest in the equipment. The lessee raises cash from the
sale/leaseback.

Acquirers should note several points:

- Price can be negotiable. If the value of the leaseback is expressed as
  a percent of the equipment price, beware. The lessor will most likely
  want to value the equipment only at its liquidation value, which
  may be significantly different from any remaining depreciation or
  book value of the equipment.
- If title is in the lessee's name, in a true sale/leaseback title must now
  pass to the leasing company, so applicable sales taxes must be accounted for.
- A finance lease acts the same as a loan against the asset. Thus the
  obligation and the yield or rate of the transaction might be greater
  than the borrower's incremental borrowing rate at its primary bank.
  The acquiring entity must weigh the benefits of leasing (such as con-
  servation of capital and credit lines for unsecured lending) as a way
  to manage its cost of funds or available capital instead of pledging
  the same assets in other forms of borrowing.
- In any leaseback scenario, there are tax and accounting implications.
  These must be reviewed with an eye to maximizing the benefits of
  the transaction.

Some sale/leasebacks offer an option to buy. How does this type of transaction affect an acquirer?

In this type of leaseback, the leasing company is purchasing the equipment at a
fixed amount, then leasing back to the entity. The stream of payments may or
may not equal the value of the equipment and interest charged over the term. In

this instance there is a residual position in the equipment on behalf of the leasing company (the lease is not a full-payout lease). Thus, at the end of the term of the lease, the leasing company is looking for one of two things to happen:

1. The original entity makes the leasing company whole on its residual position.
2. The original entity returns the equipment so the leasing company can remarket the equipment to another user, thus recapturing its residual position.

Why would an acquirer want to do a leaseback?

Let's say an acquirer has bought a company that has assets suitable for a sale/leaseback, and has found a leasing company that is willing to take a residual position on the equipment. Let's also assume that the acquirer is able to sell the equipment for 100 percent of its value to the leasing company, and promises a stream of payments, not including the end purchase option, that equals only 90 percent of the transaction. At the end of the lease, the lessee must either exercise its purchase option or return the equipment. If the lessee elects to return the equipment (in effect using the leasing company as a remarketing agent as well as a funding source), it has raised relatively inexpensive capital by paying only the stream rate versus the full yield of the transaction (stream plus residual). Table 4–1 shows the math for a three-year sale/leaseback with a 10 percent purchase option (written as a finance lease).

T A B L E   4–1

Three-Year Sale/Leaseback With 10 Percent Purchase Option

Asset value at time of sale/leaseback	$100,000.00
Residual position at three years taken by leasing company	$ 10,000.00
All-in yield required by leasing company, including residual 12%	
Payment terms: 36 payments at	$ 3,089.28
Purchase option	$ 10,000.00
Total payments if lessee does not exercise purchase option*	$111,214.08
Effective interest rate paid by lessee would be 7.9%	
Total payments if lessee exercises purchase option	$121,214.08
Effective interest rate paid by lessee would be 12%	

*Leasing company remarkets the equipment looking for at least its residual position plus remarketing expenses.

What paperwork is involved in a sale/leaseback?

To prepare for a sale-leaseback, a detailed appraisal, an as-built survey, and title insurance of the real estate must be ordered, preferably at least six weeks in advance of closing. The other loan documents must be drafted to permit the sale/leaseback. The leaseback may be financed by a mortgage loan. The lease and the mortgage loan documents must clarify that the borrower or tenant continues to own, and the senior lender continues to enjoy a first and prior lien upon all equipment and fixtures used in the borrower's or tenant's business.

How common is it for an acquired company to have a lot of leases, and how important are they?

In recent decades, leasing has increased as a source of financing, as companies (particularly smaller ones) lease their equipment, vehicles, and other valuable property in order to leverage their cash and equity. As mentioned in Chapter 1, a recent survey showed that 16 percent of small businesses use leasing as a source of capital.[19] Conversely, these lessors have found a ready market: A full 80 percent of companies lease the equipment they use.[20] Although such lease obligations are not material to the overall balance sheet position of large companies, they can greatly affect the value of small and midsized firms.

Suppose an acquirer wants to buy a company that has many valuable leases, but the leases contain a lot of fine print about cancellation in the event of a change of control. How serious is such fine print?

The seriousness of the fine print, as with everything in M&A life, depends first and foremost on the size and nature of the entities involved and the past relationship between them. Beyond this general rule, the situation will vary according to whether the company being acquired is a heavy lessee, a lessor, or both.

What advice do you have for the acquirer of a heavy *lessee*?

If the company being acquired has signed one or more important lease agreements as a lessee, the first decision to be made will be whether the acquirer will be assuming the lessee's obligations. This is usually what happens. Note, though, that the original lessee will almost always need to get approval from the lessor before it can assign its lease obligations or sublease to a new owner.

Therefore, the first order of business for any acquirer is to contact the lessor and inform it of the pending transaction. The lessee should also contact the lessor. The importance of this contact cannot be overemphasized. Almost every lease includes a requirement that the funding source must be notified if there is a change in ownership. (This is done to enable the lessor to look at the credit history and worthiness of any new owners before allowing the previous owners to assign their obligations over to it.) On almost any lease, *nonnotification of change in ownership or location of the equipment is generally considered a technical default of the terms of the lease.* If the new and old owners are in technical default, the funding sources may call the remaining payments due.

Of course, if the company that is leasing survives, and is at least as strong as it was before the merger, there won't be any issues. At the end of the day, it is not so much the change in ownership as the change in credit risk that is of concern. Generally (hopefully), the credit of the acquiring company is better than that of the existing entity, so the acquirer can make its own decision as to whether to assume the lease, renegotiate it, or pay it off.

In leveraged buyouts, the financial ratios of the company generally change dramatically and thus the creditworthiness of the new entity may not be sufficient for the original funding source. In this case, the obligations to the funding source could be fulfilled through a prepayment of the lease with monies raised in the leveraged buyout. Alternatively, some sort of additional collateral can be pledged in order to give the funding source sufficient comfort from a credit perspective.

Differing funding and lending sources have different tolerances and/or policies for rewrites, buyouts, and refinancing. On any substantive lease, it is important to understand what the options for early termination are and whether the funding source sells or discounts its paper and/or maintains the servicing of the lease after the inception.

What advice do you have for the acquirer of a heavy *lessor* with major lease receivables?

Buying a company with major lease receivables raises a different set of issues. Many companies have contracts with customers whereby those customers agree to pay for their equipment in a lease or lease style of acquisition. Companies that have a perishable or consumable component to their sales may rent equipment (which is longer lasting) along with their consumables in order to tie their customers up over time. In this type of company, an acquirer will find accounts receivable from bundled lease papers or installment contracts. Also, companies that manufacture capital equipment may offer a lease alternative to customers that can't afford to pay up-front cash. In such a company, acquirers will also find significant lease receivables carried on the balance sheet.

In either case, prospective acquirers should perform a due diligence on the portfolio of leases. On the upside, there may be options to discount the leases to third parties, generating a possible premium—or at least a vehicle to reevaluate the asset values of the receivables given by the company being acquired. On the downside, leases may not be included in the lessor's delinquency, days' sales outstanding, or bad debt accounts, thus giving a higher level of performance of the overall company than they should. For example, some capital equipment leases are really sales that the lessor would not take for credit or documentation reasons—so as a liquid asset they are suspect.

Sometimes lease accounting varies, so how the company "books" its lease may not give a true picture of the company's balance sheet or revenue stream. Say the company being acquired is a subsidiary of a large entity with a low cost of capital, and that this subsidiary historically wrote contracts with its customers as leases at current market rates, but booked the deals by discounting the stream at its (much lower) cost of funds. Since the company books these transactions by discounting the paper, the booked sales amounts or present value amounts may in fact be higher than the actual sales price.

A company that looks great as an acquisition candidate may turn out to be a very poor choice after the deal because of such a practice. For example, one company (recently purchased by a client of the expert who was consulted for this chapter) leased internally about 15 percent of its capital sales, and then discounted the stream up front at the corporate cost of funds. This elevated the apparent sales amount by 110 percent! The company's good-looking revenues on the books did not take into account a differing cost of funds. Revenues after the acquisition were lower, since the new entity could not borrow at the same rates and/or discount the deals below market.

TAX-EXEMPT BONDS

What should be done if existing debt includes tax-exempt industrial development bonds?

First, the acquirer should gain a general understanding of bonds (discussed earlier in this chapter). Then, the acquirer should study tax-exempt bonds in particularly, which give the borrower the advantage of low interest rates but also carry disadvantages: They encumber assets better used to support new borrowings, and they may carry with them old parent company guarantees that must be lifted as a condition of the acquisition. Often these bonds can be "defeased" under the terms of their trust indentures; that is, high-quality obligations (usually issued or guaranteed by the U.S. government) can be deposited with the trustee bank for the bond issue in an amount high enough to retire the bonds over their term through scheduled payments on the obligations.

If the interest rate on the bonds is low enough, the amount of obligations required to defease them may be less than their face amount, and once the bonds are defeased, their covenants and liens cease to have any effect. Note, however, that the defeasance of high interest rate bonds is expensive, and the defeasance of variable rate bonds is impossible, because they lack a predictable interest rate for which a sufficient sum can be set aside. In addition, tax problems can arise: Are the earnings on the defeasance fund taxable, and does the defeasance give rise to discharge of indebtedness income for the borrower?

Tax-exempt bond issues are likely to be complex, and any transactions involving them may require special attention from the bank serving as bond trustee and the issuer's original bond counsel. Such issues involve a two-step process: The funds are borrowed by a government body and are then reloaned to the company to build a facility or are used to construct a facility that is leased to the company, normally but not necessarily on terms that permit a purchase for a nominal price at the end of the lease term. Check with a tax or leasing expert for hidden problems.

Suppose that an acquisition candidate is leasing a facility under terms that guarantee purchase for a nominal price at the end of the lease (say under a tax-exempt bond deal). How easy is it for an acquirer to assume the lease and get the same purchase rights?

This is very hard to answer as a general rule. Most leases issued under tax-exempt funding involve very large sums of money, and as with all large transactions, each lease tends have some unique terms and conditions. A few points of advice may be in order here nonetheless.

First, it should be noted that the nominal end-of-term price generally does not matter as much as the original structure and reason for issuing the tax-exempt funds. Changes in ownership more often than not signal changes in the conditions of the lessee—and, thus, the primary reason tax-exempt funding was available. Remember, just because an entity is tax-exempt does not always mean that it is qualified to received tax-exempt leasing or funding. For these reasons, under the terms of most agreements, the issuing authority must be notified of any changes in the status of the lessor.

In general, both the lessor and the lessee will hope for continuation of a lease of this type. Although tax exemption was given originally to the lessee, it winds up (through the economics of leasing) being enjoyed by the lessor. Tax-exempt leases enable the lessor to offer a lower cost of funds to the lessee, since the lessor does not have to pay tax on the profit from the interest charges within the lease.

What are the pros and cons of keeping existing debt in place?

Review carefully the existing debt of the company being acquired and determine whether prepayment may be necessary or advisable. In some cases, the acquisition may entitle the lender to prepayment, perhaps at a premium. In other cases, even where prepayment is not required, it might be a good idea to repay existing debt because of high interest rates or burdensome covenants in leases, loan agreements, or indentures.

Restrictive covenants in leases or loan agreements may prohibit a sale of assets without the lessor's or lender's consent, a condition that could hamper postmerger restructuring or spin-offs. Restrictions on sale of assets provide important protection to a lessor or lender that otherwise cannot prevent major changes in the structure or operations of its lessee or debtor, and courts have interpreted such restrictions liberally in favor of lessors and lenders. Although many covenants use the language "all or substantially all" in describing this restriction, even modest asset sales may be challenged. Any sale of more than 25 percent of the assets raises questions, particularly if the assets being sold constitute the major revenue-producing operations of the historical core business.

Indentures for unsecured borrowings also typically contain covenants prohibiting the imposition of liens on assets of the lessor or debtor and may prohibit more than one class of debt or interlayering (e.g., both senior and subordinated debt). Such financing must be done on an unsecured basis and without recourse to some of the techniques for layering of debt discussed later in this chapter.

Debt of this kind is deceptively simple. It may first appear that the lack of elaborate and specific covenants, such as those contained in the typical secured loan, offers many opportunities to substantially restructure the company without lenders' consents. It is likely to turn out, however, as the buyer analyzes the loan agreements, that the broad prohibitions on sale or encumbrance of assets and on the making of dividend payments or similar payments defeat most financing plans. Just as the technically tight, detailed loan agreement encourages and legitimizes loopholes on the basis of technicalities, so the broadly written loan agreement makes lawyers and other technicians less willing to rely on highly refined justifications for arrangements that may violate the spirit of the existing debt agreement.

In addition to restrictions on sales of assets or liens on assets, the selling company may be subject to preexisting covenants prohibiting a change of control of the lessee or debtor. In such cases, preservation of existing debt may require changing the structure of the acquisition. A common legal issue that arises in such cases is whether the merger of the lessee or debtor into another corporation constitutes a transfer of ownership requiring the lessor or lender's consent. In most cases, it is possible to conclude that the merger is not a transfer to another entity, because the original lessee or debtor continues as part of the surviving entity, although the conclusion varies according to state law.

JUNK BOND BASICS

What are junk bonds?

Junk bonds are medium-term to long-term obligations of an acquired company that (1) are subordinated to its senior debt, (2) are normally unsecured, and (3) bear high interest rates. Their rather inelegant name, reportedly coined by Michael Milken in a conversation with Rik Riklis,[21] comes from the fact that they are riskier than senior debt: They get a below-investment-grade rating from one or more of the bond rating services.[22] They generally deserve a better label, however, and are thus called by some underwriters "high-yield securities." Indeed, the term *junk* arguably had the effect of discounting the price, which helped some purchasers realize enormous returns, to the detriment of issuers. Junk bonds are normally not prepayable for an initial period (three to five years), and thereafter prepayable only at a premium.

In 1997, $120 billion in new junk bond issues came to market—an all-time record. This compares with only $54 billion in new issues five years before.[23]

The main purpose of junk bonds is to provide extra financing for acquisition transactions, filling in the gap between senior secured debt, which pays a lower interest rate, and the seller's takeback financing or the buyer's equity financing, which is the last to be paid back. There is sometimes more than one layer of junk debt—one being senior subordinated and the other junior subordinated debt.

To whom and how are junk bonds sold?

Junk bonds are commonly sold to large financial institutions—insurance companies, pension funds, and mutual funds, including overseas investors—usually in blocks of $500,000 or more, and are primarily for the sophisticated investor. Funds that invest in junk bonds often attract money managers, who are known to go in and out of the junk bond market rapidly, causing volatility in prices. Often, but not necessarily, the offerings are registered under the federal securities laws to increase their marketability and are sold in a package with *warrants* to acquire common stock in the acquired company. Warrants are rights to buy stock from the company at a specified price for a future period of time. If the offerings are privately placed, they often carry registration rights that will enable the holders to require the borrower to register the debt for sale in a public offering. (See the discussion of registration rights below.)

How do the warrants relate to the junk bonds?

The junk bonds offer some of the same high-risk/high-reward characteristics of equity, and it is a natural combination to offer them together with an equity kicker in the form of warrants (discussed in Chapter 6). Frequently, the institutions buying the bonds sell the warrants (sometimes back to the underwriter), thereby obtaining the junk bonds at a discount.

What is a bond indenture?

An *indenture* is the basic agreement setting forth the terms of the junk bonds. It is entered into between the borrower and a bank, acting as trustee for the bondholders. An indenture serves the same function as the credit or loan agreement executed with the senior secured lender and the note purchase agreement executed with an institutional mezzanine lender. The indenture contains the covenants, events of default, and other material terms of the transaction, including the various responsibilities and rights of the issuer, trustee, and bondholders. If the bonds are issued or subsequently sold pursuant to a public offering, the indenture must qualify under the Trust Indenture Act of 1939. Much of the boilerplate in the indenture is derived from requirements under that law.

The principal objectives of the covenants are to prevent disposition of the assets of the borrower (unless the sale proceeds are reinvested in assets used in the same business by the borrower or used to pay off the junk bonds or senior debt); to ensure that if any merger, consolidation, or change of the borrower occurs, the successor entity is obligated to repay the bonds on the same terms and is in as strong a financial position after the transaction as before; to limit the creation of additional debt and liens (particularly secured debt senior to the bonds); to limit payments of dividends and distributions to stockholders ("restricted payments"); and to restrict transactions with affiliates.

CONCLUDING COMMENTS

Acquirers who wish to use debt to finance their transactions have a wealth of possibilities before them. Charles Lamb, in our opening quote, observes that there are "two distinct races" of human beings—those who borrow and those who lend. This may well be true—and an interesting observation to contemplate. Yet it is also true that we humans enjoy an infinite number of ways to borrow and lend. We hope that our brief guide to the major sources of debt-based capital has been useful to you in building your company through acquisitions.

But before you borrow or issue a note, consider also the two chapters ahead—on equity-based financing and on hybrid sources. If you have not found your ideal source of financing in the preceding pages, you are sure to find it ahead!

E N D N O T E S

1. Forecast of Average Prime Rate Charged by Banks, NSA (Percent)

	June 1999	July 1999	August 1999
Value	7.75	7.25	7.25
Standard Deviation	0.47	0.73	0.45
Correlation Coefficient	0.9857	0.9696	0.9714

Source: Financial Forecasts Center, Applied Reasoning, Inc., Decatur, Alabama (forecasts.org).

2. One such funding source is called *purchased federal funds*—unsecured advances of immediately available funds from excess balances in reserve accounts held at Federal Reserve banks. Another such funding source is advances at the Federal Reserve discount window, a Federal Reserve facility for direct loans to a financial institution with a deficiency in its reserve account. See: Thomas Fitch, *Dictionary of Banking Terms*, 3rd ed. (New York: Barron's Educational Series, 1997).

3. This description of mixed debt is based in part on a discussion by attorney Douglas L. Batey, cited in Chapter 1, note 1.

4. See: J. Fred Weston and Thomas E. Copeland, *Managerial Finance*, 9th ed. (Los Angeles: Academic Press, 1998), p. 851.

5. The subject of bank guarantees came up in an M&A financing bulletin board (mergersdaily@e.com) in mid-December 1998. Some participants expressed skepticism, saying that there is no such thing as a bank guarantee for deal financing. Others claimed that this does occur, but that it is done on a confidential basis. Here is a typical exchange: Q: *Why don't these European banks just fund the loan? A: Basically because the banks don't want to use their own money. With a guarantee, the money stays in their bank but because it is accounted for, they do not have to pay taxes on it. The banks aren't doing this from the goodness of their hearts; they get something for it. And if you think taxes are high in the United States . . . . Bank guarantees are basically like insurance wraps—a more common term in the United States.*

6. Batey, op. cit. (note 3).

7. Weston and Copeland, op. cit. (note 4), p. 887.

8. The full case citation is *BFP v. Resolution Trust Corp.*, 114 S. Ct. 1757 (1994), and the Bankruptcy Code section in question is Section 548(a)2. See: Martin D. Ginsburg and Jack S. Levin, *Mergers, Acquisitions, and Buyouts: A Transactional Analysis of the Governing Tax, Legal, and Accounting Considerations* (New York: Aspen Publishers, 1998), vol. 2, ch. 15, p. 152.

9. Source: Fitch, op. cit. (note 2). When and if the U.S. Congress ever repeals the Glass-Steagall law separating banking from commerce, the banks themselves may be underwriting notes. For now, however, this must be done through holding companies or nonbank subsidiaries.

10. For the full story, see Bruce Wasserstein, *Big Deal: The Battle for Control of America's Leading Corporations* (New York: Time Warner Books, 1998), p. 33.

11. Ibid., pp. 540ff.

12. Ibid., p. 541.

13. This is a direct quote from Ginsburg and Levin, op. cit. (note 8), vol. 2, ch. 13, p. 95. Our discussion of Section 163(l) and Section 279 summarizes a much more detailed account in Ginsburg and Levin.

14. Commercial paper sometimes appears as part of a buyout, but only as an element of working capital financing.

15. A classic case in this regard is *K. M. C. Co., Inc., v. Irving Trust Co.*, 757 F. 2d 752 (6th Cir. 1985).

16. For a general overview of tax aspects, see Stanley Foster Reed and Alexandra Reed Lajoux, *The Art of M&A: A Merger/Acquisition/Buyout Guide*, 3rd ed. (New York: McGraw-Hill, 1999), pp. 255ff. For a more technical, detailed discussion, see Ginsburg and Levin, op. cit. (note 8).

17. The main source of expertise in this leaseback discussion is Robert Neal, managing director of Newcourt Capital, in Brookfield, Connecticut, a subsidiary of the Toronto-based Newcourt Credit Group, which is planning to merge with The CIT Group as we go to press.

18. The rules for the accounting treatment of leases are covered by Financial Accounting Statement 13 (U.S.), which distinguished between an operating lease, which can be treated off the balance sheet, and a capital lease, which should be treated as a balance sheet transaction. Both finance leases and installment contracts are forms of capital leases.

19. See note 1 above.

20. Robert Neal, op. cit. (note 17).

21. Milken, of course, is the financier who rediscovered and popularized junk bonds in the 1980s. Through him, his employer Drexel Burnham Lambert became famous, and then notorious—at least in some circles. (Milken may be a scoundrel in some eyes, but others see him as a hero.) Rik Riklis is known best as the CEO of Rapid American Corp. This story is told in Connie Bruck, *The Predators' Ball* (New York: Penguin Books, 1989).

22. The major bond rating services—Duff & Phelps, Moody's Investor Services, and Standard & Poor's—use different symbols and sometimes arrive at different conclusions. The most well-known rating system is S&P, which is, from the top, as follows: AAA, AA, A, BBB for investment grade; BB, B, CCC, and lower for noninvestment grade. In July 1994, S&P added an "r" rating for bonds of any grade that carry a relatively high-risk factor.

23. The 1998 number is from Securities Data Publishing, as reported by the Securities Industry Association. Worldwide and cumulatively, the total is much higher, especially when counting the high-yield debt issued by entities other than corporations. For a good discussion of junk bond dynamics, see "Junk Bonds Have Grown Up," *Business Week,* May 18, 1998, which reports on the "$120 billion" market for junk bonds. Currently, the amount of new money in junk bond funds (which invest in both corporate and noncorporate issues, domestically and worldwide) is about $105 billion, according to the Investment Company Institute, cited in "Junk Lures Some Nontraditional Investors," *The Wall Street Journal,* March 5, 1999, pp. C1ff.

CHAPTER 5

Dynamics of Equity-Based Financing

Fortune is like the market, where many times, if you can stay a little, the price will fall.

Francis Bacon, *Of Delays*

INTRODUCTION

On September 15, 1998, the Financial Relations Board, a national public relations firm, sent out a press release declaring "Clark/Bardes Taps Public Market to Fund Its Growth." Clark/Bardes/Holdings had recently completed an initial public offering (IPO) on the Nasdaq exchange (ticker symbol CLKB), and the release was drumming up interest in the new stock.

The timing of the IPO, completed when a bearish market was scaring away many would-be new issuers, showed that Clark/Bardes, a national designer, marketer, and administrator of insurance-financed employee benefit programs, wanted more than quick money from its IPO. Clearly, it had a long-term strategic purpose for raising money by selling its shares—but what?

The press release revealed the company's driving reason to go public, describing Clark/Bardes as a company "whose goal is to grow through acquisition to become the premier distribution company in the industry." The newly public company had already merged with a community banking pay consultant (Bank Compensation Strategies Group) in September 1997, and had signed a letter of intent to acquire another compensation consultant (Shoenke & Associates Corporation) in May 1998. But all this was just the beginning. "We are at the forefront of the consolidation trend in our industry," said Tom Wamberg, Clark/Bardes chairman. "To sustain this effort requires capital. This is our major reason for going public—to raise the money in order to gain market share before others see the beauty of our vision." In November 1998, Clark/Bardes acquired Wiedeman & Johnson Company for $4 million in cash and $2 million worth of common stock. And in April 1999, the company bought Management Compensation Group/HealthCare for $31 million in cash and assumed liabilities, plus $5.3 million in stock.

As Clark/Bardes' IPO vividly illustrates, the sale of equity is one important way to seek funds for a merger, acquisition, or buyout. Owners of private companies can sell equity through a private offering or, like Clark/Bardes, in an IPO. Pursuing an IPO, companies can use their own stock to pay for acquisitions. Alternatively, they can sell the equity to third parties, and use the money to buy other companies for cash, or to pay down debt from previous acquisitions. Companies that are already publicly held can raise money by issuing more stock.

In this chapter, we will explain the fundamentals of equity-based financing (as opposed to debt or hybrid financing). We set forth the fundamentals of private and public stock offerings. We will also look at reverse buybacks, partial spin-offs and carve-outs, and employee stock ownership plans. Later on, in Chapter 8, we will take a closer look at the role of various equity sources in all this, providing guidance on how to work with equity professionals.

EQUITY FUNDAMENTALS

What exactly is equity, and how is its value realized?

In finance, equity is the value of a company (shown on a balance sheet as net worth) after liabilities have been subtracted from assets. Equity is expressed in units called *shares* or, collectively, *stock*.

When a company is operating, the value of equity can be realized in two ways: (1) in the form of any dividends the company chooses to pay stockholders, and (2) in any gain the stockholder may make by selling off shares.

When a company ceases to operate (is declared insolvent and files for bankruptcy), then equity represents claims on assets after all other claims have been paid.

Shares of stock are a type of *security*—a financial instrument "secured" by the value of an operating company or a government. Securities may be issued as equity securities (shares of company stock) or as debt (company or government bonds, notes, or paper).

In the United States, securities are regulated by both state and federal authorities.

What is common stock?

Common stock is a type of stock that grants its owners the right to vote and to receive dividends.

What is preferred stock?

Preferred stock is a hybrid security having some of the characteristics of both debt and equity. Payments to owners of preferred stock are called preferred dividends. Being of fixed size, these dividends are contractual just like interest payments on debt. However, if cash flow is insufficient to cover preferred dividends, the firm cannot be forced into bankruptcy or reorganization. Instead, the preferred dividend payments are deferred. Cumulative preferred dividends must be paid before any dividends can be declared to shareholders. So in terms of risk, preferred stock is riskier than debt, but less risky than equity.

What are the basic rights of a holder of common stock in a corporation, and who exactly grants them?

As mentioned, stock is a security offered by a business entity. The security represents an interest in the entity, so its holder has certain rights. The nature of the rights will depend on the nature of the entity (e.g., partnership versus corporation) and the nature of the security (e.g., common versus preferred).

The rights of holders of common stock in a corporation are established by the laws of the state in which the corporation is chartered and by the terms of its charter, which is granted by the state.[1] Charters are relatively uniform on the subject of shareholder rights, which have two aspects: collective and individual.

Collectively, shareholders have the right to:

- Elect the directors of the corporation
- Amend the charter with the approval of the appropriate officials in the state of incorporation
- Adopt and amend bylaws
- Authorize the sale of fixed assets
- Change the amount of authorized common stock
- Issue securities, including preferred stock, debentures, and bonds
- Propose (or approve/reject a board proposal for) a merger with another company

Individually, shareholders have the right to:

- Vote in the manner prescribed in the corporate charter
- Sell their stock certificates
- Inspect the corporate books (often with restrictions)
- Claim assets of the corporation left over after a liquidation (after all other claimants have been paid)

Can equity holders "make or break" M&A financing and refinancing, and if so, how?

Equity holders can exercise a powerful influence on M&A financing and refinancing, if they take full advantage of their rights.

First, the shareholders' right to nominate (and vote for) directors can be used, via a proxy fight, to put new directors on the board. This changing of the guard may affect financing and refinancing decisions—particularly if the proxy fight is being run by a dissident shareholder who wants the company to enter into a merger, acquisition, or divestiture. If the dissident slate wins, then the division will most likely be spun off.

Also, the shareholders' collective right to amend the charter or bylaws of the company can affect the company's ability to finance and refinance M&A activity. This is because many charters and bylaws include restrictions on issuing new stock or on selling assets. By adding such restrictions, shareholders may make it more difficult to finance a merger internally, through the company's own wealth. Conversely, by subtracting such restrictions, they may make it easier to do internal financing for a merger. (Note, however, that having such restrictions may actually help a company obtain external financing, since the lenders will have assurance that the balance sheet will remain strong.)

By the same token, shareholders' collective rights to affect the capital structure of a corporation (by authorizing the sale of fixed assets, changing the amount of authorized common stock, and issuing securities of various kinds) obviously has a direct impact on a corporation's financing decisions.

Finally, the shareholders have a collective right to:

- Vote to enter into mergers or to sell company units
- Opt and amend bylaws with respect to mergers, asset sales, and other matters

The collective right of shareholders to determine merger policy is a complex area governed by state and federal securities laws as well as individual company bylaws. The extent of shareholder power depends in large part on the laws of the state where a company is incorporated, the nature of the transaction proposed, and the bylaws of a company.

What impact does state law have on the power of shareholders to influence merger decisions?

One dominant influence is in the area of unsolicited ("hostile") tender offers for the stock of "target" public companies. Although such transactions are rare—comprising only about 1 percent of all merger activity—they can involve large companies that are major employers in particular regions or states. As a result, at least 41 states have passed at least one "antitakeover" law in the past 12 years, ever since the U.S. Supreme Court upheld the constitutionality of such laws in *CTS Corp. v. Dynamics Court of America* in April 1987.

Here is a quick summary of the most common antitakeover laws in order of frequency:

- *Control-share acquisition* laws require approval of voting rights for stockholders whose ownership interests exceed certain thresholds; approval must come from disinterested stockholders—that is, stockholders not affiliated with the bidder or with target company management.

- *Stakeholder* laws permit boards of directors to take constituencies other than shareholders into consideration when weighing the benefits of a proposed merger.

- *Business combination freeze-out* laws set forth long waiting periods before unsolicited acquirers may complete mergers with unwilling firms.

- *Fair-price* laws require bidders to pay a legally defined fair price to all shareholders, unless the transaction is approved by the board or by holders of a specified supermajority of shares. A variation of this is the *cash-out law,* which requires the buyer of a certain percentage of a company's shares to buy the rest at a legally defined fair price.

- *Poison pill* laws affirm the right of corporation directors to pass shareholder rights plans that can deter hostile takeovers. In a typical poison pill plan, a tender offer for a certain percentage of a company's stock (say, 20 percent), automatically triggers the right of existing shareholders to buy the stock at a predetermined discount.

All the above laws are common; they are used in about half of all states or more. Other (much more rare) antitakeover laws include laws banning *greenmail* (preventing raiders from buying stock as part of an implied plan to take a company over, but then selling the stock back at extortionate prices), or laws addressing specific business or governance issues such as *labor contracts* (protecting employees from the negative effects of postmerger changes such as plant closings), *recapture of profits* (enabling companies to recapture profits made by putting company stock into play), *compensation re-strictions* (prohibiting corporate officers from receiving lucrative golden parachute payments in the event of a hostile takeover), and *mandatory classi-fied boards* (requiring all companies to have staggered board terms to prevent takeover via proxy vote).[2]

How is equity bought and sold?

Equity can be bought and sold through a *private placement* or *public offering.*

PRIVATE EQUITY OFFERINGS

What is a private placement?

A *private placement* (also known as a *direct placement*) is the sale of an entire is-sue of securities (which may be equity securities or debt securities) to a small group of investors. The placements are called private because they are exempt from the regulations that cover larger or public offerings.

In the United States, private placements to 35 or fewer investors are ex-empt from Securities and Exchange Commission (SEC) registration require-ments, under the Securities Act. Also, resales of privately placed securities to institutional buyers are exempt (under Rule 144A) from registration require-ments.[3] Buyers of securities in private placement transactions sign an *invest-ment letter* stating that the securities will not be resold for a stated period of time—typically two years.

How does a private placement work?

In a private placement, a brief notice of sale on federal Form D (promulgated under the Securities Act) must be filed with the SEC for informational pur-poses. There is, however, no federal review or comment process for a Regula-tion D private placement.

Recent changes to Regulation D broadened the availability of the exemp-tion from registration by permitting up to 35 nonaccredited investors to par-ticipate in a Regulation D private placement and an unlimited number of "ac-credited" investors. An "accredited investor" is defined under Regulation D Rule 501(a) to include wealthy individuals, entities with substantial net worth, certain institutional investors, and executive officers and directors of the issuer. Anyone who does not fit within the definition of "accredited" is considered nonaccredited.

What is a private equity partnership?

A *private equity partnership,* also known as a private equity fund, is a limited partnership formed to invest in a private company, such as a debt-funded leveraged buyout or a start-up. Investors in such funds include public pension funds, private pension funds, endowments and foundations, banks, finance companies, family trusts, insurance companies, money managers, and individuals.[4] Private equity funds are discussed in more detail in Chapter 6, on the dynamics of hybrid financing.

What regulatory controls are imposed on private equity funds and other investment funds?

The principal regulatory control is the Investment Company Act of 1940, a particularly complex statute that even the experts find challenging. It is likely to apply to any investment fund that raises money from the public and uses the proceeds primarily to acquire securities of other companies, other than operating subsidiaries held and managed in a classic holding company manner. The Act prohibits dealing with affiliates, requires a primarily equity-based capital structure, and imposes various public reporting and fiduciary obligations on the fund's principals. To avoid the effect of the Act, most leveraged buyout funds raise their capital from private placements.

Investment funds that are structured as limited partnerships are subject to a growing body of state and federal law governing these structures. (For more on limited partnerships, see Chapter 10.) A word of warning: Anyone who is in the business of buying companies, holding them short term (particularly under two years), and selling them, all without actively engaging in their day-to-day management, should check to be sure that activity is not subject to regulation under the Investment Company Act. Problems can arise even if no investment fund is involved, especially if the buyer uses the proceeds of publicly held junk bonds for financing.

PUBLIC EQUITY OFFERINGS

What is a public offering?

A *public offering* is the sale or offer to sell securities (stocks or bonds). The offering must follow a formal registration of the securities with the appropriate authorities. In the United States, securities—including securities issued in connection with a merger or acquisition—must be registered with the SEC.[5] Public offerings are usually managed by an underwriter (as discussed in Chapter 8).

What is an initial public offering?

An *initial public offering* (IPO) is a company's very first sale of stock (or offer to sell stock) to the general public. An IPO may be an offering of common or preferred stock. For example, Tejas Securities Group of Austin, Texas, has done both types of IPOs during 1998.[6] All issuers of U.S. initial public offerings must file a registration form with the SEC.[7]

What kind of registration form must be filed for an IPO?

Form S-1 is the basic registration form used by all companies. For all registrations, the companies obtain an exemption and qualify for different forms, as described below. The form has two parts. Part 1 is the prospectus (legal offering document) that must be offered to all purchasers of the securities. Part 2 contains additional information that is filed with the SEC, such as the articles of incorporation.

Notable alternatives to S-1 include SB-1, for businesses offering up to $10 million worth of securities per year, and SB-2, for issuers that have less than $25 million in annual revenues. Also of note is form 1-A, which privately held companies can use (under Regulation A) to test the waters for an offering worth $5 million or less. There is also form 2-A, a more complex version of form 1-A. If the securities are being issued expressly for a merger or acquisition, the acquirer can also use the short form S-4, described below.

How common are IPOs?

The frequency of IPOs has always been highly variable. Some years there are over a thousand, and other years only a handful.[8] In the late 1990s, there have been both highs and lows, based on Securities Data Publishing data (as reported by The Securities Industry Association). In 1995, U.S. markets saw 575 IPOs for a value of $30.3 billion. In 1996, the total was 872 offerings for $50 billion; in 1997, there were 625 IPOs worth a total $43.9 billion; and in 1998, which began with a strong market, experienced a weak third quarter, and ended with strength, there were 374 IPOs worth $43.7 billion. With hundreds of IPOs in the pipeline as we go to press, 1999 promises to be a year of greater vigor.

Can a small company with no profits go public?

As for small companies, yes, they can do IPOs. There is even a term for this—*microcap investing* (investing in public companies with a total market value of under $300 million).[9]

As for unprofitable companies, the answer is yes as well. This is a typical situation for the so-called penny stocks. Consider Noram Gaming and Entertainment, Inc. As of mid-1997, the company, with revenues under $1 million, had a market capitalization of $14.2 billion (with over 13 million shares outstanding, each share selling on Nasdaq for $1.09), with a trading range of $0.25 (25 pennies) to $3.00. Yet Noram reported the following other financials:

Book Value Per Share: Nil

Dividend: Nil

Return on Equity: Nil

Earnings per share: ($0.01)[10]

Even more striking is the story of Ticketmaster Online–CitySearch, a merger of two companies followed by an IPO that sold 7 million shares to the public for $98 million—and then saw its $14 per share stock triple in days. Yet in its prospectus, it reported a loss of $330,000 for the eight months ending September 30, 1998, on revenue of $14.3 million.[11]

If a company decides to do an IPO, but changes its mind because of a bear market, can it convert the offer into a private placement?

A company can do a private placement after attempting an IPO, but it must wait six months. When a company files a registration statement, its statement quickly becomes public via the Internet, making it in effect a general solicitation. In a private placement, a company may make no general solicitation or advertising. In the colorful words of Marc H. Morgenstern, managing partner of Kahn, Kleinman, Yanowitz & Arnson, a Cleveland-based law firm, "Today, because of the broadcast power of the Internet, there is no such thing as a quiet filing like the olden days just three years ago."[12]

Speaking of full disclosure, isn't it true that public companies have to file all their basic SEC filings electronically now, and that these files are on view around the clock to any Internet user?

Yes. Most important filings must be filed onto the EDGAR system, which stands for electronic data gathering, analysis, and retrieval. EDGAR is the SEC's computer system for the receipt, acceptance, review, and dissemination of documents submitted in electronic format. General rules and regulations for electronic filers are set forth in Regulation S-T.

Can a company accomplish an IPO over the Internet?

Yes. This process began several years ago when several companies formed to enable investors to use the Internet to buy securities. One company, called E*Trade, applied this process to IPOs. In July 1996, E*Trade announced that it intended "to begin raising equity capital through public and private offerings via [its] Web site and other electronic media."[13] The floor for such transactions, said the company, would be $5 million. (This low ceiling is prompted no doubt by the liberal exemptions accorded those using Form 1-A under Regulation A, mentioned above.) Today, there are dozens of companies that facilitate IPOs and securities sales over the Internet.

Are Internet IPOs regulated, and if so, what are the rules?

Offerings accomplished over the Internet, called direct public offerings (DPOs), fall under the same rules as other public offerings—with some supplemental requirements owing to the electronic medium.[14] This is the main message of the October 1995 SEC publication entitled *The Use of Electronic Media for Information Purposes*. According to this philosophy, the company must disclose in its offering circular that the final offering document is available in both e-mail and printed form. An offering available via the Internet must be updated just like a printed document, and the information must be accessible to the Internet-based investor. Investors must be able to download, retain, and print out the information provided. Companies may need to document this capability and the investor's use of it, so experts recommend establishing a confirmation process for all communications.[15] The SEC continually warns against DPO fraud; following these rules can be an important step in preventing it.

Could you name some online brokers?

First, many old-line securities brokerage firms have Internet sites with broad capability to send and receive information online. Brand names such as American Express, Fidelity, and Schwab have begun to sell securities online. In addition, some new brokerage firms exist primarily online. Here is a current list of firms including some, such as E*Trade, that can help firms do IPOs online:

1800Daytrade.com	Ameritrade (merger of Aufhauser,
A. B. Watley	Ceres, and eBroker)
Accutrade	Andrew Peck Associates
AFTrader.com	Benson York Group
American Express Financial Direct	BHI Securities Limited

Bidwell and Company
Bull & Bear Securities
Burke, Christensen & Lewis
   Securities
CompuTEL
CrestarInvest
Datek Online
Delong, Friedman, and Sukenik
Discover Brokerage Direct
DLJ Direct
Ira Epstein (for futures and options)
E-Commodities
e.Schwab
E*Trade
Executioner
Fidelity Web XPress
InvestExpress Online
Jack White
J. B. Oxford
Marquette de Bary & Co.
Max Ule & Co.

Mr. Stock
Muriel Siebert & Co.
National Discount
Net Investor
NowTrade
Pacific Brokerage Services
Pacific Continental/US Invest
ProTrade Securities
Quick & Reilly
Scottsdale Securities–Scottrade
Stocks4Less
Suretrade.com
Trading Direct
TradeStar Investments
TruTrade
Wall St. Access
Waterhouse Securities
Web Street Securities
Wyse Securities
Xpresstrade
Ziegler Thrift Trading[16]

If a company does another public stock offering after an IPO, must it go through the whole registration process again?

No, there is an accelerated process. After one year as a public company, a company may register for an offering using an S-3 wraparound form, rather than the form S-1 required for an IPO. Since SEC review of S-3 forms tends to be cursory (the entire review is done at the S-1 filing stage), firms are not subject to 30-day waiting periods and associated compliance costs.[17]

USING STOCK TO PAY FOR A TRANSACTION

What are the basic ways stock can be used to pay for a deal?

There are two main ways. First, a company can sell stock and use the money raised from the stock offering to pay for the deal. Second, a company can use stock itself to pay for the deal.

How common is stock as an acquisition currency, and what are the pros and cons for it?

Stock is a fairly common acquisition currency. As mentioned in Chapter 1, over half of all deals in 1998 were in cash, and the rest were either in stock (29 percent) or stock and cash (17 percent). By contrast, 10 years before, nearly 70 percent were in cash, and only 8 percent was in stock, with the rest in a combination. Most of the cash in the 1980s deals were borrowed. Most large transactions are stock for stock. In fact, between 1995 and through the early part of 1999, 90 percent of all transactions valued at over $1 billion were stock for stock. When all the smaller transactions are included in the data, the pure stock deals decline to under 50 percent. This contrasts with the decade of the 1980s, when two thirds of all transactions appeared to be in cash. But this appearance is misleading, because debt was raised largely through junk bonds. Although cash proceeds were used in the acquisitions, really they were financed by debt rather than cash.

On the positive side, the hard costs of stock are relatively low. Even if an IPO is involved, stock costs a company nothing beyond the expense of registration and the administrative and promotional costs of becoming a public company. To be sure, these costs can be substantial. They include expenses for underwriting, legal and accounting services, transfer services, broker commissions, and printing. But these are usually a fraction of the amount of money that comes in as a result of a stock offering. By contrast, debt is in a sense pure cost; every penny borrowed is owed back—usually with interest.

On the negative side, stock sales cost more in terms of management time and energy. Moreover, there is a lot of uncertainty about outcome. A company's stock price (and, thus, its price/earnings ratios) can change during the deal, changing the economics of a transaction. Market volatility is also a concern. If the stock market as a whole drops during a stock transaction, chances are that the acquirer's stock will drop with it.[18]

What exactly happens when an acquirer pays stock for another company?

The acquiring company must come up with the stock. To do this, it can:

- Issue new shares
- Buy stock back from shareholders
- Use treasury stock
- Use stock put "on the shelf" from a previous registration

Of course, the acquirer using stock does not have to use stock alone. As mentioned earlier in this book, some deals are paid for in stock, some in cash, and some in a mix of stock and cash (including notes and/or assumption of debt). Let's take a few recent examples.

In some transactions, the acquirer pays in stock while assuming debt. According to a mid-1998 press release, Frontier Natural Gas Corp. of Houston, Texas, acquired partial interests in some oil and gas projects from Aspect Resources for an estimated $24.1 million in May 1998. The acquirer paid 4,266,000 shares valued at $20.3 million, and assumed $3.8 million in liabilities of the company. On the same day, Frontier closed a very similar deal with Esenjay Petroleum in a transaction valued at $25.5 million. It paid 5,165,000 shares valued at $24.5 million, and assumed $1 million in liabilities.[19]

What is treasury stock?

Treasury stock is previously issued shares that are repurchased and held by the issuer.

What do you mean by stock that is "on the shelf"?

Acquirers can also avail themselves of the *shelf registration* regulations of the SEC. These rules allow companies to file a statement for a large number of shares, distributing some at that time, but reserving the rest "on the shelf" for future distributions. In general, the stock is not supposed to stay on the shelf very long, but the SEC does allow companies engaged in a continuing program of acquisitions to register a reasonable number of securities for these future purposes, periodically amending the registration statement to keep it current.

What kind of red tape is involved in the issuance of new stock to pay for a merger, and how can this be minimized?

As mentioned earlier in this chapter, the Securities Act of 1933 requires (absent exemptions) that the securities issued be registered. The registration process can take months if registrants have to file form S-1, which requires disclosure of a great amount of financial details about the company issuing the shares. Similar rules apply under the Trust Indenture Act of 1939 for issuance of debt securities in a transaction, as discussed in Chapter 4.

Fortunately, the SEC has created S-4, a shorter form to be used for securities issued as part of a business combination or exchange offer.[20] If a company has already filed an S-1 form, it can reference that form in the shorter S-4 form, speeding up the process. Also, it can avail itself of shelf registration rules, as discussed above.

If the shareholders of the selling company must approve the merger, the transaction may be delayed. But this cloud has a silver lining in terms of disclosure obligations. A lot of the necessary information will already be in the proxy statement. Acquirers can use a combination of the selling and acquiring companies' statements, and the two together are considered a prospectus for the new securities.

Do all stock-based acquisitions involve ordinary registered common stock?

No, some involve restricted and/or unregistered stock.

For example, when International Casino Cruises of Houston, Texas, acquired the Green Mount Power Corp. subsidiary of Mountain Energy Inc., it paid 50 million in restricted common shares. Restricted common stock has voting rights, but the timing of its sale is restricted. (For more on restricted stock, see Chapter 6.) Also, note that some stock used to pay for deals (or exchanged for an acquirer's stock in a pooling) is unregistered. Some companies are too new and small to get through the registration process at the SEC. They usually sign an agreement that their stock will be registered in one, two, or three years from the time of the merger.

Can you give some examples of how IPO funds can be used to finance acquisition programs and/or to pay down debt from past acquisitions?

When Lexington Healthcare Group Inc. went public in late 1996, one of its stated purposes was to buy Professional Relief Nurses, Inc. And when Mercury Waste Solutions went public around that same time, one of its stated purposes for the IPO capital was repayment of the company's debt, which had grown as a result of its purchase of U.S. Environmental, Inc., a Minnesota-based mercury recycling company.[21]

Sometimes, an IPO occurs simultaneously with an acquisition. In April 1998, National Equipment Services sold some $234 million worth of shares and used the proceeds to pay for Falconite, Inc., a rental equipment company.

Prior to the offering, the company reclassified its previous mix of common and preferred shares into all common shares, and then did a stock split.[22]

What are public company shells?

A public company *shell* is an entity that has gone through the registration process, but that has no significant operations or assets. Its value is limited to the value of the time and money its buyer saves by not having to go through registration. Of the some 15,000 public companies in the United States, over 10 percent are shells.

Do companies ever buy public company "shells" to accomplish acquisitions?

Yes. We do not know how common this practice is, but we often see advertisements like the following:

> *Go Public!*
> *PUBLIC SHELLS*
> *Your company can be publicly traded*
> *Call_____*

or

> *Clean Public Shell Available*
> *Raise Money*
> *Do Mergers & Acquisitions*
> *Call _____*

Shell prices seem to run around $25,000.[23]

Is equity-based financing relatively secure for the issuing company?

It depends on the arrangement that the issuer has with the underwriter. If the underwriter makes a firm commitment, then the issuer gets the full price anticipated. But if the underwriter promises only a best effort, then a drop in the price just prior to the issue can hurt the issuer.

Once an issue is out, of course, it is the public that owns the shares, and that wins or loses on the basis of share price appreciation. But the issuer can also gain from share price appreciation. If its share price is high, it can issue new shares, either for direct sale to the public or for use in stock-based compensation plans.

Issuing new shares can be a double-edged sword. On the one hand, the company receives the funds (or, in the case of stock grants to executives, saves the cash compensation costs). On the other hand, if the market value of the company stays the same while the total number of shares increases, dilution results—and current and potential investors are wary of that.

BEYOND IPOs—EQUITY-BASED FUND-RAISING STRATEGIES

In addition to IPOs, what are some equity-based techniques for raising funds?

These include *reverse buybacks, carve-outs, employee stock ownership plans (ESOPs), undervalued share transactions,* and *financed equity issuance transactions.*

What is a reverse buyback?

It is the opposite of a buyback. A buyback is the purchase of one's own shares. A reverse buyback is the sale of the shares bought in a buyback. Incidentally, the new Regulation M, which took effect in early 1997, makes it easier for corporations to buy and sell their own shares. Old regulations that make it very expensive to buy back odd lots of securities (100 or less) have been streamlined.

What is a carve-out?

A carve-out, also known as a partial spin-off, is the sale of a minority stake in a company through an IPO.

Could you give examples of recent carve-outs?

In September 1998, Barnes & Noble, the largest bookseller in the United States, announced plans to sell a minority stake in its online operations through an IPO.[24] This was one of 32 such deals in that year, and like many, it did well.

The transaction brought the firm approximately $100 million in new funds, all without giving up control over the unit. Other companies involved in 1998 carve-outs include CBS (carve-out of radio and outdoor advertising properties), General Motors (two-step spin-off of parts maker Delphi Automotive Systems), and Keebler, the cookie maker (which sold 16 percent of itself to the public in January 1998). The Keebler carve-out preceded (and helped finance) the company's current acquisition program.

How does a two-step spin-off work?

In a two-step spin-off, a company starts with a carve-out, selling a minority interest in a unit. Then it gives (spins off) the rest of the unit to shareholders. This is the current plan of General Motors—following in the footsteps of AT&T, which spun off Lucent Technologies in 1996. (The $2.647 billion spin-off was the largest IPO of that year.[25]) The first step not only raises capital for the parent, but enables the market to set the unit's value before the rest of the unit is handed over to shareholders, typically a few months later.

What impact does a two-step carve-out have on the value of parent company shares?

It depends entirely on the circumstances at hand. Sometimes—as in the case of Lucent—the shareholders wind up with stock in two companies (the unit's and the parent's) worth more than the parent's stock beforehand. After the offering, the stock of the spun-off unit may then outperform the parent's stock. (For example, in the two years following its 1996 spin-off, Lucent's share price grew from $13.50 to more than $108, while AT&T's shares did not even double.)

Sometimes, however, the parent that spins off the unit (or the fraction of a unit) increases in value as a result of the spin-off. According to a recent account in *Business Week,* Barnes & Noble hopes its online unit, like its rival Amazon.com, will "command a market multiple akin to the more than 10 times estimated 1998 revenue." That would give a market value of at least $500 million, or more than one quarter of the parent's total capitalization, even though it contributes less than 2 percent of total sales.

How well do the shares of carve-outs perform for their owners?

In recent research, three professors—Heather Hulburt of West Virginia University and James Miles and J. Randall Woolridge of Pennsylvania State University—found that both carved-out units and the parent companies' shares returned more on average than the shares of peer companies. The group examined 83 carve-out deals from 1981 to 1990, and found that those companies, on average, saw faster growth in sales, operating income, capital expenditures, and assets than their industry rivals, producing higher returns on assets and sales. One reason is that a high percentage (80 percent) of the carved-out units paid their managers in stock.

It is important to note that the returns are long term, not short term. The carve-out does not offer the quick returns available in a regular spin-off. First, there are none of the automatic sales that sell-offs usually trigger. Moreover, when the carve-out shares enter the marketplace as a new IPO, investment bankers talk them up, improving their price and limiting the chance for a buyer's gain. And unlike a regular spin-off, the carve-out is still linked to the parent, problems in the parent company at the time of the transaction can affect the subsidiary. Finally, in dividing up assets, liabilities, and personnel for the carve-out (or eventual spin-off), the parent may be tempted to keep some of the best for itself—a process that requires judgment calls.[26]

What exactly is an ESOP, and how can it help a company raise money to acquire other companies?

An ESOP (as mentioned earlier, an employee stock ownership plan) is a tax-qualified employee benefit plan that invests primarily in the stock of the employer. In order to encourage ESOPs, the U.S. Congress has provided a variety of special tax benefits to stockholders who sell their stock to an ESOP, to companies that have ESOPs, and to lenders that provide financing for ESOPs.[27]

Shareholders who sell their stock to an ESOP may qualify for tax-free rollover treatment under Section 1042 of the Internal Revenue Service Code (the Code), with additional benefits for estate taxes. That section permits deferment of payment of a capital gains tax upon the sale of stock, provided the shareholder reinvests the sale proceeds in stock of another active business corporation within one year after the sale. (In addition, if the selling shareholder is an estate or other entity holding the employer's stock at the time of the decedent's death, as much as one half of the proceeds of the sale of the stock to an ESOP may be deducted from the gross estate for federal estate tax purposes.)

Companies that have ESOPs can accomplish several goals, including some financing goals. For example, ESOPs can help a company divest a subsidiary through an ESOP buyout, repurchase shares from the public equity market using pretax dollars, and acquire capital by having the company borrow through the ESOP and repay the loan with pretax dollars.

Under some circumstances, institutional lenders (such as banks, insurance companies, investment companies, and the like) can exclude from income taxation 50 percent of the interest earnings on an ESOP loan. This tax deduction used to be much broader until 1996, when the Small Business Job

Protection Act repealed a part of the Code that offered more incentives to lenders.

What is an undervalued share transaction, and how can it help a company raise money?

An undervalued share transaction is a type of derivative financial instrument.[28] In an undervalued share transaction, a company buys a *cash-settled call* on its own stock, and then sells a call on its own stock at a higher price. When the price of the stock rises above its exercise price (is in the money), the company may take its profit in cash. When the stock rises further, to put the higher-priced call in the money, the company issues new shares, once again receiving cash—though less than the market value of the stock.

What are financed equity issuance transactions?

In this type of transaction, an underwriter purchases shares from a company, which agrees to risk exposure to movements in its stock for up to one year. If the stock price rises, the underwriter pays the difference to the company; if the stock price drops, the company delivers additional stock.[29]

What is alphabet stock, and what role can it play in acquisition financing?

Alphabet stock, also called special class stock, is a variation on series class stocks that have been used by mutual funds for many years. It was first used for a standard business organization when General Motors acquired Electronic Data Systems Corporation (EDS) in 1984. GM again used the device a year later when it acquired Hughes Aircraft Company. Although neither EDS nor Hughes remain as GM subsidiaries today, the acquisitions are instructive. In those two deals, GM issued new class E and class H stock, respectively. Holders of these stocks had the same basic rights under state and federal law as common shareholders, but they received dividends that were more sensitive to the fortunes of their unit.

CONCLUDING COMMENTS

In this chapter, we have merely scratched the surface of an extremely dynamic and complex area. Equity markets involve broad and deep questions of accounting, finance, and law. A full answer to many of the questions posed here could fill a book. Nonetheless, we have tried to orient the reader toward a few basics in equity-based financing. These basics should suffice for a mastery of our next subject: hybrid financing.

ENDNOTES

1. For more details, see J. Fred Weston and Thomas E. Copeland, *Managerial Finance*, 9th ed (Los Angeles: Academic Publishers, 1998), pp. 932ff.

2. This list is based on a summary of state antitakeover laws appearing in *Mergers & Acquisitions*, September–October 1998, pp. 44ff. The most detailed, current, and authoritative source of this information is Investor Responsibility Research Center (IRRC), in Washington, D.C. IRRC, a not-for-profit research center, publishes annual reports on these developments and also reports on them in its various newsletters.

3. An institutional buyer is defined under Rule 144A as an entity "acting for its own account or the accounts of other qualified institutional buyers, that in the aggregate owns and invests on a discretionary basis at least $100 million in securities of issuers that are not affiliated with the entity." A variety of types of institutional buyers are included and defined in Rule 144A. In order of appearance, they are insurance companies, investment companies, small business investment companies, public employee benefit plans, private employee benefit plans, trust funds, business development companies, investment advisers, dealers, banks, and savings and loans. See: *Securities Act Rules: Rules 100 Through 236—General Rules and Regulations Under the Securities Act of 1933* (New York: Bowne & Co., 1998), printed September 15, 1998. See also Regulation D of the Securities Act of 1933, covering "Rules Governing the Limited Offer and Sale of Securities Without Registration Under the Securities Act of 1933." Since enactment of the 144A exemption in 1990, private placements have grown. For example, as of early 1997, one out of every five bond issues was a private placement, and about two thirds of all junk bond issues were done through private placements. See "Private-Placement Market Is Proving Popular," *The Wall Street Journal*, April 1, 1997, p. C14.

4. As of late 1996, private equity partnerships were attracting the following sources of funds: public pension funds (29 percent); corporate pension funds (21 percent); endowments and foundations (15 percent); banks, savings and loans, and finance companies (11 percent); insurance companies (10 percent); money managers and other strategic investors (7 percent); and family trusts and individuals (7 percent). See *The Private Equity Analyst*, Wellesley, Massachusetts, cited in "Pension Funds Target Buyout Funds' Big Fees," *The Wall Street Journal*, October 3, 1996.

5. In "Preliminary Notes to Rule 145," the SEC notes that Rule 145 is designed to extend "the protection provided by registration under the Securities Act of 1933, as amended, to persons who are offered securities in a business combina-

tion of the type described in paragraphs (a) 1, 2, and 3." Those paragraphs cover stockholder votes on reclassifications (other than stock splits or changes in par value), mergers or consolidations, and transfers of assets. See *Securities Act Rules,* op. cit. (note 3), Rule 145. Note, however, that not all such transactions must be registered. The exemptions covered under Regulation D may be extended to include "business combinations that include sales by virtue of Rule 145 (a) or otherwise." See *Regulations D, E, and CE: Including Rules 501, 601, 701, and 1001 Under the Securities Act of 1933* (New York: Bowne & Co., 1999), dated March 15, 1999.

6. From a press release posted July 10, 1998, by Tejas Securities Group and picked up by Business Wire.

7. The following discussion has been adapted from James B. Arkebauer and Ron Schultz, *Going Public: Everything You Need to Know to Take Your Company Public, Including Internet Direct Public Offerings,* 3rd ed. (Chicago: Dearborn Financial Publishing, 1998).

8. For example, in 1969 there were over 1,000 IPOs, and in 1975 there were only five. Ibid.

9. "Betting Small: How Fund Managers Buy Microcap Stocks in Hopes of Big Profits," *The Wall Street Journal,* December 1, 1997, p. A1.

10. (EPS was negative.) See "Noram Gaming & Entertainment, Inc.: Special Research Report," *Global Penny Stocks,* www.pennystock.com, April 21, 1997.

11. "Ticketmaster Is Latest Rocket from Internet," *The Wall Street Journal,* December 4, 1998, pp. C1ff.

12. Quoted in a company press release dated October 5, 1998.

13. Advertisement for www.etrade.com appearing on p. C20, *The Wall Street Journal,* July 29, 1996.

14. The main source for this answer is Arkebauer and Schultz, op. cit. (note 7).

15. According to Arkebauer (ibid.), "It is felt that the use of passwords, e-mail confirmation, and in some cases, documentable evidence is needed to confirm that the investor has successfully accessed [offering information]."

16. This list is provided by Professor Brian Betker of Saint Louis University. It is posted online as part of Professor Betker's Finance 363 course.

17. For a good article on this subject, see Gabor Garai and Susan Pravda, "One Year After Your IPO: Is Your Board Keeping Pace with Opportunities?" *Director's Monthly,* May 1997, pp. 9ff.

18. The most dramatic example of this is seen in the IPO market, which can "dry up" almost overnight.

19. See the May–June 1998 roster of *Mergers & Acquisitions* magazine, as published in the September–October 1998 issue. Following this transaction, Frontier changed the name of the unit to Esenjay Exploration.

20. We thank Bruce Wasserstein, chairman and CEO, Wasserstein Perella & Co., for contributing to this discussion of regulatory aspects of securities issued to fi-

nance deals. Our answer here is based in part on his highly readable commentary in *Big Deal: The Battle for Control of America's Leading Corporations* (New York: Warner Books, 1998), pp. 539ff.

21. *Going Public: The IPO Reporter,* January 13, 1997, p. 10 and p. 13.

22. *SEC New Registrations Report,* April 1998, p. 3. This newsletter is a publication of Commerce Clearing House (CCH) Washington Service Bureau.

23. These are both ads from *The Wall Street Journal.* The authors have also noticed similar shell ads on the Internet.

24. Robert Barker, "When a Carve-Out Is a Good Deal," *Business Week,* September 21, 1998 (Personal Business: Investing), from the Internet. As mentioned, carve-outs have been doing well. Here are the numbers (from Securities Data Publishing) comparing initial prices to year-end prices: 1995, 34 carve-outs, average run-up 23.3 percent; 1996, 54, run-up 18.9 percent; 1997, 46, run-up 14 percent; and 1998, 32, run-up 26.6 percent.

25. The $11.334 billion spin-off of Deutsche Telekom AG was the largest IPO in the world that year, but only $1.605 billion of its paper was placed in the U.S. See "Carve-Outs Seen as Largest 1996 Public Offerings," *Going Public: The IPO Reporter,* op. cit. (note 9), p. 1.

26. In August 1998, Cincinnati Bell carved out its billing and customer service unit, Convergys, and sold 10 percent to the public with plans to spin off the remainder in a few months. Speaking of the divvying up process, former Cincinnati Bell CEO John LaMacchia once observed: "You try to be as fair as possible, but you can't just close your eyes and cut the baby in half." (LaMacchia named Richard Ellenberger as his successor, as announced on November 19, 1998, in the *Cincinnati Courier.*)

27. For more details on all three points, see Stanley Foster Reed and Alexandra Reed Lajoux, *The Art of M&A: A Merger/Acquisition/Buyout Guide,* 3rd ed. (New York: McGraw-Hill, 1999), pp. 421ff.

28. This instrument is offered by at least one firm—SBC Warburg Dillon Read. See Joan Ogden, "Behind the Boom in Equity Derivatives," *Global Finance,* June 1998, pp. 46ff.

29. This derivative instrument is offered by at least one firm: Merrill Lynch. See Joan Ogden, ibid.

CHAPTER 6

Dynamics of "Hybrid" Financing

The most general definition of beauty . . . Multeity in Unity.

Samuel Coleridge, *On the Principles of Genial Criticism*, 1814

INTRODUCTION

One of the fundamental tenets of financing—and the tax codes of many countries—is the distinction between debt and equity. As explained earlier (first in Chapter 1 and then again in Chapters 4 and 5), these two instruments—debt and equity—are as different as night and day. Debt is an unconditional obligation to repay principal and interest, has a fixed maturity date, and is not convertible to or attached to any other instrument; neither the principal nor the interest owed by the debt instrument is contingent on profits or other variable factors. Equity, in contrast, represents ownership of shares in a corporation. The value of equity is realized through exchange—by buying low and selling high. In a liquidation situation, equity is what would be left of a company if all debts (liabilities) were paid, so it represents a residual claim on assets.

All these distinctions sound great in theory, and they work fairly well in reality. But beyond this "black and white" distinction between debt and equity, there is also a very large gray area—debt instruments that have equity features, and equity instruments that have debt features. These so-called *hybrids* play a critical role in M&A financing.

In this chapter, we will briefly discuss the most common types of hybrids—namely, securitized credit, convertible bonds, preferred stock, and warrants—and then we will discuss the vehicles through which these hybrids travel: mezzanine financing, registration rights in security holder agreements, and seller takeback financing.

THE HYBRIDS

What is securitized credit?

Securitized credit is a loan that has been turned into a security. In Chapter 4, we mentioned this phenomenon when introducing two key terms: *securitization* (the conversion of assets into securities for sale to investors) and *securitized credit* (the conversion of bank loans such as mortgage loans into marketable securities for sale to investors). These are also referred to as *asset-backed securities*. The asset backing the security may be almost any type of financial asset—a situation that has led to enormous creativity in this field.[1]

The borrower usually does not feel the effects of the securitization. No matter who owns the loan, the borrower and the lender must still honor the terms of any contracts they have signed. From the point of view of the lender, however, securization makes a tremendous difference: It enables the lender to convert a loan to cash (having sold the loan to an investment pool), thus receiving money now rather than later. The existence of securitization as an option, therefore, might make lenders more willing to lend money, including money for an M&A transaction, knowing that if they need to recoup their cash quickly, they can.[2]

How might loan securitization help support M&A activities?

In January 1997, First Union, a commercial bank (which later that year merged with Corestates Financial Corp. in a $16 billion transaction), announced that it had helped Newcourt Credit Group, Inc., issue $519.2 million in asset-backed notes. Newcourt has used the proceeds from this issuance to strengthen its capital position following the acquisition of AT&T Capital in 1996.[3]

What are some other common types of hybrid instruments?

Some common types of hybrid instruments include *convertibles, exchangeables, preferred stock,* and *warrants.* All these are used in *mezzanine financing,* and they are often secured through *registration rights.*

What is a convertible?

A *convertible* is a financial instrument that can be exchanged at a set price for a set number of equity shares. A *convertible bond* is a bond that includes a call option on a stock. Some preferred stock has this feature, as do some debentures.

The convertible bond market has been growing in recent years (it now exceeds $140 billion),[4] and today there are even mutual funds that invest in it.

What is an exchangeable?

An *exchangeable* is a financial instrument (usually a convertible bond) that uses shares of companies other than the issuer's for its call option. An exchangeable provides a vehicle for issuers to unload equity holdings in other companies, often with tax savings, such as deferral of capital gains until redemption of the notes. Companies that want to ensure the sale of their holding may issue *mandatory exchangeables*. These instruments require buyers to take shares (or their cash value) but they carry a smaller premium for the issuer. Companies can also use options to defray the cost of issuing regular debt, a practice that has the same effect as a convertible bond.[5]

What is preferred stock?

Preferred stock is stock that pays a fixed dividend and has claim to assets of a corporation ahead of common stock in the event of liquidation. Preferred stock usually does not carry voting rights.

What is a warrant?

A *warrant*, also called a *subscription warrant*, is a certificate giving the bearer the right to buy securities or other commodities at a stated price for a stated period or at any time in the future. Warrants may be used in private financings, typically at a bargain price, or they may be sold to the public at higher prices, and traded on stock exchanges.

What is the difference between stock options and warrants?

They are very similar, but stock options are usually granted only to the issuer's employees, whereas warrants may be offered to a variety of players, such as providers of merger financing. In fact, warrants may even be sold to the general public.

What is the role of warrants?

One increasingly popular alternative to preferred or common stock is a warrant to acquire common stock at some time in the future. This has a double advantage for the buyer. First, it avoids making the seller a common stockholder entitled to receive information and participate in stockholders' meetings during the immediate postacquisition period. Second, unlike stock, it does not adversely affect the eligibility of an acquired company for S corporation status.[6]

What are the key terms generally found in warrants?

Key provisions will address the following issues:

- The number of shares that can be acquired upon exercise of the warrant
- The "exercise price" (the amount to be paid to acquire the shares)
- The period of time during which exercise may occur (which, to prevent interference with any future sale of the company, should not extend beyond the date of any such sale)
- Any restrictions on transfer of the warrant
- Any rights that may be accorded to the warrant holder when and if it participates in registrations by the company for a public stock offering

There are also lengthy and technical provisions for adjustment in the number of shares for which the warrant can be exercised. These provisions aim to prevent dilution if there are stock splits or dividends, or if shares are sold to others at less than full value.

Does the *seller* ever receive security as a subordinated lender?

Occasionally, but not typically. The seller may take a subordinated note either on an unsecured basis or with security. Security interests strengthen a seller's bargaining power with senior lenders in the event of bankruptcy or refinancing. The collateral gives the seller a right to foreclose as well as a seat at the bankruptcy table, even if under the subordination provisions the seller has no immediate right to payment. Possession of a security interest also gives the subordinated lender leverage to initiate and influence a refinancing.

MEZZANINE FINANCING

What is mezzanine financing?

As mentioned earlier in this book (Chapter 1), *mezzanine financing*, sometimes called *second-tier* financing, is unsecured subordinated debt that also allows the lender to receive some rights to acquire equity at a later date.[7] The loan is usually a term loan of 5 to 10 years, and often it will require interim payments of interest only, with the principal being due in a balloon payment at the end of the term. The opportunity to take stock can be in the form of convertible bonds, convertible preferred stock, or warrants.

How does the financing actually work?

Let's use warrants as the example, since these are the most common equity component of a mezzanine debt issue. The exercise price of the warrants is usually nominal, or at least substantially below the market value of the company's stock. The warrant will, therefore, have value at least equal to the difference between the market value of the stock and the exercise price. These warrants will usually have at least a 10-year term. The mezzanine lender may also require a "put" option on the warrant and on any stock purchased with the warrant.

Why is it called mezzanine financing?

Mezzanine means middle, and it provides an additional layer of financing between the senior debt and the company's equity. Mezzanine investors are junior (subordinate) to collateralized senior lenders, but are senior to the equity investors.

What is the main function of mezzanine financing?

Mezzanine financing is a way to borrow funds over and above what secured lenders will loan, although at somewhat higher interest rates. In this it is very much like junk bonds (discussed in Chapter 4), except that it has more equity features, and it is almost always privately placed. Mezzanine financing is used in highly leveraged transactions, either for operations or for acquisitions.

Is mezzanine financing debt or equity?

Mezzanine capital looks like equity to the debtor's commercial bank lender and it looks like debt to the company. It combines cash flow and risk characteristics of both senior debt and common stock.

In the risk/reward spectrum, it occupies a middle ground between debt and equity, with a higher risk/reward ratio than debt, but a lower risk/reward ratio than equity. It also costs more than debt and less than equity—although some of its costs are hard to quantify.

Who provides mezzanine capital?

Mezzanine capital is typically supplied by venture capital limited partnerships and other nonbank financial institutions.

What kinds of restrictions do lenders put on mezzanine loans?

Mezzanine lenders usually insist on the same protective covenants that venture capital investors do, including rights of cosale, preemptive rights, rights of first refusal, limitations on issuing additional shares and dividends, one or more board seats for the mezzanine lender, limiting the number of insiders on the board, veto rights over certain corporate actions such as increases to top management's compensation, and registration rights (see below). All these are important considerations in mezzanine financing, particularly when it involves an equity investment fund.

What is an equity investment fund?

An *equity investment fund*, also known as a *private equity fund*, is a type of financing vehicle often used to provide the mezzanine financing in a business recapitalization or management buyout (MBO). The investment fund raises equity capital from private investors and uses the capital to make equity and subordinated debt investments in a portfolio of companies that are in need of extra financing. In return for their capital, investors in an investment fund typically receive income from the debt the fund provides to its portfolio of companies and the potential for capital appreciation from the fund's equity investments. (For more on the techniques of MBO financing, which often involve multiple financial sources, see Chapter 10.)

The dominant players have been Kohlberg Kravis Roberts and Forstmann Little, but there are others: Adler & Shaykin, Apollo Advisors, Blackstone Capital Partners, Clayton Dubelier & Rice, Foreman Associates, Hicks Muse Tate, Kelso & Co., Thomas H. Lee, Texas Pacific Group, and Warburg Pincus Investors. Other funds may be organized for specific deals. Also, funds hang shingles at various brokerage firms such as Donaldson, Lufkin & Jenrette, Merrill Lynch, Morgan Stanley, and the brokerage operations of Citigroup (notably its Lehman unit). For more on the role of these funds, see Chapter 9.

How are investment funds structured?

Generally, investment funds are organized as limited partnerships.[8] The interests in the partnerships are considered securities under federal and state securities laws and, consequently, are offered and sold in a registered public offering or in reliance on an exemption from the registration requirements.

Most commonly, the investment funds have been marketed to a limited number of sophisticated, wealthy individuals, financial institutions, and public and private pension funds in a private placement offering.[9] Proceeds of the offering are used by the funds to acquire common equity, preferred stock, and subordinated debt in a series of management buyouts.

Do investment funds generally make majority investments?

They have done so traditionally, but in the early 1990s, following a drop in available bank financing, many began to take on minority investments.[10]

How do the fund investors share in the benefits of the investment?

Fund investors do not directly own any stock or other interests in the company to be acquired. Instead, each participant, or investor, in an investment fund contributes capital to each acquisition vehicle formed and will become a limited partner in the acquisition vehicle, receiving a return on investment in accordance with the partnership agreement. For example, in two private funds sponsored by Forstmann Little & Co. and KKR, respectively, the general partner receives 20 percent of the realized profits from the investments made by the fund, and the remaining balance is distributed to the limited partners. In certain public funds, income and gain may be distributed 99 percent to the limited partners and 1 percent to the general partner until the limited partners have received distributions of an amount equal to a 10 percent cumulative annual return on their capital contributions. Thereafter, the general partner is permitted to take a larger share of the profits.

Are the acquisitions in which the fund will invest identified in advance?

No. Investment funds are typically structured as "blind pools," meaning that the portfolio of companies in which a fund will invest will not be identified or known at the time each investor purchases an interest in the fund. The general partner of the fund will have complete discretion in selecting the companies in which the fund will invest. Generally, the funds do not invest in companies when management is opposed to the acquisition.

What kind of time frame and returns can an investor in an equity fund expect?

Private investment funds are often structured so that each investor enters into a commitment, for an average period of five to six years, to make a capital contribution upon the request of the general partner. The commitment is usually quite large, ranging from $5 million to $10 million; however, investors have control over and use of their capital until it is actually invested in a particular acquisition vehicle upon request of the general partner. Returns on equity fund investments vary, especially between equity and debt investors.[11]

What other investments do funds make besides mezzanine and equity financing?

Occasionally, an investment fund will provide bridge financing rather than mezzanine financing. Bridge financing is provided for a short term, typically nine months or less, to supply funds during the interim period before permanent financing is arranged. After the bridge loan is repaid, the fund remains with an equity interest in the acquired company and can roll the loan proceeds over into another acquisition.

In addition, investment funds may be structured to allow the fund to use its capital to finance a friendly tender offer for stock of a publicly held company whereby 51 percent of the stock is acquired in the tender offer and the remaining stock is acquired in a cash merger. This structure permits leveraged purchases of public companies, despite the margin requirements that prohibit acquisition financing secured by more than 50 percent of the value of the securities acquired. The initial 51 percent of the stock acquired in the tender offer is financed half by borrowings and half by equity from the fund. When the cash merger occurs, the additional financing can be supported by the assets of the company being bought, and all or a part of the initial equity investment can be repaid.

REGISTRATION RIGHTS

What are registration rights?

Registration rights are rights given to an owner of debt or equity securities (1) to require the issuer of the securities to register such securities for public sale under federal and state securities laws or (2) to participate in any such public sale initiated by the issuer or another security holder. Registration rights are key provisions of warrants, preferred stock, and privately placed subordinated debt issues and thus deserve special attention here. They also appear in stockholders' agreements and agreements with management.

Why do security holders want registration rights?

Registration rights give security holders more liquidity.[12] Absent such rights, debt or equity privately placed in connection with an acquisition usually cannot be resold freely to the public. To resell securities (whether debt or equity) to the public, holders must (1) do another private placement, (2) get an exemption from the applicable registration provisions of federal and state securities laws, or (3) hold on to their securities for a certain time, in compliance with the holding period and other limitations of Rule 144A of the Securities Act of 1933.

What exactly is Rule 144A and what restrictions does it impose on securities sales in the merger context?

Rule 144A is a part of the Securities Act relating to private resales of securities to institutions. Fundamentally, it exempts certain securities sales to qualified institutional buyers under certain conditions.

The Rule 144A exemption, however, is riddled with restrictions. It limits the amount of "control" an entity may amass as a security holder. Second, it restricts the amounts of restricted or unregistered securities that can be sold at any one time. Finally, it controls the way in which those securities may be sold.

For example, Rule 144A(d)3(i) says that to qualify for a Rule 144A exemption in a deal involving exchangeables or convertibles, any issues that have an effective conversion premium of less than 10 percent will be treated as securities of the class into which they are convertible or exchangeable. Similarly, warrants that may be exercised for securities within less than three years from date of issuance, or that have an effective exercise premium of less than 10 percent, shall be treated as securities of the class to be issued upon exercise.[13]

These restrictions are more than just an administrative nuisance and, because of the decrease in the liquidity of the investment represented by such securities, may substantially reduce their market value.

In order to minimize the effect of these restrictions, holders of acquisition debt or equity—including holders of privately placed junk bonds, preferred stock, warrants for common stock, or common stock—are usually interested in obtaining from the buyer a promise to include the securities in a registration statement under the Securities Act at the security holders' request. This may be a shelf registration, which, as described in Chapter 5, allows a company to register securities in advance of their sale.[14]

Note that shelf registration is not an all-or-nothing process: Each registration statement relates only to a particular, specified number of shares or amount of debt obligation of a particular type, so some securities of a company may be freely available for sale while others, even if otherwise identical, may still be restricted. In order to protect a security holder, it is not enough to require that securities of the kind held by the holder be registered; rather, the holder's particular securities must be registered.

Why wouldn't the buyer automatically grant registration rights?

There are considerable costs to the company in granting registration rights. The registration process involves substantial expense for preparation of the registration statement, including the fees of accountants, attorneys, and financial printers. These costs usually amount to several hundred thousand dollars.

In addition, the registration process is an arduous one for the issuing company and its officers and directors, and it requires company employees to spend a significant amount of time and attention that would otherwise be focused on management of the company and its business. Perhaps most important of all, the buyer wants to control when and if the company goes public. The exercise of registration rights may cause the company to become a "reporting company" under the Securities Act, necessitating the filing of periodic reporting documents with the Securities and Exchange Commission (SEC) and resulting in additional expenses. Through the registration process, the acquired company subjects itself to various potential liabilities as well as a host of regulations under federal and state securities laws. If the registration rights relate to common or preferred stock, the buyer will, furthermore, not want to go to the public market until its acquisition debt has been paid down and it is sure that the offering will be a success.

What are demand registration rights?

Demand registration rights entitle a holder of securities of a company to cause the company to register all or a part of such securities for resale by the security holder. Usually, the company is required to effect such registration promptly upon demand of the security holder, or within some other reasonable time frame.

What are piggyback registration rights?

Piggyback registration rights entitle a security holder to cause the company to include all or a part of its securities in a registration of the same or other classes of securities of the company undertaken at the request of a third party, such as a lender. Piggyback registration rights might allow a lender holding warrants, for example, to have the shares of common stock for which its warrants can be exercised included in a registration of common stock or subordinated debt of the company that was undertaken by the company with a view toward raising additional capital.[15] Piggyback registration rights generally are not exercisable, however, in the issuance of securities in connection with an acquisition or exchange offer, or pursuant to employee benefit plans, including employee stock ownership plans (ESOPs), covered in Chapter 5.[16]

How many times should security holders be entitled to exercise their registration rights?

Generally, the number of registration rights that security holders receive is a function of the relative bargaining powers of the buyer-borrower and its security holders. It is fairly common for lenders with common stock warrants or privately placed junk bonds to receive one or two demand registration rights. It is often the case, however, that for demand registration rights other than the first demand, certain other terms and conditions of the registration rights, such as payment of expenses and limitations on the number of shares allowed to be included, become more restrictive with respect to the security holder and more favorable to the borrower.

A greater or unlimited number of piggyback registration rights are often granted to security holders, with the primary limitations being the time during which such rights are exercisable and the amount of securities that the security holder can include in the registration.

What time restrictions should apply to demand registration rights?

The company's desire for a period of stability after the acquisition must be balanced against the selling security holder's desire for liquidity. Therefore, demand registration rights usually will not be exercisable for some fixed period of time, often several years, after the acquisition. In addition, demand registration rights are often not exercisable until after the company has conducted its own initial public offering of its common stock. In this way, the company can control the key decision whether and when to go public. Sometimes, if the company has not gone public before a certain extended deadline, perhaps the date on which warrants will expire, the security holder can compel registration.

Registration rights should not be exercisable during a stated period, usually six to nine months, following a prior registration of securities by the company. The restriction helps prevent an "overhang" problem—marketing of the prior offering can be hurt if a large block of additional securities is entitled to go to market in the near future.

As mentioned in Chapter 5, securities are sometimes put on a "shelf"—registered by a company for a sale to take place at a future time, without knowing the exact date and terms of the sale. Demand registration rights usually do not entitle a security holder to demand registration of its securities in a shelf registration until after the company has already effected such a shelf registration of its own securities, if at all.

What about timing for piggyback registration rights?

Piggyback registration rights raise additional timing issues, since they may be exercisable upon a registration by the company of securities of a type other than the securities to which the rights attach. A holder of common stock, for example, could require inclusion of some or all of its shares in a registration statement that covers debt securities of the company. In the acquisition context, in which the company's ability to sell debt securities during the first months or years after the acquisition may be crucial, care must be taken that piggyback rights do not create competition for the company's own offering. It is, thus, normal for piggyback registration rights to be restricted only to registrations of equity securities for several years after the acquisition.

When do registration rights terminate?

The exact termination date for registration rights is a matter for negotiation, but it is common for such rights to terminate under any of the following conditions: when the securities of the issuing company are widely held; when the security holders could otherwise make use of the existing market for such securities to sell their shares without significant limitations; or when a security holder has sold, or has had the opportunity through piggyback rights to sell, a specified percentage of securities held.

What benefits can accrue from registration rights agreements?

Registration rights agreements usually provide that the holders of a certain percentage, often as high as a majority, of the securities must join together in order to exercise their demand registration rights. The agreements may also provide that a threshold dollar amount must be reached before the offering will be large enough to be marketed efficiently by underwriters. Demand registration rights are usually not exercisable unless the aggregate offering price (or market price, if a market exists for such securities) of the securities to be registered exceeds a certain amount, which may be $5 million or more.

Without such agreements in place, the company could be forced to undertake the expensive and time-consuming process of registration for relatively small amounts of securities. Conversely, even with such agreements in place, the company can forestall an offering by persuading a substantial number of security holders that an offering would be inadvisable at any particular time.

What amount of securities may each security holder include on a demand or piggyback basis in any particular registration statement?

This issue arises when the number of securities sought to be included in the registration is so great that the underwriter cannot place such a large number of securities at a suitable price. Registration rights agreements usually provide that the underwriter is the final arbiter of the question of just how many securities may be included in the registration statement. In such a case, the registration rights agreement should spell this out and set priorities. If the registration is being carried out as part of a demand registration, those making the demand usually have priority. Security holders with piggyback registration rights often have the next priority, the includable shares being allocated among them on a pro rata basis, depending on the relative bargaining positions of the security holders. In demand registrations, the company is often the last one that is able to participate and, thus, may be unable to sell for its own account.

These priorities usually change, however, with respect to registrations of securities initiated by the company in which security holders are exercising piggyback rights. If the registration involves an underwritten distribution of securities, then the priorities will generally be as follows: first, securities that the company proposes to sell for its own account (this is important in order to permit the company to raise needed capital), and second, shares of selling security holders, who may be either members of the investor/management control group or outside security holders exercising piggyback registration rights. Such selling shareholders will generally participate pro rata according to the relative numbers of shares held by them or the relative number of shares sought to be included in the registration statement by them, although it is a matter of negotiation between the control group and those with piggyback rights as to who gets priority.

Who pays the expenses of registration?

The company generally pays the expenses of registering securities pursuant to demand registration rights. This is true at least with respect to the first demand registration right exercised by a security holder. These expenses include SEC filing fees, accountants' and attorneys' fees, and expenses of financial printers. The security holders including securities in the registration statement will, if such shares are sold by an underwriter, have to pay underwriters' and broker-dealers' commissions from the sale of their shares, as well as applicable stock transfer fees.

An open item for negotiation is the payment of any applicable fees and expenses relating to the sale of securities under various state securities laws ("blue sky" fees). Responsibility for payment of expenses of registering securities pursuant to exercises of demand registration rights (other than the first such exercise) is often the subject of negotiation. Expenses may be payable in whole or in part by the security holder demanding registration, in order to put some limitation on the exercise of such subsequent demand rights. Sometimes state blue sky commissioners will insist that the selling stockholder pay a pro rata share of expenses, particularly if they feel that insiders would otherwise get a free ride; such a possibility should be provided for in the registration rights provision.

Expenses incurred in registering securities included in a registration pursuant to the exercise of piggyback rights are usually relatively small and, except for underwriters' and brokers' commissions, are typically paid by the company.

What indemnification will a security holder seek in negotiating a registration rights agreement?

Registration rights agreements, because of the potential liabilities involved under federal and state securities laws, generally provide that the company will indemnify the security holders, including their shares in a registration statement, against liabilities arising through any misstatement or omission of a material fact in the registration statement and the prospectus. This indemnification should not, however, include statements supplied by the selling security holders themselves for inclusion in the registration statement or prospectus. A mirror image of this indemnification should be included in the registration rights agreement to provide for indemnification of the company by the security holders including securities in the registration statement with respect to the information provided by them.

The SEC and several court decisions have maintained that indemnification against liabilities under federal and state securities laws is against public policy and, therefore, unenforceable. In the event that such indemnification is unenforceable, "contribution" (i.e., a right to require pro rata sharing of liabilities) between the company and the security holders may be allowed, however, and is customarily included in the registration rights agreement as an alternative to indemnification.

Who picks the underwriter?

The company. This right is customary even in demand registrations, although sometimes an institutional security holder will try to get it.

What special problems arise with respect to registration rights of debt securities and preferred stock?

The company and the debt holders may have planned from the start to sell the debt publicly, in which case the initial placement is really a bridge loan pending the registration, and the registration rights provisions serve to lay out the next stage in the proposed financing sequence. In the alternative, the debt holders may plan to continue to hold the debt, but with a shelf registration in place so as to be able to sell publicly at any time. Under either circumstance, the registration rights provision presents no problems, and the subordinated debt should be issued from the start in a publicly held junk bond format with appropriate covenants and other indenture provisions.

Sometimes, however, the mezzanine debt has been structured to be privately held. The covenants may be tight, so that the company knows that it can operate only on the basis of repeated requests for waivers. This is particularly likely to occur if the subordinated debt holder has also taken a substantial equity position in the company and plans to operate effectively as a business partner of the company. Under such circumstances, the loan agreement with the subordinated debt holder must be completely rewritten before a public registration can occur. It will be necessary either to negotiate in advance and include an entire alternate indenture in the registration rights provisions or to have a brief, more informal understanding that registration of the debt can occur only under certain conditions—for example, only if the loan covenants are adjusted to a conventional format for a public issue and/or the company has otherwise issued some class of publicly held securities.

Preferred stock raises some of the same issues, since a private placement of preferred stock may contain provisions, such as special exchange or redemption rights, not suitable for publicly held preferred. In addition, demand or piggyback registration rights create marketing problems when they compel the simultaneous offering of different classes of securities, particularly at the time of an IPO of common stock. The company should consider offering the preferred stock holder a right to redeem preferred stock from a specified percentage of the proceeds of the common stock offering in lieu of granting preferred stock registration rights. In the alternative, a demand preferred stock registration should not be permitted until a reasonable time (120 to 180 days) following an IPO of common stock, and no piggyback rights should arise on such IPO or thereafter without the approval of the common stock underwriter.

SELLER TAKEBACK FINANCING

What is seller takeback financing?

Many leveraged acquisitions involve some takeback of debt or stock by the seller. This is particularly likely to occur if the seller is a major corporation divesting a minor operation. If debt is taken back, it may be structured as a simple installment sale, or it may involve accompanying warrants. In either case, the claims of the seller are generally junior to those of other creditors, such as the senior lenders to the buyer. A seller takeback is not always possible. In particular, it may be necessary to pay stockholders of publicly held companies the acquisition price entirely in cash because of the delays and disclosures involved in offering them debt or other securities that require a prospectus registered under federal security laws.

Why do sellers consider takeback financing, including junior class financing?

Sellers are generally reluctant to take back stock or debt that is junior to all other debt. Still, a seller benefits from such subordinated financing by receiving an increased purchase price, at least nominally, and obtaining an *equity kicker*. This is an extra demand by a lender for payment of equity, in addition to repayment of principal and interest. Sometimes a buyer will take a kicker as well.

Both lenders and sellers should remember that the kicker note or stock will realize full value only if the acquired company prospers, and that there is a real risk that this part of the purchase price will never be paid. By the same token, if the company does prosper, the upside potential can be very high—much higher than if no part of its purchase price were contingent on results.

There may also be cosmetic advantages to both buyer and seller in achieving a higher nominal price for the company being acquired, even though a portion of that price is paid with a kicker—such as a note or preferred stock with a market value and a book value below face. Thus, for example, if a seller has announced that it will not let its company go for less than $100 million, but has overestimated its value, the seller may eventually be pleased to settle for $60 million cash and a $40 million 10-year subordinated note at 4 percent interest. The note will go onto the seller's books at a substantial discount. (The amount of the discount will be useful for the buyer to discover if he or she later wishes to negotiate prepayment of the note in connection with a restructuring or a workout.)

How can a seller obtain an equity kicker in the company it is selling?

Sometimes a takeback note has the same effect as an equity kicker because it serves to inflate the sales price beyond the company's real present worth, and it can be paid only if the company has good future earnings. It is also quite possible for the seller simply to retain common stock in the acquired company. In the alternative, the seller can obtain participating preferred stock, in which dividend payments are determined as a percentage of earnings or as a percentage of dividend payments made to common stock holders, and in which the redemption price of the preferred rises with the value of the company. Some of these choices have tax significance, which may be assessed in light of the general principles introduced in Chapter 3.

CONCLUDING COMMENTS

It may seem from the foregoing that M&A financing and refinancing knows no bounds when it comes to new and complex financial instruments and arrangements. This is certainly true. This chapter has listed only a few of the hybrids that have been created in the M&A hothouse. More than one has flourished, rising from the level of the "gimmick" to become a true "asset class," in the words of Mark Seigel, head of global new issues at Morgan Stanley Dean Witter.[17] Only time—and many trials and errors—can tell what the next new class will be.

Whether considering debt, equity, or a hybrid instrument, deal makers need to master the basics of each of these financing types. Then and only then will they be prepared for the next stage of the M&A financing journey: approaching sources, the subject of our next chapter.

ENDNOTES

1. Consider the property income certificate, or PINC, a two-part security traded as one. One part is debtlike, entitling the holder to a portion of the rental stream from a property pool. The other is equity, reflecting the property's capital value. For a look at these in London, see "Reason to Think PINC," *The Financial Times*, September 26, 1997, p. 17.

2. For more information on this subject, see Tamar Frankel, *Securitization: Structured Financing, Financial Asset Pools, and Asset-Backed Securities* (New York: Aspen Law & Business, 1998).

3. First Union announced this securitization as part of a full-page ad it published on January 30, 1997, in *The Wall Street Journal*, p. C12. Robert Neal, a vice president of Newcourt credited earlier as our expert source in leasing-based finance, told us that "securitizations can be used as an acquisition tool from a standpoint of funding a premium out of an acquisition by having a lower cost of funds, thereby increasing the value of the acquired assets to the acquirer."

4. "Convertibles Seen as 'Bungee Cord' Being Put to the Test," *The Wall Street Journal*, April 24, 1998, pp. C1ff.

5. Joan Ogden, "Behind the Boom in Equity Derivatives," *Global Finance*, June 1998, pp. 46ff. Summarized in *Bowne Review for CFOs and Investment Bankers*, July–August 1998, pp. 5ff.

6. As mentioned in an earlier chapter, with a few exceptions, S corporations may not have more than 75 stockholders, stockholders must be individuals, and a corporate seller cannot remain as a stockholder of an S corporation, though the corporate seller can remain as a warrant holder. It is important, however, that the warrants not be immediately exercisable, since their exercise will cause a loss of S corporation status. Thus, certain "triggers" are established as preconditions to the exercise of warrants. These are basically events that entitle the stockholder/investors to extract value from their stock: a public sale of stock, a sale of substantially all the stock or assets, or a change of control of the acquired company. Once one of these events occurs, S corporation status is likely to be

lost anyway, and it is logical to let the warrant holder cash in and get the benefit of equity ownership. Note: The Taxpayer Relief Act of 1997 changed rules involving ESOPs, making it more desirable for an ESOP to own an S corporation.

7. The answers to the questions on mezzanine financing are based on a discussion by Douglas L. Batey, as credited in Chapter 1, note 1.

8. Another type of fund increasingly—although still rarely—used for investment is a tax-exempt money market or mutual fund. The federal tax code and the Investment Company Act of 1940 require a mutual fund to be at least 75 percent diversified, but up to 25 percent of the fund may be invested in a single company, leaving the door open for control-seeking investments.

9. For a guide to sources, see *Directory of Private Equity Investors 1999* (New York, Securities Data Publishing, 1999). Traditionally, public pension funds avoided speculative control-oriented investments such as LBOs, but in the 1980s, as reported by Sarah Barlett in *The Money Machine: How KKR Manufactured Power and Profits* (New York: Warner Books, 1991), KKR broke the barrier and other funds followed.

10. Examples include Blackstone Group's 35 percent offer to Six Flags, Forstmann Little & Co.'s 33 percent stake in Whittle Communications L.P., and Kohlberg Kravis Robert's offer to buy 17 percent of Fleet/Norstar Financial Group Inc.

11. For example, *equity* investors in Forstmann Little & Co.'s pioneering 1985 investment in the buyout of FL Industries (formerly American Electric) had made a 50 percent annualized return on their investment by the time Forstmann sold its stake to Thomas & Betts six years later. This was in part because of a large dividend. During the same period, *debt* investors made an annualized return of about 21 percent, according to Forstmann Little executives.

12. The benefits of investor liquidity can be seen in the case of ICF International Inc. of Fairfax, Virginia. During one major equity offering, seven insurance companies that were ICF investors announced their intention to convert warrants to stock, and then sell the stock to underwriters, who would then sell to the public.

13. Paraphrased from Rule 144A(d)3(i) in *Securities Act Rules—Rules 100 Through 236: General Rules and Regulations Under the Securities Act of 1933* (New York: Bowne Red Box Service, 1998), p. 29 (printed September 15, 1998).

14. In October 1992, the SEC expanded the range of companies qualified to participate in the shelf registration process. Now 2,000 companies, including some over-the-counter issuers, may register their offerings with the SEC and then offer their securities for the next two years without obtaining additional approval.

15. Banks should note, however, that when they provide both lending and underwriting services, they may be sued for violation of the Bank Holding Company Act. Under that law, regulators and bank customers may sue banks on these grounds.

16. ESOPs in and of themselves can be used to finance a deal. For thorough guidance on structuring ESOP-financed transactions, see National Center for Employee Ownership, *Leveraged ESOPs and Employee Buyouts* (Oakland, CA: National Center for Employee Ownership, 1998). For an excellent guide to ESOP-based financing from the founder-owner's perspective, see Dickson C. Buxton, *You've Built a Successful Business—Now What? A Guide to Perpetuating Your Business* (Glendale, CA: Griffin Publishing, 1996).

17. Seigel was speaking of a particular type of bond that Morgan Stanley invented in January 1998. The new instrument includes a put option giving the holder the right to sell the bond at a preset price and date. He was quoted in "Innovative Use of 'Puts' Wins Avid Following," *The Wall Street Journal,* January 26, 1998, p. C1.

PART THREE

A Closer Look at Sources

The art of M&A financing requires mastery of the numbers, as seen in the previous two parts of this book. But it also requires a human element. Deal makers must engage and sustain the interest of flesh-and-blood lenders, underwriters, and backers—real people in real suits. This part of our book takes a closer look at these sources, often called financial middlemen or intermediaries.

Financial intermediaries play a valuable role in our economy. Collectively, they bring together, through transactions in the financial markets, the savings of individuals and entities, so that these funds can increase in value, bringing fees to the intermediaries and income to the principals (which in some cases include intermediaries).

Some $18 trillion is involved in what might be called the "intermediary economy"—the dollars and cents that are received, held, and invested day in and day out in order to facilitate financial transactions. Of these dollars, the largest percentage is held by commercial banks (26 percent), followed by private pension funds (17 percent), mutual funds (13 percent), life insurance companies (12 percent), and public pension funds (10 percent). Other intermediaries include savings institutions (6 percent), finance companies (5 percent), non-life insurance companies (5 percent), money market funds (5 percent), and credit unions (2 percent). Investment banks and merchant banks act as the *intermediaries'* intermediaries, funneling savings to investment in various ways.

In this part of our book, we will explain the roles of the various intermediaries in M&A financing, grouping them by role as lenders, underwriters, or

backers. We owe thanks to several experts in the field. Russell Robb, an entrepreneur turned investment banker, who serves as the editor of *M&A Today*,
provided much useful information on the current practices of investment
bankers in the burgeoning middle market. Craig Breed, owner of the cbex.com
Web site for middle market deal making, helped us compose our review of online sources for debt capital (a list that includes his competitors).

We hope you find a wealth of information in these pages!

Working with Debt Sources

Lend me the stone strength of the past, and I will lend you the wings of the future, for I have them.

Robinson Jeffers, *To the Rock That Will Be a Cornerstone,* 1924

INTRODUCTION

"Neither a borrower nor a lender be," said Polonius in Shakespeare's *Hamlet.* This philosophy would certainly not fly in today's highly leveraged business environment, where most sages agree that lending is consistent with economic progress. True, prudent lenders and borrowers alike avoid making loans at high interest rates with little or no collateral, but few would agree with Polonius today. In fact, many modern-day advisers would argue that without responsible borrowers and willing lenders, the wheels of commerce would quickly grind to a halt.

As noted in Chapter 1, there are various types of lenders, ranging from commercial banks to venture capital firms. In this chapter, we will take a closer look at how these lenders operate, focusing particularly on commercial banks and insurance companies. At the end of this chapter, we will discuss the special dynamics of junk bond financing (introduced in Chapter 4).

OVERVIEW OF LENDERS

What are the various types of lenders?

All the basic sources of external financing, as listed in Chapter 1, can provide debt-based financing, whether cash, bonds, or notes. Here is a brief recap:

- Asset-based lenders
- Commercial banks
- Commercial finance companies
- Insurance companies
- Investment banks
- Investment companies
- Merchant banks
- Private buyout investment firms
- Small business investment companies (SBICs)
- Venture capital firms[1]

Each of these plays a distinctly different role in the financing process. In previous chapters, in focusing on instruments, we mentioned all these sources. Now, in this chapter, we will focus on the role these sources play and the relationships they have.

What are asset-based lenders?

Asset-based lenders are any entities, including banks, factors, and finance companies, that engage extensively in asset-based lending. (Though factors are often included as asset-based lenders, they do not always lend money. Rather, they often buy accounts receivable, as explained in Chapter 4. Similarly, leasing companies do not usually lend, but instead buy and lease back equipment.) As stated in Chapter 4, asset-based lending is based on assets owned by the borrower, such as business inventory or accounts receivable. Some companies pledge their accounts receivable as collateral and draw against a line of credit that is less than the full amount of the receivables. The interest charged is generally above prime rate

What is a commercial bank—and what is a nonbank bank?

Today the word *bank* is used extremely broadly to cover a great range of financial institutions, including commercial banks, investment banks, merchant banks, so-called nonbank banks, and of course savings banks. What most ordinary citizens think of as a bank, however, remains the commercial bank—still the only place where money deposits can be withdrawn on demand (demand deposits).

The identity of commercial banks has been obscured in recent years for two reasons.

- Many banks have formed holding companies that own financial institutions other than commercial banks.[2] As a result, commercial banks have virtually no limit on the services they may offer their customers, as described below.[3]
- Financial institutions other than commercial banks have made tremendous inroads into the services traditionally offered by banks, such as loans.

A nonbank bank—also called a limited service bank—is one that provides depository services or lending but not both. In the 1980s, hundreds of industrial companies applied to the Federal Reserve System to establish nonbank banks. In 1987, the Competitive Equality in Banking Act limited growth of such banks to 7 percent in most states.[4]

What are commercial finance companies?

A commercial finance company is primarily defined by what it is not: It is not a commercial bank, a stock brokerage firm, or an insurance company. Rather, it is a firm that acts as an intermediary between borrowers and lenders. Commercial finance companies derive their income not only from obtaining loan capital for borrowers, but also from investing in transactions such as leveraged buyouts.

Insurance companies obviously sell insurance, but do they also lend?

Yes. Insurance companies have joined the list of those providing loans to business, including merger, acquisition, and buyout loans. Toward the end of the chapter, we will provide more information on this type of lender.

Investment banks, investment companies, and merchant banks are more involved in equity; can they also function as lenders?

They do not function directly as lenders, but they can be a bridge to lending, as discussed in Chapter 9, or "backers."

What are private equity funds?

As explained in the last two chapters, these are firms (typically partnerships) that form in order to invest in private companies. They often function as backers, and are therefore discussed more fully in Chapter 9.

What are small business investment companies (SBICs)?

These are firms that are licensed by the U.S. Small Business Administration (SBA) to provide equity capital and long-term loans, subsidized by the SBA, to small businesses. An SBIC may lend money to or buy stock or convertible debentures in firms with less than $5 million in assets, net worth of not more than $2.5 million, and after-tax net income of not more than $250,000 per year. The SBA matches the capital contribution of investors in an SBIC, which is permitted to make loans equal to four times its initial capital.[5]

What are venture capital firms?

Venture capital firms are entities formed for the express purpose of channeling investments into new companies at one or more of three stages: start-up, mezzanine, or initial public offering (IPO). At the start-up stage, venture capital firms offer initial capital to a firm even as it is forming; at the mezzanine stage, venture capital firms provide midlevel financing that is senior to the original venture capital financing, but junior to commercial bank financing. As the company matures, the venture capital firms take it public to cash out their investments. (As explained in Chapter 4, these terms refer to the order of repayment in the event of a default on the loan. *Junior* means that in the event of default, the lender will be repaid after another party; *senior* means the lender will be paid before another party. The term *mezzanine* is reserved for the lender in the middle.)

COMMERCIAL BANKS

How important is commercial bank lending to the economy in general and to businesses?

Although commercial banks are not as dominant as they were decades ago, they remain the number one provider of loan capital, both from a macroeconomic and a microeconomic perspective.

From the macroeconomic perspective, banks occupy a pivotal position in the short-term and intermediate-term "money markets"—a miniature economy in which traders buy and sell the loans made by banks. From a microeconomic perspective, banks occupy a critical role because they are the main source of short-term business loans. As a firm's financing needs increase, it requests additional loans from banks—sometimes in order to acquire another company. If the request is denied, often the alternative is to slow down the rate of growth or to cut back operations. Commercial bank lending, which appears on the balance sheet as *notes payable*, is the most important type of short-term funding for any business other than credit extended by suppliers.

How prominent are banks as financial intermediaries today in comparison with past eras?

As mentioned in the introduction to this section on sources, commercial banks are the single most prominent financial intermediary when it comes to assets held. They control over one quarter (26 percent) of all financial assets held in the intermediary market.

This dominance pales in comparison with past years. In 1950, commercial banks held over half (52 percent) of all intermediary assets. Life insurance companies and savings and loan companies also had sizable shares of the market (22 percent and 14 percent respectively), but commercial banks were clearly dominant as holders of the nation's funds. Other financial institutions controlled 4 percent or less.[6] Today, as explained in the opening to Part Three, the wealth of financial intermediaries is far more evenly distributed, thanks in part to deregulation. Nonetheless, banks still hold a commanding lead.

With all the deregulation that has occurred, why do commercial banks still control more money than other financial institutions?

Commercial banks are defined by their ability to lend with only fractional reserves. In addition, the preponderance of check writing is on commercial bank demand deposits. Check writing is still a widely accepted medium of exchange, accounting for over 90 percent of all financial transactions.

As for the deposit aspect, another important factor is federal deposit insurance. Only deposits in banks, credit unions, and savings and loan associations (S&Ls) are covered by this guarantee. The amount of coverage, which is backed by the U.S. government, considered a stable, deep-pocket guarantor, can be up to $100,000.

Finally, commercial banks have no set limits on the amount of money they may loan out—although international guidelines do ask banks to hold a capital cushion.[7] By contrast, thrifts have restrictions on the percentage of assets they may loan out.[8]

Speaking of savings and loans and credit unions, what exactly is their function, and how prominent are they in the financial intermediary market?

S&Ls traditionally received funds from passbook savings and invested them primarily in real estate mortgages for individuals. New laws passed in the early 1980s broadened the lending powers of S&Ls, encouraging them to take risks, while at the same time cushioning those risks by continuing to cover deposits with insurance. Knowing that the safety net was there, S&L managers took very big risks—often unwisely, given their relative lack of sophistication. Lack of experience, excessive risk taking, and outright fraud resulted in the multibillion-dollar failures and bailouts of the late 1980s. Today, burned by this experience and hemmed in by new laws, S&Ls no longer play a prominent role. Their market share, traditionally at double-digit levels, is only 6 percent today.

Credit unions are not-for-profit financial cooperatives that make personal loans. They may also offer other banking services, such as residential mortgages and credit cards, if they have a federal charter. Their market share as financial intermediaries has averaged 2 percent in the 1980s and 1990s—double what it was in the 1960s and 1970s.

What kinds of restrictions do banks have on making loans outside their charter areas? Can a bank chartered in Texas loan to a business located in Nevada?

Federal law, through the Glass-Steagall Act of 1933, imposes some restrictions, while state laws may impose others. Under current law, commercial banks may acquire one another, even if they are located in different states. This is the main message of the Interstate Banking and Branch Efficiency Act of 1994, which was signed into law on September 29, 1994, and became effective on June 1, 1995.[9] Although this law left considerable room for states to impose limitations on acquisitions and expansion across state borders, it nonetheless opened the doors to a new wave of bank acquisitions and alliances in the late 1990s—a trend that will continue well into the new millennium.

What about underwriting securities. Can banks do that?

Yes, within limits. The Glass-Steagall Act of 1933 (within the Banking Act of the same year) set up a wall between commerce and banking by, among other things, forbidding banks to underwrite securities. Ever since that time, changes at both the federal and state levels have chipped away at this and other restrictions on banks and their competitors. Today, banks may do a limited amount of securities underwriting through their holding companies. Some believe that as this deregulatory movement continues, it may eventually lead to the outright repeal of Glass-Steagall.[10] In Chapter 11, we outline this and other aspect of ongoing financial services deregulation.

BANK LENDING

What exactly is a commercial bank loan, and what are the main types of loans?

In the classic bank loan, the borrower obtains the loan by signing a conventional promissory note. Loans may be made charging *regular interest* or *discounted interest;* they may be paid at *maturity* or in *installments.* Alternatively, banks may extend a *line of credit.* As explained in Chapter 4, all these types of loans may be secured in part through a *compensating balance.*

What kinds of firms do banks finance, over what term, and with what level of security?

Banks make loans to firms of all sizes and in all industries. By dollar amount, the major proportion of loans from commercial banks is obtained by large firms. By number of loans, small and medium-size firms account for over one half of bank loan borrowers. In general (with some notable exceptions), large banks are less likely than small banks to lend to small businesses. Thus mergers between banks—especially those that create very large banks afterward—tend to dry up credit for small businesses.

Fortunately, though, for small businesses seeking bank financing, there is a countertrend—the growth of the independent "new bank." Small, local commercial banks, the main suppliers of credit to small businesses, will never be an endangered species (despite consolidation), thanks to constant "new bank" start-ups.[11] Small banks tend to offer lines of credit, mortgage-based lending, leasing, and equipment loans.

The continuing creation of small banks, combined with the continued willingness of some larger banks to make small business loans, has ensured a substantial flow of bank loan capital to small businesses.[12] This is significant for M&A financing, because smaller companies are more likely to use debt than equity to finance their acquisitions.

As for the industry distribution of commercial bank loans, these vary from quarter to quarter and from lender to lender. An excellent source for quarterly data on this trend is Phoenix Management Services in Chadds Ford, Pennsylvania, a turnaround management company. Ever since November 1995, Phoenix has surveyed approximately 100 representative lenders (including commercial banks, commercial finance companies, and factors) every quarter to find out their first and last choices for lending. The Phoenix surveys, combined with other evidence such as lender advertisements, show that no one sector is sacred. While some lenders still prefer firms rich in hard collateral—the "smokestack" sector that attracted buyout capital in the 1980s—others prefer service companies.[13]

In terms of loan maturity, commercial banks concentrate on the short-term lending market. Short-term loans make up about two thirds of bank loans by dollar amount, whereas term loans (loans with maturities longer than one year) make up only one third.

In terms of loan security, if a potential borrower is a questionable credit risk, or if the firm's financing needs exceed the amount that the loan officer of the bank considers prudent on an unsecured basis, some form of security is required. In terms of the number of bank loans, two thirds are secured through the endorsement of a third party, which guarantees payment of the loan in the event that the borrower defaults. As mentioned in Chapter 4, commercial banks require collateral on over half (60 percent) of the dollars they lend, and this occurs in nearly all (90 percent) of the term loans they make. Insurance companies are more lenient as lenders, requiring collateral on less than a third (30 percent) of the loans they make.

What are the going percentages on various types of collateral?

It is well known in mortgage lending that most lenders will lend against 60 to 80 percent of the market price of real estate (land and/or buildings), not the full value. Other rules of thumb (provided by Russell Robb, editor of the newsletter *M&A Today*)[14] include:

- Accounts receivable (90 days or less): 70 to 85 percent

- Inventory (not work in process): 25 to 60 percent
- Machinery and equipment: 50 to 80 percent

How do these ratios average out in relation to all of the borrower's assets?

One key ratio is equity to total assets. This ratio is a kind of cushion for lenders. It shows the percentage by which assets may shrink in value on liquidation before creditors will incur losses.[15] For example, consider two corporations that plan to combine, New Corp. A and New Corp. B.

- The ratio of equity to total assets in New Corp. A is 80 percent. Total assets, therefore, would have to shrink by 80 percent before creditors lose money.
- The ratio of equity to total assets in New Corp. B is 40 percent. Thus, total assets would have to shrink by only 40 percent before creditors lose money.

Therefore, all else being equal, New Corp. A would be a better lending prospect than New Corp. B. (See Table 7–1.)

How do bankers analyze debt coverage when making an M&A or buyout loan?

This varies according to the bank involved and the current market. According to Russell Robb, most traditional lenders base their loans on the cash flow of the borrower. Depending on the stability of the business and the risk tolerance of the bank, bankers look for coverage of between 1.2 and 1.8 times

T A B L E   7–1

Balance Sheets for Corporations A and B

New Corp. A				New Corp. B		
	Debt	$ 20			Debt	$ 60
	Equity	80			Equity	40
Total assets	$100	Total claims	$100	Total Assets	$100	Total claims	$100

debt. Table 7–2 shows an analysis of debt coverage done on a pro forma basis—that is, accounting for these items as if the companies were already combined.

T A B L E 7–2

Pro Forma Analysis of Debt Coverage

Operating income	$ 600,000	
Add back interest	$ 200,000	
Add back taxes	$ 200,000	
	$1,000,000	
Reorganization add-backs (e.g., savings from cutbacks in key areas)		
Excess compensation	$ 100,000	
Vehicles, travel, etc.	$ 100,000	
	$ 200,000	
		$1,200,000
Less:		
Bank interest	$ 300,000	
Shareholder return	$ 200,000	
Noncompete agreement (e.g., consideration given to enhance enforceability)	$ 100,000	
Bank repayment	$ 200,000	
		$ 800,000
Debt coverage ($1.2 million ÷ $800,000) = 1.5		

Source: Russell Robb, *Buying Your Own Business* (Holbrook, MA: Adams Media, 1995), p. 140.

Could you give an example of a real-life lender and what it is looking for?

Here is what a typical lender looks for (as of early 1999) when lending to a proposed leveraged buyout transaction:

Minimum annual sales of company to be purchased: $50 million

Performance of company to be purchased: must be profitable

Minimum size of investments or loans to be considered: $10 million

Preferred size of investments or loans: over $10 million

Requirements for management team: must be in place before acquisition

Equity participation of management: required

Technology focus: prefer low-technology deals

Interest rate policy: floating rates only

Financing requirements for equity participants: at least 20 percent of total acquisition cost

Lending criteria:

- Ratio of loan to collateral: moderately important
- Ratio of cash flow to debt service: very important
- Ratio of debt to equity: very important
- Historical earnings: very important

Collateral advance rates:

- Accounts receivable: 80 percent average, 85 percent maximum
- Raw materials inventory: 50 percent average, 55 percent maximum
- Machinery and equipment: 40 percent average and maximum[16]

How can a borrower choose among potential lenders?

A potential M&A borrower should consider the relative financial strength of the bank funding it. Furthermore, it should note the following important differences among banks:

Banks have different attitudes toward risk. Some banks follow conservative lending practices, requiring a great deal of high-level collateral, while others lend on the strength of business plans alone. These differences stem in part from the personalities of officers, but they also reflect the growth profile of a bank's community and the stability of the bank's deposit liabilities, which is determined by its mix of demand and time deposits. A bank can take risks if its community is booming and its deposit liabilities are stable (with a relatively low level of demand deposits and a relatively high level of time deposits). Conversely a bank will tend to be more cautious if its local economy is stagnant and its deposit liabilities are volatile (with a high level of demand deposits and a low level of time deposits).

Banks offer different degrees of support and loyalty to customers.   Some banks offer considerable counseling to borrowers, and stay with them during hard times, using liquidation only as a last resort. Others let customers fend for themselves, calling loans and liquidating collateral at the earliest opportunity. In assessing lenders, support is obviously of critical importance.

Banks differ in their degree of loan specialization.   Larger banks have separate departments specializing in different types of loans, such as real estate, installment, and commercial loans. Within these broad categories, they may specialize by line of business, such as steel, machinery, and textiles. Smaller banks are likely to reflect the nature of the business and economic areas in which they operate. They tend to become specialists in specific lines, such as financial services, health care, and utilities. When M&A opportunities come along in their special fields, they are already attuned to the strategic issues.

Bank size can be an important characteristic.   Large banks prefer to make large loans to large customers, while small banks prefer to make small loans to small customers. Of course, if you set aside the risk factor, large loans have a natural appeal to any banker, since fees are larger for relatively the same amount of work (i.e., there are economies of scale in lending). But because of the risk of nonpayment, it makes more sense for small banks to lend only small amounts. In fact, the maximum loan a bank can make to any one customer is generally limited to 10 percent of a bank's capital accounts (capital stock plus retained earnings).

APPROACHING A SOURCE OF DEBT FINANCING: THE BANK BOOK AND COMMITMENT LETTER

How is an acquisition or buyout transaction presented to prospective lenders?

The normal medium of communication about a proposed deal is the so-called *bank book* or *business plan,* a brief narrative description of the proposed transaction and the company to be acquired. The bank book indicates what financing structure is contemplated and includes projections of earnings sufficient to cover working capital needs and to amortize debt, along with a balance sheet setting forth the pledgeable assets. Since the balance sheet will typically value assets according to generally accepted accounting principles (GAAP), an appraisal of actual market and/or liquidation value, if available, may be attached or referenced.

What happens after the bank book is presented to a lender?

If the bank appears willing to make a loan that meets the dollar amount and general terms requested by the buyer, the loan officer will seek to obtain as much information as possible about the company from the buyer. This information will include proxy statements, 10-Ks and 10-Qs if the acquisition candidate is a public company, and audited financials or tax returns if it is not. The loan officer will also send out a team of reviewers to visit the company's facilities, interview its management, and obtain an internal or outside appraisal of the assets. This review can take from half a week to a month or more. Banks are aware that they are in a competitive business and generally move quickly, particularly if the loan is being simultaneously considered by several institutions.

The loan officer will then prepare a write-up recommending the proposed loan and will present it to the bank's credit committee. The committee may endorse the recommendation as made, approve it with changes (presumably acceptable to the borrower), or turn it down. If the proposal is approved, the bank will prepare a commitment letter (sometimes with the assistance of its counsel, but often not) setting forth the bank's binding commitment to make the loan. This letter, thereafter, becomes the bank officer's governing document in future negotiations.

What does the commitment letter contain?

Apart from the bare essentials (the amount of the loan, the proportions that will be term and revolver, the maturity of the term loan and amortization provisions, and interest rates), the commitment letter will set forth the bank's proposals on the following:

- Fees to be paid to the bank
- Voluntary prepayment rights and penalties under the term loan
- What collateral is required; whether any other lender may take a junior lien on any collateral on which the bank has a senior lien; and

whether the bank is to receive a junior lien on any other collateral
subject to another lender's senior lien

- How the funds are to be used
- The amount of subordinated debt and equity that may be required
  as a condition to making the senior loan
- Payment of the bank's expenses

The commitment letter may also set forth in some detail lists of *reporting
and filing requirements, conditions to closing, financial covenants,* and *default provisions*—all described below. The letter usually contemplates additional closing
conditions and covenants that may be imposed by the bank as the closing process evolves. The commitment letter will also contain an *expiration date,* typically a very early one. For example, it may provide that the offer to make the
loan will expire in 24 hours if not accepted in writing by the borrower, or it
may allow as much as two weeks.

The commitment letter, if it provides for a revolving line of credit (usually called a *revolver*), will generally state both the maximum amount that may
be borrowed under the line (the *cap*) and a potentially lower amount that the
bank would actually lend, sometimes expressed as a percentage of the value of
the collateral pledged to secure the revolver. This lower amount is called the
borrowing base. The difference between the amount actually borrowed on the
revolver at any time and the amount that could be borrowed (i.e., the lower of
the cap or the borrowing base) is called *availability.*

How is the borrowing base determined?

If receivables are pledged, the commitment letter may distinguish between
"eligible receivables" and "other receivables." Both are subject to the bank's
lien, but the bank may consider only "eligible receivables" as assets against
which borrowings may be made.

In a typical situation, eligible receivables will be those that are not more
than 90 days old or past due, have been created in the normal course of business, arise from bona fide sales of goods or services to financially sound parties unrelated to the borrower or its affiliates, and are not subject to offset,
counterclaim, or other dispute. The bank will lend up to a specified percentage
(typically 70 to 90 percent) of eligible receivables. This percentage is known as
the *advance rate.* Thus, notwithstanding the maximum amount of the line theoretically available to the borrower, revolving loans outstanding may not at
any time exceed that stated percentage of eligible receivables, determined
monthly or even weekly.

Inventory is also usually used as collateral. To be eligible, inventory will generally have to be of the kind normally sold by the borrower (if the borrower is in the business of selling goods) and will be limited to finished goods boxed and ready for sale, not located in the hands of a retail store or in transit. In such circumstances an advance rate of 50 percent is not uncommon. In addition, in some circumstances banks will lend against work in process or raw materials. However, a rather low advance rate—perhaps 15 percent—will be applied against such unfinished goods because of the problem a bank would experience in attempting to liquidate such collateral. The bank may also impose an "inventory sublimit"—an absolute dollar ceiling on the amount of inventory-based loans.

What does this method of determining the amount of the loan imply for company operations?

It is important to estimate carefully the need for working capital at the time the loan is committed for and then to operate within the ceiling and borrowing formulas imposed by the revolving loan. A heavy penalty falls on the manager who allows inventory to build up, or fails to collect receivables promptly. Only 50 or 60 cents can be borrowed for every dollar tied up in finished inventory, and every dollar of uncollected receivables costs the company 10 to 30 cents of inaccessible borrowing ability. Chief financial officers can get in trouble after the closing if they don't understand the business implications of their loan terms.

Are the terms of the commitment letter negotiable?

Yes. However, the best (and often the only) time to negotiate is when early drafts of the commitment letter are circulated or when the loan officer sends the buyer an initial proposal letter before credit committee approval. Buyers should be careful to involve their lawyers and other advisers at that stage and not wait until later to get into details. It is important that the borrower understand the lender's procedures. The proposal letter may be the only opportunity to negotiate a document in advance; sometimes commitment letters appear only after the credit committee has met. After that, expectations of the lender become set, and the loan officer will find it awkward to resubmit the proposed loan to the credit committee. The borrower typically does not know how much latitude the loan officer has to modify the commitment without returning to the credit committee. Because a new credit action can result in delay, it is rarely in the interest of the borrower to return to the credit committee.

Once the commitment letter is signed, how long will the commitment remain open?

The lender's commitment to make a loan will typically provide that definitive documentation must be negotiated, prepared, and signed by a certain date. Sometimes the time allowed is quite short: 30 or 45 days. Sometimes closing takes longer, because of the need to obtain administrative approval, such as Federal Communication Commission (FCC) consent to change of ownership of television stations. In such cases, the termination date of the commitment must be pushed back to allow reasonable time to accomplish all the actions necessary to effect the closing of the acquisition.

Earlier you mentioned that reporting and filing requirements are often spelled out in loan agreements. What exactly is involved?

A typical loan agreement will specify that financial reports must be in conformity with GAAP. Furthermore, it may stipulate that any necessary filing be done in a timely manner. Filing must be coordinated in each of the jurisdictions so that it occurs contemporaneously with the funding of the new loan and the payoff of the old loan. In a complex, multijurisdictional transaction, such coordination, if it is to be done successfully, requires a combination of monumental effort and plain old good luck. Frequently, lenders have some flexibility about the filing of termination statements in connection with the old loan being discharged and will allow a reasonable period after closing for this to be accomplished.

What about conditions for closing? Which of these are the most commonly encountered?

Here is a checklist:

- *Requirements regarding perfection and priority of security interests in collateral.*   If, for example, first liens are to be given to the lenders on inventory in various jurisdictions, certain events must occur. *First,* lien searches have to be completed and reports received and reviewed (professional companies can be hired to conduct computerized searches of liens on record in any state or county office); *second,* documents terminating old liens have to be prepared, signed, and sent for filing; and *third*, documents perfecting new liens have to be prepared, signed, and sent for filing.

- *Counsel opinions.*   Few deals crater over the failure of counsel for the borrower to deliver required opinions, but it is not unheard of for a closing to be delayed while final points in the opinions are negotiated between counsel for the bank and the borrower. Problems typically occur in local counsel opinions and relate to the validity of the bank's lien in a particular jurisdiction. There is no magic solution, but early involvement of local counsel for the borrower is always a good idea.

- *Auditor opinions.*   In early 1988, the American Institute of Certified Public Accountants banned the formerly common practice of comfort letters from auditors. Ever since this ban, auditors have become increasingly reluctant to opine as to the solvency of borrowers, an opinion that banks have often requested as a way of limiting their fraudulent conveyance risk. Comfort letters were statements by auditors as to the solvency of their client, made without an actual audit. Similarly, auditors may be reluctant to address the reliability of financial projections provided by the borrower to the bank. Banks need to determine at an early stage what the auditors will, and will not, agree to say in writing at the closing.

- *Government consents and approvals.*   In certain transactions, approval of a government entity is a central element in the transaction. For example, a sale of a television station cannot be effected without requisite approvals from the FCC. The timing of such approvals, even if they are reasonably assured, is outside the power of the parties, and the failure of a government agency to act when expected can wreak havoc on the schedule for closing.

- *Material litigation and material adverse changes (MACs) affecting the company.*   Some loan agreements give the buyer and/or lender the right to back out if the company being acquired gets hit by a major lawsuit or other event that could seriously harm its business. If a MAC-like contingency does occur, the burden is on seller's counsel to persuade both the buyer and the bank that the suit is unlikely to succeed or, if successful, would not be material to the company or its operations. Similarly, bad economic news can cause either the buyer or the bank to halt the process, resulting in either a negotiated price reduction or a termination.

How serious are these material adverse change (MAC) clauses? Can they actually break a deal? What are some examples?

The MAC clause typically contains language assuring all parties that "no material adverse changes shall have occurred" in capital markets that would "adversely affect" a bank's ability to syndicate or sell the credit facility planned in the agreement.[17] Such occurrences are fairly rare, but they do happen.

For example, capital market crunches in the fall of 1998 caused two providers of debt-based financing to invoke MAC clauses in restructuring or postponing financing for merger deals. In September, Credit Suisse First Boston said that because of the state of the high-yield debt market, it would not provide financing as originally planned to fund Stone Rivet Inc.'s bid to acquire shares of Envirotest Systems Corp. Stone Rivet is an acquisition vehicle controlled by Alchemy Partners, a private equity investment partnership controlled by Alchemy Partners in the United Kingdom. In mid-October 1998, Merrill Lynch Capital, a unit of Merrill Lunch, informed Welsh, Carson, Anderson & Stowe that it might not fund its planned $1.31 billion acquisition of Centennial Cellular Corp.[18]

Returning to the subject of conditions to closing in general, are there *continuing* conditions that apply to subsequent draws on the revolving line of credit?

Yes. In most loan agreements, the bank's obligation to honor subsequent draws upon the revolver is subject to a variety of conditions. Chief among them is reaffirmation by the borrower that the original warranties and representations made in the loan agreement are still true (including those stating that there have been no material adverse changes in the business since a date generally preceding the closing date) and a requirement that no covenant default exists. If the foregoing conditions are not met, the bank is not required to lend.

Covenants in loan agreements for highly leveraged mergers, acquisitions, or buyouts frequently appear more intrusive than those in most commercial loan agreements. Why?

Because in a typical leveraged deal the lenders are significantly more at risk than they are in a normal business loan. Both from a balance sheet standpoint (because of the absence of a substantial equity "pad" under the senior debt) and an operating standpoint (because of the burden that debt service will place on the borrower's cash flow), the lender is likely to view itself as significantly exposed. Lenders attempt to address this problem by imposing covenants on the borrower in order to:

- Protect collateral
- Provide early warning of divergence from the business plan or of economic bad news
- Obligate the borrower, by express contractual provision, to operate the acquired business in accordance with the business plan submitted to and approved by the bank
- Prevent the leakage of money and property out of the borrower, whether as "management fees" or other payments to related parties, costs of new acquisitions, capital expenditures, or simply dividends
- Enable the bank to exercise its remedies at as early a stage as possible if things go awry by exercising its right to declare a default as a result of a covenant breach

This said, however, borrowers should remember that financial covenants *are not written in stone.* As the borrower repays its debt, it gains an ever stronger financial position, making the covenants increasingly less binding. Even if the borrower gets into financial trouble, lenders may be willing to revise the terms of an agreement, as explained in Chapter 12.

What are the covenants a borrower is most likely to be confronted with?

When borrowing funds in a leveraged transaction, the buyer is often asked to sign off on promises that it will comply with the business plan, provide early warning of potential economic trouble, protect collateral, and control expenditures.

How can a seller in a contingency payment deal make sure the buyer will comply with the business plan?

The buyer is typically asked to promise to:

- Use the proceeds of the loan only for the stipulated purposes
- Engage only in the kinds of business contemplated by the lenders
- Refrain from merging or selling all or substantially all of its assets, or any portion thereof in excess of a specified value, without the bank's consent

- Limit capital expenditures, lease payments, borrowings, and investments in affiliates and third parties to agreed amounts
- Prevent change in ownership or control of borrower without lenders' consent
- Bar acquisitions of other businesses
- Make changes in the acquisition agreement, subordinated debt instruments, or other material documents

What about covenants designed to give early warning of economic trouble?

The seller typically asks the buyer to promise to:

- Remain in compliance with financial covenants (discussed below)
- Provide periodic (monthly, quarterly, annual) financial reports, with
  annual reports to be audited
- Give prompt notice of any material adverse development affecting
  the operations of the business
- Provide revised and updated projections, on at least an annual ba-
  sis, prior to the commencement of each new fiscal year
- Permit visits and inspections by bank representatives

How can the seller protect its collateral?

The buyer must typically promise to:

- Keep the business and property adequately insured
- Limit sales of property to merchandise sold in the ordinary course
  of business
- Require property to be kept free of liens (a "negative pledge")
- Bar leases of property by the borrower
- Provide life insurance for principal executives of the borrower

What loan agreement covenants can discourage financial leakage from the borrower?

Lenders will often ask the borrower to agree to:

- Cap executive compensation and management fees
- Limit, or often prohibit (at least for a specific time period, or until
  specified financial tests are satisfied), dividends and other distributions to equity holders

- Prohibit transactions with affiliates, except as expressly agreed upon and except for those provided on an "arm's length" basis for services definitely required by the borrower
- Lend money or guarantee the obligations of other parties

What kinds of financial covenants are likely to be imposed?

The financial covenants that lenders are most concerned with relate to the company's cash generation and cash distribution. Lenders are vitally concerned about monitoring the company's ability to service current and future obligations to the lender. Thus, in general, they want to limit "unnecessary" cash outflows such as dividends, excessive capital expenditures, and future payment obligations (i.e., additional debt) until their claims are satisfied. In addition, lenders want sufficient advance information about the company's cash inflow relative to debt service requirements. If this ratio starts to deteriorate and approach default levels, the lender will increase monitoring activity and notify management of relevant default consequences. Therefore, the borrower may be required to maintain stipulated ratios for:

- Interest coverage (earnings before interest and taxes to interest expense)
- Debt to net worth
- Current assets to current liabilities
- Fixed charges to net income (or cash flow)

In addition, the borrower may be required to attain stipulated minimum goals for:

- Net worth
- Cash flow

The borrower may also be required not to exceed stipulated maximum limits for:

- Capital expenditures
- Total debt

How do lenders determine financial covenant levels?

Lenders use information provided by the borrower and their own lending experience combined with regulatory guidelines[19] to set financial covenant levels. The projected financial statements serve as the basic data for establishing covenant levels. Since financial covenants are usually designed as early warning devices, lenders want covenants that are good indicators of debt service capability. Contrary to popular belief, lenders do not want financial covenants as high as possible. What they try to achieve is an effective filter system, identifying problem loans that merit special attention. If covenants are too high, the lender may waste valuable administrative time on a relatively low-risk situation.

For example, assume a senior lender provides $2 million at 12 percent fixed interest to be paid over five years. The company's projected cash flow and debt service requirements appear in Table 7–3. The projected coverage ratio is calculated by dividing projected cash flow by total debt service.

Given these data, the lender will make a judgment about the projected volatility of the company's cash flow. Assuming the company's prospects satisfy the senior lender's loan committee, a projected coverage ratio covenant must be determined. The level selected will probably be a simple discount on expected performance that still provides the lender with reasonable security. Once the company is out of the woods, the lender should be comfortable and should not keep increasing the level of required performance even if the projections indicate that enhanced performance can be achieved.

The covenant level will probably rise over time to reflect the lender's desire to see the company's cash flow continue to increase. A sample of minimum cash flow to prevent default appears in Table 7–4. The covenant levels shown in this table require the company in effect to increase cash flow each year until the last, when the lender's risk has been significantly reduced.

Borrowers are faced with an interesting dilemma when presenting a prospective lender with the projected financial performance of the company they wish to buy. A borrower may be motivated to make the firm's future performance look good in order to obtain the loan. However, these same projections will form the basis for the lender's financial covenants. If the projected performance was inflated, the company could continually be in default on the loan agreement. On the other hand, if the borrower downplays the future performance of the company to avoid this possibility, the borrower runs the risk of making the loan relatively unattractive to the lender. Ultimately, both sides benefit the most when forecasts are submitted that genuinely reflect the buyer's expectations for the company.

When are financial covenants usually negotiated?

Very late in the negotiating process, usually just before closing. The typical buyer prefers to get the commitment for the loan before negotiating these provisions in detail. Often the most reliable financial projections become avail-

T A B L E   7–3

Sample Company's Projected Cash Flow and Debt Service Requirements (Thousands of Dollars)

Year	1	2	3	4	5
Loan balance at 1/1	2,000	1,700	1,250	800	350
Interest	240	204	150	96	42
Principal payments	300	450	450	450	350
Total debt service	540	654	600	546	392
Projected cash flow	1,000	1,200	1,400	1,600	1,800
Projected coverage ratio	1.85	1.83	2.33	2.93	4.59

T A B L E   7–4

Sample Covenant (Thousands of Dollars)

Year	1	2	3	4	5
Covenant ratio	1.4	1.4	1.8	2.1	2.5
Minimum cash flow (covenant ratio × debt service)	756.0	915.6	1,080.0	1,146.6	980.0

able only at the last moment, and they provide the base for the covenants. Sometimes, the bank sets the covenants too tightly at the closing, and the negotiating process continues through the initial months of the loan in the form of waivers. This should be avoided if possible.

Loan agreements typically include default provisions. Where do these appear and what do they accomplish?

Default provisions, which are usually spelled out in representations and warranties, corroborate and complete the acquired company information upon which the lender based its credit decision. They constitute, in effect, a checklist of potential problem areas for which the borrower is required to state that no problem exists, or to spell out (by way of exceptions or exhibits) what the problem is. Thus, typical warranties will state the following:

- The financial statements of the borrower that have been submitted to the bank are correct. (Although it is comforting to have this conclusion backed by an auditor's certification, usually the auditor's report is laced with qualifications.)
- There are no liens on the borrower's assets, except as disclosed to the bank or permitted pursuant to the loan agreement.
- The transactions contemplated will not conflict with any laws or contracts to which the borrower is a party or by which it is bound (the so-called noncontravention representation).
- No lawsuits pending or threatened against the borrower are likely to have a material adverse effect on it if they are decided against the borrower, except as disclosed to the bank.
- The loan will not violate the "margin rules."
- The borrower has no exposure under the Employee Retirement Income Security Act (ERISA).
- The borrower is not a regulated public utility holding company or investment company (since, if it were, various government orders would be required).
- The borrower is "solvent" (so as to mitigate concerns about fraudulent conveyance risks).
- The borrower's assets (and principal office) are located in the places specified. (This information is needed to ensure that perfection of security interests in the collateral is effected by filing notices in the correct jurisdictions.)

What happens if a representation is wrong?

A breached representation can have two practical consequences for a borrower: (1) if such a breach occurs, the bank may refuse to make a requested advance, either at or after the closing, and (2) breach of a representation or warranty can trigger a default under the loan agreement.

The first consequence—bank refusal to fund—should not be surprising. The truth and accuracy of the representations are typically a condition to the initial loan made at the time the loan agreement is signed and also to any subsequent draws on the revolving line of credit. If, for example, the borrower has warranted in the loan agreement that it has no significant environmental problems, and subsequently it is discovered that the borrower has been guilty of illegal dumping of hazardous wastes, the bank will probably have the right under the loan agreement to shut off further draws on the line of credit. Such a decision could be catastrophic for a company precluded from financing itself from cash flow because its loan agreement also provides for the "lock boxing" of revenues and mandatory paydown—that is, a requirement that revenues be deposited in a lock box under the lender's control and used to pay off bank debt.

The second consequence—a default under the loan agreement—triggers the remedies a lender typically has under a loan agreement, one of which is the right to "accelerate" the loan—that is, to declare all moneys loaned immediately due and payable, even though the amounts due under the term portion may not be otherwise due for several years, and the revolver may not expire until the end of the current year.

The right to accelerate is, in a practical sense, the right to trigger the bankruptcy of the borrower and for that reason is unlikely to be exercised except in those cases where a lender determines that its interests will be better protected by putting the borrower in bankruptcy than through other means. Since bankruptcy is viewed by most secured lenders as risky, slow, and a last resort (and a potential liability for the bank), a breached warranty is generally unlikely to bring the house down. But unless the breach is waived by the lender, its existence in effect turns what was originally conceived of as a term loan into a demand loan, callable by the bank at any time.

Frequently, highly leveraged transactions result in the bank having a demand loan even in the absence of a default, so going into default does not make matters much worse. Also, some lenders and their counsel try to negotiate loan agreements that are so tight that the company is arguably in default from the moment the agreement is entered into. Banks also impose default rates of interest in some cases, so that the cost of borrowing can go up on a warranty breach. This is a more effective sanction for the bank, provided that the company's fiscal health is not endangered.

What events typically trigger default?

- Breach of one or more of the covenants described above (sometimes subject to a right to cure certain breaches within a specified cure period and/or to the qualification that the breach be "material" or have a "material adverse effect" on the borrower)
- Payment defaults (failure to pay interest, principal, or fees when due or, in the case of interest and fees, sometimes within a stipulated grace period—see below)
- Breach of a representation or warranty (sometimes subject to the qualification that the breach be material—see below)

- Cross default (default in the loan agreement triggered by a default in another loan document, such as a security agreement, or in another unrelated but material agreement to which the borrower is a party, such as a subordinated debt instrument). Typically, for a cross default to be triggered, the default in the other instrument must be "mature"—that is, all cure periods must have expired and the other lender must have the right to accelerate. In addition, defaults on other debts below a specified dollar threshold may be expressly exempted from a loan agreement's cross-default provisions

- Insolvency or voluntary bankruptcy, or involuntary bankruptcy, if not discharged by the borrower within a stipulated period (typically 60 days)

- An adverse final court judgment above a stipulated dollar amount that is not discharged or stayed on appeal within a prescribed period

- The imposition of a lien (other than a lien permitted pursuant to the loan agreement) on assets of the borrower

- The occurrence of an event triggering ERISA liability in excess of a stipulated amount

- The death of the chief executive officer or an individual guarantor or other termination of the employment of certain specified managerial employees

What techniques can be used to take some of the bite out of default provisions?

There are basically two default softeners: the use of *grace* or *cure* provisions and the concept of *materiality*.

A *grace period* is a period of time, following the due date for the making of a payment, during which payment may be made and default avoided. It is rare, but not without precedent, for a grace period to be accorded to a principal repayment obligation. More common are grace periods for interest payments or fees. Five days' grace beyond the due date is common; sometimes 10 or even 15 days may be granted.

Cure periods apply to defaults triggered by covenant breaches. Generally, the lender will attempt to limit their application to those covenants that are manifestly susceptible of cure (the duty to submit financial reports at specified dates) but deny them for covenants designed to provide early warning of trouble (breach of financial ratios). Sometimes, the cure period will not begin to run until the lender has given the borrower notice of a failure to perform; in other cases, the cure period will begin to run when the borrower should have performed, whether the lender knew of the borrower's failure or not. Cure periods vary greatly from transaction to transaction and from provision to provision. However, 5-day, 10-day, and 30-day cure periods are seen from time to time, and sometimes the concept of counting only "business days" is used to extend the period by excluding Saturdays, Sundays, and nationally recognized holidays.

The concept of materiality is more commonly applied in the case of defaults triggered by warranty breaches. The borrower will assert that default should not be triggered if a representation turns out to be untrue, but the effect of such inaccuracy is not materially adverse to the borrower or the collateral, or to the lender's position. In some cases, where the loan agreement does not afford the borrower the right to cure a breached covenant, it provides that such a breach will not trigger a default unless the effect is material and adverse.

Understanding these points can help a borrower prevent future problems—and do a better job of negotiating fees.

What fees are typically charged by commercial banks?

Bank fees for lending services tend to be as varied as the ingenuity of lenders can devise and as high as borrowers can accept. In some cases, the lender may charge a fee upon the delivery of a *commitment letter* signed by the bank (the "commitment letter fee") and a second commitment letter fee upon its execution by the borrower. Both such fees may be credited against a third fee due from the borrower at closing on the loan (the "closing fee").[20]

If the loan has been syndicated, the bank may charge an agency or management fee for its services in putting together the syndicate. This will typically be an ongoing fee (as opposed to the one-time commitment letter and closing fees), payable quarterly or monthly as a percentage of the total facility (0.25 percent per annum is not uncommon).

The total amount of fees charged by a bank at the closing ranges from 1 to 2.5 percent. The percentage depends on the speed demanded of the bank, the complexity of the transaction, the size of the banking group (the more lenders there are, the more expensive it is), and the degree of risk. The front-end fee for a short-term bridge loan is usually higher than the fee charged up front for a long-term loan, since the bank has less opportunity to earn profit by way of interest over the life of the loan. Usually, the New York money center banks charge fees at the higher end of this range. In addition to the front-end fees, there will usually be a commitment fee or facility fee (typically 0.5 percent) on the amount from time to time undrawn and available under the revolver.

If the borrower will need letters of credit, the bank will typically assess a letter of credit fee (typically 1 to 1.5 percent per year) on the amount committed under a standby or commercial letter of credit.

Finally, the bank will often seek early termination fees on the unpaid balance of the term portion of the financing. These fees are intended to compensate the bank for economic losses it may suffer if the borrower terminates the term loan prior to its maturity because of a cheaper financing source, thus depriving the bank of the anticipated profit on the loan for the balance of the term. These fees may step down in amount the longer the term loan is outstanding. It is usually possible to get the bank to drop these termination fees or at least limit them to terminations occurring in the first year or two. This is worth spending some chips to achieve. If the company does well, the buyer will probably want to refinance the senior loan as quickly as possible to escape burdensome covenants, and these fees are likely to be a problem.

You mentioned a letter of credit. Can a letter of credit facility be combined with a merger, acquisition, or buyout loan?

Yes. If the business uses letters of credit in its ongoing operations (for purposes such as ensuring payment for raw materials or foreign-sourced goods), it can generally obtain a commitment from the lenders to provide such letters of credit up to a stipulated aggregate amount. The letter of credit facility will typically be carved out of the revolving line of credit, will be collateralized by the same collateral that secures the revolver, and will have the effect of limiting availability under the revolver to the extent of the aggregate letter of credit commitment. Draws on letters of credit will be treated, in such circumstances, as draws on the revolver. Separate fees (the usual 1 to 1.5 percent per year) may be charged for outstanding standby letters.

Sometimes companies have a practice of issuing a large letter of credit for all shipments in a certain period and then securing specific orders as they arise. In such cases, it may be possible to limit availability by the amount of claims that can be or have been made against the letter of credit for specific orders, and not by the larger unused balance of the letter of credit.

What bank expenses is the borrower required to pay?

Typically, whether the loan is made or not, the commitment letter will require that the borrower be liable for all the lender's out-of-pocket expenses and obligations for fees and disbursements of the bank's outside counsel. This provision is not negotiable; banks never expect to pay their own counsel for work done in connection with a loan. Such fees are always assessed against the borrower or, if the loan does not close, the intended borrower.

Are there problems in having more than one lender participate in a loan?

Frequently, loans are made by bank syndicates—that is, several commercial bank lenders. In some cases, the banks involved in making the loan will all be parties to the loan agreement, with one of their number designated as the agent bank. In other cases, only one bank will sign the loan agreement, but it will sell off participation interests to other banks. Although the number of participants in a loan makes no difference to the borrower from a legal standpoint, the practical implications of having to deal with multiple lenders can be serious and troublesome.

When a high degree of leverage is involved, lenders tend to limit their risks by imposing an intrusive array of covenants—negative and affirmative, financial and operational—upon the borrower. These covenants are designed to ensure that the business will be conducted as represented to the bankers and in accordance with the financial projections submitted to the bankers by the borrower. Any deviation, any change in the manner of operation of the business, or any bad financial development may trigger a default.

Because it is not always possible for a buyer to foresee all future developments in the way the business will be conducted, it is generally not possible, even in the absence of bad financial news, to operate at all times within the requirements imposed by the loan covenants. Hence, the borrower will generally find it necessary, from time to time, to go back to the lenders to have certain covenants waived or amended.

(In upcoming chapters—particularly Chapters 11 and 12, we will provide some detailed guidance on dealing with multiple sources in financing and refinancing.)

Can junior lenders ever be paid back before senior lenders?

Not generally. Under a longstanding principle in bankruptcy law called the *absolute priority rule,* junior creditors may not go ahead of senior creditors. There are exceptions—such as the "new capital" exception for junior lenders that invest—but the rule generally prevails.[21]

What is a negative pledge covenant, and why do lenders seek them?

A negative pledge covenant is a promise by the borrower not to pledge to someone else the assets considered or used as collateral—that is, assets that are lien-free or subject to the bank's lien. It is generally used to bar junior liens on collateral that is subject to the bank's senior lien. Although in theory the rights of a junior loan holder should not impinge on the senior lender's rights in the collateral, in practice lenders strongly prefer not to be accountable to a second loan holder with regard to their stewardship over the collateral on which they have a first lien. A junior loan holder is someone who can second-guess the senior lender's actions in realizing upon the collateral and sue.

What kinds of problems are most likely to be encountered in attempting to perfect liens on the collateral?

- Prior unsatisfied liens may be discovered. For this reason, as well as for general due diligence considerations, it is prudent to begin a lien search as promptly as possible in all jurisdictions in which record filings may have been made affecting the collateral.

- Liens on patents, trademarks, and trade names, and copyright assignments require special federal filings, which may be time-consuming and require the services of specialized counsel.

- Collateral assignments of government contracts and receivables from the U.S. government require federal approval, which involves a potentially time-consuming process.

- Uniform Commercial Code (UCC) filings giving notice to the world of security interests that must be made at state and, sometimes, local government offices where the company and its assets are located. Filing requirements in Puerto Rico and Louisiana, the two non-UCC jurisdictions in the United States, are markedly different from, as well as more elaborate than, filing requirements in other U.S. jurisdictions. Local counsel should be contacted early and will play key roles.

- Security interests in real estate and fixtures require separate documentation and recordation in the localities and states in which they are located. Lenders will often require title insurance and surveys, both of which involve considerable lead time.

- Lenders will often want local counsel opinions as to perfection and priority of liens, and obtaining these can be a major logistical task.

For interest rate and fee calculations, bankers typically treat the year as having only 360 days. Why?

Because a 360-day year produces a slight increase in yield over the stipulated rate or fee. This practice has acquired the status of a convention and is not generally subject to negotiation.

What are default rates?

Loan agreements typically provide for an increase in interest rates in the event of default, or at the time of acceleration of the loan. A premium of two or three percentage points above the rate normally in effect is common. A borrower should try to have a default rate go into effect only after the lender makes a formal declaration of default, since minor technical defaults are all too easy to stumble into and should not be a source of profit to the lender.

Why are mandatory prepayment obligations imposed by lenders?

Reasons for mandatory prepayment requirements vary depending on the bank's perception of the transaction. In some transactions, the lender is anxious to recoup and redeploy its money as swiftly as possible. This desire, and the anticipated availability of cash derived from cash flow projections, will tend to drive in the direction of an aggressive amortization schedule on term debt. (In some cases borrowers may also be asked to "amortize" revolving lines of credit as well by accepting scheduled reductions in availability over a period of time and making any principal payments required by such reductions.)

In addition, a bank may schedule amortization payments to match the buyer's plans for selling off assets or terminating pension plans, in effect forcing the buyer to honor its promises to break up and sell off parts of the acquired business or to terminate such pension plans as represented to the bank. Finally, lenders may require that all or a portion of excess cash flow be paid down to reduce senior term debt. The bank may permit distributions of dividends to stockholders of an S corporation for the purpose of paying federal, state, and local income taxes on income of the company and retaining some earnings for capital expenditures. At the same time, however, it may also require that the buyer use everything left over after satisfying junior debt to pay off any outstanding balance on the term loan.

TABLE 7-5

Installment Sale Models
Cash Requirements for 10-Year Payout (in thousands), Purchase Price = $1.0 Million[a]

Year	1	2	3	4	5	6	7	8	9	10	Cum.
No depreciation											
Gross earnings	$145	$165	$189	$214	$244	$276	$308	$350	$395	$447	$2,733
Interest	53	47	42	37	32	26	21	16	11	5	289
Pre-tax earnings	93	118	147	177	213	250	287	334	385	442	2,444
Tax 38%	35	45	56	67	81	95	109	127	146	168	929
After-tax earnings	57	73	91	110	132	155	178	207	238	274	1,515
Amount retired	75	75	75	75	75	75	75	75	75	75	750
Net cash flow	**(18)**	**(2)**	**16**	**35**	**57**	**80**	**103**	**132**	**163**	**199**	**765**
Cumulative cash flow	(18)	(20)	(4)	31	88	168	271	403	567	765	
With depreciation[b,c]											
Pre-tax earnings	$93	$118	$147	$177	$213	$250	$287	$334	$385	$442	$2,444
Depreciation (10% per year)	69	69	69	69	69	69	69	69	69	69	690
Net earnings	24	49	78	108	144	181	218	265	316	373	1,754
Tax 38%	9	19	30	41	55	69	83	101	120	142	667
After-tax earnings	15	30	48	67	89	112	135	164	196	231	1,088
Amount retired (net of depreciation)	6	6	6	6	6	6	6	6	6	6	60
Net cash flow	**9**	**24**	**42**	**61**	**83**	**106**	**129**	**158**	**190**	**225**	**1,028**
Cumulative cash flow	9	33	75	136	219	325	454	613	803	1,028	

a Assumes down payment of $250,000, plus balance in 10 annual installments of $75,000 plus interest of 7% on the unpaid balance. Down payment covered by $300,000 cash and securities held in current assets. Tax rates vary.
b Assumes depreciation of $690,000 value of copyrights over 10-year period of contract.
c Net worth is $310,000.

Cash Requirements for Five-Year Payout (in thousands), Purchase Price = $1.0 Million[a]

Year	1	2	3	4	5	6	7	8	9	10	Cum.
No depreciation											
Gross earnings	$145	$165	$189	$214	$244	$276	$308	$350	$395	$447	$2,733
Interest	53	42	32	21	11						159
Pre-tax earnings	93	123	157	193	233	276	308	350	395	447	2,575
Tax 38%	35	47	60	73	89	105	117	133	150	170	978
After-tax earnings	57	76	97	120	144	171	191	217	245	277	1,596
Amount retired	150	150	150	150	150			750			
Net cash flow	**(93)**	**(74)**	**(53)**	**(30)**	**(6)**	**171**	**191**	**217**	**245**	**277**	**846**
Cumulative cash flow	(93)	(166)	(219)	(249)	(255)	(84)	107	324	569	846	
With depreciation[bc]											
Pre-tax earnings	$93	$123	$157	$193	$233	$276	$308	$350	$395	$447	$2,575
Depreciation (10% per year)	69	69	69	69	69	69	69	69	69	69	690
Net earnings	24	54	88	124	164	207	239	281	326	378	1,885
Tax 38%	9	21	33	47	62	79	91	107	124	144	716
After-tax earnings	15	33	55	77	102	128	148	174	202	234	1,168
Amount retired (net of depreciation)	81	81	81	81	81				405		
Net cash flow	**(66)**	**(48)**	**(26)**	**(4)**	**21**	**128**	**148**	**174**	**202**	**234**	**763**
Cumulative cash flow	(66)	(114)	(140)	(145)	(124)	5	153	327	529	763	

[a] Assumes down payment of $250,000, plus balance in five annual installments of $150,000 plus interest of 7% on the unpaid balance. Down payment covered by $300,000 cash and securities held in current assets. Tax rates vary.

[b] Assumes depreciation of $690,000 value of copyrights over 10-year period of contract.

[c] Net worth is $310,000.

Why do banks insist on applying prepayments first to the last installments due (in inverse order) rather than the other way around?

Banks reverse the order of loan payments in a highly leveraged transaction in order to keep the flow of cash coming into the bank and to get the loan paid off as swiftly as possible. If borrowers could prepay the next payments due they would, in effect, be buying themselves a payment holiday. Sometimes prepayments may result from sale of income-producing assets (or the bank's application of casualty insurance proceeds to prepay principal in lieu of making such proceeds available to the borrower), because such events can reduce the subsequent capacity of the borrower to pay debt service. In such cases, the loan should be recast to lower proportionately the combined total of subsequent interest and principal payments. For an example of an installment loan schedule, see Table 7–5 (on preceding pages).

So far, we have been talking about commercial bank loans. What other major sources of financing are there?

In addition to commercial banks, leveraged acquirers can turn to insurance companies (for loans), or underwriters (to do *junk bond issues*). Equity investment funds also make loans as backers—a special relationship discussed in Chapter 9.[22]

INSURANCE COMPANY FINANCING

What kind of financing is usually available from insurance companies?

For many years, insurance companies have provided senior fixed term financing—both secured and unsecured—for terms of up to 10, 12, or 15 years through "private placements." If a company's capital requirements are sufficiently large, one or more additional insurance companies may participate in the transaction as lenders. Frequently, these groups are assembled by investment bankers. Because the behavior and practices of insurance company lenders differ somewhat from banks, they deserve special attention.

Loans may be secured, unsecured, or a combination of each. All, or any portion, may be senior debt, the remainder being subordinated debt generally bearing a greater rate of interest. Rates are usually fixed for the term of these financings.

Does it make a difference which insurance companies are solicited?

It may, for several reasons. Although lending terms tend to be somewhat standardized, some companies will lend into a riskier credit, with a rate premium and perhaps a somewhat more onerous set of covenants. In addition, over the years, several life insurance companies and their counsel have devised and perfected lengthy, onerous forms of note purchase agreements (essentially the equivalent of loan agreements), with which many borrowers became disenchanted, taking their business elsewhere. Since then, in an effort to regain the lost business, some companies have developed a new, streamlined, and more readable form of agreement that is definitely preferable to its predecessors, from the borrower's point of view. It may be appropriate to agree in advance of documentation that a streamlined form of agreement will be used.

How long does it take to obtain insurance company funding?

Insurance companies are generally more bureaucratic than banks, and decision making often seems to take longer. In-house counsel to insurance firms can, in some cases, march to a different drummer, delaying legal responses, but their input is required notwithstanding the presence of an outside law firm.

Although substantial acquisitions have been closed with insurance company funds, these closings did not break any records for speed. Often, if time is of the essence, it is prudent to arrange for a bridge lender to fund initially and be taken out within a period of several months by an insurance company private placement. The bridge lender can even be the bank providing the revolving financing. Even this solution can be difficult to achieve, however, since the principal terms of the takeout financing must be negotiated in advance with the insurance company, and often between it and a senior lender, to be sure the takeout financing can be closed in the future.

How are insurance company private placements generally negotiated?

The deal is negotiated and, frequently, put in the form of a "term sheet" that is "circled" (approved) by each insurance company, or commitment letters may be issued, particularly if enough pressure is placed on the lenders by the borrower or its counsel.

Once the borrower and its bank agree to a term sheet or commitment letter, the lead lender (usually the insurance company taking the largest percentage of the total loan) will have its outside counsel prepare a first draft of the note purchase agreement; such counsel generally acts for the entire lending group, although with varying degrees of authority and effectiveness. The other participants (and their in-house counsel) will generally review this draft before it is forwarded to the borrower and its counsel. The content of this agreement has the potential to change significantly for the worse—from the borrower's perspective—as it progresses through successive drafts and in-house counsel for each participant gets additional bites at the apple. A strong lead lender, however, can often prevent this from occurring.

How should the borrower or its counsel respond if, during the negotiation of a note purchase agreement, a representative of the insurance company refuses to strike an objectionable covenant, saying that the borrower can request a waiver at a later date if necessary?

These agreements should be negotiated as fully as possible prior to closing. Although subsequent waivers are obtainable, a borrower should not be surprised if some payment is required in connection with the waiver, particularly if interest rates have risen significantly since the funding of the transaction. Even when rates have not risen, some companies have been known to impose fees when waiver requests are made, frequently in order to compensate for their staff time spent in evaluating the requests; of course, the cost of any outside counsel will be the responsibility of the borrower. Furthermore, waivers are generally more readily obtainable from banks and less so from insurance companies. One should act accordingly in negotiating the initial insurance company documentation.

Is it possible to provide for optional prepayments without incurring significant prepayment premiums?

Yes. Generally, prepayment provisions in note purchase agreements have followed a formula that allows for optional annual prepayments in any year in the amount of any specified annual mandatory prepayments, without additional charge. If, however, the loan is to be prepaid in any given year by an amount in excess of this permitted optional prepayment, a percentage premium (typically around 9.5 percent) would be applied to this excess, with the amount of the percentage declining annually and reaching zero within a year before maturity. The applicable percentage would then be multiplied by the amount prepaid in excess of any permitted optional prepayment; the resulting product is the dollar amount that must be paid, in addition to the outstanding principal balance, in order to prepay the principal indebtedness evidenced by the note purchase agreement or an appropriate portion.

Recently, many life insurance companies have become wary of the fixed premium method for prepayments and are moving toward a *make-whole* arrangement. This consists of a formula that pays to the lender the net present value of the lost return during each year that the notes issued under the note purchase agreement would have been outstanding, compared with a theoretical reinvestment at an agreed formula rate.

Are other prohibitions on prepayment typically found in insurance company financings?

Yes. Prepayment is usually prohibited if the source of funds for such prepayment is borrowings, or proceeds from the sale of preferred stock, having a lower after-tax interest cost to the company than the company's after-tax cost of interest at the rate payable under the insurance company's notes.

Is there any way to structure the borrowing in order to reduce the amount of prepayment premiums?

Yes. If a portion of the amount borrowed is at a variable rate tied to prime or Eurodollar rates, prepayment premiums on that portion can be avoided.

Do insurance companies provide revolving loans, takeout commitments, or other forms of guarantees?

Insurance companies don't do revolving loans. For this reason, they are not suitable for working capital lending. Insurance companies are not organized for the continuous financial monitoring required for revolving lending. Also, unless operating as a surety, insurance companies do not give guarantees. They may not make a loan unless it would be prudent at the time made. Thus, they may not give enforceable commitments to take out or back another lender if the borrower gets into trouble.

What material covenants would you expect to find in a more streamlined insurance company note purchase agreement?

- Typical financial reporting covenants, including requirements for a statement of the principal financial officer of the company setting forth computations pertaining to compliance with financial covenants (including long-term and short-term debt incurrence, secured debt incurrence, and the making of restricted payments)

- Maintenance of corporate existence, payment of taxes, and compliance with statutes, regulations, and orders of government bodies pertaining to environmental and occupational safety and health standards or even broader government statutes and regulations with a materiality standard

- Maintenance of specified types of insurance

- Restrictions on debt incurrence, including limits on short-term debt and long-term debt, each of which may be restricted to specified dollar amounts or by formulas relating to consolidated tangible net worth and consolidated net earnings available for fixed charges

- Limits on liens and encumbrances, sale/leasebacks, and some types of payments

- Maintenance of financial condition—minimum amount of consolidated tangible net worth, minimum ratio of consolidated net tangible assets to consolidated debt, minimum current ratio, maximum long-term rentals, restriction on subsidiary stock dispositions, and issuance of shares by subsidiaries

- Limitations on amounts of annual capital expenditures

- Restrictions on mergers and consolidations affecting the company and subsidiaries, and disposition of company or subsidiary assets

SPECIAL CONSIDERATIONS IN JUNK BOND LENDING

One special type of loan made by both commercial banks and insurance companies is junk bond lending. What covenants do junk bonds normally contain?

Compared with senior debt agreements, unsecured junk bond indentures are simpler, fitting the classic bond indenture mold. Senior debt instruments provide for total information flow to lenders, hair-trigger default provisions, and, often, extensive second-guessing and approval of management decisions. Junk bond indentures, by refreshing contrast, tend to rely more on the borrower's good judgment and the value of the company as a going concern. The indentures limit themselves to protecting against major restructurings or asset transfers or increases in amounts of senior or secured debt. This difference in approach reflects the longer-term nature of such debt and the impracticality of obtaining consents from a large, diverse group of public bondholders. In the very rare case that the junk bonds are secured, however, a more elaborate set of covenants relating to the protection of collateral will be included.

Generally, borrowers should try to limit the financial covenants in junk bond issues to "incurrence" tests rather than "maintenance" tests. In other words, the covenants should not require that any specified level of financial health be maintained and should be breached only by a voluntary act, such as (these are the four normal circumstances) paying a prohibited dividend, incurring prohibited debt, merging or combining with another company or selling assets unless certain tests are met, or dealing with affiliates other than at arm's length. These covenants will often closely restrict operating subsidiaries of the borrower to ensure that all debt is incurred on the same corporate level.

In many transactions the covenants go much further. They may include detailed financial maintenance covenants relating to net worth, current ratios, interest coverage, limitations on investments, and application of asset sale proceeds.

Which bond covenants are particularly subject to negotiation?

The following key issues should be covered in the indenture:

Restrictions on Mergers and Asset Sales   There are a variety of such restrictions. The most onerous require that the surviving entity in the merger or the purchaser of all or substantially all the assets have a net worth not lower than the borrower had before the merger and that the fixed charge coverage ratios (generally the ratio of debt payments to cash flow [predebt service]) equal a certain percentage of the ratio that pertained before the merger. The effect of this type of provision is to preclude a sale of the business in a leveraged transaction that will cause a material increase in total debt of the company after the merger. The borrower thus has fewer means available for disposing of the business.

Some indentures require the borrower to offer to prepay junior debt from asset sale proceeds that are not used to prepay senior debt. (It must be an "offer," because the debt is usually not prepayable without the consent of the lender.) Senior lenders object to this provision because they believe that it may be necessary for the proceeds to be left in the business, particularly if there is trouble and the asset sale was used to gain needed liquidity for the business. The dispute can usually be solved by allowing, until the senior lender is paid in full, a limited amount of such proceeds to be left in the business before a prepayment offer must be made.

A borrower should always check in advance to learn what the investment banker's standard format is (best done by reviewing indentures from previous transactions). Once you've locked in with an investment banker, you'll hear over and over again that it can't market the debt without the restrictions it is used to. Be prepared with examples of other junk debt with less onerous provisions. If you have any specific plans to sell off assets, be sure they don't violate this provision.

Debt Incurrence   Many junk bond indentures have very tight restrictions on debt incurrence by the issuer. The simplest form of restriction is that the issuer cannot issue "sandwich debt" or "interlayer debt"—that is, debt subordinated to the senior debt but senior to the junk debt. This restriction allows the issuer to borrow as much senior debt or debt junior to the junk debt as the lenders are willing to lend. The holders of the junk debt are relying on the limitations senior lenders will place on the amount of senior debt that can be incurred.

Other types of restrictions limit the incurrence of debt to a percentage of the original amount of debt or require the achievement of certain financial ratios before incurring additional debt. The ratios, and any particular provisions necessary for a particular business plan, are all subject to negotiation with the lender. The senior lender will want the borrower to be able to incur new senior debt somewhat in excess of the unpaid amount of the existing senior debt in order to permit minor workout arrangements and to finance some expansion.

Restrictions on Prepayments   To avoid the adverse selection problem of losing the high interest rates on good loans and suffering defaults on the others, junk bonds restrict prepayment. Most junk bonds preclude prepayments for several (often five) years and thereafter may permit prepayments only on payment of substantial premiums. This restriction is not as troublesome if the covenants in respect of mergers and debt incurrence are not too strict. A long nonprepayment period means that the issuer can't rid itself of the debt except through *defeasance* of the bonds, if the covenants become too burdensome. (Defeasance is a refinancing technique in which the bond issuer continues to make coupon interest payments rather than redeeming the bonds at their call date.)

Subordination Provisions   These are provisions that show the subordination of the various levels of debt. (For more on this topic, see Chapter 10.)

Restricted Payments   These restrictions prohibit dividends and other distributions as well as stock redemptions unless specified conditions are satisfied. The conditions usually prevent payments until a specified minimum net worth level has been attained; thereafter, payments may not exceed a certain percentage (25 to 50 percent) of accumulated net income.

Be careful of this provision; it may have the effect of precluding a sale of the company through a leveraged transaction unless the junk bonds are also prepaid. Such a transaction normally requires the borrower, or a successor obligor under the junk bond indenture, to borrow the acquisition debt and pay the proceeds to the acquired company's shareholders. Such payments probably constitute a restricted payment that may not be made unless the tests are satisfied (and in most such cases they won't be). Even if all the other tests for the merger are satisfied (such as net worth and coverage ratios), this test may present another and often insurmountable hurdle.

But won't it be possible just to waive these covenants if they prove to be too restrictive?

No. Prepaying the junk bonds will very likely be either impossible or very expensive because of prepayment restrictions and penalties. In addition, unlike the case of senior lenders, it is often impossible, or at the least very difficult, to obtain waivers of covenants from a multitude of public bondholders. Therefore, the restrictions contained in the junk bond indenture should be something the borrower can live with for a long time. Special care must be taken to ensure that the covenants fit the long-term plans of the company with respect to acquisitions, dispositions of assets, expansions, and so on. Once the covenants are in place, the borrower has to live with them pretty much unmodified.

From the point of view of bondholders, how have junk bonds been performing?

The junk bond market took off in the mid-to-late 1980s, dropped precipitously in the very late 1980s and early 1990s, and has headed toward a middle course for the remainder of the 1990s.[23] Interest rates also play a part in junk bond demand: Low rates increase the appeal of junk bonds' high potential return.[24] Within these general trends, individual junk bond issues respond to specific company events or rumors, and these in turn cause variations in the market for junk bonds.

What about default rates for junk bonds?

Recently (in the late 1990s), they have been low—less than 1 percent (as a percentage of all bonds outstanding), compared with 10 percent in 1991.[25] But each bond issue must be analyzed according to its particular generation. Default rates vary over time, with a very *low chance* of default for a year or so, a *higher likelihood* in the next two years, and then a *decreasing chance* after four years.[26]

What is a quasi-junk bond?

A quasi-junk bond is a junk bond that gets a split rating—that is, one credit rating service gives it a lowest investment grade (BBB or higher) and another calls it junk (BB or lower).

What recourse do bondholders have in the event of poor bond performance?

Creditor lawsuits against parties involved in overly leveraged transactions have targeted numerous parties, including issuers of junk bonds. Many of these cases are filed under state fraudulent conveyance laws. Few are brought to trial. Many are settled out of court.[27] Junk bondholders often have a say in restructuring or changes of control.[28]

Is there ever insider trading in junk bonds?

Some investors believe there is widespread insider trading—trading based on material nonpublic information—in various debt securities including junk bonds, municipal bonds, government securities, commodities, and futures. A common symptom of such trading, often seen in junk bonds, is a sharp increase in price prior to a positive announcement. Investigation, pursuit, and punishment of such trading has been limited to date, though, because the federal agency with explicit authority to go after insider trading in securities, the Securities and Exchange Commission, fears that it may not have jurisdiction to pursue such cases. There are also detection problems. Junk bond trading, done only over the counter, is more difficult to track than equity trades, which occur on the major stock exchanges.

CONCLUDING COMMENTS

Obtaining money to buy a company requires a thorough understanding of the players as well as the rules. Obviously, lenders and other sources of debt are key players in the merger, acquisition, and buyout process. Understanding where these sources are, how they operate, and what they seek marks an important stage in mastering the art of M&A and refinancing. In the next chapter, we will turn our attention to sources of equity financing.

E N D N O T E S

1. This list is based on the categories given by Securities Data Publishing in its annual *Directory of Buyout Financing Sources* (New York: 1999). The directory is divided into three sections: U.S. senior lenders; U.S. mezzanine providers and equity investors; and foreign senior lenders, mezzanine providers, and equity investors. The 10 categories listed were derived from the self-descriptions offered in the first two sections.

2. The activities of such holding companies have been regulated (and deregulated) under the Bank Holding Company Act of 1956 and amendments to that law. Under this law, a registered bank holding company may own or control nonbanking companies (if approved by the Federal Reserve Board), but only if they are closely related to banking or have a public benefit.

3. A recent "Relationship Banking Survey" sent out by First Virginia Bank asked the following question: "Which of these services have you ever used at a bank or other financial institution, and which of these services would you like to have from us?" The survey then listed 34 different services, including annuities, discount brokerage services, insurance services, and mutual fund investments.

4. The only exception was Utah.

5. This definition is based in part on Thomas Fitch, *Dictionary of Banking Terms,* 3rd ed. (New York: Barron's Educational Series, 1997). As mentioned previously, Fitch consulted numerous authorities for his dictionary, including major accounting and banking groups.

6. *Flow of Funds Accounts* (Washington, DC: Federal Reserve Board of Governors Third Quarter, 1998).

7. For over a decade, banks around the world have respected an 8 percent capital adequacy guideline from the Bank for International Settlement in Basle, Switzerland. The model is based on the general risk of each type of asset. Government debt instruments are considered under the BIS guidelines to have zero risk, while loans are counted fully. In September 1997, the investment bank J. P. Morgan announced the development of a different system more sensitive to the particular risk of individual instruments.

8. Interestingly, thrifts have fewer restrictions than banks on their ability to sell insurance. This and other differences have caused some commercial banks to convert to thrifts in recent years. Also, in a reverse of the 1980s trend, some thrifts are now buying banks. See "Blurring the Lines Between Banks and Thrifts: Legislation Has Widened Opportunities," *The Washington Post,* December 1, 1996, pp. H1ff. Nonetheless, from the perspective of a commercial borrower, commercial banks remain a more significant source of capital than thrifts.

9. Public Law No. 103-328, 108 Stat. 2341.

10. This repeal may occur within the shelf life of this book. Although the 105th Congress adjourned in October 1998 without repealing Glass-Steagall during its two years at the helm, the new Congress has put repeal on its agenda for 1999–2000.

11. There is ample research showing that local banks are indispensable as providers of capital to small business. One classic study is by Gregory E. Elliehousen and John D. Wokers, "Banking Markets and the Use of Financial Services by Small and Medium-Sized Businesses," *Federal Reserve Bulletin,* October 1990, pp. 801–817. Some people worry that the bank merger trend will wipe out small, local banks and thus choke off capital for small businesses (including those that wish to grow through acquisition). Fortunately, there is a countertrend of the "new bank." This trend was first noticed in the mid-1990s. See "Back to the Fray: Displaced by Mergers, Some Bankers Launch their Own Start-ups," *The Wall Street Journal,* March 4, 1996, pp. A1ff.

12. "Small Businesses are Getting More Loans from Banks," *The Wall Street Journal,* April 8, 1997, p. B2.

13. Consider Sirrom Capital Corporation. In the first six months of 1997, Sirrom loaned $104 million to 43 small businesses in the United States and Canada. These were senior and subordinated loans from $1 milion to $5 million that were concentrated in "service businesses with an emphasis on cash flow and intangible assets." See *The Wall Street Journal,* July 22, 1998, p. B3. Sirrom is not alone. A Phoenix Management Services survey released in April 1999 showed that lenders in 1999 are most interested in light manufacturing (81 percent), industrial distribution (78 percent), and service companies (68 percent). Other sectors, such as construction, healthcare, and retail, received much lower marks.

14. This list appears in Russell Robb, *Buying Your Own Business* (Holbrook, MA: Adams Media Corporation, 1995), p. 283.

15. This example comes from J. Fred Weston and Thomas E. Copeland, *Managerial Finance,* 9th ed. (Los Angeles: Academic Publishing Service, 1998), p. 932.

16. From the very first entry in Securities Data Publishing's 1999 *Directory of Buyout Financing Sources,* op. cit. (note 1), p. 45, featuring ABN Amro Bank N.V. of Chicago.

17. For an example of the use of such a clause, see "Banks Balk at Financing Merger Deals, *The Wall Street Journal,* October 16, 1998, pp. A3ff.

18. Ibid.

19. Ibid. at note 7.

20. Borrowers should pay fees only to reputable institutions. Advance-fee loan rackets have proliferated in recent years. Complaints about such scams made up the largest number of complaints to local Better Business Bureau offices—at the rate of 1,000 per month in some locations.

21. The U.S. Court of Appeals for the Fourth Circuit recently refused to uphold a "new capital exception" ruling by a U.S. District Court. The Appeals Court refused to grant priority to a limited partnership that had defaulted on a mortgage loan granted by Travelers Insurance Co., the senior lender. The partner-

ship had submitted an impressive plan to bankruptcy court, but the appellate panel said the group had "carried their opportunity for self-dealing too far." See James Lyons, "A Creditor's Comeback," *Fortune,* June 8, 1992.

22. Note also that in rare circumstances, public pension funds—which are usually strictly equity investors—may make a loan. For example, the public employees pension fund for the state of Minnesota loaned Northwest Airlines $740 million for expansion in late 1991, boosting the fortunes of Northwest's parent company, NWA Inc., which had gone private in 1989. Today, Northwest Airlines Corporation is a public company, traded as NWAC on the Nasdaq stock exchange. The company, which has grown through related diversification, reported $10 billion in operating revenues in 1997.

23. Even in the early 1990s, there were signs of a junk bond market recovery. According to Lipper Analytical Services, mutual funds investing in "high current yield" bond funds realized a 36.36 percent return on investment in 1991, much of it in the second half of the year, when the market was rebounding.

24. A January 8, 1992, *New York Times* article, "Junk Bonds and Mark Funds Excel," by Leslie Wayne, states that "high-yield funds benefited from lower interest rates, which allowed many issuers to refinance their balance sheets, and from the scarcity of new issues of junk debt, limiting the available supply and raising the prices of some bonds."

25. "In Bonds, the Junkier the Better," *Business Week,* July 7, 1997, p. 116.

26. The latest scholarship shows a bell curve for annualized cumulative default rates of non-investment grade bonds rated BB, B, and CCC, in descending order of quality. Studies by Merrill Lynch, Moody's Investor Service, and Bond Investors Association support the bell curve idea.

27. In mid-1992, Merrill Lynch & Co. was faced with a newly formed "litigation trust" formed by bondholders in a failed $800 million LBO of Insilco. Burned holders of $400 million in bonds were reportedly planning to sue Merrill Lynch on the grounds that the prospectus for Insilco's junk bonds didn't disclose all the risks associated with the buyout.

28. For example, when Six Flags was contemplating a 1991 bid by Time Warner and two investment groups, the arrangement had to be approved by holders of Six Flags junk bonds issued in connection with a $600 million leveraged buyout by Wesray Capital Corp. in 1987.

Working with Equity Sources

The only credential the city asked was the boldness to dream. For those who did, it unlocked its gates and its treasures, not caring who they were or where they came from.

Moss Hart, *Act I*, 1959

INTRODUCTION

It is now the time and place to consider equity-based financing. To provide perspective let us recall the setting for this discussion. We take the point of view of a company considering a range of possibilities for financing mergers and acquisitions. Such a company may be an established global colossus, or it may be new and small—as MCI was at its inception in the early 1970s. MCI's earliest growth was financed through venture capital, extended terms of payment from its main supplier of equipment, and alliances with larger, well-established companies. A decade later, MCI was using the public financing markets.

This chapter begins with the equity financing spectrum, giving overviews of three types of sources: *venture capital,* which is used by new companies; *private placements,* which are used by more mature companies; and *public offerings,* another venue used by mature companies. The majority of the chapter will focus on this third category, discussing the underwriting process in general. Our discussion of financing via equity sources in the early stages will be brief, since the following chapter on working with backers develops the material more fully.

THE EQUITY FINANCING SPECTRUM: FROM VENTURE CAPITAL TO PRIVATE AND PUBLIC OFFERINGS

What kind of equity financing can a new company find?

Most new companies will find it difficult to attract financing—whether debt or equity—from a typical commercial bank or investment bank. Instead, most new companies need to reach out to a special form of financing called *venture capital*. The venture capital firm, discussed more fully in the next chapter, takes a stake in a company in return for equity.

Why do new companies require special equity financing sources?

The mortality rate for new companies is quite high. They are very risky. The survivors and the successful companies strive to produce high returns to the equity sources for the high risks that they bear. A venture capital source—whether an individual, a group of individuals, or an institution—has sufficient wealth to bear such risks. In addition, venture sources of equity financing generally have considerable business experience and have staff to help them evaluate whether the new business venture makes sense.

What are the major benefits of financing from venture capital sources?

There are two principal benefits. First, the venture capital firm offers financial support as progress is demonstrated. Second, the principal investors offer counseling and advice along the way.

If venture capital offers these benefits, what is the role for initial public offerings (IPOs)?

IPOs are a method of gaining broader public participation in the equity risks and rewards. By its very nature, involving investment in an enterprise that is typically new and small, venture capital involves relatively small amounts of money. When larger amounts are needed—and when the need for advice diminishes—it may be time to consider an IPO. When a new company has established a record of progress, the risk of further equity investments become lower, so IPOs become possible.

Are several years always required to be able to obtain broader public financing?

Not always. In the late 1990s, equity financing sources became wildly enthusiastic about Internet companies. Netscape, America Online, and Amazon.com paved the way. It seemed that any company whose name ended in ".com" received financing virtually as soon as its concept was publicized. Furthermore, its stock increased many-fold within days of the IPO.

What other equity sources are available for companies that have established a track record?

Pension funds and insurance companies can be sources of equity financing. This is sometimes called private placement with financial institutions. These sources have the expertise to evaluate a new company's prospects in a professional way. It is a valued stamp of approval to receive financing from this type of source.

What are some of the advantages of the private sale of equity with financial institutions?

A private sale of equity offers several advantages in financing a deal. First, it represents a valuable endorsement of the prospects for the proposed merger, acquisition, or buyout. Second, the deal can be done relatively quickly. Third, the issuance costs are likely to be relatively lower. Finally, the buyer and seller have greater flexibility in negotiating security arrangements.

Are there any disadvantages of a private equity placement?

Yes. These sophisticated financing sources will require more restrictive terms to protect their investments. In addition, because there will be no public market for the securities, the sources will require higher prospective returns. Whether those returns are measured simply as increased value of the stock's selling price or, more exactingly, as the security's actual yield (annual dividend per share/market price), they are likely to be higher than the returns sought by the typical investors in a public equity placement.

Why might a seasoned company contemplating M&As be interested in an equity offering?

The equity offering may further strengthen its equity base. With more equity, its debt/equity ratio—a key indicator of long-term debt-paying ability—will be lower. This will give the company more flexibility for financing in M&A transactions, as well as for its own internal growth.

After a company has been in business for a number of years, what is likely to represent the major source of its historical equity growth?

A company that has been operating successfully for 15 to 20 years is likely to have used internal financing in the form of retained earnings and depreciation to finance from 60 to 70 percent of its funding requirements. The remainder of its funding will have come from external sources. As mentioned in Chapter 1, the rest is divided fairly equally between debt and equity sources, with larger companies tending to use more equity than debt, including sales of equity to foreign investors. The larger the transaction, the more likely it is that the acquirer will consider paying at least partly in stock. In 1998, for example, 42 percent of transactions worth $100 million or more were funded entirely in stock, versus only 27 percent of transactions worth between $5 million and $10 million.

When an established company seeks to increase its equity base through a public offering, what types of firms can assist it in these efforts?

This is a good question, because although established companies tend to use a variety of sources, they may develop close relationships with only one type of financing provider—either a commercial bank or an investment bank. In fact, both are necessary.

As mentioned in Chapter 7, the main functions of a commercial bank are to accept deposits, which it can insure, and to make loans. Although banks today, thanks to deregulation, can participate in equity financing as well, this has traditionally been the province of investment banks. As explained in more detail below, an investment bank has the main function of underwriting the sale of all types of financing instruments. The expertise and relationships required to carry out these functions usually mean that an investment banking firm has a number of other activities that are related to its underwriting activities. For example, an investment banking firm might have a securities brokerage unit, or might sponsor an investment company such as a mutual fund.[1]

Over a period of years, a company should seek to develop both strong commercial banking and investment banking relationships. That is, over time, a company can and should communicate its worth to both commercial bank lending officers and investment banking executives. These professionals need time and information to develop an understanding of the performance and future prospects of the companies they are financing. The first step in an underwriting, then, is to develop a working relationship with a potential underwriter.

We should also mention custodians—the banking institutions that settle and safeguard securities. For more on global custodians, see Chapter 14.

THE ROLE OF UNDERWRITERS

What is an underwriter?

Technically speaking, *underwriting* is the insurance function of bearing the risk of adverse price fluctuations during the period in which a new issue of securities is begin distributed. In plain English, an underwriter is a firm—typically an investment banking firm affiliated with a stock brokerage firm—that shows confidence in or "underwrites" the securities offered in a stock issue. The underwriter does this by buying the newly issued stock from the company.

After buying the stock, the underwriter may keep it in the hopes of appreciation, or sell it to other dealers (*wholesale*) or to the investing public (*retail*). The underwriter and the broker, if separate, split the fees.[2]

What is a broker-dealer?

Let's parse the phrase. A *broker* acts as an agent for an entity, getting others to buy what that entity is selling (e.g., securities), and getting paid a commission for this work. A *dealer* actually buys the entity's product (securities) and then resells it, hopefully at a profit. When an entity fulfills both roles, it is called a *broker-dealer*. The equity marketplace has a wealth of brokerage channels. In North America alone, there are 5,000 securities brokerage firms.[3]

What is an underwriting *lead manager?*

A *lead manager*, also called a *managing underwriter*, is an entity—typically an investment bank—that represents an *underwriting group*, also known as *syndicate*, in the purchase and distribution of a new securities offering. The managing underwriter helps form the selling group, acts as an agent for it (as authorized by an agreement among underwriters), decides the allotment each group member will have, and engages in buying and selling during the offering period in an attempt to reduce the volatility of the share prices. As such, the managing underwriter acts as a broker-dealer for the securities, as explained above.

Lead managers (typically large investment banking firms) may buy large blocks of stock and then place them with institutional investors or with retail brokerage firms. Alternatively, they may put together selling syndicates of retail brokerage firms that in turn sell the stocks to their individual customers.

In return for the service it provides, the lead manager of an underwriting is paid a fee from the syndicate's gross profits. Lead managers can earn substantial amounts for performing these services. In 1996, a strong IPO year, Goldman Sachs served as lead manager for 50 issues, worth a total of $9.6 billion.

What are underwriting *comanagers*?

Sometimes there may be more than one lead manager. For example, in the $904.5 million IPO of Heller Financial Inc. in April 1998, Goldman Sachs and J. P. Morgan both served as lead manager.[4]

Do underwriters also typically offer advisory services?

Many large firms involved in underwriting offer advisory services to their clients, but smaller firms tend to concentrate on underwriting. Advisory services include advice about what to buy, how to approach the buyer, and how to structure the transactions. Some underwriters, in their broad role as investment bankers, offer fairness opinions on transactions.

According to a study by the National Association of Securities Dealers (NASD), the percentage of underwriters also offering advisory services breaks down as follows:

- 43 percent of firms underwriting $20 million or more
- 14 percent of firms underwriting $10 million to just under $20 million
- 8 percent of firms underwriting less than $10 million[5]

Smaller firms that offer advisory services tend to specialize by industry.

What kind of risk do underwriters generally run, and what kinds of returns do they generally make?

Underwriters often buy, or take responsibility for selling, the full amount of an offering at a guaranteed minimum price—a practice called *firm commitment*. If the actual sale price collected from broker-dealers or investors is lower than the guarantee, underwriters lose money, and if it is higher than the guarantee, they gain money. The potential risk or return from an issue depends, then, on the difference between the actual sale price when the shares first enter the market and the underwriter's guarantee—a difference called the *underwriting spread*.

Don't underwriters have a natural interest in making a very low guarantee? How can issuers make sure that the underwriter's guarantee is as high as the market will bear?

Underwriters want to attract all categories of investors—both those who know the value of an issue and those who do not—so they tend to underprice. The average underpricing is as low as 5 percent for very large issues and as high as 40 percent for very small issues. On the other hand, there are some natural limits to underpricing. If underwriters overprice too much, they will lose investors. If they underprice too much, they will lose issuers.[6]

In most offerings, pricing is a matter of negotiation between the issuer and the managing underwriter, who has an exclusive bid on the sale of the securities. In fact, *negotiated underwriting* is a technical term, which means the sale of securities through a single managing underwriter, as opposed to *competitive underwriting* through several underwriters. These terms are somewhat misleading, since market dynamics ensure that negotiated underwritings are as competitive as those called "competitive" because they involve multiple underwriting bids. Multibidder underwriting is very rare in corporate securities offerings and even in municipal offerings—except for municipal general obligation bonds, which by law may require multibidder underwriting.

How can underwriters reduce the risk of losing money if the underwriting spread is low or negative?

Instead of working on a *firm commitment* basis, underwriters can work on an *agency* basis, also known as a *best-effort* basis. In both of these cases, the offering price is assured and the maximum number of shares is specified. But in a best-effort offering, the underwriter pledges to sell as much as it can, but not to buy (or promise to sell) the full offering. If, for example, the underwriter sells only half the issue, it receives only half its commission.

Could you elaborate on the difference between a firm commitment basis and a best-effort basis?

The typical firm commitment offering involves a large company making a large issue. Even if the underwriter/broker fails to sell the minimum, its offer to buy the shares will stand. Underwriters are usually from major investment banks, and buyers are usually major institutional investors. The initial value of the issue is fairly certain, and there is relatively low volatility in the *aftermarket*—that is, the earliest period of market trading.

The situation is precisely the opposite for a best-effort offering. This type of offering typically involves a small company making a small issue. If the underwriter cannot sell the minimum, it may refuse to buy the shares, thus in effect canceling the IPO. Underwriters tend to be from smaller investment banks, and buyers may be individuals. The initial value of the issue is relatively uncertain, and aftermarket volatility is relatively high.

What if a company offers to sell its shares, but only some of the shares get bought?

If the shortfall is too great, it may not be worth the cost of the underwriting. This is why some new issuers have an "all or none" agreement that entitles them to cancel the entire offering unless it is fully subscribed.

What kinds of fees are involved in an IPO of equity?

In IPOs, the combined costs of underwriting, advisory, and indirect costs can reach as high as 21 percent for smaller issues—even higher in some cases.[7] Table 8-1 shows each typical IPO cost as a percentage of total offering sales. It contrasts large issues (over $100 million) with very small issues (under $2 million). The results show that the total for underwriting fees plus expenses can range from 11 percent to 24 percent, depending on whether the issue is large or small (small issues are more expensive, percentage-wise), and depending on whether the issuance is a done on a firm commitment or best-effort basis (best-effort issues tend to be more expensive). The underwriter and the broker split the fee.[8]

Aside from underwriting fees, what other costs can an issuer incur?

Perhaps the most important cost is the opportunity cost—what the company's management would be doing with its time if it were not involved in the process of issuing the securities. In the case of an IPO, these costs include the value of the considerable time the company spends in going public and then operat-

T A B L E 8–1

Cost of Initial Public Offerings

	Firm Commitment Basis		Best-Effort Basis	
	Large Issues	Small Issues	Large Issues	Small Issues
Underwriter fees	7%	10%	8%	11%
Other direct expenses	2	10	2	10
Indirect expenses	1.5	3	1.5	3
Total	10.5	23	11.5	24

Source: J. Fred Weston and Thomas Copeland, *Managerial Finance*, 9th ed. (Los Angeles: Academic Press, 1998), p. 902.

ing as a public company. Expert James B. Arkebauer, a source for this chapter as noted throughout, says that 30 hours a week for six months is not unusual.

Beyond opportunity cost, the issuing company may incur various fees, including those for accountants, attorneys, financial printers, and transfer agents, as well as the costs of promotion and registration. The best way to estimate these costs is to use *percentages*, as suggested in Table 8–1. This is because dollar amounts vary so widely. For example, here are the going dollar ranges for IPO services as of 1998.[9]

- *Accountants' fees.* The simplest start-up IPO will cost at least $5,000 and may rise to $15,000. Accounting work for existing companies, according to Arkebauer, range from $20,000 to $60,000—with extremely complex audits of large companies rising up to $100,000.
- *Lawyers' fees.* On a small IPO (defined as $8 million and under), this expense can vary between $30,000 and $80,000. Legal fees for a start-up shell can be as low as $20,000. This service involves filing for incorporation prestructured for public company operation, followed by a registration statement and IPO.
- *Printers' fees.* Printing costs can range from $10,000 to $100,000.
- *Transfer agents' fees.* These agents issue shares when the orders come in. This service requires an initial setup fee of $1,000 to $10,000, plus a continuing maintenance costs.

- *Registration fees.* There are several of these, including a fee to the Securities and Exchange Commission (SEC) (.029 percent of maximum dollar amount of securities being registered), state filing fees, called Blue Sky regulations (from $10 to $1,000), and fees for stock exchange listing. For example, the NASD's fee is $500 plus 0.01 percent of the offering's maximum amount, up to $35,000, and listing on the association's automatic quotations board, or Nasdaq, is $5,000 plus a maintenance fee.

Obviously, with such wide ranges in fees, the percentage approach is best when trying to gauge cost.

INVESTMENT BANKS

You mentioned that investment banks often underwrite securities sales. What exactly is an investment bank and what does it do?

An investment bank is neither an investor nor a bank. That is, it does not invest its own money permanently, and it does not act as a repository for other people's funds.

Rather, an investment bank is an intermediary between saving and investing. An investment bank, in its broadest definition, is a financial institution that helps operating companies raise debt and equity capital in securities markets.

One common function of an investment bank is underwriting—the purchase and resale of a new offering of equity securities, as mentioned above. Investment banks also help market the new stock, distributing it to retail stock brokers, often through a retail brokerage unit affiliated directly with the bank. These brokerage units in turn may have securities analysts who make buy, sell, or hold recommendations on particular issues.

In addition to their involvement in initial public offerings of stock, other common investment banking functions include:

- Advice on private placements
- Structuring and execution of equity and equity-based transactions
- Financing, structuring, and execution of mergers, acquisitions, buyouts, and spin-offs

In addition, some investment banking houses are affiliated with retail brokerage firms that sell stocks to clients, sometimes offering securities analysis—recommendations on whether to buy, hold, or sell particular stocks.

Could you give a step-by-step explanation of how an underwriting might work at an investment bank?

A business needs $10 million to buy another company. It interviews a number of investment bankers, selects one, and holds initial planning meetings for a new offering of equity securities. (This example works equally well if the securities issued are debt securities—that is, bonds rather than stock.)

On a specific day, the investment banker presents the company with a check for $10 million, less commission. In return, the investment banker receives stock in denominations of $40 each to sell to the public. (Bond denominations would typically be $1,000.) The company receives the $10 million before the investment banker has sold the stock.

Between the time the business is paid the $10 million and the time its stock is sold, the investment banker bears all the risk of market price fluctuations in the stock. This risk can be high, because in the time it takes to sell the shares, there may be a market downturn. If an investment banker counts on selling the shares of a new high-tech company for $40 over a period of a few weeks, but there is an overnight market sell-off of high-tech stocks, then the investment banker will sustain a loss. If underwriters see this coming, they may cancel a planned initial public offering of stocks (or a new bond offering).

What are the basic steps of an underwriting?

First, the key officers of the issuing company and the investment banker hold meetings or *preunderwriting conferences* at which they discuss the amount of capital to be raised, the type of security to be issued, and the terms of the agreement. The treasurer of the issuing company will write memoranda to the company's board of directors and senior management describing proposals suggested at the conferences.

Directors of the issuing company (or a standing or special committee of the board) discuss the alternatives at a scheduled or special meeting and, eventually, make a *go or no-go decision.*

If the decision is a no-go, the would-be issuer should receive a thorough explanation for this decision, and guidance on "coming back to the well" at a later time.

Before giving up, the potential issuer should seek a second opinion and sometimes even a third. If there is broad consensus that this is not the time for an equity offering, the issuer needs to respect this professional judgment and follow the advice received.

If the decision is a go, then the next step is for the issuer and the investment banker to enter an *agreement* (which may be done by handshake or in writing) to proceed with a flotation. The investment banker then begins to conduct an underwriting *investigation*.

This investigation, also called due diligence, requires looking at *operations, accounting, legal,* and *strategic* aspects of the company, among others. If the company is proposing to purchase a company and/or additional assets with the proceeds of the stock issuance, the underwriter's engineering staff may analyze the proposed acquisition. A public accounting firm is called upon to make an audit of the issuing company's financing situation and also helps prepare the registration statements (see below) in connection with these issues for the SEC. A law firm is called in to analyze the legal aspects of the flotation. In addition, the originating underwriter (who is the manager of the subsequent underwriting syndicate) makes an exhaustive investigation of the issuing company's overall strategic prospects.

When the investigation is over, the issuer and the investment banker draw up an *underwriting agreement*. Terms of the tentative agreement may be modified through continued discussions between the underwriter and the issuing company, but in the end, there will be a *final agreement*. This will cover all underwriting terms except the price of the securities.

The next step is the filing of a *registration* statement with the SEC. Applicable law (the Securities Exchange Act of 1933) sets a 20-day *examination period* (also called a waiting period), which may be shortened or lengthened by the SEC. The SEC staff uses this time to analyze the registration statement to determine whether there are any omissions or misrepresentations of fact. During the examination period, the SEC may file exceptions to the registration statement, or ask for additional information from the issuing company or the underwriters. The investment bankers are not permitted to offer the securities for sale at this time, although they may print a *preliminary prospectus* with all the customary information, except the offering price.

At the end of the registration period, *pricing* for the offer is determined. There is no universal practice, but in one common arrangement the investment banker charges a *gross underwriter spread,* which is a percentage of the offering price for equity issues. It can range from a few percentage points for large offerings to 11 percent for small offerings.[10]

What are the main steps of underwriting?

Thee 10 basic steps of underwriting are shown below.

10 Steps of Underwriting

1. Preunderwriting conferences
2. Go or no-go decision
3. Agreement to proceed with the flotation (by handshake or in writing)
4. Investigation (operations, accounting, legal, *and* strategic)
5. Initial underwriting agreement (in writing)
6. Final underwriting agreement (in writing)
7. Filing of registration statement
8. 20-day examination period
9. Printing of preliminary prospectus
10. Pricing of the offering

Could you give an example of the pricing process?

Sure. The stock of Wilcox Chemical Company was selling at $38.00, and had traded between $35.00 and $40.00 per share during the previous three months. The company and the underwriter agreed that the investment bankers would buy 200,000 shares at $2.50 below the closing price on the last day of registration. The stock closed at $36.00 on the day the SEC released the issue, so the company received $33.50 per share.

How can an issuer avoid getting locked into a bad deal?

Typically, pricing agreements have an escape clause that provides for the contract to be voided if the price of the securities falls below some set figure—called an *upset price*. In the case of Wilcox, this price was set at $34.00 per share. Thus, if the closing price of the shares on the last day of registration had been $33.50, Wilcox would have had the option of withdrawing from the agreement.

How long does it typically take to do a stock offering?

From start to finish, the typical initial public offering takes approximately six months. It is important not to drag it out too long. As middle market investment banker Russell Robb has observed, "For any given deal there is a limited window of opportunity. If you spend too much time raising equity after the target company is in play, the window will close."[11]

Any comments on the timing of doing an M&A deal?

The legendary average is six months, but it may take less or more depending on several factors. One important factor is the reason for the transaction. If the participants are joining forces because they need to beat a competitor to the punch, the deal may be struck in days and closed in weeks. At the other extreme, if a relatively young founder is selling out to a large company in which he or she will have no future management role, the deal may drag on for months while the buyer courts the founder and the founder wrestles with doubts. Also, regulatory problems can slow any transaction. In major transactions challenged by antitrust authorities, it can take well over a year before the parties receive a green light. And in all these cases, there is always an even chance that the deal may never close.[12]

You have explained how investment bankers are paid for underwriting an offering. Suppose they also help the issuer use the proceeds of the offering to buy a company. How are they paid then?

Investment bankers that advise in the acquisition of a company charge fees in one or more of four ways: an accomplishment fee using some formula based on purchase price, such as the Lehman formula (see below) or a modified version of it; retainers; flat fees; and/or a piece of the action.

What is the Lehman formula?

The Lehman formula, which dates back to the 1950s, is named after the Lehman Brothers, who founded the company bearing their name—now a unit of American Express. Nicknames for the formula include the "Lehman scale," the "M&A formula," and the "Wall Street rule." This is a sliding scale—generally the 5-4-3-2-1 formula: 5 percent of the first $1 million of the price of the transaction, 4 percent of the second, 3 percent of the third, 2 percent of the fourth, and 1 percent of the balance.

In the 1950s and early 1960s perhaps 75 percent of the fees were computed in this manner. Thus, a $5 million deal would call for a fee of $150,000, a $25 million deal would call for a $350,000, and a $50 million deal would call for $600,000. In larger transactions, the final 1 percent might drop down to 0.5 percent at the $50 million to $100 million level, or $850,000 for a $100 million deal. As the deals got larger, sometimes a cap was put on the fee by agreement, such as "no fee to exceed $2 million." Generally, in transactions above $100 million, the fee was and is negotiated. An $800 million transaction might call for a base fee in the $2 million to $5 million range rather than a fee of $8.1 million dictated by the straight 5-4-3-2-1 Lehman scale.

What is a modified Lehman formula?

This is a fee scale that is based on Lehman, but with some difference. Variations include the double Lehman, of 10-8-6-4-2, and the stuttering Lehman of 5-5-4-4-3-3.

Here is how a $5 million deal would look using all three types of fees.

T A B L E 8–2

Commission Amounts For a $5 Million IPO

Type of Commission	Amount	Overall Percentage
Double Lehman (10-8-6-4-2)	$300,000	6.0
Stuttering Lehman (5-5-4-4-3-3)	$201,000	4.2
Lehman (5-4-3-2-1)	$150,000	3.0

Source: Reprinted with permission from Russell Robb, *Buying Your Own Business* (Holbrook, MA: Adams Media Corporation, 1995), p. 115.

Why are retainers charged, and what kind of money is involved?

Retainers are fairly common in smaller transactions involving smaller, independent investment banks, since unlike major multibillion-dollar banks, the advisers cannot afford to risk nonpayment.

According to one report,[13] monthly retainers for such transactions may run from $5,000 to $15,000, or there may be a one-time up-front retainer payment between $20,000 and $50,000. Another issue to negotiate is whether the investment banker deducts all, half, or none of the retainer from the accomplishment fee. Alternatively, an investment bank might say that it will deduct the retainer from the accomplishment fee, as long as the minimum fee is not less than, say, $200,000.

What about flat fees—what's the story there?

Many finders who build themselves up as "investment bankers," though they have only a phone number and an office, try to get Lehman scale for their services, but usually are forced to settle for a flat fee or to sue. Some have successfully sued and collected very large fees using the Lehman scale.

Fees are sometimes modified by the type of deal. Now, in the late 1990s, many of the deals are done with an exchange of securities. These deals are relatively uncomplicated and call for reduced fees. By contrast, a very complicated leveraged buyout (LBO) may require a high fee.

Hostile deals carry much larger fees than friendly deals, especially when they are successful. In a hostile deal, bankers might be involved for many months or even years. In such deals, however, in the heat of battle, many a tendering corporation has failed to reach a final fee agreement with the bankers, lawyers, consultants, accountants, and others that may be involved until after the deal is closed. Then there may be problems, which sometimes wind up in court with a judge or jury making the fee decisions. Juries are particularly tough on finder's and broker's fees that are legally due; they find it hard to believe that the simple act of introducing a potential seller to a potential buyer is worth a large sum.

The fee payment often depends on the final price paid in the deal. But determining the final "price" in a complicated, highly leveraged deal with equity kickers such as detachable warrants and rights, simultaneous spin-offs or spin-outs, or sales of subsidiaries can be very difficult. As a result, more and more fees are negotiated ahead of time in round numbers.[14]

During the 1980s, when the LBO movement was on, it was common practice for the finder or broker, as part of or in addition to its fee, to make a "bargain purchase" of some of the original stock—say, 1 percent of the equity—as an added inducement to bring a deal to a successful closing. As we move into the next millennium, we may see a recurrence of this practice as consolidation in advisory firms (such as investment banks) leads to layoffs. As former employees become entrepreneurs, there was a boom in the independent finder-broker population—and a consequent rise in such creative fee making.

Taken all together, what kinds of fees can major investment banks and other M&A advisers generate in a year?

In 1998, advisers disclosed fees on 498 deals for a total of $2.7 billion, with sellers paying most of that amount ($1.8 billion versus some $900 million). The top 10 M&A intermediaries that year generated an annual total of $2 billion, with the top performer, Goldman Sachs, making over $403 million. Others in the top 10 for the year were, in descending order: Merrill Lynch; Morgan Stanley/Dean Witter; Salomon Smith Barney; Credit Suisse First Boston; Lehman Brothers; Donaldson, Lufkin & Jenrette; Lazard Freres; B. T. Alex Brown/Wolfensohn; and J. P. Morgan. All the intermediaries in this top-grossing group were investment banks—and almost all were securities firms as well. The 10 next biggest earners of M&A advisory fees were primarily investment banks, but the list also included two commercial banks—Bank of America and Chase Manhattan.

Judging from this list, one would think that most M&A intermediary work is done by investment banks. Is this true?

The majority of fees are indeed paid to investment banks, which dominate in the largest deals. Other advisers (particularly for smaller deals) include commercial banks and accounting firms. For example, in 1998, Bank of America, KPMG Peat Marwick, and PricewaterhouseCoopers ranked among the top 10 highest-earning advisers for transactions under $100 million.

Aren't there conflicts of interest among these roles of advising, underwriting, and analysis?

Clearly there can be. That is why investments banks construct "Chinese walls" between their advisory and securities side. Managers working on the advisory side have inside information that is not supposed to reach the analysts on the securities side. Conversely, analysts are presumed to be neutral, a stance that could be weakened by deal brokering. Sometimes, however, the Chinese walls are thin—or even internalized, with the same person fulfilling two or more roles.[15]

Are investment banking firms the sole source of underwriting activity?

No. Through special Federal Reserve grants of permission, commercial banks have developed a strong presence in underwriting activities. On any list of the top 20 underwriting firms for a given year, the underwriting departments of commercial banks are likely to have at least two or three spots on the list.

M&A ACTIVITIES AMONG FINANCIAL INSTITUTIONS

What has been happening in the relationships between commercial banks, investment banks, and other financial institutions?

A high level of M&A activity has been taking place. Mergers between commercial banks and between investment bankers have been among the largest M&As announced in recent years. The merger between Dean Witter and Morgan Stanley, a $10 billion deal, was the combination of a large retail brokerage firm (Dean Witter) with a large investment banking operation. The Travelers Group combination with Citicorp was a $70 billion deal. The Travelers Group consisted of investment banking, consumer finance, and a wide range of insurance activities. Citicorp was engaged in global consumer and global corporate banking. Hundreds of mergers between commercial banks have been taking place. The largest was combining NationsBank with Bank of America, a $59 billion deal.

What is driving all these mergers between financial institutions?

This increased competition puts pressure on fees that can be charged and the necessity for lowering costs to protect profit margins. The use of computers and other high-tech equipment requires large investments which the banks seek to spread over larger volumes of business in different kinds of activities.

What is the significance for the broadening of financial institutions into large department stores of financial services for M&A financing?

There is more competition among financial institutions to provide new and innovative financial services, including online services through the Internet. M&A financing is facilitated by a large range of equity sources and increased competition among them to get the deals done. We will explore this topic further in upcoming chapters, particularly Chapter 11, which covers the controversial topic of "one-stop shopping" for financing.

CONCLUDING COMMENTS

In December 1997, economist George Newman wrote the seventieth and, alas, the last of an unbroken series of brilliant columns for The Conference Board.

The series, entitled "Uncommon Sense," revealed the many facets of Newman's genius as a financial thinker.

Significantly, the last column was a ringing defense of investment bankers, one of the chief sources of equity-based financing. Entitled "Blessed Are the Deal Makers," this column defended so-called paper shuffling, especially the work of underwriters and others who help create markets for financing, including merger financing.

In his opening, Newman sets up the problem: "Critics of the 'greedy '80s' reserved their most virulent attacks for Wall Street 'paper shufflers' who created no tangible product and were, therefore, useless parasites. On top of that, they siphoned off potentially productive capital to sterile paper transactions."

Newman's essay refutes all these negative accusations, which often used as their straw dog the lessons of *Other People's Money*, a stage and film classic featuring financier "Larry the Liquidator." Newman redeems Larry and other financiers.

All in all, Wall Street does have an impact on ownership and management and that, in turn, influences behavior and performance. To the uninitiated, Larry and all the Larries on Wall Street appear only to shuffle papers with no consequence. But by facilitating mergers and LBOs and financing small business, the Larries very much affect the quantity of oil discovered, the number of airlines that stay in business, and the emergence of Apples, CNNs, and Microsofts.

In conclusion, let us consider the equity-financed growth of thousands of businesses in the United States and beyond. Whether this growth occurs through independent expansion or through M&A, it is certainly a positive force.

E N D N O T E S

1. In France, for example, Morgan Stanley offers a Société d'Investissement à Capitale Variable (SICAV), which is in effect a mutual fund. In promoting its SICAV, Morgan Stanley has stated (for example, in a *Financial Times* ad of December 30, 1996), "The exclusive purpose of the Company is to invest the funds available to it in transferable securities and other assets permitted by law with the purpose of spreading investment risks and affording its shareholders the results of the management of its assets."

2. Whether the deal is done in house or split, the usual breakdown is about 30 percent for the underwriter and 70 percent for the broker. If the deal is syndicated, the syndication members keep 10 percent of the deal, leaving 60 percent for the broker.

3. This is the number of brokerage firms listed in the 1998 edition of Standard & Poor's *Security Dealers of North America.*

4. *IPO Journal,* August 1998. This is a new publication—in fact, August 1998 was its Volume 1, No. 1.

5. James B. Arkebauer and Ron Schultz, *Going Public: Everything You Need to Know to Take Your Company Public, Including Internet Direct Public Offerings,* 3rd ed. (Chicago: Dearborn Financial Publishing, 1998).

6. See Randolph P. Beatty and Ray R. Ritter, "Investment Banking, Reputation, and the Underpricing of Initial Public Offerings," *Journal of Financial Economics,* 15 (1986), pp. 213ff. In this classic paper, Beatty and Ritter discover an equilibrium in IPO pricing, despite seemingly chronic underpricing.

7. One study showed a high of 41.14 percent for these combined expenses. Ibid.

8. See note 2.

9. Ibid.

10. Part of this expense is called the nonaccountable expense allowance, a flat fee that the underwriter or broker takes off the top regardless of cost. This allowance is between 1 and 3 percent of the total cost, with smaller issues costing the higher percentage. Ibid.

11. Russell Robb, *Buying Your Own Business* (Holbrook, MA: Adams Media Corporation, 1995), p. 283.

12. Robb, ibid., states that 50 percent of all deals never close. This figure is consistent with the deal fallout rates tracked by Securities Data Publishing in *Mergers & Acquisitions.*

13. Russell Robb, "Some Thoughts for Investment Bankers," *M&A Today,* October 1998, pp. 10ff.

14. See "M&A Services," *Mergers & Acquisitions,* March/April 1998, pp. 62ff.

15. For example, at Solomon Brothers Inc., the same individual played the role of securities analyst and deal broker. See "Jack of All Trades: How One Top Analyst Vaults 'Chinese Wall' to Do Deals for Firm," *The Wall Street Journal,* March 25, 1997, pp. 1ff.

CHAPTER 9

Working with "Backers"

But at my back I always hear;
Time's winged chariot hurrying near.

Andrew Marvell, "To His Coy Mistress" (1650–1652)

INTRODUCTION

Backers form the third basic source of capital, providing debt or equity capital as needed. Although some backers might be strictly classified as providers of debt, and others as providers of equity, the true backer is not wedded to one type of financing, but does whatever it has to do to achieve returns. As such, the backer provides, almost by definition, a "hybrid" of capital sources in order to ensure growth during a time of change.

The most common type of backer is the private equity fund, but this is by no means the only type. Backers may be individuals somehow affiliated with a venture—a backer may be your brother; she may be your sister—or any other relative or friend. Or backers may simply be "angels"—wealthy individuals who invest in new or struggling ventures. Alternatively, backers may be suppliers who give extended credit terms to a customer. At a greater remove, backers may be credit card companies that give a generous credit limit for the self-employed owner of a small new company, or finance companies that offer nontraditional loans.

With such a great variety of backers in existence, we cannot hope to cover them all in this brief chapter. We can, however, paint a fairly representative picture of the kinds of resources that may be available for M&A financing beyond traditional sources of debt and equity capital.

BACKERS AND PRIVATE EQUITY FINANCING

What is a backer, and what types of financing sources get involved as backers?

Backers provide financing to private companies or to public companies going private. They may do this by buying equity, or by making a loan in return for an additional equity position. They often do so in the hopes of making a large return on their investment when those same companies go public or return to being public.

Any type of M&A capital source may participate in "backing" a company through the private equity or lending route. As listed in Chapter 1 and echoed in Chapter 7, these range from asset-based lenders such as factors and leasing companies to venture capital firms.

Literally hundreds of detailed examples are listed in leading directories. For example, the *Directory of Buyout Financing Sources* (New York: Securities Data Publishing, 1999) lists 1,002 firms. Each one has its own unique combination of requirements and characteristics.

Could you give an example of a backer?

Take the firm Houlihan, Lokey, Howard & Zukin (HLHZ). In the Securities Data directory, given a choice of 10 categories, it classifies itself as a "merchant bank" and an "investment division of an investment bank." It also names Churchill ESOP Capital Partners as an affiliated investment partnership.

Founded in 1972, HLHZ began backing leveraged buyouts (LBOs) in 1994. Since that time, it has bought into at least nine companies, often beginning as a mezzanine capital provider. It will function as either a deal originator or an investor in deals created by others. It can act independently, or through coinvestments with limited partners in particular transactions.

Since its inception, HLHZ has invested some $188 million in LBOs. It provides mezzanine financing through notes and/or securities in private placements, and it obtains equity participation through warrants ("preferred" but not required). In a 1998 press release, it calls itself an "appraisal firm, a valuation firm, an employee stock ownership plan (ESOP) firm, a solvency firm, a restructuring firm, and an investment banking firm."

This is not to say that all backers defy categories. Other backers include a *venture capital firm*, a *private equity fund*, an *insurance company investment unit*, and a *commercial finance company*. All these different providers of finance may be referred to as backers, or more technically, as providers of *private equity fi-*

nancing. For a sample announcement of a start-up private equity fund, see Appendix 9–A. For profiles of various types of equity sources, see Appendix 9–B.

What is private equity financing?

Private equity financing (a technical term for the activities of backers) is investment raised through private offerings or other nonpublic means in order to buy equity in private companies, or in public companies in order to take them private. The most common type of private equity financing is known as venture capital.

What is venture capital?

Venture capital is money invested at a relatively high risk and potentially high return in a newly formed company or a small company specializing in new technologies. The venture capitalist typically seeks capital gain, rather than interest income or dividend yield. In 1997, some 113 venture capital funds raised $10.4 billion, according to *Private Equity Analyst*, a trade journal. The individual venture capitalist or the venture capital group typically takes a major stake in the high-risk company in return for common stock, often supplemented by common stock warrants, or convertibles. (As explained in Chapter 5, common stock warrants are rights to buy the company's common stock at a set price, and convertibles are debentures or preferred stock purchased with an option to convert to common stock.)

Venture capital goes through several stages—from "seed" capital on a trial basis to the "exit" stage when a stake is sold. At each stage, the stake increases. By the time the object of investment goes public (or returns to being a public company), the venture capitalist may own as much as 80 percent of its equity. We discuss this point below in more detail.

The venture capitalist may also help the company obtain debt financing, by helping it seek a commercial bank loan, or by providing the funds itself. When loans are made, the repayment is generally in the form of the right to exercise convertibles or warrants.

As a type of private equity financing, the venture capital investor makes investments in privately held companies (or public companies that are going private). It holds the investment long enough to experience appreciation of share price—usually five years, which has earned it the nickname "patient capital." As a *Forbes* article once noted, the venture capital investor is "patient, but not too patient."[1] The big payoff can be when the company goes public.

This may mean going public for the first time in an initial public offering (IPO), or it may mean returning to public ownership in a *reverse buyout*.

Venture capital expects a relatively high return for its investment, because of the riskiness of venture capital investments. Many venture capital funds require a 35 percent return on investment (see for example the first profile in Appendix 9–B). This high target is set in part because the rate of loss in overall investments is so high—with approximately one third yielding negative returns. The average return on venture capital investments (taking into account both investments that exceed high targets and those that lose money) has ranged between 12.5 and 24 percent in recent years.[2] The return is often realized when the company receiving the venture capital money goes public—whether in an initial public offering or, in the case of a company that has gone private using the venture capitalists' money, in a reverse buyout.

What is the difference between venture capital and private equity capital?

The terms are often used interchangeably, but each has its own nuance. The term venture capital, as mentioned, refers to a significant investment made in a new venture or technology—often by an individual person or entity. (When an individual person makes an investment, he or she is often called an "angel," as described below.) The term private equity capital, by contrast, generally refers to funds raised to buy equity via a private offering—that is, an offering that is exempt from registration under the Securities Act of 1933.

In recent years, the two terms have intersected somewhat. In the past, venture capitalists worked without a formal structure. Increasingly (ever since the 1980s LBO boom and the entrance of pension funds into the venture capital arena), they are forming funds to make their investments along with other investors. One common vehicle is a private equity fund, such as an LBO fund, which make equity investments in multiple companies. Private equity funds that came to market in 1998 raised over $30 billion for LBOs alone.[3] This was up considerably from most previous years.[4] Less than one third of all private equity funds can be considered "venture capital" funds.[5]

Investors in these funds may be individuals or institutions, but over the past two decades, the role of institutions has grown while the role of individual venture capitalists has diminished. Individual investors are now the smallest source of capital for private equity funds, and taken together with families, they are one of the smallest sources. In 1981, for example, individuals and families invested 23 percent of all venture capital funds. They were rivaled only by pension funds, which had begun such investments in 1980 because of changes in pension law—a liberalization of investment policy for corporate pension funds subject to the Employee Retirement Income Security Act of 1974 (ERISA). Today, individuals and families contribute only 12 percent of venture capital funds compared to 46 percent for pension funds.[6]

Another force separating venture capital from its entrepreneurial roots has been the trend for large commercial or investment banks or even large corporations to form venture capital subsidiaries. The parent-subsidiary relationship in these cases tends to increase the conservatism of investments. So does the involvement of public and private pension funds, which have held about 40 percent of all venture capital funds for the past decade.[7]

Pension funds are under legal obligation to maximize returns to beneficiaries. Pension funds for public sector employees, called *public pension funds,* are regulated under the Taft-Hartley Act of 1947, and pension funds for private sector employees, called *private pension funds,* are regulated under ERISA. Both of these laws say that fiduciaries of funds and the agents of fiduciaries (such as investment managers) must safeguard the wealth of fund beneficiaries.[8] This is very different from an individual venture capitalist investing in a company to enhance his or her own wealth.

Thus the role of the individual "venture capitalist"—both as a lone investor and as an investor within a fund—has been waning, while the role of institutions has been increasing. In turn, the old truism about venture capital (and, by association, private equity) being a "high risk, high return" type of investment no longer holds. Since the role of individuals has declined, so has the level of both risks and returns. Scholars have noted that returns have declined since the 1980s for many reasons, including the "rising valuation of deals caused by increased competition, greater focus on late-stage investments with lower risks and expected returns, and, possibly, a reduction in the quality of venture capitalists' decision making."[9]

What is a private equity fund?

As stated in Chapter 5, a *private equity fund* is a limited partnership formed to invest in a private company, such as a start-up or a buyout—that is, a unit of a formerly public company that has been taken private. Investors in such funds include public pension funds, private pension funds, endowments and foundations, banks, finance companies (either owned independently by venture capitalists or owned by a larger corporation such as AT&T or GE), family trusts, insurance companies, money managers, and individuals. Of all these investors, finance companies are the most likely to work as venture capitalists, typically taking a 20 percent position, with other investors, typically institutional investors (as listed above), dividing the remaining 80 percent.[10]

If I have a deal to propose to a private equity fund, what are my chances of success?

About 1 percent, on average. According to one study, these funds invest in about one out of every 100 deals they study.[11]

How long do private equity funds normally last before being liquidated—that is, sold off or distributed in kind to investors?

A decade is fairly typical. During the first five years, the fund monitors all the investments closely. Over the next five years—give or take two years—the fund sells off investments gradually, with all investments sold or distributed in kind to investors by the end of the period.

Some funds keep rolling forward, buying stock in companies and selling off enough stock to pay off investors, but keeping the remainder of the stock in their growing portfolio.

In discussing backers so far, you have focused on buyouts. What is the connection?

A *buyout* by definition involves a change in ownership that puts a company in the control of a few dedicated lenders or investors. The buyout may involve a private company, a public company, or a unit of a public company. Most buyouts involve a large amount of debt capital—hence, the term *leveraged* buyouts. Securities Data Publishing in Newark, New Jersey, uses these three categories to classify LBOs as *going-private, divestiture,* and *private market* LBOs.

If an LBO involves a public company or unit, it is a true "buy *out*" from public equity markets into the private domain. This can be a significant shift. By their very nature, backers do more than lend money or buy equity; they usually provide advice along with their capital. This is clearly a rare occurrence in the public company milieu, where broadly held ownership dilutes the potential control that might be achieved by any owner—or lender, for that matter. Yet there are public companies—or units within companies—that can benefit from a backer's attentions.

Here is where a buyout comes in. By buying all the shares of a public company and thus taking it private, or by buying a unit from a public company, a group of backers can gain control of a company and then make it benefit from their advice.

In most LBOs, the previous managers stay on. When they also become owners, investing in the company through their own cash or through sweat equity (receiving reduced pay in return for an up-front ownership position), the arrangement is called a management buyout (MBO). MBOs can occur in all types of LBOs—going-private, divestiture, and private market.

How common are these various types of LBOs, and how much money do they involve?

First, in terms of the percentage of the entire M&A market, LBOs are becoming rare. In 1989, they comprised 8 percent of all M&A deals and 23 percent of all M&A dollars. Now, a decade later, they constitute about 1 percent of all deals and 1 percent of all dollars. The greatest decline has occurred in the transactions that take public companies private. This is happening more rarely now because of strong stock prices. (As we go to press, the Dow Jones Industrial Average just rose above 10,000 for the first time ever.) Despite their increasing rarity, however, LBOs are considered a major component in private equity financing, and LBO funds are considered to be a very important source of backers.

What is an LBO fund?

An LBO fund is a private equity fund that uses bank debt to acquire companies—typically by taking public companies, or units of public companies, private.

Funds tend to invest in firms with a guaranteed cash flow and/or valuable collateral. Looking at the top 20 industries involvd in LBOs over the last 10 years, this is the trend we see. Consider this list of the top five:

- Business services (including leasing firms) (150 leveraged buyouts worth $4 billion)
- Metal and metal products (115 deals worth $4.6 billion)
- Printing and publishing (88 deals worth $4.2 billion)
- Machinery (83 deals worth $2.8 billion)
- Food (74 deals worth $6.6 billion)

In all these instances, the buyers financed the deal in large part with debt collateralized by the acquired company's assets and revenues.

How can a buyer finance an acquisition with the acquired company's assets and revenues?

As this question implies, LBOs seem to defy conventional buy-sell wisdom. How, one might ask, can the buyer borrow against the assets of the acquired company when it is a different entity and needs the money as a precondition to the acquisition? If a person wants to buy stock in IBM, IBM won't finance it; why is a leveraged buyout different?

The typical leveraged acquisition is not simply a stock purchase, although it often starts as one. A key structuring objective is to cause the assets and revenues of the acquired company to be located in the buyer-borrower. This can be achieved in three different ways:

1. The buyer can acquire the assets and business of the company.
2. The buyer can acquire the stock of the company and immediately thereafter merge with it.
3. Skipping the stock acquisition stage, the buyer and the company can simply merge directly.

If the buyer and company merge, a problem of timing arises at the closing: Payment for the stock purchased by the buyer must be made *before* the merger places the assets of the acquired company in the buyer's possession, but the loan to the buyer cannot be funded until *after* the merger is consummated. To resolve this problem, the parties to the closing agree that all transactions will be treated as occurring *simultaneously* or, for the sticklers, that the seller of the stock will get a promissory note, which is repaid minutes later when the merger documents are filed. Sometimes lenders prefer to have both the buyer and the company named as borrowers on the acquisition loan. Tax or contract compliance questions may be raised by these timing issues, and they should be thought through carefully.

Why would a buyer want to do a highly leveraged buyout? Doesn't this leave the acquired business in a very exposed position?

Certainly it does—this was the great lesson of the 1980s, the era of overleverage. According to *Fortune* writer Gregory Smith, roughly half the magazine's "Deals of the Year" from 1985 to 1990 were experiencing financial troubles by 1991—with some in bankruptcy. Prudently undertaken, however, a high level of debt need not harm postmerger performance. Indeed, there is some evidence that debt-driven mergers do as well as or better than stock-driven mergers.[12] Furthermore, as a mode of payment, debt is an equalizer. Few have the cash or stock already in hand to buy a company, but many can borrow; debt financing enables a buyer with limited resources—in particular, a management group—to own a company. It also gives an investor a chance to reap an enormous return on equity.

One classic example is Thomas H. Lee's 1985 purchase of Sterling Jewelers for $28 million, 90 percent borrowed. He sold the company two years later for $210 million—for a return of 24 times equity. Other LBO successes range from the many successful small and midsize investments by Forstmann Little[13] to successful KKR deals including Duracell, Inc., Owens-Illinois, Inc., and Safeway Stores, Inc. KKR has invested over $10 billion in equity during more than two decades, and has averaged a compound annual return in the mid-20s, compared with a return in the midteens for the Standard & Poor's 500.

But for every example of easy success there is one of precarious struggle. Some investors have experienced both. Investor Donald P. Kelly, who joined with KKR to buy Beatrice Cos. in 1986 with other shareholders, made $3 billion in profits by breaking it up and selling off many of its parts. But Kelly did not do as well with another LBO investment, the 1989 purchase of Envirodyne Industries Inc. (Today, the company is doing better after many transmutations—it went public in a reverse buyout in the mid-1990s, and was renamed Viskase in 1998.)

What have been the largest LBOs in history?

The three largest LBOs in history were 1980s deals engineered by Kohlberg Kravis Roberts & Co. They were the buyouts of RJR Nabisco (a $29.8 billion 1989 buyout in tobacco and food), Beatrice Cos. (a $6.3 billion 1986 buyout in food), and Safeway Stores, Inc. (a $5.3 billion 1986 buyout in grocery stores). No recent deal has reached these levels.

What are some LBO funds currently active in the United States?

In the United States, current leaders include Apollo Advisors; Blackstone Group; Clayton Dubelier & Rice; Forstmann Little; Hicks, Muse Tate, & Furst; Kohlberg Kravis Roberts; Thomas H. Lee; and Texas Pacific Group. Some securities brokerage firms, such as Donaldson, Lufkin & Jenrette, and Lehman Brothers, are also active in this market.

What is a management buyout fund?

A *management buyout fund* is a leveraged buyout fund that has among its principals the managers of the company it is buying. Many leveraged buyout funds are management buyout funds.

244 PART 3   A Closer Look at Sources

Why are LBO and MBO funds considered to be backers?

As mentioned, a backer is a source of capital that makes a direct investment and often provides guidance along with money. This is very typical of LBO and MBO funds—for two reasons.

First, private equity capital in general tends to include a close watch by investors, who take a somewhat higher risk by avoiding the public company registration process in making their investment; to compensate for that risk, they seek a somewhat higher level of control.

Second, when a funding source provides so much capital that the company becomes highly leveraged, it will want a close involvement to ensure responsible postdeal management. As stated in Chapter 7, whenever a high degree of leverage is involved, lenders tend to limit their risks by imposing an intrusive array of covenants—negative and affirmative, financial and operational—upon the borrower. Lenders that receive an equity kicker as part of their deal have a way to stay at the "back" of the borrower to make sure it follows through.

An LBO or MBO combines both of these dynamics, being a private equity deal that includes a high degree of leverage. As such, it is bound to have the traits of a "backed" deal, rather than a passive investment.

Are all funds that invest in private ventures themselves privately held?

No. Although most are structured as partnerships or as investments companies, some are publicly held corporations. The general term for such publicly held investment corporations is investment development companies. The American Research and Development Corporation, one of the first investment development companies, made its fortune by investing $70,000 in 1957 in Digital Equipment Corporation. By 1971, that investment was worth nearly $400 million—and today it would be worth billions.

Another notable example of a publicly held investment fund is Investcorp, a $240 million fund traded on the Bahrain stock exchange. Investcorp, which uses a combination of debt and equity to buy its portfolio companies, has some 300 investors, mostly based in the Middle East. Its targets have included luxury retail names such as Gucci's, Saks Fifth Avenue, and Tiffany's, as well as humbler endeavors such as Prime Service, Inc., a company that rents industrial equipment.[14]

You mentioned that a venture capitalist might loan money and take warrants or convertibles. This is also the case with sources of mezzanine financing and sometimes even senior lenders. What is the difference between a venture capitalist and these lenders?

It's all a matter of risk, with the most senior lender taking the least risk and the venture capitalist taking the most risk.

Some senior lenders take no risk at all, but function just like normal commercial bank term lenders, extending a loan with a stated rate of interest, fixed or variable. Other senior lenders take a small amount of risk, by providing more favorable interest rates in return for a small equity "kicker" in the form of warrants or convertibles. The mezzanine lender takes a more significant portion of its yield through an equity kicker to add to its interest income.

The venture capital or private equity investor, by contrast, has much more invested in the common stock itself. Purchase of junior securities are designed to "fill a hole" in the financing or to ensure some priority over equity holders in the event of liquidation.[15]

Venture capital investments are often characterized as "active." Why?

The venture capital professional will often serve as a board member or as a financial adviser to the company receiving its capital. This differentiates the venture capitalist from other types of investors—both institutional and individual—that hold stocks passively in public companies.

To be sure, institutional and individual investors may take activist stances in particular companies. The 100-plus members of the Council of Institutional Investors certainly take such stances, as do the thousands of individuals who belong to the Investor Rights Association of America. But this activism is a hit-or-miss, issue-oriented process. Not all companies receiving investment capital from these investors ever hear from them, and when they do, it is through proxy resolutions. Such resolutions address particular governance issues such as shareholder voting rights or social issues such as investment in countries that violate human rights—not business matters.[16]

By contrast, the issues that venture capitalists care about and get involved in are supremely ordinary—from pricing to profits. The venture capital investor does not normally insist on voting control via shares (as mentioned, it may own merely warrants or convertibles, rather than common stock), but it does typically insist on active participation as a voting member of the company's board of directors.

How are venture capital and other types of private equity financing used in the M&A process? Isn't such funding normally just devoted to the start-up phase?

Venture capital money usually begins at the start-up phase, but it eventually arrives at the M&A financing stage. In fact, there is a technical term for the process from start-up to M&A—*staged capital commitment*. In this kind of commitment, the venture capitalist agrees to provide capital throughout the life of a company, including its time of growth through M&A activity.

For example, in the first round, it might provide $1 million for the purpose of assembling a management team, developing a business plan, completing engineering specifications, conducting market research, and testing the feasibility of the process. In the second round, it might provide $5 million to build a full-scale manufacturing facility and to market the product. Then, in the third round, with rising revenues, it might provide capital for further expansion and for working capital needs. At this time or a later date, the venture capitalist may want to support an acquisition, a buyout or split-off (purchase of all or part of a subsidiary), or a strategic alliance.

At each round of financing, the original venture capitalist may reevaluate its position and withdraw. Other venture capital sources may be sought for the new level of financing. Venture capital funding may continue into the refinancing stage—even after a merger, buyout, or alliance. (For comments on the role of venture capital groups in equity refinancing, see Chapter 12.)

Some entrepreneurs receive continual backing from venture capital sources over a period of decades, either in the form of second-round financing for their ventures or as they start new ventures.

How does private equity finance fit into "M&A finance"? Can a company use this type of financing in order to buy another company?

Not exactly. The company that receives an infusion of private equity financing is hardly in a position to go out and acquire companies. It is typically in need of cash just to continue operations. But the fund that buys it is itself a mini-M&A machine, often buying and selling a series of companies as a financial acquirer. Although these financial acquirers do not operate their investments over the long term, or integrate them with other acquired companies, they often provide managerial guidance, whether through a board seat (a typical venture capital move) or by providing expert hands-on managers.

Sometimes, financial acquirers will spend a stint of time running a company—and may begin to look like regular operating managers. Consider the time Ted Forstmann, cofounder of Forstmann Little, has put into Gulfstream Aerospace Corp. He could have sold the company at a profit before its full recovery, but "it would have torn my insides out," he told a *Business Week* reporter. Today, Gulfstream is a very profitable company. It reported net profits of $243 million in 1997 after being nearly insolvent in 1993.[17]

What kinds of investment criteria do private equity sources have?

Above all, private equity sources look for a good product or service. They also want good management. However, the turnaround-type funds are prepared to replace management. Beyond this, funds have particular requirements. As suggested earlier, a small financial management company run by a classic "venture capitalist" interested in big returns will be different from a fund composed entirely of institutional investors. In between these two extremes are a variety of financing attitudes.

How can a seeker of M&A financing get a feel for what different funding sources want?

Fortunately, the private equity financing industry has grown large enough to support a minipublishing industry, with numerous directories, guides, and even Internet sites to inform companies of what these sources seek.

For example, Spencer Kleusner's datamerge.com Internet company offers an interactive CD-ROM called Venture Track 2000 that matches users with the venture capital firms most likely to invest in their industry or company type. The software instructs users on custom-tailoring their business plan and presentation to each venture capital firm. It also lists specific questions, concerns, and objections that a given firm may raise, and suggests appropriate responses to each. The software also gives insight into the firm's likely areas of interest; personal/individual preferences of principals; best methods of approach; things to say or not say to particular individuals; investment philosophies or strategies based on past experience; firm background, relationships, and working atmosphere; case studies of past investments; and key contacts.

In the print medium, the *Directory of Buyout Financing Sources*, mentioned earlier, gives a good profile of what sources are looking for, including minimum annual sales of the company to be bought, minimum size of investments or loans considered, preferred size of investments or loans, requirements for management teams, level of equity participation required from management, technology focus (high, medium, low), industry preference, and industries not considered. The directory also indicates the source's geographic coverage.

Some entries (e.g., for insurance firms and banks) list policies of the senior lenders and the mezzanine providers. For senior lenders, the directory lists interest rate policy, maximum size of syndication participation, and lending criteria—for example, loan-to-collateral ratio, ratio of cash flow to debt service, debt-to-equity ratio, and historical earnings. For mezzanine lenders, the directory lists mode of mezzanine financing (notes, private placements, etc.), investment criteria (e.g., total annualized return on investment), and whether warrants are required. Entries for banks and commercial finance companies include collateral advance rates, and loan terms granted on collateral.

For four profiles adapted from the *Directory of Buyout Financing Sources*, see Appendix 9-B.

What are some Web sites I can contact for information?

As mentioned, there is datamerge.com. Also, try these:

- Angel Capital Electronic Network: ace-net.sr.unh.edu (no www. preceding)
- National Venture Capital Association: nvca.org
- Angel Investors Institute: angelinvestors.org
- Venture Capital Resource Library: vfinance.com

This is only a partial list, but as with any Internet search, one good site leads to another.

EXIT STRATEGIES

Commentary on private equity financing often speaks of their "exit." What does it mean to "exit" an investment?

An investor "exits" an investment by selling its shares. The main idea here is to buy low when entering the investment, and to sell high when exiting the investment.

What are the most common exit strategies used by backers?

There are two: IPOs and acquisitions (including LBOs). Between 1984 and 1996, for example, there were 1,137 IPOs of companies that had been backed by venture capital, and at least 1,105 acquisitions (sales) of venture capital-backed companies.[18] Activity has been growing in both areas. In 1980, there were only 27 IPOs involving venture-backed companies and only 28 sales of such companies. In 1994, there were 134 venture-backed IPOs and 97 exits via sale.

It is not surprising that acquisitions and buyouts should rival IPOs as an exit strategy. After all, acquisitions are more common than IPOs. Yearly acquisitions number in the thousand, while IPOs number in the hundreds. Of the nearly 15 million companies operating in the United States (including the tiniest start-ups), only about 1 percent (15,000) are public companies, and the annual number of new public companies is often only about 1 to 10 percent of that number (150 or so per year in a down year—with great years never more than 10 times that number). This gives an investor a very tiny chance of hitting the IPO jackpot. By contrast, every year there are several *thousand* mergers—many of them paying good returns to investors in the companies being bought.

The meaning for backers is clear. Backers of a troubled company can work with it to improve management, then convince the owners to sell to another company—or perhaps to buy it themselves at a premium.[19] By selling their shares to an acquirer (including an MBO group), investors in the purchased company can realize high returns. For example, one investor invested $100,000 in Think Systems in the fall of 1996, and then convinced the company to sell to another company, i2 Technologies Inc. The following spring, the investor doubled his money in just half a year.[20] (For more about angel investors, see below.)

BEYOND PRIVATE EQUITY FINANCING: OTHER TYPES OF BACKING

Do all backers insist on buying private companies or on taking public companies private? Aren't there ways to back public companies?

There are, but they are not common, since the whole notion of backing involves control, and it is very hard to control a public company without converting it into a quasi-private (closely held) entity. It is possible, however, to work with the subsidiary of a public company through a special arrangement.

Could you give an example of backer financing involving a public company?

Here are two recent ones.

In July 1998, Accel Partners, a venture capital firm that specializes in the Internet and communications industries, acquired 15 percent of HireSystems, a subsidiary of Kaplan Educational Centers, which in turn is a subsidiary of the Washington Post Company, a publishing company listed on the New York Stock Exchange. In the typical venture capital mode, the managing partner of Accel began serving on the board of the subsidiary. The venture capital infusion occurred just eight months after Kaplan had acquired HireSystems, which offers Web-based services to help companies recruit and hire personnel. Interestingly, this transaction had an impact similar to a carve-out. As discussed in Chapter 5, a carve-out is the sale of a minority stake in a company through an IPO. The difference here is that no IPO was involved; rather, the transactions was structured in the typical mode of an early venture capital private equity investment.

In September 1998, AMBI Inc., a Nasdaq-listed nutritional products firm, announced the following agreement with American Home Products Corporation (AHP), a New York Stock Exchange-listed corporation:

- AMBI granted to AHP's health care division an exclusive license to sell a particular AMBI product (the Cardia™ salt alternative in retail markets in the United States).

- AHP agreed to make equity investments in newly issued shares of AMBI common stock (buying $4 million worth after making an up-front payment of $1 million).

- AMBI granted a first negotiation option for exclusive rights and licenses for additional AMBI nutrition products for retail distribution in the United States.

According to investor relations manager Gerald Shapiro, the transaction was considered after the company rejected the more traditional alternatives. Issuing new equity, whether in a public or private offering, would have been too dilutive and therefore unfair to long-term stockholders who had "suffered with us." Debt would have created too much leverage; the company already had negative working capital. This solution offered the cash the company needed without dilution or excessive leverage. In January 1999, AMBI was able to buy another company, Lite Bites-R-Nutrition Bars, for $6 million in cash and 1.3 million shares of AMBI.

ANGELS

You mentioned angels earlier. How are they different from venture capitalists?

An *angel* is a wealthy individual who offers both investment capital and management expertise to a company. One estimate says that some $20 billion in financial backing is provided by angels.[21] This amount is not easy to track; it is composed of many small investments. Angels take a minority position—typically 5 percent—not the controlling positions often amassed by venture capitalists and other private equity sources. Each angel may invest only once or just a handful of times. As mentioned earlier, one exit strategy may be merger.

What is the difference between and angel and a "name"?

An angel will invest in one company at a time, typically in a start-up private company, whereas a "name" might make many investments, often in public companies.

How can I find an angel?

The best way, as always in business, is to ask around. There are organizations that specialize in matching angels and businesses. One such organization is the Chicago Partnership Board (cpboard.com), which calls itself a "limited liability companies auctioneer." It conducts auctions for companies in need of angel financing.

SUPPLIERS AS BACKERS

How can a company use its suppliers as a source of capital?

As mentioned in Chapter 8, a company's suppliers—the other companies providing goods and services—may be considered a form of capital. Simply by extending the time of payment beyond the typical 30 days, the supplier is in effect providing the company with the use of its cash beyond the normal time horizon. This cash infusion functions very much like a loan—and some suppliers do charge interest and or penalties for late payment. In other cases, the grace period functions more like equity, with the supplier agreeing to support ongoing business operations as a partner. In some cases, the supplier takes a piece of the action outright.

Could you give an example of a company using a supplier as a financial partner?

Sure. Consider the relationship between Cain Energy, a small Scottish oil exploration outfit, and Halliburton Co., a $7.4 billion Dallas-based oil service firm. Cain found a huge natural gas field off the coast of Bangladesh in 1996, and needed capital to exploit it. It asked Halliburton, an oil services firm to supply its services for the field for the usual fee, and at the same time invest $85 million. In return for the investment, Halliburton got 25 percent ownership of the venture. In a previous deal with British Petroleum, Halliburton received a cut of the cash flow. Other oil services firms such as Reading & Bates, Schlumberger, Seitel, and Western Atlas are also obtaining stakes in customers' projects—sometimes by providing services at discounted rates.

A *Forbes* article has declared that these oil services companies are becoming "more like banks." However, from a risk management perspective, they are in fact becoming more like backers. Unlike the bank lender, which typically earns a guaranteed stream of interest payments backed by collateral, the vendor-backer takes on the risks of the business enterprise it supports. As the article notes, "With participation, of course, comes risk. In June [1997], Reading & Bates wrote off dry-hole costs of $7 million, knocking nearly 5 percent off the $145 million analysts had previously expected it to earn this year."[22]

Suppose a company that has been receiving supplier credit is acquired by another company. What guarantees does a supplier have that the credit it has extended will be repaid?

The bulk sales law, subject to variations among states, requires the purchaser of a major part of the material, supplies, merchandise, or other inventory of a seller whose principal business is bulk sales—the sale of merchandise from inventory—to give at least 10 days' advance notice of the sale to each creditor of the seller. The notice must identify the seller and the buyer and state whether the debts of the seller will be paid as they fall due. If orderly payment will not be made, further information must be disclosed. In addition, many states require the buyer to ensure that the seller uses proceeds from the sale to satisfy existing debts, and to hold in escrow an amount sufficient to pay any disputed debts.

Although the requirements of the law are straightforward, its applicability to particular sellers and to particular transactions is ambiguous, so acquirers should consult qualified legal counsel to ensure compliance when necessary.

CONCLUDING REMARKS

From asset-based lenders to venture capital firms, backers can be an important source of capital in all stages of a company's life, including its years of growth through mergers and acquisitions. The close relationship between the givers and the receivers make this a special form of financing support, sometimes compared to friendship. Indeed, "Stand by Me" could be the theme song for such a relationship.

Yet despite the loyalty that backers may show for the firms they back, all good things must come to an end. For the backer, there is always an end in sight: profitable exit from the investment. Hence, our opening quote from Andrew Marvell. At the "back" of every business one hears not only words of encouragement, but also the wings of time's ever-moving chariot.

A P P E N D I X   9–A
Sample Announcement of a Start-Up Private Equity Fund

Mergers and Acquisition—Investment Opportunity List Members:

Our client is establishing an exclusive Venture Capital Cooperative Fund with membership restricted on a first come-first serve basis.

Below is a short overview of this initiative, which is listed on our special investment page at http://www.bbean.com/investsp.htm

BBCOM 258—Venture Capital Cooperative Fund!

Seeking limited number of members to establish fund—
$12,500 per single unit membership! Two unit ($25,000) minimum!

The Fund:

The Fund will provide bridge financing and arrange longer-term equity or debt financing for approved projects. Projects requiring financial investment or funding may be sponsored by members or by third parties. It is anticipated that the membership not only will provide the initial start-up investment, through the membership unit purchase, but will participate from time to time in the assessment of projects to be funded, based on a member's background and expertise. For this reason the principals are seeking participation of a diverse group of professionals and are not receptive to the bulk acquisition of membership units by few investors.

Fund Income/Revenue:

The Articles of Organization for the Fund require that the majority of all distributed revenues is to be shared first by the Membership. This profit sharing will continue until the Members have received double the amount of capital invested in the Fund. At that time, each of the total of 100 Units of Membership will be entitled to a 1 percent ownership of the Company and the profits. The Company is projecting revenues of $3,360,000 to $6,560,000 total cumulative income in years one to three. A single $12,500 Unit of Membership could receive approximately $48,600 to $80,600 or more over one to three years. The Company intends to continue funding projects for the foreseeable future.

Project Principals:

The principals of the Fund are experienced accomplished professionals with a proven track record of performance and a demonstrated ability to assume new challenges and get the job done. The principals have previously participated in transactions ranging from $5,000,000 to $150,000,000. They stand ready to answer any and all questions you may have.

    If this unique investment opportunity is of interest, please contact _____.

Member of the Netcheck Commerce Bureau
(http://netcheck.com—netcheck@netcheck.com)
"Promoting Ethical Business Practices Worldwide on the Internet"

Excerpted verbatim from a communication to subscribers to mergersdaily@egroups.com (mergers and investment opportunity listing) sent October 1998. This listing does not constitute endorsement.

A P P E N D I X   9-B
Profiles of Backers*

PROFILE 1: VENTURE CAPITAL FIRM

Vital Statistics

Year founded: 1992
Year began buyout activities: 1992
Number of buyout professionals on staff: 3

Primary Areas of Participation

Equity investor
Senior lender

Role in Financing

Prefer role as deal originator but will also invest in deals created by others

Transactions Financed

Leveraged acquisitions/management buyouts
Recapitalizations
Buy and builds/roll-ups
Growth financings

Sources of Group's Capital

Funds managed on behalf of limited partners

Fee Structure

Return on investment is most important but also charge commitment, closing, and other fees.**

---

*Adapted from *Directory of Buyout Sources, 1999 Edition* (New York: Securities Data Publishing, 1999).
** Of the four profiles in this appendix, the venture capital firm was the only one that listed fees.

Transaction Criteria

Minimum annual sales of target company:
No minimum—can show losses

Preferred size of investments or loans:
$5 million to $25 million

Requirements for management team:
Vary by transaction

Equity participation required of management:
Preferred but not required

Preferred industries to work in:
Computer and electronic products
Finance and insurance
Industrial machinery and equipment
Medical/health related

Geographic Coverage

United States

Equity Investors' Policy

Investment policy:
Do not require controlling interest
Target period to exit investment: 3 to 7 years
Provide coinvestment opportunities to limited partners

Investment criteria:
Minimum return on investment: 35 percent

Range of equity offered to management:
11 percent to 25 percent

Role as investor:
Very active before closing
Very active after closing

PROFILE 2: PRIVATE EQUITY FUND

Vital Statistics

Year founded: 1979
Year began buyout activities: 1979
Number of buyout professionals on staff: 10

Primary Areas of Participation

Equity investor
Mezzanine provider
Senior lender

Role in Financing

Prefer role as deal originator

Transactions Financed

Leveraged acquisitions/management buyouts
Recapitalizations

Sources of Group's Capital

Funds managed on behalf of limited partners

Transaction Criteria

Minimum annual sales of target company:
Based on EBIT (earnings before interest and taxes)

Preferred size of investments or loans:
$50 million to $100 million

Requirements for management team:
Vary by transaction

Equity participation required of management:
Required

Technology focus:
Prefer low technology deals

Preferred industries to work in:
No preference

Businesses will not consider:
Finance and insurance
Oil and gas, mining, other natural resources
Utilities
Real estate construction
High technology

Geographic Coverage

United States, Canada, Europe, Australia and New Zealand, Mexico

Mezzanine Providers' Policies

Mezzanine financing provided by:
Purchasing notes and/or securities in private placements

Investment criteria:
EBIT/total interest coverage ratio required: 1.5:1

Equity participation through warrants:
Warrants required

Minimum ratio of equity to mezzanine:
11 percent to 50 percent

Equity Investors' Policies

Investment policy:
Require controlling interest
Target period to exit investment: 3 to 7 years

Investment criteria:
EBIT/total interest coverage ratio required: 1.5:1

Range of equity offered to management:
1 percent to 25 percent

Role as investor:
Very active before closing
Very active after closing

PROFILE 3: INSURANCE COMPANY

Vital Statistics

Year founded: 1860
Year began buyout activities: 1980
Number of buyout professionals on staff: 5

Primary Areas of Participation

Equity investor
Mezzanine provider
Senior lender

Role in Financing

Prefer role in deals created by others

Transactions Financed

Leveraged acquisitions/management buyouts
Recapitalizations
Refinancings
ESOPs

Sources of Group's Capital

Allocations from parent or affiliated company

Transaction Criteria

Minimum annual sales of target company:
$50 million

Minimum size of investments or loans considered:
$10 million

Requirements for management team:
Must be in place before acquisition

Technology Focus:
Prefer low-technology deals

Geographic Coverage

United States, Canada, parts of Europe, Central and South America

Senior Lending Policies

Interest rate policy:
Fixed and floating rates

Lending criteria:
Cash flow to debt service: moderately important
Debt-to-equity ratio: very important

Equity Investors' Policies

Investment policy:
Do not provide coinvestment opportunities to limited partners

Role as investor:
Very active before closing
Very active after closing

PROFILE 4: COMMERCIAL FINANCE COMPANY
(subsidiary of a publicly traded commercial bank)

Vital Statistics

Year founded: 1970
Year began buyout activities: 1970
Number of buyout professionals on staff: 14

Primary Areas of Participation

Senior lender

Role in Financing

Will function as either deal originator or investor in deals created by others

Transactions Financed

Leveraged acquisitions/management buyouts
Recapitalizations
Refinancing
Turnarounds

Sources of Group's Capital

Allocations from parent or affiliated company

Fee Structure

All fees negotiable

Transaction Criteria

Minimum annual sales of target company:
$25 million

Preferred size of investments or loans:
$5 million to $50 million

Requirements for management team:
Must be in place before acquisition

Equity participation required of management:
Preferred but not required

Technology focus:
No preference

Preferred industries to work in:
Business products and services
Computer and electronic products
Consumer products
Consumer services (including retailing)
Electronic media
Industrial chemicals and materials
Industrial machinery and equipment
Medical/health related
Publishing
Telecommunications
Transportation
Wholesaling/distribution

Businesses will not consider:
Construction

Geographic Coverage

United States and Canada

Senior Lenders' Policies

Interest rate policy:
Prime plus 2.5 percent

Equity participation should finance at least:
5 percent of total acquisition cost

Loan syndication policies:

Prefer to lead syndications, but will also purchase parts of syndications led by others

Maximum size of syndication participation:

$20 million

Creditor voting rights in syndications:

Prefer to have but may waive

Lending criteria:

Loan-to-collateral ratio: very important

Ratio of cash flow to debt service: moderately important

Debt-to-equity ratio: minor importance

Historical earnings: minor importance

Total interest coverage ratio required:

EBIT/total interest: 1.2:1

Collateral advance rates:

Accounts receivable: 80 percent average, 85 percent maximum

Raw materials inventory: 30 percent average, 60 percent maximum

Finished goods inventory: 40 percent average, 60 percent maximum

Machinery and equipment: 70 percent average, 80 percent maximum

Real estate: 60 percent average, 70 percent maximum

Loan terms granted on collateral:

Accounts receivable: evergreen

Inventory: evergreen

Machinery and equipment: 7 years maximum

Real estate: 10 years maximum

E N D N O T E S

1. See "Patient, But Not Too Patient," *Forbes*, March 10, 1997, pp. 134ff., a profile of Investcorp, a publicly held fund that invests in private companies, turns them around, and takes them public at a profit, typcially after five years but "hopefully less." Some payoffs occur after 18 months, the article notes. Successful investments have paid investors seven times their original participation, although of course not every investment is successful.

2. Here are some precise numbers on venture capital trends. Although they are from different time periods (unfortunately), they do give a general idea of the "high roller odds" a venture capitalist faces. As of 1997, venture capitalists were targeting returns of 32 to 48 percent. (See "Fishing for Venture Capital," *Business Week,* October 13, 1997, p. 70–E1, a "special report.") But in earlier years, average annual returns were lower: 1991 (24 percent), 1992 (12.5 percent), 1993 (19.7 percent), and 1994 (16.2 percent), in part because of a high rate of losing investments—with 34.5 percent of all investments losing money according to one study. (See Edgar Parker and Phillip Todd Parker, "Venture Investment: An Emerging Force in the Southeast," *Economic Review,* Federal Reserve Bank of Atlanta, Fourth Quarter 1998, pp. 36ff., esp. pp. 36 and 42.)

3. By late 1997, *Forbes* declared it a $30 billion year for new money being poured into buyouts. Leaders at that time were Kohlberg Kravis Roberts ($6 billion raised in 1997); Blackstone Group ($3.8 billion raised); Forstmann Little ($3.2 billion); Thomas H. Lee ($3 billion); Donaldson, Lufkin & Jenrette ($3 billion); Apollo Advisors ($2.5 billion); Hicks, Muse, Tate & Furst ($2.5 billion); Texas Pacific Group ($2.5 billion); and Lehman Brothers ($2 billion). See "Tom Lee Is on a Roll," *Forbes,* November 17, 1997.

4. Rounded LBO fund figures for the previous years were $35 billion (1997), $23 billion (1996), $18 billion (1995), $12 billion (1994), and $6 billion (1993). See Kopin Tan, "State of the Buyout Market," in *Directory of Buyout Financing Sources, 1999 Edition* (New York: Securities Data Publishing, 1999), pp. 5ff.

5. As mentioned earlier, in 1997, a total of 113 self-described venture capital funds raised $10.4 billion (source *Private Equity Analyst*). By contrast, the total amount of private equity money raised was nearly $30 billion (see note 3).

6. See Parker and Parker, op. cit. (note 2), p. 41. Despite their low numbers, wealthy individuals who invest do have some clout, at least in the United States, if their investment interests are not respected In the bankruptcy of Lloyds of London, "names" were given standing to sue the insurer for securities fraud. See "Lloyds Faces U.S. Setback: Appeals Court Allows Names to Sue," *The Financial Times,* March 10, 1997, p. 1, about a suit brought by the American Names Association.

7. Bernard S. Black and Ronald J. Gilson, "Venture Capital and the Structure of Capital Markets: Banks Versus Stock Markets," *Journal of Financial Economics,* 47 (1998), pp. 243ff.

8. The conservatism of involvement by large institutional owners or investors can be seen by any regular reader of *Pensions & Investments,* the weekly magazine for the field. See, for example, "Wilshire Wants LBO Data for Risk Evaluation Co-Op," *Pensions & Investments,* August 4, 1997, pp. 3ff. The article notes that pension fund managers have invested $100 billion in LBO funds over the past several years, despite the fact that the funds are missing "such basic tools as measuring the volatility of the investment and value added brought by managers." Other articles in *P&I* have focused on the fact that some funds, as invest-

ment companies, charge fees; the articles ask why that is necessary. *P&I* has reported that CalPERS was disappointed when one fund's "internal rate of return" fell behind that of CalPERS' other partnership investments. See "CalPERS Blasts Hicks, Muse Fund," *Pensions & Investments,* September 15, 1997, p. 51. In short, institutional involvement is adding more discipline to this formerly entrepreneurial phenomenon.

9. Parker and Parker, op. cit. (note 2), p. 42.

10. Jack S. Levin, *Structuring Venture Capital, Private Equity, and Entrepreneurial Transactions* (New York: Aspen Law and Business, March 1, 1998), p. 3. For guidance on how to start a private equity partnership, see Geoffrey L. Fiszel and Randall G. Peterson, *How to Start Your Own Private Investment Partnership* (New York: McGraw-Hill, 1998).

11. Paula Kaufman, Executive Director, Finance Division, International Quality and Productivity Center, Little Falls, New Jersey, in a brochure for a June 1997 conference on "Middle Market Private Equity Sourcing and Finance."

12. Tim Loughran and Anand M. Vijh, "Do Long-Term Shareholders Benefit from Corporate Acquisitions?" *Journal of Finance,* December 1997.

13. Of the first 18 companies Forstmann Little acquired since its founding in 1978, it sold 11. By the mid-1990s, the $2.67 billion it invested in these companies had returned 32.2 percent to investors in debt and 86.4 percent to investors in equity. Goldman Sachs' $25 million stake in the 1989 buyout of Hospital Corporation of America was valued at $162.5 million by December 1991, when it did a partial "reverse buyout" by selling shares to the public. Another investor success was AFG Industries. In 1988, 30 investors paid $13 million to buy 41 percent of AFG. In 1992, they made over 10 times that amount—$150 million—by selling to Asahi Glass Co.

14. "Patient, But Not Too Patient," *Forbes,* op. cit. (note 1).

15. This answer is paraphrased from Jack S. Levin, op cit. (note 10), p. 5. Other prominent sources on this topic include Michael Hallowand, *Venture Capital and Public Offering Negotiation* (New York: Aspen Law and Business, 1998); and Joseph W. Bartlett, Esq., *Equity Finance: Venture Capital, Buyouts, Restructuring, and Reorganization* (New York: John Wiley Law Publications, 1998).

16. Indeed, the main proxy resolution filing rule under the Securities Exchange Act of 1934 (Section 14-a-8) includes a provision that allows companies to exclude resolutions from a proxy vote if they concern "ordinary business."

17. "Gulfstream's Pilot," *Business Week,* April 14, 1997, pp. 64ff., and the December 21, 1998, issue of *The New Republic* (posted on the Internet).

18. *Venture Capital Journal,* cited in Bernard S. Black and Ronald J. Gilson, op. cit. (note 7). See also Parker and Parker, op. cit. (note 2), p. 40.

19. Black and Gilson (ibid.) recognize the MBO as a desirable form of exit for a "mature, cash-generating company."

20. "The Guardians: New Breed of Investors Brings More than Cash to Hopeful Startups," *The Wall Street Journal*, August 25, 1997, pp. A1ff. This brief article focuses on a profile of M. R. Rangaswami, an angel active in the Silicon Valley area of California.
21. Ibid.
22. Toni Mack, "A Piece of the Action," *Forbes*, August 11, 1997, p. 60.

PART FOUR

Strategies for Financing and Refinancing

Putting It All Together

When preparing for a piano recital, an artist might work with the left hand, then the right, practice one refrain again and again, sound out a chord, rehearse the prelude, then the finale. But sooner or later, it will be time to play the entire piece through from beginning to end.

So it is with deal financing.

In mastering the art of M&A financing, there are times to focus on differing sources; times to focus on differing instruments; times to do the paperwork and the planning. But sooner or later, the time comes to "play"—actually spend the money that the company has worked so hard to obtain.

In this part of the book, we will show what it means to put it all together. In Part One, we discussed preliminaries, in Part Two instruments, and in Part Three sources. Here in Part Four it is time to see how to manage multiple instruments* and sources—and eventually the multiple contingencies that can lead to refinancing, this section's closing subject.

All this requires great discipline. How the money is spent, over what time period, and with what results—all this must be tracked, measured, and at times second-guessed.

But far more important is how the whole process plays out. So much depends on forces beyond a company's control. One thing is certain, though. To master the art of M&A financing, all you really have to do is learn the notes, and then summon the courage to play—and, if necessary, play it again.

---

*The authors wish to express special appreciation here to Robert Neal, of the CIT Group (recent acquirer of the Newcourt Credit Group) for the leaseback portion of Chapter 10.

C H A P T E R 10

Managing Multiple Instruments–Planning Points

I warrant you, if he danced till doomsday, he thought I was to pay the piper.

William Congreve, *Love for Love,* 1695

INTRODUCTION

When planning to acquire a company, managers naturally concentrate at first on possibility: What financing can we obtain? Then they focus on feasibility: Who can provide this financing? Eventually, however, they must consider a third dimension: How should we structure the financing?

In most M&A transactions, the key elements of structuring the deal will be a simple choice between the use of cash or stock. These are plain vanilla deals. About half of all deals are in pure cash; and another third are in pure stock.

If cash is used, there will also be a choice of using the firm's own cash or borrowed cash (debt). If stock is used, there may be a question of whether to use existing treasury stock or to issue new stock. Still, in these cases, the choices are fairly simple.

However, when the acquired firm is privately controlled by a few individuals, it may be necessary to work out some complex arrangements to overcome the seller's reluctance to agree to the deal. This accounts for the "combination" transactions that make up a little under one fifth of all transactions.[1]

Leveraged buyouts (LBOs) and management buyouts (MBOs) are examples of such complex transactions. They generally employ a combination of fi-

269

nancial instruments. Some circumstances may require multiple instruments to satisfy the diverse goals of different parties to the transaction. In such cases, structuring the deal may involve many moving parts with lots of bells and whistles.

In this chapter, we will begin very practically with the postmerger impact of different types of financing. By comparing different types of financing, we can better understand how they work in combination with each other. Then, as an example of a transaction using multiple financing instruments, we will focus on one type of complex transaction—a management buyout financed by an employee stock ownership plan. Finally, in an appendix, we will explain how to calculate the cost of capital, analyzing the costs of debt, preferred stock, common equity, and their weighted average—a useful skill to have when choosing among these instruments, or when combining them in a complex transaction.

POSTMERGER IMPACT OF FINANCING INSTRUMENTS

Could you review again the modes of payment used in M&A deals today?

As mentioned in Chapter 1, based on the most recent figures available, about half of all deals these days are paid for in cash, a third in stock, and the rest with a combination of the two that sometimes includes a "note" of some kind (a regular promissory note, or a promise to pay on contingency).[2] Assessing the impact of all these modes can be critical for any company.

How can the mode of M&A financing (cash, stock, or both) affect shareholder relations?

How can they not? In 1997, 41 percent of all liability insurance claims against directors and officers (429 out of 1,046) originated from suits by shareholders, and many of the suits involved merger and/or financial decisions. Plaintiffs protested a decision to merge with another company or to divest a company unit, or they alleged inaccurate or inadequate disclosure.[3] Shareholder suits also protested various types of financial decisions (stock repurchase, investment or loan decision, recapitalization, dividend declaration, or derivatives investment) or sued over poor financial performance. The average payment made to shareholders in 1997 was $7.51 million.[4] Merger financing transactions, although not specifically named as a source of shareholder suits, are vulnerable to such litigation.

Can the choice of a particular mode of financing—for example, borrowed cash—have an impact on postmerger performance?

Yes. The use of cash, versus stock, versus a combination, can have some affect on the postmerger performance of a newly combined company. Of course, other factors are important, too. The strategic reason for buying a company, the price actually paid, and the general ability of the company to support the price—all these can affect postmerger performance. But the impact of these factors can be magnified by the type of financing used. Each of these payment strategies—cash, stock, or a combination—will have a different impact on the value of a company's equity.[5]

Equity Impact of an All-Cash Deal. This impact can vary, depending on whether the acquirer used its own cash or borrowed it. Overall, when compared with share-financed deals, cash-financed deals have a more positive impact on share prices over a long (five-year) term.[6] Positive results cannot be assumed for cash-financed deals that have been made with borrowed capital. As explained in Chapter 4, a debt-financed transaction that causes the acquirer to have a debt/equity ratio of 75 percent or more[7] is considered a heavily leveraged transaction (HLT). Such transactions often have a negative impact on share values. Some companies refrain from acquisitions because they do not want to become too highly leveraged.[8]

Equity Impact of an All-Stock Deal. Two factors are relevant. The first is whether the terms of the deal result in dilution in earnings per share for the acquirer. The second is whether the use of stock is taken as a signal that the acquirer knows its stock is overvalued (since otherwise it might prefer to use debt or cash). Both of these possibilities can explain why share values may not do as well overall following stock deals as following cash deals.

Equity Impact after a Cash and Stock Deal. If the acquirer combines cash and stock in the payment, the impact on postmerger returns may be positive or negative, depending on the factors described above. Sometimes acquirers offer notes to the seller promising additional payments or "earn-outs" based on meeting certain financial goals. Obviously, for shareholders of the acquired firm, this mode of financing is ideal. If the goals are not met, the company and its shareholders pay nothing extra. If the goals are met, the company and its shareholders benefit from this improved performance—even if they do have to make the additional payment promised in the contingency deal.

The shareholders benefit especially when the performance goals for the earnout relate to share price, rather than to some accounting-based measure.

In summary, an acquisition may have a negative or a positive effect on the acquirer's share prices, and this effect depends in part on how the deal was financed. It is up to postdeal managers to do what they can to ensure the most positive outcome for shareholders and to admit, explain, and work to correct any negative result to existing shareholders, rather than hoping for a new generation of owners to come along.

What kinds of things do shareholders look for in debt-financed deals?

Of course, everything depends on the quality of the transaction, but here are some very basic generalities. Shareholders will look at sales growth and earnings growth as well as several key ratios based on numbers from the balance sheet, the income statement, and/or stock prices.

In debt-financed acquisitions (deals using borrowed cash), shareholders may focus on ratios involving debt, namely:

- Current ratio (current assets/current liabilities)
- Debt ratio (total liabilities/total assets)
- Debt/equity ratio (total liabilities/total equity)
- Net working capital (current assets minus current liabilities)

Another concern has to do with the technicalities of accounting. If you pay by cash, or even just partly by cash, your deal by definition is not a pooling, which requires stock payment. Pooling is desirable to some acquirers because of its positive impact on earnings. Purchase accounting may involve goodwill amortization in subsequent years that will decrease reported earnings per share.

Could you give an example of accounting for restructuring charges in connection with a merger transaction?

Consider, for example, the following lead paragraphs of a postmerger press release distributed by Aspect Telecommunications following an acquisition.

> San Jose, CA, April 15, 1996—Aspect Telecommunications Corporation (Nasdaq: ASPT) reported today record highs for net revenues, income from operations, net income, and earnings per share for the quarter ended March 31, 1996.

Net revenues for the quarter ended March 31, 1996, were $65.8 million, an increase of $23.1 million or 54% compared to the same period of the prior year. . . . Compared to the quarter ended December 31, 1995, net revenues increased by 8%. Income from operations also increased by 8% during the same period, excluding a non-recurring accounting charge of $1.8 million recorded in the quarter ended December 31, 1995, associated with the acquisition of TCS Management Group. Excluding this same charge, fully diluted earnings per share increased from $0.32 to $0.34 per share.

What are some special challenges in equity-financed deals?

In equity-financed transactions, shareholders may focus on ratios involving equity:

- Earnings per share (net income minus preferred dividends/common shares outstanding)[9]
- Price/earnings (market price per common share/earnings per share)
- Equity ratio (total stockholders' equity/total assets)
- Return on common stockholders' equity (net income minus preferred dividends/average common stockholder equity)

In transactions combining debt and equity payments, shareholders will focus on all the above ratios.

DILUTION CONCERNS IN TRANSACTIONS INCLUDING STOCK

If a company uses stock to pay for a merger, won't this automatically dilute share value?

No. Another company is being acquired. Usually, it will have earnings or earnings potential.

What determines whether dilution will occur?

It depends on the number of shares used to pay for the acquired company in comparison with the earnings it adds to the earnings of the combined company. An example will illustrate how this works. Assume the facts in Table 10–1.

T A B L E   10–1

Dilution Following a Merger

	Company A	Company B	Combined
Total earnings	$60,000	$50,000	$110,000
Number of shares of common stock	5,000	10,000	15,000
Earnings per share of stock	$6	$5	$7.33
Price/earnings ratio per share	20 times	10 times	
Market price per share	$120	$50	

The bottom line of the table shows that the market price per share for the acquirer, Company A, is $120 and for the acquired company, Company B, is $50. If A accepts the 20 percent premium for B, it pays $60 per share, which represents a deal price/earnings ratio of 12 times. It is the P/E ratio of the acquirer compared with the deal P/E ratio of the acquired company that determines whether earnings dilution occurs. Since the P/E of the acquiring firm (A) is 20 and the deal P/E of the acquired company (B) is 12, we can predict that the deal will be accretive for A and dilutive for B. The new EPS per old share for A is $7.33, which represents 22.2 percent earnings accretion. The B shareholders now hold 1/2 share of the combined company stock for every share they held before the acquisition. So the new EPS per old share for B is 1/2 of $7.33, or $3.67, which represents an earnings dilution of 26.7 percent.

Why would the shareholders of the acquired company agree to a deal in which they suffer earnings dilution?

One possibility is that the P/E ratio of A will apply so that the new market price per share of the combined company is 20 times $7.33, or $146.60. This represents a market price accretion of 22.2 percent for A. The market value per old share of B is half of $146.60, or $73.30, representing a 46.6 percent market price accretion for the B shareholders. So long as the P/E ratio of the combined company is at least equal to 13.63, the B shareholders will not suffer market price dilution. However, for the A shareholders the combined P/E ratio has to be above 16.37 to avoid market price dilution.

So are the effects on earnings and market price accretion or dilution simply the result of these arithmetic calculations?

The results depend fundamentally on whether the acquisition makes sense from a business standpoint. If A and B combined represent a good strategic fit so that future growth in earnings will be higher, even if there were initial earnings dilution for the B shareholders, in the longer-run future, earnings accretion will be achieved. If the market recognizes the basic synergies achieved by combining the two companies, leading to improved earnings growth in the future, the postacquisition P/E ratio will produce market price accretion for both the A and B shareholders.

The example shows earnings dilution for the acquired company. Does earnings dilution ever occur for the acquirer?

Of course. If the deal P/E ratio for the acquired company is higher than the predeal P/E ratio of the acquirer, it is the acquirer that will suffer initial earnings dilution and possible initial market price dilution as well.

Why would it make sense for an acquirer to suffer initial earnings dilution or market price dilution?

What matters for valuation and market prices are the projections of future growth rates in earnings and cash flows. The situation is similar if a company embarks on a major new product program. An investment is made representing an initial cash outflow, but the major cash inflow may occur over a period of years in the future. As a result, new investment programs might be associated with initial earnings dilution, but be rewarded by higher stock prices. Studies of announcements of new investment programs find a significant association with higher market prices.

What about the effects of stock options?

Another element in all this is the impact of the stock option programs the company has. Such programs used to involve 1 percent of all stock; today, they take up an average of 10 percent. The method for calculating the dilutive effect of stock option programs, called overhang, is rather complex —although compensation experts have demystified it to some degree.[10]

How can a company mitigate shareholder concerns about initial dilution?

First, the company should be straightforward about the dilution. Shareholders will notice it, so management might as well point it out and explain it as soon as feasible after the merger is announced. If future earnings prospects are good, the company should say so—and explain how they will be achieved.

Could you give an example of a successful postmerger communication about dilution?

The following one is a few years old, but it could be applied to any situation today. It is from the 1994 annual report of Cyprus Amax Minerals Company in the year following the company's purchase of Amax.

> **Earnings Reflect Strength of Combined Companies**
> For the year, the Company reported earnings of $175 million, or $1.69 per share, on revenue of $2.8 billion, compared to 1993 earnings of $100 million, or $1.85 per share, on revenue of $1.8 billion. While 1994 earnings included the merged operations for the full year, 1993 earnings included the Amax operations only from November 15, 1993. *The decline in earnings per share reflects the impact of the shares issued to complete the merger.*
>
> *As the year progressed, the integration of our merged operations and our many cost improvement programs began to take hold, greatly improving the earnings fundamentals of our businesses.* Each of our businesses, copper/molybdenum, coal, and lithium, succeeded in reducing costs, improving productivity, and increasing production levels. As markets improved, our earnings strengthened, with fourth-quarter copper/molybdenum and coal earnings being the highest of 1994. . . . [Emphasis added.]

USING MULTIPLE INSTRUMENTS IN FINANCING THE MANAGEMENT BUYOUT

What is a good example of a transaction that uses multiple instruments?

Perhaps the very best example is a leveraged management buyout, because it typically involves both debt and stock. The acquiring group is most likely not an operating company with a ready store of cash, so it borrows the money for the deal. At the same time, the acquiring group includes managers that take stock in the new company (sometimes a controlling stake) as part of the deal. If the acquiring group promises to give stock to the managers, rather than selling it to them, the stock in effect becomes part of the payment for the company.[11]

How is an MBO typically structured?

In a management buyout, the management of an existing company, together with any financial partner, typically forms a new company to acquire the existing one. The acquiring company may acquire all the assets or stock of the existing company, or it may merge with the existing company. Often management forms a new holding company and engages in a forward or reverse merger with the existing company. (A forward merger means the company to be acquired is subsumed into the acquirer; a reverse merger does it the other way.) If management owns stock, it can either have the acquiring company repurchase its existing shares or contribute its equity in the existing business to the acquiring company. These methods have different tax consequences, discussed below.

Should an MBO be structured as a merger, a stock purchase, or an asset purchase?

A stock purchase via a tender offer is the fastest method to purchase a majority of any public company's stock. However, tender offers have certain disadvantages. Tender offers may require the expenditure of money prior to gaining access to the cash flow of the company to be acquired, and without any assurance of ever tapping it. The margin rules of the Federal Reserve Board (Regulations G and U) restrict a purchaser from borrowing more than half the purchase price against a pledge of publicly traded securities. Because of the margin rules, tender offers are rare (about 1 percent of deals). Public companies are more often acquired through mergers.

Most MBO transactions are structured as a merger. A merger usually requires approval of the stockholders of both corporations in noncash transactions and of the nonsurviving corporation in cash transactions. A merger transaction involving a public company will require the filing of proxy materials with the Securities and Exchange Commission and a registration statement complying with federal and state securities laws when securities are to be issued. A stock purchase can be done when ownership of the stock of the acquired company is concentrated in the hands of a few people, but it typically must be consummated contemporaneously with a merger to obtain the required financing.

Can an MBO involve employees as owners?

Yes, employees can be new owners. There are some tax advantages to having the company establish an employee stock ownership plan (ESOP) as the new owner. Examples are the Weirton Steel and United Airlines ESOPs. In an ESOP buyout, the ESOP is the sole or a principal purchaser of its company's stock. Senior management can own stock in addition to the stock owned through the ESOP. The ESOP purchase of the stock is financed by a loan, either directly to the ESOP or through the company. The loan is almost always backed by the company's assets. Interest payments to the ESOP lender are given favorable tax treatment and, therefore, can be obtained at below-market rates, lowering the company's interest expense. Loan repayments are treated for tax purposes as contributions to a pension plan and are deductible in full, in effect making principal repayments deductible as well as interest. Thus, the ESOP is a powerful and efficient financing tool.

New tax laws have made it more advantageous for S corporations to have ESOPs and for ESOPs to consider S corporation elections.[12] However, because the ESOP is a tax-qualified pension plan subject to the Employee Retirement Income Security Act of 1974 (ERISA) and the Internal Revenue Code (the Code), there are limits on the size of the ESOP and the extent to which it may benefit senior management.

What special tax issues arise in a management buyout?

For the most part, a management buyout raises the same tax issues as any other leveraged buyout. In addition, there are a few issues that pertain specifically to acquisitions with equity participation by management. These issues relate primarily to the manner in which management's investment will be paid for or financed, and generally involve questions of whether significant amounts of compensation income will be deemed to be received by management. Where members of management already own stock or stock rights in a company, special care must be taken in structuring the transaction to allow a tax-free conversion of these existing equity rights.

What is the basic rule for taxation of an employee who receives or purchases stock in an MBO?

As a general rule, under Section 83 of the Code, an employee receives taxable compensation to the extent that the value of any property received from the employer exceeds the amount the employee pays for that property. If the employee has taxable income from the receipt of the property, the employer is entitled to a deduction and is required to withhold tax on the same basis as if regular salary were paid. These rules apply whether the employee is receiving stock or other kinds of property. If an employee has not paid full value for the stock and is thus taxed on the receipt of the stock, the employee will obtain a basis in the stock equal to the amount actually paid for it, plus the amount of taxable income recognized. If an employee has paid full value for the stock, the employee will have a basis in the stock equal to his or her cost and will have no compensation income. In either case, when the employee later sells the stock, the employee will have capital gain or loss measured by the difference between the sale proceeds and the basis in the stock.

There is an important exception to the general rule. If the stock is not substantially vested in the employee, there is no tax to the employee and no deduction to the employer until such time as the stock does become substantially vested. Stock is substantially vested if it either is not subject to a "substantial risk of forfeiture" or is transferable by the employee. When the risk of forfeiture or the restriction on transferability lapses, rendering the property substantially vested, the employee will be required to pay tax on the excess of the stock's value at the time the property vests over the amount paid for the stock. This rule will apply even if the employee originally paid full value for the stock, and it cannot be avoided unless the employee otherwise elects under Section 83(b) of the Code.[13]

Are there circumstances that might impel an employee to forfeit his or her stock?

Yes. Many "golden handcuff" techniques create a substantial risk of forfeiture and can, therefore, undermine the tax plans. The receipt of stock may be subject to forfeiture if the employee will be required to return the stock upon the happening of a particular event, or the failure to satisfy some condition. A typical provision creating a substantial risk of forfeiture is one requiring that the employee return the stock to the company in the event that the employee terminates his or her employment within a certain period after the receipt of the stock. A requirement that the employee return the stock unless certain earnings goals are met also creates a substantial risk of forfeiture.

Will receipt of stock by a management investor always be treated as receipt of stock by an employee?

Technically, Section 83 of the Code applies to the receipt of stock or other property by an employee only if he or she receives it in connection with the performance of services. This includes past, present, and future services. In some circumstances, a reasonably strong case can be made that the employees are not receiving stock in connection with the performance of services but are receiving stock on the same basis and in the same context as other members of an investor group. In spite of this commonsense analysis, most tax advisers recommend that planning in this area proceed on the assumption that the Internal Revenue Service (IRS) will apply Section 83 in determining the tax consequences to members of an investor group who are employees of the company.

We should mention here that management rarely has enough cash to buy as large an equity interest as it would like. The stock acquisition of management is usually financed by the company, the investor partner, or a third party. In return, the employee often gives the financier a promissory note.

If the employee's stock purchase is financed with a note, is Section 83 income avoided?

A promissory note from the employee will be treated as a bona fide payment for the stock in an amount equal to the face amount of the note, provided it meets two important requirements. First, the note should provide for adequate stated interest at least equal to the applicable federal rate. Second, the note should be with recourse to the employee.

When should the employee be treated as receiving income?

The employee's principal objective is to make sure that whatever event will trigger income to the employee will also cause the employee to have converted the stock investment into cash. Suppose an employee buys 100 shares of company stock for $100, which is its fair market value at that time. To ensure that the employee will not later be taxed on appreciation in the stock on the basis of a claim that the interest has not yet vested, he or she files a Section 83(b) election. Thereafter, the employee sells the stock for $500. Traditionally, the main planning goal would be to ensure that the $400 of appreciation is taxed at favorable capital gains rates. If the employee is in the 20 percent tax bracket, however, he or she will be largely indifferent as to whether the $400 is taxed as capital gains or as ordinary compensation income, so long as it is not taxed until he or she sells the stock. It appears that the employee's objective has been achieved.

On the other hand, the company's tax planning objectives may not have been well served. There is no benefit to the company as a result of the employee's recognition of $400 of capital gain upon the sale of the stock. When, however, the employee is able to defer the triggering of Section 83 until the stock is sold, the company will obtain a deduction in the amount of $400. The value of this deduction will be very significant for any company that is a C corporation. The employee is taxed at the capital gains rate.

In some cases, the tax problem can be solved by a company commitment to pay the employee a bonus sufficient to cover the employee's tax. The bonus is deductible to the company, of course, at rates currently higher than those paid by the employee. The combination of tax bonus plus Section 83 deduction may be better for the employer than the employer's making an 83(b) election, and the employee will be indifferent, since the tax is paid by the employer.

What happens when management borrows from third-party investors rather than from the company itself?

When stock of the company or a nonrecourse loan to buy stock in the company is made available to an employee from a party that is a shareholder in the company, the Section 83 rules make it clear that the employee will suffer the identical income tax results as if the stock or loan were made available directly from the company itself. As to the shareholder who makes the stock or loan available to the employee, any value transferred to the employee thereby is treated as having been contributed to the company by the shareholder on a tax-free basis. The only benefit obtained by the shareholder will be an increase in the basis in his or her stock of the company.

Can some of the employee's assets be protected from the recourse loan?

Yes, within limits. A management participant should be willing to risk his or her capital in a meaningful way, but not to the extent of personal bankruptcy. It might be worthwhile to consider a loan that gives the lender recourse to the borrowing employee, but specifically excludes recourse with respect to certain assets—for example, a house.

What other techniques provide management with full equity rights at a lower cost than the cost to third-party investors?

The most direct and effective means of reducing the relative cost of management stock is through a preferential rights arrangement. There are numerous variations on this theme. Here is an example of the most straightforward: Assume that a leveraged buyout is to be capitalized with $5 million in common equity, and that third-party investors are willing to put up this entire sum. The third-party investors could be given a preferred stock with a liquidation preference of $5 million and some reasonable preferred dividend rights. For a relatively nominal sum, both the third-party investors and management would purchase all the common shares of the company.

By providing the third-party investors with preferential rights equal to virtually the entire shareholder equity of the corporation, the book value, and arguably the fair market value of the common stock, will be nominal.

There are two problems with this arrangement. First, the IRS can argue that the preferred stock was in fact worth less than $5 million and that in any event the common stock was worth more than the nominal value ascribed to it because of the very low risk-to-reward ratio of the investment. Second, having more than one class of stock will prevent the company from electing to be an S corporation. When S corporation status is desired, the purchase price of the common stock can be reduced by having third-party investors purchase deeply subordinated debt instruments in addition to their common stock.

If management already owns stock, how can management convert its existing stock ownership into stock in the buyer on a tax-free basis?

There are several tax-free ways in which management (as well as other shareholders) of a company may exchange existing equity in the company for a participating interest in the acquiring company in a leveraged buyout. Depending upon the other structural goals and requirements, a tax-free rollover[14] may occur in the context of a recapitalization of the company, some other tax-free reorganization, or a National Starch transaction under Section 351 of the Code.[15]

If cash is received as part of the exchange, how is it treated?

Because leveraged buyouts involve a significant reduction in the value of the equity of the acquired company through increased debt financing, a shareholder in the existing company who wishes to retain an equity interest will seek one of two things: a significant increase in its percentage ownership of the outstanding stock, or the receipt of cash or other nonequity consideration in addition to the stock it already holds. In the latter case, management's tax advisers must analyze the facts to ensure that the receipt of nonstock consideration will be treated as a capital gain rather than a dividend to the participant. One key difference between a dividend and a capital gain is that under the latter characterization the shareholder will be permitted to reduce taxable income by his or her basis in the stock.

CONCLUDING COMMENTS

As stated in the opening to this chapter, most M&A deals are plain vanilla deals involving only one type of consideration—cash or stock. This chapter has looked at exceptional deals that involve both instruments—using as an example a management buyout with an ESOP source.

Yet even if the transaction you are dealing with is not complex, it is useful to bear all your financing options in mind. Even a simple deal can benefit from studying a complex one. We hope that this chapter has served as a starting point for such considerations, and an introduction to the chapter that follows—on dealing with multiple sources.

A P P E N D I X   10–A[16]

Calculating the Cost of Capital in a Transaction Involving Debt, Preferred Stock, and/or Common Stock

A hypothetical company, the United Corporation, has three sources of M&A financing: debt, equity, and preferred stock. This appendix will show how to estimate the weighted average cost of capital by analyzing the components costs and their market weights.

Table 10–A-1 shows the balance sheet for United Corporation in 1999. We can start by looking behind the numbers that appear in the company's balance sheet. We might see a loan payable. Since there are no "free lunches" in this world, we know that all liabilities that do not carry an explicit cost must surely have an implicit cost. What is this cost for the various liabilities of a firm? Answering this question requires considerable judgment.

T A B L E 10-A-1

Balance Sheet for United Corporation, 1999

Assets		Liabilities and Stockholders' Equity	
Current assets	$2,080	Accounts payable	$ 360
Fixed assets	2,490	Accruals	400
		Notes payable @ 12%	400
		Deferred taxes	110
		Minority interests	120
		Long-term debt @ 10%	1,000
		Preferred stock	200
		Stockholders' equity	1,980
Total	$4,570	Total	$4,570

This case illustrates how the cost of capital can actually be measured for a firm. We shall illustrate calculations of the cost of capital of the three major types of financing in a complex transaction—debt, preferred stock, and common equity—and employ the following symbols throughout the appendix:

k_b = before-tax opportunity cost of debt

k_{ps} = before- and after-tax opportunity cost of preferred stock

k_s = before- and after-tax return required by the market for equity capital

k_r = before- and after-tax cost of internally generated equity capital

WACC = weighted average cost of capital; represents a weighted marginal cost of capital

Our ultimate objective is to obtain the firm's marginal cost of capital for use in capital budgeting decisions and for application in valuation analysis. The firm's marginal cost of capital is a weighted average of the opportunity costs of its financing sources. In calculating weighted average cost of capital (WACC), all costs are expressed on an after-tax basis. This provides consistency with the after-tax cash flows used in any previous capital budgeting analysis. In using the marginal cost of capital for decision-making purposes, we are assuming that the risks of individual projects are similar to the riskiness of the firm's present portfolio of assets. This is required for WACC analysis in both capital budgeting and valuation analysis.

We shall first estimate the marginal cost of each source of capital, then the market value weights of each source, and finally the WACC. United Corporation has short-term debt, long-term debt, preferred stock, and common equity. As we already discussed, the implicit cost of accounts payable is already reflected in the cash flows of the income statement. The same is true of accruals and deferred taxes. Minority interests occur when a third party owns some percentage of one of the company's consolidated subsidiaries. Since the cash flows paid to minority interests are not part of the value of the company, the opportunity cost of funds provided by minority interests is not included in the WACC.

Cost of Debt

Although accounting statements distinguish between notes payable (short-term debt) and long-term debt, it is important to remember that they are perfect substitutes—one is *not* cheaper than the other. Short-term debt must be rolled over. If the term structure of interest rates is upward sloping, the market expects that future short-term rates will be higher than the current short-term rate. Therefore, except for liquidity premiums, the product of n short-term rates equals the n-year rate. For this reason we combine short-term and long-term debt in the capital structure and assume they have the same long-term marginal cost, *ex ante.*

The cost of debt should be on an after-tax basis because interest payments are tax deductible. Therefore, the cost of debt capital is calculated as follows:

$$k_b(1 - T) = \text{the after-tax cost of debt}$$

Here, T is the corporate tax rate as used previously. Thus, if the before-tax cost of debt were 15 percent and the firm's effective corporate tax rate were 40 percent, the after-tax cost of debt would be 9 percent.

We start with the firm's before-tax cost of debt and multiply it by the $(1—T)$ factor to obtain the relevant after-tax cost. How do we obtain the before-tax cost of debt in practice for an actual firm? Two main procedures may be used. We can look in any of the investment manuals to determine the rating of the firm's outstanding publicly held bonds. Various government agencies and investment banking firms periodically publish promised yields to maturity of debt issues by rating categories.

For our United Corporation example, its bonds were rated AA. At the time, we find that seasoned AA industrial debt issues of 10-year maturity (the remaining years to maturity of most of UC's long-term corporate debt) were 13.5 percent.

We can check this by calculating the promised yield to maturity on the cash flows from UC's long-term debt in relation to its current price. For its major issue of long-term debt, UC pays a coupon of 10 percent based on $1,000 par value per bond. Coupons are paid semiannually. UC's bonds are rated AA rather than AAA, so there is some very slight risk associated with them. We can obtain the current price of the UC bonds by looking in the daily newspaper or from various quote machines. We find that the price is $810.95. We can estimate the promised yield to maturity of UC's bonds by solving for k_b in Equation 10A.1:

$$\$810.95 = \sum_{t=1}^{20} \frac{50}{\left(1 + \dfrac{k_b}{2}\right)^t} = \frac{(1,000)}{\left(1 + \dfrac{k_b}{2}\right)^{20}} \tag{10A.1}$$

When we make the calculation, we find that the k_b that solves this equation is very close to the 13.5 percent cost of AA seasoned industrial bond issues. We shall, therefore, use 13.5 percent as the before-tax cost of long-term debt. Let us postulate that the firm's effective corporate lax rate is 40 percent. The after-tax cost of long-term debt would, therefore, be as follows:

$$k_b(1-T) = .135(.6) = .081$$

Thus, the after-tax cost of debt would be 8.1 percent. We had indicated that the coupon payment actually promised by the long-term debt of UC was 10 percent. But the coupon rate simply indicates what the cost was at the time the debt was issued. What is relevant for present decision making is the current cost of the debt, which we calculated.

Cost of Preferred Stock

Preferred stock is a hybrid between debt and common stock. Like debt, preferred stock carries a fixed commitment on the part of the corporation to make periodic payments; in liquidation, the claims of the preferred stockholders take precedence over those of the common stockholders. However, failure to make the preferred dividend payments does not result in bankruptcy as nonpayment of interest on bonds does. Thus, to the firm, preferred stock is somewhat less risky than common stock but riskier than bonds. To the investor, preferred stock is also less risky than common stock but riskier than bonds.

From the standpoint of the issuing firm, preferred stock has the disadvantage that its dividend is not deductible for tax purposes. On the other hand, the tax law provides that 85 percent of all dividends received by one corporation from another are not taxable. This 85 percent dividend exclusion makes preferred stock a potentially attractive investment to other corporations such as commercial banks and stock insurance companies. This attractiveness on the demand side pushes the yields on preferred stock to slightly below yields on bonds of similar companies. Although preferred issues may be callable and may be retired, most are perpetuities. If the preferred issue is a perpetuity, then its yield is calculated as follows:

$$\text{Preferred yield} = \frac{\text{Preferred dividend}}{\text{Price of preferred stock}} = \frac{d_{ps}}{p_{ps}} \qquad (10\text{A}.2)$$

Returning to our example for United Corporation, we find that its only preferred stock issue outstanding carries a $9 dividend. The current price of the preferred stock obtained from newspapers or other sources is $69.23. Hence, the preferred stock yield or its cost will be

$$\frac{d_{ps}}{p_{ps}} = \frac{\$9}{\$69.23} = .13 = 13\%.$$

The result is 13 percent. Since preferred stock dividends paid by the issuing corporation are not deductible for tax purposes, this 13 percent is therefore already on an after-tax basis. No further tax adjustment need be made. It stands on the same basis as the 8.1 percent after-tax cost of long-term debt whose before-tax cost was 13.5 percent.

Cost of Common Equity

The cost of common equity is the most difficult of the major sources of financing to be determined. Four major methods will be employed. They are

1. The Capital Asset Pricing Model
2. The bond yield plus equity risk premium
3. Realized investor yield
4. The dividend growth model

The first three are based fundamentally on financial market data. The fourth model has some theoretical problems but is so widely used that we include it as one of the inputs.

Capital Asset Pricing Model (CAPM) Approach. Recall that the CAPM approach states that the investors' required rate of return on common stock is equal to a risk-free rate plus a risk premium. The risk premium is the market risk premium (which is the market return minus a risk-free rate) multiplied by the applicable beta of the firm. The Security Market Line equation is

$$k_s = R_F + (\overline{R}_M - R_F)\beta_j$$

The market risk premium has been calculated in a number of studies. Over long periods of time it appears to average out for the United States between 6 and 8 percent. We will use 7.5 percent in our calculations here. Theory calls for using the short-term Treasury bill rate as an estimate of the risk-free rate. For example we can readily determine that the short-term Treasury bill rate is 10 percent. The only information specific to the firm that is required in the use of the CAPM is the beta or the risk measure. Various investment advisory services publish beta estimates for a large number of companies. Drawing on these we find that the beta for the common stock of United Corporation is 1.05.

Short-term interest rates fluctuate with greater volatility than longer-term interest rates. This is true of short-term T-bill rates as well as other short-term interest rates. Some analysts, therefore, find it useful to use a longer-term Treasury bond rate as a check in developing a CAPM estimate of the firm's cost of equity capital. For the fiscal year (say, 1999), we would find that the 10-year T-bill rate was 12.5 percent so that we would have

$$k_s = 12.5 + 7.875 = 20.375\%$$

For 1999, use of the 10-year T-bill rate would yield a somewhat higher cost of equity capital. For some prior periods, the reverse would have been true. Thus, we have some initial estimates of the firm's cost of equity capital, but we need to test these estimates by using other procedures as well.

Bond Yield Plus Equity Risk Premium.   Under the CAPM method described, the required return on equity represents a premium over the risk-free rate measured by yields on government securities. This second method also involves a risk premium. However, in this case it represents a premium over the firm's own long-term debt cost. This method provides a logical test check since the cost of common equity should be greater than the cost of debt. Debt represents a fixed legal claim giving bondholders a senior position over holders of preferred stock or common stock. The beta of long-term debt for a firm is typically much lower than the beta of its common stock. Hence we would expect a premium over the debt return in the required return to common stock.

This method is in the same spirit as the CAPM placing both the debt and the equity on a Security Market Line with the debt having a lower beta. If we had a good estimate of the beta of the debt, the differential between the required yield on the debt and the required yield on the equity would be given by the Security Market Line. The premium of the required equity return over the long-term debt return would represent the indicated risk premium. We have estimated this to be 4.5 percent for the United Corporation. Hence, given the cost of long-term debt that we have calculated to be 13.5 percent, the indicated required return to common equity by this method would be 18 percent.

Realized Investor Yield.   The realized investor yield is the average dividend yield plus the average capital gain over some prior period such as 10 years. This measure represents what investors have, in fact, required as a return from this company's common stock. This method captures the readjustments that investors make in the price of the firm's stock to take account of changes in the outlook for the firm. However, the measure for an individual firm may be unstable. To make the measure more reliable, another test check is to make the calculation for a group of similar firms, where random individual firm instability may be averaged out.

This calculation of the average dividend yield plus the average capital gain represents the average return realized by investors. This can be related to the Security Market Line, which gives us the required return on equity. In the long, run we would expect the average return to equal the required return since stock prices will be adjusted to move the two toward equality. For the previous 10 years for United Corporation we have calculated the average dividend yield to be 4.1 percent and the average capital gain to be 14.1 percent. Thus, by this method the indicated required return on equity is 18.2 percent.

Dividend Growth Model.   The dividend valuation model can be expressed as follows:

$$p_o = \frac{d_1}{k_s - g} = \frac{d_o(1+g)}{k_s - g} = \frac{\text{EPS}_o(1+g)(1-b)}{k_s - br} \qquad (10A.3)$$

The required return on equity can be derived from this dividend valuation expression. In Equation 10A.3. b is the percent of earnings retained by the firm, r is the expected marginal return on new capital invested, and d_o and d_1 are the current and expected dividends per share, respectively. A number of assumptions underlying the dividend valuation model should be noted to understand how it may be used to estimate the required return on equity for a firm. The growth rate (g) refers to the growth in dividends. Since g is the product of the retention rate times the internal profitability rate, this indicates that the model is an all internal equity financing model. Retained earnings is the only source of financing investment in this model. Furthermore, constant growth is required. There is no period of supernormal or subnormal growth and the constant growth continues through infinity.

The logic of the model indicates that the g refers to the growth rate in dividends, but under the assumptions of the model everything else also grows at the same rate. If dividends grow at 12 percent, and the payout ratio and retention rate are constant, earnings must be growing, at the same 12 percent. Since retained earnings are the only source of growth, the total assets of the firm will also be growing at 12 percent. And over time, the value of the firm or the price of its common stock will be growing at a 12 percent rate as well. Clearly there is a relationship between p, the price of the common stock, and the growth rate in earnings, dividends, and the total assets of the firm. Thus, the model provides a somewhat ambiguous basis for estimating k_s.

Nevertheless, the dividend valuation model is widely used in practice both for valuation common stock and for estimating the cost of equity capital for United Corporation. The valuation expression is solved for k_s as shown in Equation 10A.4:

$$k_s = \frac{d_1}{p_o} + g \qquad (10A.4)$$

Equation 10A.4 states that the required return on equity is the expected dividend yield plus the expected growth rate in dividends. The expected dividend is obtained by taking the current dividend, d_o, and applying the expected growth rate. For United Corporation, the current dividend is \$2.75. It is difficult to arrive at a reliable figure for the expected growth rate. One approach is to begin with the growth over some previous period. But the position of the firm is likely to be affected by developments of the economy as a whole as well as in its own industry. Nevertheless, various financial services provide estimates of expected growth in earnings and dividends for individual firms. In addition, an independent analysis can be made by the analyst attempting to make a calculation of the cost of capital for the firm. Suppose that by a combination of all of these methods we arrive at an expected growth rate in dividends for the firm of 12 percent. Then d_1 would be \$2.75 multiplied by 1.12 to give us a d_1 or expected next year's dividend of \$3.08. The current price of UC's stock is \$69.44. The \$3.08 divided by \$62.44 represents a 4.9 percent dividend yield. When this is added to the 12 percent expected growth rate, we obtain a 16.9 percent estimate of the required return on equity.

Summarizing our results thus far we have the following results for the four methods:

1. CAPM—20.4 percent
2. Bond yield plus equity risk premium—18.0 percent
3. Realized investor yield—18.2 percent
4. Dividend growth model—16.9 percent

Note that the first three methods of estimating the cost of equity capital use information generated by the financial markets. Therefore, they may be reasonably regarded as the required rates of return on equity by external investors. Hence, they represent an estimate of the cost of external equity funds. Since the dividend valuation model is an all internal equity financing model it may be reasonably regarded as providing the cost of internal funds. It is interesting to note that the three methods that provide estimates of external equity financing cluster at a little more than 18 percent, whereas the dividend valuation model gives a somewhat lower figure at approximately 17 percent as a cost of internal equity financing.

We now have estimates of all of the costs of the individual components in financing. We next consider how we can pull all of this information together to calculate the weighted marginal cost of capital for the firm as a whole, an expression that is referred to as WACC or MCC (marginal cost of capital).

Determining Market Value Weights and WACC

Column (1) in Table 10–A–2 represents the book value of the liabilities and stockholders' equity accounts for which an explicit charge can be calculated. The first item is notes payable on a short-term basis. Short-term notes payable would carry an interest cost relatively close to current interest rate levels. Hence, their market value would approximate their face value. Therefore, in column (2), the market price factor of the notes payable is shown at 100 percent. In calculating the effective cost of long-term debt we indicated that with a coupon rate of 10 percent and a current required market rate of 13.5 percent on United Corporation's AA debt, the current price per $1,000 bond for United Corporation would be approximately $800. Hence the market price would be about 80 percent of their maturity value. We made a similar calculation for preferred stock arriving at a 70 percent factor. For common equity we would employ the price of $62.44 previously used, which is 120 percent of the $52.04 book value per share.

T A B L E   10–A–2

Calculation of Market Value Weights and Proportions for
United Corporation

	Book Value (millions) (1)	Market Price Factor (2)	Market Value (millions) (3)	Proportions (4)	Targets (5)
Notes payable	$ 400	100%	$ 400	.108	10%
Long-term debt	1,000	80	800	.215	20
Preferred stock	200	70	140	.038	5
Common equity*	1,980	120	2,376	.639	65
	$3,580		$3,716	1.000	

*38.05 million shares.

Applying the market prices to the book value figures, we obtain the indicated market values shown in column (3). When we sum the market value figures we obtain $3,716 million as compared with book values of the four items of a somewhat smaller amount. From the market value figures we can calculate the proportions of financing, shown in column (4). These are proportions at market values. The use of book value weights would have been inappropriate because they are less likely to indicate what the proportions would be in the future financing of the firm. Market proportion weights provide a better estimate of the target financing mix of the firm than book value weights. In the financial planning models of the firm, target financing proportions would be employed. These would be the best indicator of the appropriate proportions to use in calculating the firm's weighted cost of capital. In column (5), we assume that we have access to such information. The figures are closely related to the current market proportions. It is assumed that the target proportion of common equity financing would increase slightly with the expected future rise in the price of the firm's common equity shares.

We now have the component costs of financing and the target proportions. We can bring these together to calculate the marginal cost of capital or the WACC (see Table 10–A–3). Recall that we assumed a 40 percent tax rate for United Corporation so that the after-tax cost of notes payable and the after-tax cost of long-term debt represent their before-tax cost multiplied by (1 – .40). We obtain a weighted average marginal cost of financing of 14.78 percent for United Corporation.

T A B L E   10–A–3

United Corporation's Cost of Capital with Internal Equity Financing

	Before-Tax Cost	After-Tax Cost	Target Proportions	Weighted Cost
Notes payable	13.5%	8.1%	.10	.81%
Long-term debt	13.5	8.1	.20	1.62
Preferred stock	13.0	13.0	.05	.65
Common equity	18.0	18.0	.65	11.70
			1.00	WACC = 14.78%

E N D N O T E S

1. For example, according to the annual almanac issue of *Mergers & Acquisitions* (March/April 1998), p. 41, the percentages were as follows: all cash 50.6 percent, all stock 32.5 percent, combination 16.9 percent.
2. A true breakout would have four categories: cash; stock; cash and stock; cash, stock, and notes. Most if not all ongoing studies combine the last two categories, and so we do here as well.
3. *1997 Watson Wyatt Directors and Officers Liability Survey* (Chicago: Watson Wyatt Worldwide, 1998).
4. Ibid.
5. The value of equity can be measured in various ways. In this discussion, we are assuming a simple valuation—stock price appreciation or decline over a defined postmerger period.
6. Research by Tim Loughran and Anand M. Vijh, University of Iowa, cited in Roger Lowenstein, "Why All Takeovers Aren't Created Equal," *Journal of Finance*, December 1997.
7. For background, see Stanley Foster Reed and Alexandra Reed Lajoux, *The Art of M&A: A Merger/Acquisition/Buyout Guide*, 3rd ed. (New York: McGraw-Hill, 1999), p. 191.
8. For example, since its acquisition of Uniroyal Goodrich Tires for $1.5 billion in 1990, French tiremaker Michelin has taken a low-key approach, preferring internal growth and joint ventures to acquisitions. In early 1997, in an interview with journalists, the company's chief financial officer said that Michelin would not make any acquisitions until its debt/equity ratio was 1:1 or lower. (At that time, the ratio was almost 2:1.)

9. Companies that have issued instruments (bonds and/or preferred stock) that are convertible into common stock make more complex calculations.

10. See, for example, "Exploring the Dilution Problem," *Director's Monthly*, August 1998, pp. 16ff, citing Donald Gough and Gregg Passin of Sibson and Company.

11. Multiple time frames for payment are also an issue. If the acquiring company and the acquired company merge, a problem of timing arises at the closing: Payment for the stock purchased by the acquirer must be made before the merger places the assets of the acquired company in the buyer's possession, but the loan to the buyer cannot be funded until the merger is consummated. To resolve this problem, the parties to the closing agree that all transactions will be treated as occurring simultaneously or, for the sticklers, that the seller of the stock will get a promissory note, which is repaid minutes later when the merger documents are filed. Sometimes lenders prefer to have both the buyer and the target named as borrowers on the acquisition loan. Tax or contract compliance questions may be raised by these timing issues, and they should be thought through carefully.

12. The Small Business Job Protection Act of 1996, effective January 1, 1997, increased the maximum allowable number of shareholders in an S corp from 35 to 75, and the Taxpayer Relief Act of 1997, effective January 1, 1998, creating a more favorable tax treatment of the S corp's share of income passed through to a ESOP.

13. In an S corporation, there are some unique twists to this rule under Treasury Regulations Section 1.1361-1(l)(2)(iii)(B). For details, see Martin D. Ginsberg and Jack S. Levin, *Mergers, Acquisitions, and Buyouts: A Transactional Analysis of the Governing Tax, Legal, and Accounting Considerations* (New York: Aspen Law and Business, 1998), vol. 2, ch. 11, p. 28.

14. A tax-free rollover of management's equity can adversely affect other aspects of the tax structuring of the transaction. Most notably, if the management buyout is intended to be treated for tax purposes as a cost basis asset acquisition, overlapping ownership between the acquired company and the acquirer may thwart such a characterization.

15. A National Starch transaction, named after the company that invented it, is a type of acquisition with tax benefits. In this transaction, a company buyer transfers cash, and one or more company shareholders transfer stock, into a newly formed corporation in exchange for common and preferred stock in the new entity. The new corporation then uses the cash to purchase the stock of the old company. Because the initial transfer of target stock and cash to the new entity qualifies as nontaxable under Section 351, no gain is recognized to the target shareholders on the receipt of the new company's preferred stock.

16. This appendix is adapted from J. Fred Weston and Thomas E. Copeland, *Managerial Finance: Ninth Edition* (Los Angeles: Academic Publishing, 1998) pp. 608ff.

CHAPTER 11

Managing Multiple Sources

Oh, I'd accept that burden, but my name's not written down.

Elena Stuarts, "What That Street Is Called," 1993

INTRODUCTION

For some fortunate acquirers, the financial support for a transaction comes from a single source—a longtime commercial banker, a committed underwriter, or an enthusiastic backer. Other acquirers, however, must use multiple sources—not just one lender, but several; not just an underwriter, but an underwriter and a lender; not just a backer, but a backer and a lender. Acquirers who do succeed in gathering multiple means of support must build relationships that satisfy multiple goals—both the acquirer's own and those of each source.

The following pages offer information and guidance that can help acquirers form and manage relationships with multiple financial sources. In the first part of the chapter, we will recap some of our earlier definitions of sources, and investigate the new trend of source convergence—or "one-stop shopping"—in M&A financing. Then, in the second part of the chapter, we will take a close look at multiple lenders, exploring subordination issues, intercreditor issues, and intercreditor agreements.

MULTIPLE SOURCES VERSUS ONE-STOP SHOPPING

There is a new trend toward one-stop financing for M&A. What is this and why is it happening?

One-stop financing basically means that the company seeking financing works with a single firm, rather than several firms, for all its financing needs. Traditionally, if a company needed to borrow money and do an underwriting, it would work with a commercial bank to do the loan, and with an investment banker to do the underwriting. With the new one-stop trend, the company may choose one firm to do both.

One-stop shopping goes hand in hand with the famed financial services revolution—the massive deregulation and consolidation that has been sweeping the industry over the past few decades. A series of legal changes—at both the federal and state levels in both legislatures and in courtrooms—has torn down old walls separating banking and commerce. These reforms have stopped short of an outright repeal of the famed Glass-Steagall Act of 1933, which prevents depository institutions from underwriting securities. On the other hand, they have made many chinks in the Glass-Steagall "wall" between banking and commerce. Today, for example, banks may own securities brokerage firms through holding companies.

What were all the Glass-Steagall restrictions, and which ones have been lifted?

The Glass-Steagall Act is actually a part of a larger law, called the Banking Act of 1933, which made many broad changes in the national banking system—including the banning of bank-owned securities companies. The Glass-Steagall sections of the Banking Act were as follows:

- Section 16 prohibited Federal Reserve System member banks from purchasing equity securities, and barred them from dealing in any securities other than U.S. Treasury and federal agency securities and general obligation securities (bonds) of states and municipalities.
- Section 20 prohibited member banks from affiliating with firms that underwrite and sell the equity and debt securities of companies.
- Section 21 prohibited underwriters from accepting deposits.
- Section 32 prohibited directors of member banks from serving as directors of securities firms, and vice versa.

Over the past 20 years, these four prohibitions have been weakened, thanks in part to efforts by commercial bankers to enter the arena of underwriters, and vice versa. As a result, today commercial banks may engage in several types of formerly prohibited activity.

For example, under the Bank Holding Company Act of 1956, as amended in the 1970s, bank holding companies may offer financial services other than deposit taking and lending, if approved by the Federal Reserve

Board. The Fed may approve activities that meet a public need and are deemed "closely related" to banking. The holding companies may do this directly, through a subsidiary bank, or through an affiliated company. Federal Reserve Regulation Y spells out these activities, which are approved on a case-by-case basis. These reforms and others mean that today a commercial bank may offer a variety of services, including:

- Operating a consumer finance company
- Offering discount brokerage services
- Sponsoring mutual fund issues and selling mutual funds
- Leasing equipment
- Serving as investment adviser to corporate clients
- Underwriting securities (i.e., asset-backed securities, corporate bonds, and commercial paper)

These changes make it easier for companies to use a commercial bank for all its financing needs, rather than using both a commercial bank and an investment bank.

Meanwhile, financial institutions that are not commercial banks (as defined by banking law) are still prohibited from accepting deposits, but they have made inroads into another classic commercial banking function—namely, lending.

Could you give examples of firms that provide both debt and equity financing?

Examples abound, since each side is vying for crossover customers. Commercial banks such as Chase Manhattan have underwriting subsidiaries, and investment banks such as Salomon Brothers and Donaldson, Lufkin & Jenrette have their own lending operations. In listing what they have done for specific deals, commercial banks and investment banks are often indistinguishable: Both offer merger advice, both serve as lead bank on loans, and both serve as lead managers on junk bond offers. And when it comes to "backers," many of these offer help in obtaining both debt and equity capital. (See Appendix 9-A.)

Some one-stop sources specialize in financing with a high component of leverage. This was the message of a full-page *Wall Street Journal* advertisement placed by Nationsbanc Capital Markets, a subsidiary of NationsBank (now merged with BankAmerica). The ad announced—in the plain language of so-called tombstones—recent loans and new issues that the bank had supported. As part of the ad, the bank stated:

Our commitment is to provide *one-stop* leveraged financing, with creative solutions backed by the capital to ensure superior execution. We have assembled one of the most experienced and fully *integrated* leveraged finance efforts in the business. From leveraged loan syndications, bridge loans, and high-yield securities to liability management, advisory services, and direct equity investments, no other firm is better able to meet *all* of your leveraged finance needs. [Emphasis added.][1]

What are the benefits of one-stop shopping versus using multiple sources?

First and foremost, the single source offers the advantage of convenience. The company doing the borrowing and issuing has to tell its story to only one company, instead of two. The relational work of all aspects of the financing, from planning to implementation to billing and payment is cut "in half"—and so is the time from application to receipt. A single source can also offer a "holistic" perspective on a company's financial needs. If it has loaned money to a company in the past, the source may have better ideas on how to package an underwriting. Conversely, if the company has helped with an underwriting, it may have a better sense of the company's borrowing needs.

Secrecy is another benefit. The fewer phone lines humming in a deal, the fewer leaks. (True, if the walls dividing lending and underwriting are too thin, there may be internal leaks and thus eventually betrayal.[2] On the other hand, conflicts of interest can appear in nondiversified financial services firms as well.[3]) Finally, one-stop shopping can increase the certainty of approval. An institution will be more likely to commit funds to a firm it knows than to a customer coming in from out of the blue.

What are the drawbacks of one-stop shopping?

The main drawback is lack of flexibility. An institution might be doing a good job for a customer in one area, and a poor one in the other area. The customer might be reluctant to withdraw business out of the second area out of fear than it will harm the first one. And even with relatively good service overall, say critics of one-stop shopping, no firm can possibly be the best at every aspect of a complex deal. A related concern is pricing; a customer that is a "captive" for a number of services might not be as inclined to negotiate for lower prices. Finally, when an institution gets involved in both commercial banking and investment banking, the possibilities for conflicts of interest grow proportionately.[4]

DEALING WITH MULTIPLE LENDERS

One common scenario in M&A financing is the use of several lenders. What different kinds of lenders are there?

Although sometimes only one lender is needed (a secured lender in most cases, or an unsecured one in the case of a very simple business with strong cash flow), multiple tiers of lenders are normally necessary for large transactions.[5] As mentioned in Chapter 4, a complex transaction funded by debt (e.g., a multilender leveraged buyout) may include several layers of debt. Each of these may be owned by a separate lender. Let us recap the list in Chapter 4, this time highlighting sources rather than instruments:

- Senior revolving debt or commercial paper is generally provided by *commercial banks* or similar *institutional lenders*.

- Senior term debt is normally provided by *commercial banks* in conjunction with senior revolving debt, or by similar *commercial lenders* or *insurance companies*.

- Senior subordinated debt is mainly placed by *investment bankers,* the principal purchasers being insurance companies, pension and investment funds, and financial institutions (as discussed in Chapter 5).

- Sale/leasebacks or other special financing arrangements for specific facilities or equipment are usually offered by *commercial finance companies* (as discussed in Chapter 6).

Sellers may also get involved in financing through a seller's subordinated note and/or seller's preferred stock. In addition, the deal may be funded through preferred or common stock sold to an independent third party, perhaps to a *leveraged buyout investment fund* or to one of the lenders. Common stock may be sold to the *buyer* or its *principals, key managers,* and *employees.* Finally, to wrap up our recap, warrants or options to acquire common stock may be granted as financing inducements to any of the parties providing financing or to the seller.

All these different providers of finance will have special requests and expectations that must be managed.

Do all the lenders typically want similar terms?

No. Sources of capital and their expected return will vary, even within the same transaction.[6]

For example, a senior lender will often lend up to 70 percent of the purchase price, depending on the amount of assets available for collateral and the strengths of cash flows, both projected and historical. If the senior lenders are properly secured, then they may not be as difficult in the negotiation of loan covenants and minimum interest rates. The subordinated lenders, on the other hand, are typically willing to provide 10 to 30 percent of the purchase price, but will generally demand a 15 to 30 percent annual return over a 5- to 10-year investment horizon.

Both the senior lender and the subordinated lender will usually look to the buyer to provide between 15 and 30 percent of the total capital required for the transaction. The general rule is, the larger the lender's portion of the acquisition financing puzzle, the higher its expected return on investment.

How is this accomplished?

The lenders all sign a contract that has subordination provisions. These provisions basically determine which of the lenders gets paid first if the borrower does not have enough money to pay all the lenders. The subordinated lender (often referred to as the *junior lender*) is the one that gets paid after the lender to which it is subordinated (the *senior lender*).

There are two types of subordination: *substantive* (order of payment in the event of trouble) and *procedural* (when and how the subordinated lender can call the loan of the borrower in case of default). Priority of payment under subordination provisions is different from lien priority, which relates only to the question of which lender has first access to proceeds of sale or foreclosure on the particular asset covered by the lien.

What are the principal subordination provisions?

In the event of any insolvency or bankruptcy proceeding, the junior lender agrees that the senior lender will be paid in full before the junior lender receives any payment.

Payment of the junior debt is prohibited if the senior debt is in default. Sometimes only defaults in payment (or certain major financial covenants of senior debt) will block payments of junior debt, or blockage will only occur, in certain types of default, for a limited period. Since any major default in the senior debt can lead to an acceleration of the debt, in theory the senior lender can convert any major covenant default into a payment default, if necessary, to prevent payment of junior debt. Senior lenders do not want, however, to be forced into taking the extreme step of acceleration, which can quickly lead to bankruptcy. Much negotiation of subordination provisions arises from the senior lender's desire to keep the junior lender from (1) being paid even if the senior debt is not accelerated, and (2) being able to force the senior lender to accelerate.

The junior lender agrees to hold in trust for, and pay over to, the senior lender any amount received by the junior lender not in accordance with the subordination provisions. This clause, known as a "hold and pay" provision, gives the senior lender a direct right to recover from the junior lender without going through the borrower.

What issues arise in negotiating substantive subordination provisions?

Common issues include:

- Principal payments on junior debt
- Priority of extra payments to the senior lender
- Priority of refinancings of senior debt
- Priority of trade debt

Why are principal payments on junior debt an issue?

M&A and buyout are almost always arranged so that no principal payments are scheduled to be made on junior debt until after the final maturity date on the senior debt. The senior loan agreement normally prohibits payments of junior debt ahead of schedule. A common exception to this rule is that senior lenders will often permit prepayment of junior debt with the proceeds of equity offerings or other junior debt. Also, the borrower is often allowed to prepay the junior debt to the extent it could otherwise make dividend or similar payments to shareholders. When there are notes to the seller, the parties are sometimes able to negotiate financial tests that, if satisfied, will permit principal payments on the notes. This is especially true when the note involves contingent payments to the seller.

What about priority of extra payments to the senior lender? What is involved here?

The senior lender will often seek (and get) the right to have all its penalties, fees, and expenses of collection paid before the junior lender gets any payments. If there is conflict with the junior lender over this point, it can usually be resolved by setting a cap on the fees.

What does the senior lender usually insist on with respect to refinancing?

A very important clause for the borrower in a typical subordination agreement is one stating that the junior lender will continue to be junior to any refinancing or refunding of the acquisition debt. Refinancing eventually occurs in at least half of all leveraged buyouts, and borrowers want to be sure they can replace a senior lender with another one on more favorable terms. They don't want such a transaction to become an opportunity for the seller or any other junior lender to make trouble.

This provision is more often an issue with sellers in seller takeback financings than it is with junior institutional lenders, which tend to accept rather broad definitions of senior debt. Senior debt is usually defined in junk bond subordination provisions as any debt for borrowed money that is not expressly made subordinated to the junior loan. Seller subordinated debt is more likely to define senior debt in terms of specific debt instruments and any refinancings or refundings thereof. Sellers sometimes exclude from the definition of senior debt any debt owed to the buyer or its shareholders.

Both seller and junk bond subordination provisions often will limit the amount of debt to which the junior loan is subordinated to a fixed amount, say 125 to 150 percent of the senior debt on the original date of borrowing. This limitation is designed to prevent the junior lender from being buried under a growing burden of senior debt that could substantially reduce its chances of getting paid.

What about priority of trade debt? When does this come up?

This issue, again, is particularly likely to arise with sellers. Trade debt is particularly important in buyouts, because in a typical LBO the buyer is purchasing a company that has been under the credit umbrella of its parent. Company management has never worried about its trade credit security, because everybody knows that it was a subsidiary of a great big parent with all the money in the world, and now it has become a separate, heavily leveraged company on its own. All parties should consider at an early stage the impact that the acquisition will have on all the acquired company's suppliers. It may be necessary in order to preserve supplier relationships that the seller be willing to remain below the suppliers in loan priority. The senior lender may insist on this feature in order to ensure that the company can retain its suppliers if financial storm clouds start to gather.

What issues arise in negotiating procedural subordination provisions?

These tend to be particularly difficult. They can best be divided into blockage and suspension provisions.

What are blockage provisions?

The *blockage provisions* are those parts of the subordination agreement that prevent the borrower from making payments to the junior lenders under certain circumstances. Seller subordinated notes frequently provide that if there is a default of any kind to a senior lender, no payments may be made on the seller note. In the case of institutional and junk bond lenders, payments on the junior debt are usually barred indefinitely when there is a payment default on the senior loan, and for a limited period of time (anywhere from 90 to 270 days, but usually around 180 days) when a nonpayment default exists, unless the senior lender accelerates its debt, in which case the blockage continues. Such periods of blockage are often available only once each year.

The fact that a payment is blocked does *not* mean that there is no default under the junior loan. The blockage provisions do not by themselves prevent the junior lender from declaring a default, accelerating its loan, and, if appropriate, forcing an involuntary bankruptcy on the borrower, although the "suspension" provisions discussed below may prevent this. Such provisions are merely an agreement between the lenders and the company that no matter what action the junior lender takes, during the blockage period the company may not make the proscribed payments. A blocked payment will constitute a default on the junior debt and entitle the junior lender to accelerate the loan, unless prevented by the suspension provisions. Therefore, a senior lender is likely to waive its right to blockage unless the company is in serious trouble.

What are the suspension provisions?

The *suspension provisions* are the parts of the subordination agreement that limit a junior lender's rights to take enforcement actions if there is a default on the junior loan. These provisions are prevalent in privately placed subordinated debt. Enforcement actions include suing the borrower, accelerating the loan, and declaring the entire amount due or putting the borrower into bankruptcy. Depending upon the type of loan, these rights may be severely restricted until the senior debt is paid in full or for a significant length of time, or they may be subject to few or no restrictions.

The suspension provisions are also important when both lenders have security interests in the same collateral (that is, a senior and junior lien on fixed assets). In such a case, it is common for the junior lender to be required to refrain from taking any action against the collateral until (1) the expiration of a fixed period of time, (2) acceleration of the loan by the senior lender, or (3) full payment of the senior lender, whichever happens first.

What rights do the senior and junior lenders want to have if the borrower defaults?

The senior lender wants to be as certain as possible that its superior position is meaningful in a practical sense. It wants no money leaving the corporation if there is any default on its loan, and it wants to control the timing, pace, and final resolution of any workout including possible asset sales or restructuring of the business.

For that reason, it wants to restrict the junior lender to relatively few events of default (generally only those that are a signal of substantial financial difficulties, such as a payment default on the junior loan or acceleration of other significant debt) so that the junior lender will have fewer opportunities to force the borrower into a workout, or worse, bankruptcy.

If there are fewer possible events of default under the junior loan, a senior lender may be able to keep the junior lender on the sidelines by keeping the interest payments on the junior debt current while it arranges a workout with the borrower. Once there is actually a default on the junior loan, the senior lender seeks the suspension provisions to forestall efforts by the junior lender to sue the borrower, accelerate the maturity of the junior loan, or throw the borrower into bankruptcy. The effect of all these provisions is to reduce the negotiating leverage of the junior lender.

The junior lender wants to minimize the time it is not participating in the workout and the ability of the senior lender to work out matters with the borrower without its consent or, at least, participation. It basically wants a "seat at the table" of any workout as soon as possible. It also wishes to keep the blockage periods as short as possible and minimize suspension provisions so that it can pressure the senior lender not to block payments on the junior debt. To gain negotiating leverage, the junior lender will also seek to structure the sub-ordination provisions so that once there is a default it can threaten to acceler-ate its loan and bring down the financial house of cards. In actuality, however, the junior lender is unlikely to accelerate, since it would probably have more to lose than the senior lender in a bankruptcy.

What about the borrower?

The typical borrower is trapped in the middle. Its main concern is that any one of these issues may kill the deal—an outcome to be avoided at almost any cost. On the other hand, it also wants to avoid setting up a situation where it will have little or no time or leverage to work out problems with the senior lenders before financial Armageddon arrives.

The borrower will not agree to clauses that favor an unrestrained "Snidely Whiplash" senior lender that can sell off all the assets and close down the business to pay its own loan off rather than live with an extended workout that offers a better chance for ultimate survival of the borrower. The borrower particularly wants to prevent the seller from gaining the ability to compel ac-tion by the institutional lenders. A deeply subordinated seller is more likely to accept 10 cents on the dollar and go away—often a key step in a workout if the borrower's stockholders are to have any incentive to make the additional ef-fort and investment necessary to save the company.

What does the senior lender require with respect to defaults on the junior loan?

A basic objective of the senior lender is to eliminate or at least minimize oppor-tunities for the junior lender to declare a default. Thus, the senior lender will be likely to strongly oppose a "cross-default provision" in favor of the junior lender—that is, a stipulation that any default under the senior loan is a default under the junior loan. If such a provision is given, it should at least be nar-rowed to certain specific senior loan defaults and should provide that any waiver by the senior lender or cure of the default terminates the default and rescinds any resulting acceleration on the junior loan as well.

The senior lender will also wish to be sure that any default on the junior loan is a default on the senior loan; that is, the senior lender will have a cross-default provision running in its favor, so that the junior lender is never in a position to take enforcement action against the borrower at a time when the senior lender cannot. The senior lender should not object, however, to a "cross-acceleration clause" permitting the junior lender to declare a default and accelerate its loan if the senior lender accelerates the senior loan.

Are subordination provisions generally the same for all junior loans?

Definitely not. First, the subordination provisions and all other intercreditor issues are the subject of negotiation and rarely are two deals exactly the same. Second, the subordination provisions vary greatly depending upon the type of junior lender, and whether the junior debt is privately placed or sold in a public offering. The range of junior debt subordination includes (from most deeply subordinated to least) seller's notes, institutional mezzanine lenders and other privately placed funded debt, and public junk bonds.

For how long is the subordinated debt subordinated?

Usually the junior debt is subordinated throughout its term or until the senior debt, including refinancings, is paid in full.

Is preferred stock subordinate to all debt?

Preferred stock is subordinated in liquidation to all debt. But preferred stock is a creature of contract between the company and its preferred stockholders, and if it is to be subject to payment restrictions imposed by lenders, the company's articles of incorporation should specifically say so.

In what agreement do subordination terms appear?

Very often, subordination provisions are found in the junior debt instrument itself, but in many cases the lenders prefer to have a separate subordination agreement. This is especially true when the junior lender doesn't want some or all of the subordination provisions to apply after the particular senior loan has been repaid. The borrower must be careful here because, if the subordination provisions fall away, the borrower may have a hard time refinancing its senior loan. As discussed above, it is customary to expect and get continuing subordination of some kind on the part of the junior lenders.

How are subordination issues affected by corporate structure?

Corporate structure has a powerful effect on relative rights and priorities of lenders and can be used to enhance one lender's position against another's.

An oversimplified example will illustrate how this works. Suppose the acquirer wishes to buy a retail company that is structured as a parent corporation with a principal operating subsidiary. The revolving credit and term lender could lend to the operating subsidiary, secured by its current and fixed assets, except the stores. The stores could be financed through loans to a separate partnership that owns them and leases them to the subsidiary. The subsidiary can obtain its working capital by selling certain categories of its accounts receivable to a separate corporation, which would finance the purchase with notes secured by the accounts. The mezzanine debt could be loaned to the parent corporation. The result is shown in Figure 11–1.

F I G U R E   11–1

Subordination and Corporate Structure

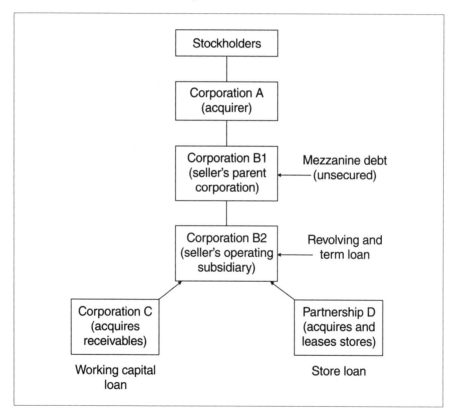

The acquirer (A) forms relationships with several lenders. Because each lender lends to a different entity, there is minimal contact between lenders and their security rights, and relative priorities are determined by the assets and corporate structure of their respective borrowers. The revolving credit and term lender to the operating subsidiary (B2) is in the senior position, except that its rights do not extend to the stores, which are owned by the partnership (D) or accounts receivable, which are sold to the separate corporation (C). Proceeds from the sale of accounts receivable are used to pay down both the revolving and term loan and to pay rent on the stores; after these needs are met, the proceeds can be paid out as dividends to the parent company (B1), which then can pay the mezzanine debt.

To the extent that the revolving loan is paid down, Corporation B (both its B1 parent company and its B2 subsidiary) gains working capital financing through its ability to borrow again under the revolver, assuming sufficient availability. Because no dividends will be paid if Corporation B's revenues cannot cover its debts to the revolving and term lender and Partnership D, the mezzanine debt is automatically subordinated to both the revolving and term lender and Partnership D. Such a structure makes the relationships between lenders clear from the start and minimizes opportunity for conflict between them.

This method of structuring priorities can, at least in theory, give one lender a very strong advantage over another in bankruptcy. (This is "in theory" because no one can predict the behavior of a bankruptcy judge, who has ample power to disregard corporate layers and combine bankruptcy proceedings of different corporations so as to sweep away even the most elegant structural devices.)

If, in this example, Corporation B goes bankrupt, the revolving and term lender will be deemed its sole creditor, other than trade credit and Partnership D (but only to the extent of overdue rent). The revolving and term lender can, thus, control the bankruptcy proceeding without even giving the mezzanine lender a place at the creditor's table. For that reason, the mezzanine debt, which is unsecured, is even more deeply subordinated than it would be if all loans were made to the same entity but subject to the subordination provisions discussed earlier in this chapter. Junior lenders may, consequently, object strongly to being required to lend at the parent level if the senior debt is at the operating level.

Lending at different levels can also present state tax problems. Some states do not permit consolidation of parent and subsidiary tax returns. Consequently, in those states, the deductions derived by Corporation A from interest payments on the mezzanine debt cannot be netted against the operating income received by Corporation B. In addition, care must be taken to be sure that loan agreements and corporate laws permit the necessary dividends to be paid so that funds can flow as required between the different corporations.

RESOLVING INTERCREDITOR CONFLICTS

What kinds of intercreditor conflicts might arise during the M&A financing process?

The major areas of difference relate to subordination provisions and rights to collateral.

Do not underestimate the importance of these issues. Intercreditor issues can give rise to serious negotiating problems and can even imperil the deal itself. Unlike buyers and sellers, both of whom usually have a strong stake in achieving a closing and therefore considerable negotiating flexibility, lenders may feel less impelled to close the deal and may condition their participation on compliance with a rather narrow and specific set of security and return criteria.

Once misunderstandings or conflicts arise as to who is to get what collateral or how subordinated the junior debt will be, they are often very difficult to resolve. For example, if two lenders' negotiators have sold the deal to their loan committees on mutually inconsistent bases, misunderstandings can take weeks to straighten out. Competitor banks or insurance companies, rather than focusing on closing the deal, may try to settle old scores, to prove their negotiating skills, to win points with their superiors, or to meet the not always appropriate standards of their lending manuals.

Nothing can be more alarming and frustrating for buyer and seller than watching lenders' loan officers or counsel come to loggerheads over major or even minor points when neither lender has much incentive or institutional flexibility to accommodate or withdraw gracefully. The situation becomes worse when each lender is not a single entity but a syndicate of banks or insurance companies. For these reasons, transactions should be structured and planned to minimize and resolve intercreditor conflicts as rapidly and as early as possible.

Why doesn't the buyer simply make clear to each lender from the start which security rights and priorities each will have?

Most intercreditor problems arise when two creditors are negotiating subordination rights or rights over collateral and encounter an issue that has not been raised and resolved as part of their respective loan commitments. Consequently, solution number one is to identify as fully as possible at the commitment stage which priorities, assets, or kinds of assets will be allocated to each lender. Some areas are clear and well accepted: Revolving lenders get a first lien on current assets; term lenders get a first position in property, plant, and equipment. Less clear is which lenders get the first position in intangibles, other than those (such as patents) necessary to use a particular piece of equipment, or licenses necessary to sell inventory, which go with the tangible assets to which they relate.

The buyer may, however, choose to keep this point unclear as a matter of negotiating tactics—in an effort not to deprive one lender of a particular piece of collateral unless the buyer is sure that another lender will insist on getting it. The lender may be more easily persuaded to get along without the additional collateral once its loan officers are fully involved and appraisals and due diligence have been satisfactorily completed. The buyer may also be trying to keep some assets unencumbered.

Or the buyer may simply miss the point. There is likely to be a lot of time pressure at the stage at which loan commitments are being negotiated, and the buyer may have clinched the deal by promising to close in two weeks. Furthermore, even if all the major terms can be worked out between the parties, the commitment letter won't cover minor issues, such as how much time the term lender will give the revolving credit lender to complete processing of or to remove the inventory (revolving credit collateral) from the premises before being free to close down and sell the plant (term lender collateral). Even these questions can be troublesome sources of delay or conflict at the late hours of the closing.

How can such intercreditor problems be avoided?

There are two cardinal rules for borrowers to follow in minimizing intercreditor issues:

1. Try to resolve the major issues in advance while there is still competition between potential lenders and before substantial commitment fees are paid.
2. Try for as long as possible to negotiate the issues via "shuttle diplomacy" between the lenders, forestalling direct negotiation between them.

How do you identify and solve intercreditor issues early in the process?

Prior to signing the commitment letter, the borrower should seek to obtain from each potential lender copies of its most recent executed (as opposed to draft) intercreditor documents. The executed documents will reflect concessions that the drafts will not. The documents should be compared to see which senior and junior lender has the most reasonable provisions, and these should be used as the basis for negotiating with all the lenders. A comparison of the junior and senior documents will reveal the areas most likely to create material conflicts—that is, those that could imperil the deal, as opposed to those that are susceptible to easy resolution in the course of negotiations.

If the borrower has decided which junior lender it will use and is choosing among competing senior lenders, it is often useful to present the typical language that the junior lender has agreed to with respect to the major intercreditor issues for review by the potential senior lenders. Before the commitment is made final, the borrower should seek senior lender approval of the most important parts of the typical junior lender language. The same process works in reverse if the senior lender has been chosen and there are several potential junior lenders.

Once the conflict areas are identified, the borrower must make a judgment: Can the differences be resolved later or must they be resolved at this stage of the negotiation? This would be the case, for example, when one lender requires provisions that are novel or likely to be provocative. When subordinated debt is to be sold in a public offering, investment bankers will often insist on subordination provisions that, they assert, the market expects and demands. If the investment banker is making a bridge loan that depends for its takeout upon having easily marketable junk debt, it will be particularly insistent on the inclusion of these basic provisions in the junk debt. If the senior lender expects substantially different provisions, the borrower is in for big problems. They must be ironed out at this stage, while there is still time to get a new lender if necessary.

Nothing helps more on such a negotiation than having an in-depth knowledge of the current practices in the marketplace. It's always easier to postpone resolving an issue if you know you can make the argument later to your senior lender that other lenders have given in on this point.

Remember that you are engaged in a balancing act between the desire to resolve intercreditor issues early and the other, more crucial economic terms of the loan, such as interest rate, fees, term, and prepayment schedule. It is foolish to press hard unnecessarily on intercreditor issues before you have commitments on basic terms, when the result could be adverse trade-offs on material terms. On the other hand, great economic terms are meaningful only if the deal actually closes.

Shouldn't lenders work out intercreditor questions between themselves?

Typically, no—at least not in the initial stages of negotiation. Especially early on, the buyer should try to avoid having the lenders communicate directly with each other about these issues. The buyer will have much more control over the negotiating process if, like Henry Kissinger shuttling between Cairo, Damascus, and Jerusalem, or Madeline Albright trying to forge peace in the Balkans, he or she filters the proposals of each party.

More important, there is a much better chance of reaching agreement if the buyer can formulate a compromise position and sell it to each party. This is especially true because the intercreditor meetings can involve a cast of thousands—each tier of lenders, the borrower, and sometimes trustees and their respective counsel, each of whom brings its own group of partners and associates. It is far harder to achieve major concessions in such a crowded environment with everyone's ego on display. If you're forced to agree to direct intercreditor negotiation, try to minimize the size of the meeting.

By the late stages of negotiating the loan agreements and the intercreditor agreement the lenders are more likely to come into direct contact, and if the transaction is well advanced and the personalities and relationships of the lenders are suitable, the final minor issues can often be resolved most efficiently directly between them. Even then, however, the buyer should be ready to continue the shuttle diplomacy process right up to the end if any of the lenders or their counsel are difficult or the negotiating atmosphere is tense.

The one exception to the no-early-direct-negotiations rule can arise when the lenders involved have worked together successfully in prior deals and agreed precedents exist between them for resolving intercreditor issues. If one lender says, when you mention the identity of the other, "Oh, is Jim doing it? We'll use the Amalgamated format," you can relax a little. But still keep a close eye on them.

DRAFTING INTERCREDITOR AGREEMENTS

What is an intercreditor agreement?

This is an agreement among lenders to loan funds to a particular borrower. It governs, among other things, the priority rights of lenders in collateral and proceeds of collateral and sets forth which lender or group of lenders shall have the right to make decisions about collateral. It is normally drafted by the most senior lender.

What issues are most likely to come up in negotiations of an intercreditor agreement?

The most common issues are:

- Equal or fair treatment

- Rights of one lender to amend the loan agreement without the consent of the other lender
- Changes in status between lenders
- Allocating shared rights over collateral
- Voting rights of lenders and others in a bankruptcy

What issues of fair or equal treatment come up in negotiating an intercreditor agreement?

When one lender has a first priority in some assets and another lender in other assets, each should have parallel rights as to priority, initiation of foreclosure proceedings, exercise of other remedies, payment for related expenses, and the like. A senior lender may seek to write in overbearing provisions with respect to junior liens. It may, for example, try to grant itself the right to foreclose on or sell collateral whether or not at market price. Such provisions should be avoided because they are probably not enforceable and raise the hackles of junior lenders.

Even in cases involving differences in the amount and quality of collateral, peace can reign if the drafter of the agreement is evenhanded. The drafter must be careful to keep the clauses of the intercreditor agreement in strict parallel—for every grant of a right to the revolving lender, there was a similar (if less valuable) grant for the term lender.

In negotiating an intercreditor agreement, where do lenders usually draw the line on later amendments by individual lenders?

Senior lenders will not want subordinated lenders paid off while senior debt is still outstanding. Therefore, it is not uncommon for a junior lender to be barred from shortening amortization schedules or the weighted average life of a financing. It is also uncommon for one lender to permit another lender to increase interest rates or rate formulas without its consent, because these terms may affect the company's ability to service all its debt.

On the other hand, a borrower should be able to agree with any one lender to ease terms of payment or to amend covenants or waive defaults without involving other lenders. Subordinated lenders frequently require that the borrower may not enter into amendments to its loan agreement that could "materially and adversely affect" the junior lender. This is a vague provision that tends to make the senior lender cautious but leaves leeway for the run-of-the-mill adjustments and corrections that normally are needed in a loan agreement after the closing. It often provides a reasonable compromise.

What about changes in status between lenders? How are these negotiated?

Sometimes one lender is prepared to take a lower priority against another only for a limited period of time or until some external event occurs. If one lender ceases to be secured, another lender may also be willing to release its security. If a senior lender agrees to extend the term of its loan past a certain date, the subordinate lender may demand the right to gain equal seniority, that is, to become *pari passu*.

When do lenders have to allocate shared rights over collateral?

Allocation should be squared away whenever an intangible right, such as a patent or copyright, is needed for realization of value for assets pledged to two different lenders. Also, allocation should be resolved in agreements where the exercise of its rights by one lender blocks another lender's rights—for example, if the term lender's right to foreclose on a factory building blocks the revolving lender's right to remove or complete processing of inventory.

What are the key issues when it comes to setting forth voting rights in the event of bankruptcy?

This is a delicate area. Senior lenders try very hard to gain control of creditors' committees in bankruptcy. They may seek to require junior lenders to waive contests of bankruptcy plans, for example. Junior lenders, if they are knowledgeable, will resist this move. Borrowers should encourage a reasonable compromise.

CONCLUDING COMMENTS

Today's deal makers enjoy a wide range of choices, not only in how they finance their transactions, but in who provides that financing. They may wish to use a single institution for all their financing needs—such as a highly diversified commercial bank. Alternatively, they may choose to engage the services of several sources, such as a group of lenders. But no matter how well deal makers select and manage their sources, they may eventually have to reconsider their selections. Hence, refinancing is our next topic.

E N D N O T E S

1. Full-page advertisement in *The Wall Street Journal,* February 21, 1996, p. C17.

2. See, for example, Stephen E. Frank, "Suit Against Chase, Role of Officers, Show Strains of Bank's Move into Wall Street, *The Wall Street Journal,* May 15, 1997. In this case, Chase's investment banking unit agreed to help one client make a hostile takeover offer against another client—from Chase's lending side. The lending client sued Chase, claiming that it was in a position to pass confidential information to the aggressor company, and so violated its fiduciary duty. This example, no matter how well Chase respected the wall of secrecy between the two areas, shows that using a one-stop source for both lending and underwriting can pose security risks.

3. In 1996, for example, the investment bank Morgan Stanley performed M&A advisory work for British Telecommunications/MCI, even though it had a long-standing relationship with the client's competitor, AT&T. See "Morgan Stanley Worries Advisory Role in BT/MCI Merger May Ruffle AT&T," *The Wall Street Journal,* November 5, 1996, p. C1.

4. See note 2.

5. This discussion of subordinated lending is adapted from Stanley Foster Reed and Alexandra Reed Lajoux, *The Art of M&A: A Merger/Acquisition/Buyout Guide,* 3rd ed. (New York: McGraw-Hill, 1999), pp. 219ff.

6. This answer is excerpted almost verbatim from Andrew J. Sherman, *Mergers and Acquisitions from A to Z: Strategic and Practical Guidance for Small- and Middle-Market Buyers and Sellers* (New York: AMACOM, 1998), p. 150.

Refinancing Strategies

You could not step twice into the same rivers; for other waters are ever flowing onto you.

Heraclitus (c. 540–475 B.C.), *On the Universe*, Fragment 1, line 41

INTRODUCTION

All the foregoing chapters have pointed to this one, because the way a deal is financed helps determine the way it will (or may) be refinanced. Indeed, good financing anticipates and prepares for refinancing. In the world of M&A financing, the last line in many stories is not "and so they lived happily ever after—*The End*." Instead, the last line is "and so they decided to seek additional financing—*To Be Continued*."

True, not every first-round financing leads to future rounds. Acquirers may find adequate postdeal support in their very first source of equity financing. Many loan agreements never get amended, thanks in part to grace and cure provisions and waivers, as discussed Chapter 7. And on the equity side, some initial public offerings are not only IPOs, but also (to coin a phrase) FPOs, or final public offerings—the only time their issuer will ever raise money by selling stock to the public. These firms borrow or raise just enough to be independent happily ever after.

Few companies, however, can avoid the need to refinance in one way or another. So all companies, including those that never do refinance, can benefit from the start from an *understanding of refinancing*—not only how to avoid or delay it, but how to plan for it as a valid contingency.

First of all, an individual loan agreement may prove to be overly optimistic on the part of the borrower. None of us can ever be sure that the promises we make today will be fulfilled tomorrow, despite our best efforts. Catastrophes, natural and created, may occur, leading to situations beyond our control. Our hopes to cross-sell newly acquired customers may be dashed when an unexpected competitor arises. The new "turnaround" managers we hired to run the troubled company we bought may turn out to be troubled themselves. To paraphrase Albert Einstein, the universe is not malicious, but it is subtle. The contingencies described above may occur in only one in a thousand deals—but that's often enough to plan for.

Second, companies grow and change—especially after a merger or buyout, when a new situation confronts all stakeholders. Like the streams that blend into and separate out of rivers, newly combined companies change as they move. Refinancing is a vital part of this flow toward the future.

In short, deal makers, therefore, must deal with the dynamic reality of refinancing from day one. The restructuring of a financial obligation is not like retreading a tire to roll down the same old roads. Rather, refinancing is like rerouting a river to irrigate new fields. Let's see how by looking at various types of refinancing.

REFINANCING OVERVIEW

What are the various types of refinancing that might occur?

Each instrument of financing has its own mode of refinancing, depending on the contract (or contracts) signed to yield the financing. In previous chapters, we discussed a variety of financing instruments including loans, bonds, and stock. Each of these is based on some type of agreement—whether a loan agreement, a bond indenture, or a stock certificate. These agreements typically include provisions that allow one or both parties to the agreement to change specific terms of the agreement. Refinancing occurs when these change-provoking terms are exercised, when new provisions are added, or existing provisions are waived or dropped.

A broader definition of M&A refinancing might include any new external financing the company obtains in order to meet the obligations of the original financing; a better term for this activity (coined by the authors) might be *serial financing* or *chain financing*.

A still broader definition of M&A refinancing might include the sale of assets after an acquisition to help pay for the acquisition (either by paying off a loan or by repurchasing stock). This is actually not refinancing per se, but merely loan repayment via sell-off.

Finally, there is another phenomenon that is often referred to as M&A refinancing—and that is the restructuring of the acquired company's working capital debt at the time of an acquisition. This is often the first step in the new company's financing journey.

What are some recent innovations in refinancing?

In the debt arena, there are several new techniques that can be used to lower the risk of credit *extended* for M&A. These are used by lenders, not borrowers.

Some commercial banks use a "good bank, bad bank" technique. This involves placing nonperforming and other lower-quality assets into a *collecting bank,* or liquidating trust, that is sold or spun off to shareholders.

Insurance companies sometimes employ *securitization,* the sale of several slices, or *tranches,* of securities backed by the mortgages or bonds below investment grade (junk bonds) held by the insurance company. A tranche is one of the classes of debt securities issued as part of a single instrument, such as a bond. This $200 billion market has some risks for buyers of the securities, since during a period of refinancing—when borrowers pay off the loans on their assets—the stream of annuity payments ends.[1]

Also, insurance companies and savings and loans can raise capital by converting from depositor-owned mutual organizations to stockholder-owned structures, a process called *stocking.* A major insurance example in 1992 was the stocking of Equitable Life Assurance Society of the United States.

Finally, to reduce the risk of M&A lending or other types of lending, a financial institution can sell a credit derivative instrument such as a credit-default swap. In a default swap, a lender pays a fee to investors in order to get them to assume the default risk of a particular loan. If the borrower defaults, investors must reimburse the bank for the loss in loan value. Similar instruments include total-return swaps—enabling lenders to sell the cash stream of a loan but not the loan—and simple options on credit risk. The market for credit derivatives exceeds $150 billion.[2]

Acquirers seeking to use any of these debt-recycling practices should exercise caution, since many of them have come under regulatory scrutiny.[3]

In the equity arena, innovations seem more rare. One new stock-based refinancing method used in private placements is called the preferred equity redemption cumulative stock (PERCS), a security designed by Morgan Stanley. PERCS offer a higher dividend than would be received in the underlying common stock. They are automatically convertible on a share-for-share basis but are subject to the issuer's earlier call.

DEBT REFINANCING:
WORKING CAPITAL, LOANS, BONDS, AND NOTES

When one company buys another one, it often inherits existing working capital debt. Should the acquirer leave it in place or refinance it?

First, let us take a closer look at working capital debt. In a company that is being considered as an acquisition candidate, this debt is likely to appear in any of at least four forms:

- A secured revolving credit loan from an outside lender
- A parent's intercompany transfers, either with or without interest
- Bank letters of credit (LCs) or guarantees to secure purchases from suppliers, principally for foreign sourcing
- More or less generous payment terms from suppliers[4]

The first two kinds of debt will almost certainly have to be refinanced at the acquisition closing. A secured revolver, or even an unsecured one, will inevitably tie up assets and stand in the way of any plans for secured acquisition financing, and the parent/seller will not want to retain what are probably short-term, rather informal financial arrangements of an in-house nature. There may, however, be some room for a buyer to argue for at least some short-term financing through a seller takeback of existing intercompany loans.

Refinancing the third type of debt is also common, but risky for all parties. A senior revolving credit acquisition lender often provides LC financing after the acquisition and will probably insist upon doing this financing as part of the deal. Sometimes such financing can be trouble, because not all lenders have experience with LCs. One solution is to put a limit on the amount of LC debt, and to charge London Interbank Offered Rate (LIBOR) on a sliding scale on the basis of the amount used. An additional solution is to include the existing LC lender in the lending group where its expertise will be accessible.

As for the fourth type of debt, it usually should not be a problem to retain existing relationships and favorable terms with suppliers. They will probably be relieved to find that the buyer doesn't plan to close the business or move it elsewhere. In some cases, suppliers have relied on the presence of a deep-pocket parent company as added security and may be looking for special assurances difficult for the postacquisition company to provide. In other cases, it is possible to structure the acquisition so that a subsidiary that purchases on trade credit has a better debt-to-equity ratio than its parent and can retain favorable trade terms.

As mentioned, these refinancing decisions must be made very close to the time of the acquisition—perhaps before it. The type of refinancing we are talking about in this chapter is refinancing of the money obtained to do the acquisition—an event that usually occurs (if it occurs at all) well after the refinancing.

What exactly is M&A loan refinancing, how common is it, and why do companies engage in it?

M&A loan refinancing is a change in one or more terms of a loan agreement signed to finance a merger, acquisition, buyout, or joint venture. The amount of money involved annually in M&A loan refinancing is roughly equivalent to the amount of money involved in the loans themselves. In other words, sooner or later, virtually every penny loaned gets refinanced.[5] Companies often make such changes because they have trouble meeting the terms of the contracts they originally sign.

Since loan refinancing is done to excuse the buyer, it is obviously good for the borrower, but what's in it for the lender?

The lender has a choice between calling the loan or renegotiating it. If the lender calls the loan, it may or may not receive all its money. If it does receive its money, it may put the borrowing company into financial distress and so limit or curtail future business with it, thus killing the proverbial "goose that lays the golden eggs."

Of course, the borrower could be a prosperous bluffer, in which case calling the loan will be wise and hardly fatal. At the opposite extreme, the company could be insolvent already, in which case calling the loan will be more a symptom than cause of this misfortune. Most situations, however, lie in the vast middle ground between these two extremes.

What kinds of changes might be negotiated between a lender and a borrower in a loan refinancing?

In rough order of magnitude (from easiest to most difficult), buyers may seek the following changes:

- Weakening and/or waiving particular covenants (bans such as the borrower's promise to freeze or gain approval for asset sales, or imperatives such as maintaining a certain cash flow to debt service ratio)
- Slowing down the pace of payments by extending the time of repayment
- Decreasing the rate of interest to be paid
- Lowering the amount of money to be repaid
- Increasing the amount of the money loaned, either with the original lender or through an additional lender
- Forgiving part or (in dire circumstances) all of the loan

Lenders will seek the opposite of these things—often as a countermeasure to some change the borrower requests. For example, the borrower may ask for more time and more money, and the lender may agree, but increase the rate of interest.

Is it really possible to renegotiate loan terms? A deal's a deal, isn't it?

Yes, a deal is a deal when it comes to leveraged transactions, as in others, but the higher the loan amount and the more sophisticated the lender, the more likely it is that the terms of a loan can be changed, despite the numerous technical provisions discussed earlier in this book. (For ample evidence of the flexibility of creditors when they are hard-pressed, consider any Chapter 11 bankruptcy case.) On the other hand, lenders too may wish to renegotiate loan terms, particularly during periods of falling interest rates.

In refinancing a loan by changing agreement terms, do all the members of a lending group have to approve every waiver and amendment?

Generally, no. But the provisions that relate to interbank matters, such as the percentage of lenders needed to grant waivers, are generally contained in a document (sometimes called the *participation agreement*) to which the borrower is not a party, and, frequently, that it may not even be allowed to see. Although lender approval arrangements are various, it is not unusual for them to provide that certain changes in the loan (such as changes in interest rates, due date, and principal amount) are so fundamental that all lenders must consent, whereas other changes can be approved by banks holding at least a 51 percent interest (or in some cases, a 66.6 percent interest) in all loans outstanding or in lending commitments.

Could you give an example of these different types of refinancings?

A recent Sunbeam refinancing used almost all of them. In July 1998, lenders to Sunbeam Corp. extended the time on a loan package the company received in order to buy three companies, but charged a higher interest rate. After weeks of negotiation, the lenders granted Sunbeam a six-month waiver on certain covenants in the loan agreements the company signed when taking out a $1.7 billion loan earlier the same year. The loan agreement was signed in March 1998 to help finance its acquisitions of Coleman Co., First Alert Inc., and Signature Brands USA Inc. The lenders were Bank America Corp. (30 percent), First Union (30 percent), and Morgan Stanley Dean Witter & Co. (40 percent). At the same time, the banks increased the interest rate they charged by a half a percent (0.5 percentage point). The initial rate on $1.2 billion of the credit now will float at 2.75 points above the LIBOR, and the remainder will float at 3 points above LIBOR.[6]

Could you cite an example of refinancing in a distressed situation?

The case of Campeau Corporation, although a decade old, shows how the refinancing of a complex transaction might occur under distressed conditions. (Good news: Not all refinancings are this scary.) Fortunately for M&A historians, the full story, which had its dénouement at the bust of the deal making decade, is summarized on a "Tenth Anniversary Page" of a major Canadian newspaper, *The Financial Post.*[7]

On April 1, 1988, Robert Campeau, the ambitious founder, chairman, and CEO of Campeau Corp., celebrated the $6.6 billion takeover of Federated Department Stores—"winning" out over R. H. Macy & Co., owner of Macy's. The deal was widely considered to be overpriced (some analysts called it "insane"). Moreover, it was funded with very little internal financing, which left the company overleveraged and diluted. Making matters worse was the fact that the deal followed on the heels of another leveraged transaction, the 1986 takeover of Allied Stores Corp. for $3.6 billion.

To help finance the Federated takeover, Campeau Corp. allowed a key shareholder, Olympia & York Developments Ltd. (now called O&Y Properties Corp.), to raise its stake in Campeau Corp. from 11.2 percent to 22 percent, but the cash raised from the sale was not enough to make the payments on the new debt.

Stock markets did not like the Campeau-Federated deal. The price of Campeau shares began to decline. Stock that had traded as high as $22¼ in September 1988 was a virtual penny stock by year's end, trading at less than $3. In January 1989, National Bank of Canada called in some 23 percent of Campeau Corp. stock, fully diluted, which had been pledged as security for a $150-million loan to a holding company owned by Robert Campeau.

Meanwhile, the strain of overleverage from the two multibillion-dollar transactions—exacerbated by the $250 million in advisory fees paid to investment bankers and attorneys for the Federated deal—forced first quarter 1989 losses of $67 million. In July 1989, Federated announced plans to reduce the company's $9.5 billion debt. It sought additional loans to meet the interest payments due on existing loans and sold off major properties in order to reduce debt principal. It even tried to sell Bloomingdale's—the jewel in the crown of Federated and reportedly the symbolic motivation for Campeau's bid—to raise additional cash.

In September 1989, Campeau was unable to meet the interest payments due on portions of its debt. In January 1990, Campeau's real estate operations were split off from its retail department store operations, which filed for bankruptcy protection. The real estate operations, now owned by both O&Y and the Campeau family, went through a restructuring as O&Y sold off noncore property, and changed the name of the company (in late 1997) to Camdev Corp.

The Campeau story is a very interesting example, but it's hard to separate the drama of it all from the mechanics. From the point of view of financing and refinancing, what happened and what lessons were learned?

To recap the above, we would simply point out that Campeau used both debt and equity financing to pay for an overpriced takeover that the company could not afford to buy. Both financing strategies would require correction. The pledged stock was recalled, and the loan terms changed when the company tried to restructure its obligations. In the end, bankruptcy brought a new situation altogether. The Campeau story shows that it may be easy to obtain financing for a transaction, but it is not always wise to pursue one. Deals must be well planned and well priced and well as adequately financed.

Do M&A borrowers ever change lenders?

Some M&A borrowers do change or add on banks, sometimes by adding them to their boards of directors. Adding bankers, however, is not the only way to "switch horses in midstream." In considering a change or expansion of lenders, refinancing teams should not forget corporate sources, including potential future acquirers that might be willing to loan funds or take over loans in exchange for an option to acquire.

You mentioned covenants banning postacquisition divestitures. Why ban this practice? Isn't this a good way to pay down acquisition debt?

Yes, it is. Many leveraged acquirers include specific asset sales in their strategic plans approved by lenders. As long as such sales do not come as a surprise and are priced well, they generally meet with lender approval. On the other hand, the kind of wholesale dismantling of going concerns for mere cash flow purposes has fallen into disfavor even at the planning stage.

What are the drawbacks of assets sales as a means of restructuring?

Asset sales often involve the sale of entire business units—not just hard collateral such as real estate or equipment. As a result, they can cause people to lose their jobs or at least relocate. This effect, however, tends to be exaggerated, since many jobs that are "lost" in postmerger or postbuyout asset sales are in fact preserved under the new owners.[8]

Could you give an example of a recent asset sale done to refinance acquisition debt?

In December 1996, Johnson Controls agreed to sell its plastic container operations to a unit of the German conglomerate Viag Group AG for $650 million. It said that it would use the proceeds of the sale to pay down the heavy debt it took on to its acquisition of Prince Automotive, which closed October 1996. The cash infusion from the sale reduced the company's debt-to-capital ratio, which was over 50 percent after the Prince deal. Johnson sold the unit rather than making a new stock offering, which it had been contemplating.[9]

Suppose, though, that a lender really does not want the borrower to sell anything after the deal is done. What then?

One way to preserve company integrity and still generate cash from assets is to pursue sale/leasebacks. As discussed at length in Chapter 4, this is when the owner of an asset sells it and then leases it from the buyer. A common practice in small company loans, this has also been employed in major cash-raising efforts.[10]

Another way to raise money after a deal is to sell debt instruments (rather than assets). This leads to the subject of bond and note refinancing, which we will now discuss.

How can selling debt—corporate paper—help pay back other debt? Isn't it just another leverage burden?

Selling corporate paper can be preferable from the point of view of interest obligation. In a given month, for example, 90-day AA commercial paper might be paying interest rates of 5.5 percent, while the equivalent LIBOR, which is a baseline for much bank lending, might be over 5.7 percent.

So high-grade commercial paper issuers can get away with paying low interest rates. What's the catch? Why don't all companies use this approach?

First, not every company can achieve and sustain a high credit rating from the credit rating agencies. Second, the paper is issued with short maturities, ranging from 14 to 270 days. Issuers must find new buyers or convince present buyers to roll over their investments. This is why many companies take out standby lines of credit from banks to back up their paper in the event that they have trouble in rolling over their commercial paper lines.

What are some ways companies can restructure the debt they issue?

With so many types of corporate debt finding their way to market, opportunities to restructure obligations are limited only by an issuer's imagination—and the quality of underlying company values. Some strategies include:

- Offering to buy back debt from holders at less than its original price[11]
- Offering to trade debt for new issues that mature later
- Asking bondholders to trade their holdings for equity

How exactly (and why exactly) are bonds or preferred stock refinanced?

In an era of falling interest rates, a firm may find itself with bonds or preferred stock outstanding that pays a coupon rate higher than the prevailing market rate. A net present value analysis will reveal whether the outstanding securities should be called or, if they are not callable, repurchased on the open market. Almost all public bond issues and many preferred stock issues have a call provision allowing the firm to force recall of the securities at a call premium. This process is called a *refinancing* or a *refunding*.

How can a firm decide to refinance its bonds or preferred stock?

This is a capital budgeting decision and the usual procedures apply. (They apply to both bonds and preferred stock, but for purposes of simplicity, we will use an example of bonds only.)

The firm needs to determine the net present value of calling the outstanding bonds and replacing them with new bonds of equivalent maturity and risk. The changes in the after-tax cash flows should be discounted at the appropriate after-tax discount rate. In this case, the appropriate rate is the after-tax rate on debt of equivalent risk. We use the after-tax rate because all refinancing costs (such as the call premium) are assumed to be financed with debt capital. This debt provides an interest tax shield. Hence, the relevant discount rate is the after-tax rate.

Two additional issues are pertinent. First, the debt refinancing may slightly alter the capital structure of the firm because the market value of the new debt issue exceeds the market value of the outstanding debt. This may create a tax gain from leverage. The second issue is that callable debt should never sell for more than the call price plus a small premium approximately equal to the flotation costs of exercising the call. No investor would rationally pay $1,100 for a bond that might be called (any minute) at $1,050.

EQUITY REFINANCING

What do you mean by postmerger equity refinancing?

In the strictest sense, postmerger equity refinancing is a change in the terms of a shareholder agreement drawn in the context of a merger, or an action triggered by such an agreement. A pure example of postmerger equity refinancing is the issuance of new shares to retire a generation of special stock issued in a merger.[12]

More broadly, however, equity refinancing might include an infusion of equity that helps a company reconfigure its balance sheet. This might occur shortly after an acquisition in order to provide working capital for the acquisition. For example, a venture capital group might buy a percentage of a newly acquired subsidiary, just as Accel Partners bought Kaplan's recruitment software subsidiary (see Chapter 9).[13] Also, as noted in Chapter 9, some entrepreneurs receive continual backing from venture capital sources over a period of decades, either as they need second-round financing for their original ventures or as they start new ventures.

Weiss Peck & Greer, which describes itself as a "private buyout investment firm, venture capital firm, and money management firm," has a small stable of entrepreneurs it will invest in repeatedly. For example, it funded start-ups Bridge Communications, Inc., Network Computing Devices, Inc., and Precept Software, Inc., all started by the same couple (William Carrico and Judith Estrin). Weiss Peck managing partner Philip Greer once said, "I can't imagine them doing a deal without us." This is a good example of going "back to the well" in the case of an equity source. Although these examples do not involve refinancing a particular company, they show a kind of refinancing of an ongoing entrepreneurial phenomenon.

What are the chief benefits and drawbacks of selling stock as a means of refinancing if a company is already a public company?

On the upside, there is financial flexibility. When a company issues stock, it receives cash for it but incurs no obligation. The deal can seem like free money. On the downside, stock sales may decrease:

- Control of original owners
- Earnings per share (as the "shares" denominator increases, the "earnings" numerator may not increase as fast)
- Market value (when management sells, the market may, too)

Of course, the state of the IPO market has a good deal to do with how well initial public offerings fare. As we go to press, the IPO market is in a slump, but history shows that these periods of inactivity never last very long.

If a company is privately owned as a result of a leveraged buyout, what are the pros and cons of going public again (reverse LBOs)?

The burdens, risks, and rewards of being a public company are treated exhaustively in other sources, but the best teacher is experience. To get a good sense of the private versus public trade-off, study the fortunes of the public companies that went private and then returned to public markets. There is no lack of examples, both good and bad. Basically, two types of situations may be involved. The LBO may have performed really well and made great improvements. This success can be rewarded by going public again at stock prices that provide large capital gains. Or the LBO may be performing poorly, so it may return to a publicly owned firm with stronger corporate governance and controls.

Classic examples from both Big Board and smaller exchanges include Ann Taylor Stores, Burlington Industries, Coltec Holdings Inc., Duff & Phelps, Duracell International Inc., Enquirer/Star, Forstmann & Co., Equity Coleman Co., Gulfstream Aerospace Corp., Haemonetics, Holopark Technologies Inc., Hospital Corporation of America, International Specialty, Owens-Illinois, Perrigo, Reliance Electric Co., R. P. Scherer, Scotts Co., Stop & Shop, Toastmaster Inc., Warnaco, and York International Corp.

More recently (in the second half of 1998), reverse buyouts have included the following companies: Allegiance Telecom, Crown Castle International, Information Holdings, National Equipment Services, New American Healthcare Corp., and Software AG Systems.[14]

REFINANCING VIA HYBRID INSTRUMENTS: BRIDGE LOANS

In previous chapters, you have mentioned bridge loans as a mode of built-in refinancing. Could you tell more about them now?

As noted in a recent issue of *Bank Loan Report*, "in many scenarios, a company that is buying another will use a combination of bank debt and high-yield bonds to finance the purchase." In leveraged buyout loans, this combination is the most common financing method. A bridge loan is a way of linking the bank debt and high-yield bond sources. It is an immediate short-term loan offered by an underwriter—often in league with a lender—in exchange for the right to replace that loan with a later bond issue. Underwriters will sometimes offer a buyer immediate short-term financing for an acquisition in exchange for the right to replace that financing with a later bond, typically a junk bond. There is often an up-front cash fee involved. The risk in bridge lending is that the market will go sour before the loan is repaid and the bonds are sold.

Could you give an example of a bridge loan?

In late 1998, Republic Engineered Steels entered into a one-year bridge facility with lenders Chase Manhattan; Donaldson, Lufkins & Jenrette, and BankBoston. In a Securities and Exchange Commission (SEC) filing, Republic said that it anticipated it would need approximately $209 million to complete scheduled "note purchase agreements." Pricing will increase by 50 basis points every three months to a maximimum interest rate of 15.5. percent.

Why do lenders want to do junk bond bridge lending?

Junk bond bridge lending began as a marketing device for both investment banks and commercial banks trying to break into the market previously dominated by a single firm—Drexel Burnham Lambert, an investment banking firm specializing in junk bonds. Drexel's practice had been to issue "highly confident" letters stating that it had reviewed a transaction and was sure that it could place the financing. Bridge loan financing gained popularity initially in 1986, during the year-end rush to beat a new tax law deadline. Ever since then, except for periods immediately following stock market declines, junk bond bridge lending, and bridge lending in general, has continued to be used in M&A because it can give buyers immediate funding. (Bond issues, after all, take time—especially those issued to the general public.)

Over the past decade, the connection between commercial bank lending and junk bond syndications has grown—not only through bridge loans but also through ordinary term or revolving credit loans to LBO groups. Although an active junk bond sector means that some borrowers will rely less on bank debt, it also brings more borrowers into the marketplace, thus increasing bank transaction volume overall.[15]

What should the interest rate be on a bridge loan?

The interest rate on the bridge loan, being short-term financing, should initially be 5 to 8 points over the Treasury or federal funds rate, lower than the expected rate on the junk bonds that will be sold to repay the bridge loan. This rate should rise by 0.5 percent or more per annum if the underwriter cannot refinance the bridge loan in a three- to six-month period. The increasing interest rate compensates the underwriter for the bridge financing risk, as does a warrant for a small amount (normally 3 to 5 percent) of the common stock of the company being acquired. The underwriter will also receive substantial fees: commonly 2 percent—1 percent upon execution of a commitment letter for the bridge loan and another 1 percent or more when the loan is funded.

What issues arise in the negotiation of a bridge loan/junk bond financing?

The bridge lender is most concerned about ensuring that it will be able to market the refinancing debt—that is, the junk debt that will be used to repay its loan. Thus, it will seek to clarify in advance any potential issue that could arise with the borrower or with other lenders. The bridge lender will also seek utmost flexibility in the terms of the refinancing debt that it can offer. For example, it may want the freedom to offer its customers interest rate and equity kickers such as warrants. The bridge lender will also require that the borrower use its best efforts to get the offering done as soon as possible. The bridge lender's prime concern is to get its debt refinanced, and it will seek to build into the contract strong incentives to motivate the borrower toward that end.

The borrower, on the other hand, wants to be sure, if possible, that its permanent mezzanine debt is borrowed on terms it can repay. The borrower should seek to place limits on the terms of the refinancing debt and also to ensure that the bridge lender's debt will roll over into longer-term debt if the refinancing debt can't be placed.

These general concerns are reflected in the most common points of negotiation in a bridge loan refinancing: the terms of the bridge loan, the terms of the refinancing debt, and the covenants and *events of default* of the bridge loan.

What bridge loan terms must be negotiated?

In many cases, the bridge loan falls due at the end of a fixed period, usually three to nine months. If the refinancing debt is not placed by then, the bridge loan is in default. The senior lenders are often unwilling to accept this risk, and the borrower should be concerned as well. The refinancing debt may not be marketable on reasonable terms even though the company is doing extremely well; the problem may simply be a downturn in the markets (following a market drop like the one that occurred in the fall of 1998) or in the marketing efforts of the bridge lender. The other parties will have made financial commitments based on the confidence level of the investment banker that the refinancing debt would be available.

For the foregoing reasons, the bridge lender can often be persuaded (particularly in a competitive environment) to commit to a longer-term investment if the refinancing debt doesn't get placed. This often takes the form of a "rollover" provision where the terms of the note change after the maturity date and it becomes long-term subordinated debt with covenants and other provisions, similar to subordinated junk debt. Another technique is to cast the original bridge note as a long-term note that the borrower is obligated to prepay with the proceeds of refinancing debt or other cash proceeds such as equity offerings. In either case, the extended bridge note will have higher than normal, or increasing, interest rates to encourage refinancing of the bridge debt at the earliest possible time.

What about the terms of the refinancing debt—what should be negotiated here?

The borrower should obtain reasonable limits on the terms of refinancing debt that it will be obligated to accept. The usual formulation is something like "at prevailing market rates and terms," subject to limitations on the interest rate, the term, scheduled principal payments, and the amount of equity that the purchasers of the refinancing debt will be entitled to receive. The borrower may seek a limitation on the amount of cash interest payable annually or, alternatively, on the average yield on the instrument, although it is difficult to bar access of the bridge lender to takeout financing, even if there has been a major interest rate move in the market. The senior lender also want to ensure that the terms of the refinancing debt include appropriate coverage ratios and limits on other indebtedness.

Finally, what covenants and events of default need to be negotiated in a bridge loan?

The senior lender and the borrower will generally try to make the bridge loan covenants, events of default, and subordination provisions similar to the refinancing debt that will take out the bridge loan. They resist, often successfully, attempts by the bridge lender to make the bridge loan agreement a tighter, restrictive document or to have the bridge lender ride on the covenants of the senior lender. Avoidance of overly tight default triggers is especially important where the obligation of the bridge lender to sell the refinancing debt is conditioned on absence of a default under the bridge note. The tighter the covenants, the greater the risk of a default that could prevent the rollover into the longer-term note and thus could put the company into a financial crisis soon after the acquisition.

FRAUDULENT CONVEYANCE AND OTHER LITIGATION CONCERNS

Lenders worry about fraudulent conveyances in LBOs. Why?

Leveraged acquisitions and buyouts have an unfortunate tendency to attract lawsuits. At least part of the problem is that both the potential rewards and risks are high. When buyouts are successful, parties may sue to get a larger share of success; when unsuccessful, parties may sue to reduce their exposure to the failure. Parties suing or sued may include bondholders (senior and junior), shareholders (majority and minority), underwriters, and, of course, lenders.

A bank that lends money to finance the acquisition of a business needs to be assured that, in the event of a bankruptcy of that business, its lien on the assets will secure the loan and the note given by the acquired company will be enforceable. However, the lien can be set aside and voided, and even the note can be rendered worthless if the pledge of assets and the giving of the note are determined to be "fraudulent conveyances or transfers" under the Federal Bankruptcy Code or under comparable state law—either the Uniform Fraudulent Conveyance Act or its successor, the Uniform Fraudulent Transfer Act (UFTA). Shareholders in leveraged buyouts are also at risk: If a transaction is judged to be a fraudulent conveyance, they may have to return the proceeds received from selling their shares.

Can a note, guarantee, or pledge of collateral be a fraudulent conveyance even though there is no intent to defraud anyone?

Yes. Both the Bankruptcy Code and comparable provisions of state law permit the voiding of a lien or obligation as "fraudulent" without the requirement of malign intent. These laws may, in effect, be utilized to protect the interests of general creditors of acquired companies where the transactions financed by the banks have the effect of depriving the acquired company of the means to pay its debts to its general creditors, whether those transactions are actually intended to do so or not.

Is there a special risk of creating an unintended fraudulent conveyance in an LBO loan as opposed to an ordinary corporate loan?

Yes. Under Section 548 of the Bankruptcy Code and comparable provisions of state law, a lien given by the acquired company on its assets, or the note secured by that lien, will be deemed "fraudulent" if the company receives less than "reasonably equivalent value" in exchange and one of the following three conditions exists:

- The company was "insolvent" at the time of such transfer or became "insolvent" as a result of the transfer.
- The company was left with "unreasonably small capital" as a result of the transfer.
- The company incurred or intended to incur debts beyond its ability to pay.

In an LBO loan, no matter how the transaction is structured (whether as a cash merger, stock purchase, or asset purchase), most of what the bank lends winds up not in the hands of the acquired company, but in the pockets of the sellers. On the date after closing, the acquired company is, by definition, "highly leveraged." It has a great deal of new debt, and liens on all its assets, but a large portion of the money raised by such debt (which the company is required to repay) has gone to the previous stockholders. It is not hard to see why an unsecured creditor of the company, viewing the new debt obligations of the company and the encumbrance of its assets, would complain that the company (as opposed to its former owners) did not receive "reasonably equivalent value" in the transaction.

Assuming that the lack of reasonably equivalent value may be a problem in all LBO loans, can't the problem be solved by showing that none of the other three conditions that would trigger a fraudulent conveyance exists?

It can, if each of the three conditions can be shown not to exist, but that is not always easy to do in the typical LBO. Of the three conditions—insolvency, unreasonably small capital, and ability to pay debts—the last two are the easiest to overcome. To the extent that the company and the bank can demonstrate, through well-crafted, reasonable projections, that the company will have sufficient revenues and borrowing capacity to meet its reasonably anticipated obligations (including servicing the acquisition debt), it should be possible to establish that the company's capital, although small, is adequate, and that the company will be able to pay its debts. Solvency, however, is another matter.

Why is it difficult to show that an acquired company is solvent for fraudulent conveyance purposes?

The difficulty arises because the definition of solvency as used in the Bankruptcy Code and state counterpart legislation is different from that used under generally accepted accounting principles (GAAP). Solvency under GAAP can mean having sufficient assets to pay debts as they mature, or having book assets that are greater than book liabilities. In the typical LBO, at least one of the tests for GAAP solvency can usually be met. But for fraudulent conveyance purposes, a company is solvent only if the "fair, salable value" of its assets is greater than its probable liabilities. In valuing assets, the approach should be conservative—using liquidation value rather than book value or other measures. Probable liabilities are not limited to GAAP balance sheet liabilities. All liabilities, contingent as well as direct, must be considered. This is a tall order, given the current regulatory push toward disclosure of such contingencies. (Consider, for example, the SEC's 1993 Staff Accounting Bulletin No. 92 on reporting and accounting for environmental loss exposure.)

Why is the "fair, salable value" test a problem for LBO loans?

In the early days of LBOs, companies were generally sold at prices that reflected the actual cash value of hard collateral—plant, machinery, and equipment—rather than a relatively high multiple of earnings. As the LBO field became more crowded and stock market multipliers increased as well, prices were bid up, with the result that pro forma balance sheets for acquired companies began to reflect more and more goodwill. In addition, companies with relatively little in the way of hard assets, such as advertising agencies, came into play.

Although such deals could be financed on the basis of their cash flow performance and projections, they would typically flunk the GAAP balance sheet test for solvency with the acquisition debt loaded on. Although they might be able to meet an alternative GAAP test based on capacity to service debt, they would inevitably lack hard assets having "fair, salable value" at least equal to their direct and contingent liabilities.

Are there structural arrangements in LBOs that can trigger fraudulent conveyance problems?

Yes. In addition to the issue of lack of "reasonably equivalent value" to the company, lenders and borrowers can get into trouble in transactions involving multicompany groups. These problems are not unique to LBOs, but they can occur in such transactions. Typically, they occur when collateral is provided by a subsidiary to secure a borrowing by its parent (upstreaming) or when collateral is provided by one subsidiary to secure a borrowing by a sister subsidiary (cross-streaming). Similarly, upstream and cross-stream guarantees can run afoul of the fraudulent conveyance prohibitions. By contrast, guarantees and pledges by a parent to support a borrowing by its subsidiary (downstreaming) do not present fraudulent conveyance problems.

Why are upstreaming and cross-streaming bad?

The donor entity—the one providing the collateral or the guarantee—is not getting "reasonably equivalent value," which is going instead to its affiliate. Thus, one of the triggers (although not the only one) for fraudulent conveyance is tripped. In addition, each subsidiary is typically asked to guarantee all the senior debt of its parent, yet the assets of the subsidiary represent only a fraction of the total acquisition. The result is that each subsidiary, taken by itself, cannot repay the full acquisition debt and may be rendered insolvent if the guarantee is called against it alone. This illogical result would be avoided if the test of solvency took into account that all the subsidiaries would share in meeting the guarantee obligation. Some cases give support for this conclusion, but the law is unfortunately not clear enough to eliminate the risk.

Are there ways to solve upstreaming and cross-streaming problems?

Yes. If the transaction passes each of the three additional tests—no insolvency, not unreasonably small capital, and ability to pay debts—there is no fraudulent conveyance. However, to guard against the risk of flunking one of the tests, two kinds of additional solutions can be explored:

- Merging the entity providing the collateral or guarantee with the borrower before the acquisition is consummated
- Dividing up the loan into two or more distinct credit facilities, each collateralized by (and commensurate with) the collateral provided by each borrower

Care should be taken, if the latter course is used, to avoid having the loan proceeds simply pass through one of the borrowers into the hands of another borrower or affiliated entity. The loan proceeds can be used to pay off bona fide intercorporate debt, but if the cash flow among the borrowing entities indicates that the separate loans are shams, the transaction runs the risk of being "collapsed" in a bankruptcy proceeding. In such a case, the liens and guarantees could be voided.

Are upstream or cross-stream guarantees that are limited to the net worth of the guarantor fraudulent conveyances?

No. Indeed, limiting the guarantee (and the lien collateralizing it) to the amount of the guarantor's net worth at the time of delivery of the guarantee can ensure that the guarantor is not rendered insolvent by delivery of the guarantee and consequently should eliminate any fraudulent conveyance problem. However, the guarantor must have the requisite "net worth" in the bankruptcy sense, and not just GAAP net worth, in addition to being able to pay its debts and not having unreasonably small capital. Net worth guarantees have yet to be tested in a bankruptcy proceeding, and although they appear conceptually sound, there are no certain predictions on what the courts will say.

Will accounting firms give solvency opinions?

No. As mentioned earlier in this book, after adverse outcomes on some such opinions in early 1988, the American Institute of Certified Public Accountants (AICPA) prohibited all accounting firms from rendering solvency letters. Some appraisers or valuation consultants will give such opinions, however.

Will law firms give opinions that fraudulent conveyance laws have not been violated?

Almost never. Law firms generally refuse to give fraudulent conveyance opinions, largely because they cannot evaluate the question of solvency and because lawyers have traditionally refused to predict what actions a bankruptcy court may take under a set of unforeseeable circumstances. Lenders usually understand and accept this reluctance, although sometimes some skirmishing occurs at the closing on this point.

Is the "fraudulent conveyance" problem inescapable for all LBOs? What are the landmark decisions in this area?

Each sophisticated lender that is willing to extend an LBO loan has made a bottom-line decision that it can live with the risk of unclear law in this area. The classic case on the subject, *United States v. Gleneagles* (1983), actually involved intentional misconduct, although the court's reasoning in that case cast a cloud over innocent LBOs as well. A number of commentators in the late 1980s, supported by court decisions such as *Credit Managers Association of Southern California v. Federal Co.* (1985) and *Kupetz v. Wolf* (1988), held that the fraudulent conveyance doctrine should not be employed as a blunt instrument against LBOs.

Courts in the 1990s have also shown a range of opinions in the matter. On the one hand, fraudulent conveyance laws have been used to remedy perceived frauds in leveraged transactions. Early in the decade, the Massachusetts Bankruptcy Court used fraudulent conveyance laws to subordinate claims of a lender in *In re O'Day Corporation* (1991). In *Crowthers McCall Pattern Inc. v. Lewis et al.* (1991), the court refused to dismiss most of the causes of action brought by a creditor's committee against the equity investors, lenders, and directors. In *O'Donnell v. Royal Business Group* (1995), the court enjoined a selling shareholder from transferring the cash proceeds received in an LBO on the grounds that the LBO may have been a fraudulent transfer under UFTA.

Most recently, in the pending case of *Zahn v. Yucaipa Capital Fund* (1998), defendants argued that the UFTA "does not apply to LBOs that are 'above board' or not otherwise intentionally fraudulent and . . . a creditor whose claim arises after the consummation of an LBO may not bring a constructive fraudulent transfer claim [under the California UFTA] where the LBO was highly publicized and was not actually fraudulently concealed." The court disagreed on all counts, putting deal makers on notice that even honest and well-publicized transactions may be vulnerable to the fraudulent conveyance charge in the hindsight of insolvency.

On the other hand, courts have shown some restraint in this area—refusing to find fraud under every failed LBO. In *Kaiser Steel Resources, Inc. v. Pearl Brewing Co.* (1991), the U.S. Court of Appeals for the 10th Circuit held that a debtor in possession or trustee cannot recover payments, even if made as a fraudulent conveyance to stockholders in an LBO. Also, in two fairly recent cases—*Munford v. Valuation Research Corporation* (1996) and *Brandt v. Hicks, Muse & Co.* (1997)—courts cited the business judgment rule to uphold the actions of directors in approving transactions that, in hindsight, may have contributed to a company's insolvency. (The business judgment rule is a legal doctrine that protects directors from lawsuits by those who would second-guess decisions made in good faith and with due care.[16])

Although it is not possible yet to say how the law will develop in the twenty-first century, a reasonable compromise might be this: Creditors that predate the acquisition and did not consent to it have a right to exact realistic standards for solvency at the time of the acquisition, while subsequent creditors that knew or could have known of the terms of the acquisition loan and its security arrangements should not be entitled to the benefit of fraudulent conveyance laws.

CONCLUDING COMMENTS

This chapter has covered a broad range, from debt and equity refinancing, to bridge loans, to ever-evolving case law on fraudulent conveyance suits—which often happen when a company faces refinancing's worst-case scenario: insolvency.

One might ask why we have chosen to end this chapter, and this section, on such a sobering note. Our goal is not to discourage deal makers. Rather, it is to encourage them to plan ahead. Due care in the financing and refinancing arena can go far in reducing the liability exposure of all parties in the event of insolvency. More important, by selecting the right amount, instruments, and sources of financing, and by remaining aware of refinancing options before, during, and after the deal, managers can avoid insolvency altogether, and increase their chances of financial success in both the short and long term.

A P P E N D I X 12-A

Sample Description (for 10-K Filing) of a Complex Financial Restructuring*

The following sample of a financial restructuring, excerpted from the "Recent Developments" section of a public company's 10-K filing, shows how complex this area can become. This unique case involves a business combination, a financial restructuring encompassing numerous parties and instruments, an acquisition, and a plan to seek a revolving credit.

BUSINESS COMBINATION WITH XYZ COMPANY INC.

On _____, ABC Company Inc. (ABC) and XYZ Company Inc. (XYZ) announced that they agreed in principle to a combination of the two companies (the "Business Combination"). The Business Combination will be structured as a tax-free exchange whereby each ABC stockholder will receive 1 share of newly issued XYZ common stock for each 5.5 shares of ABC common stock currently held. The exchange ratio will be adjusted on the basis of the market price of ABC common stock prior to the consummation of the Business Combination, subject to two limitations designed to limit the effect of market fluctuations on both ABC and XYZ stockholders.

    The number of ABC shares to be exchanged for each share of XYZ will be adjusted upward, if necessary, so that the market value of ABC shares to be exchanged for 1 share of XYZ is at least $3, but in no event will more than 6.5 shares of ABC be exchanged for each share of XYZ. Likewise, the number will be adjusted downward, if necessary, so that the market value of ABC shares to be exchanged is no more than $4, but in no event will fewer than 4.5 shares of ABC be exchanged for each share of XYZ. As a result, the current XYZ stockholders will own between approximately 22 and 29 percent of the surviving corporation and the remainder will be owned by the current ABC stockholders. Therefore, the Business Combination, if consummated, will be treated as a reverse merger/acquisition of XYZ by ABC for accounting and financial re-

---

*Based on information in the public domain. Except for the numbers, which are retained verbatim, all other facts are disguised.

porting purposes. The corporation resulting from the Business Combination will be named A-to-Z Inc.

The Business Combination is subject to a number of conditions, including the redemption of XYZ's Series B Cumulative Convertible Preferred Stock, certain amendments to various public and private securities of XYZ, and the availability of financing commitments prior to the combination. The Business Combination is also subject to the execution of a definitive Business Combination agreement, the approval of the combination by the nonaffiliated common stockholders of both companies, and other customary conditions to closing. The definitive agreement will be subject to approval by both companies' boards of directors and the receipt of fairness opinions from independent investment firms for both companies.

On _____, the Advisory Companies Incorporated advised the ABC Board of Directors that, on the basis of then current conditions, it would be prepared to deliver its opinion that the financial terms of the Business Combination are fair to the unaffiliated stockholders of ABC. Financial Advisors Inc., an affiliate of _____, has delivered its opinion to the XYZ Board of Directors that, on the basis of the conditions and assumptions contained therein, the financial terms of the Business Combination are fair to the unaffiliated stockholders of XYZ. There can be no assurances that the Business Combination will be consummated or, if consummated, will be consummated on the terms set forth above. A purported class action was brought by an alleged shareholder of XYZ against XYZ, ABC, and certain of ABC's and XYZ's past and present executive officers immediately following the announcement of the Business Combination.

FINANCIAL RESTRUCTURING

On _____, ABC completed its financial restructuring (the "Restructuring"), which had been proposed in order to reduce or satisfy certain of ABC's then current and future financial obligations and to provide ABC with additional capital to permit the continuation of ABC as a going concern. The following is a description of the consummation of the main components of the Restructuring, certain actions taken in conjunction therewith, and certain of the agreements entered into in connection therewith.

Consummation of Exchange Offers

The holders of $22,496,000, or 66.6 percent, in principal amount of ABC's outstanding 14% Senior Notes due _____ (the "14% Notes") exchanged such notes, which were past due, and received $1,000 in principal amount of 11.5%/10% Reducing Rate Senior Notes due 2000 (the "New Senior Notes") plus $102.08 in accrued interest for each $1,000 in principal amount of 14% Notes exchanged. In addition, the holders of $12,700,000, or 78.7 percent, in principal amount of ABC's outstanding 13% Senior Subordinated Notes due _____ (the "13% Notes") exchanged such notes and received $1,000 in principal amount of 13%/12% Reducing Rate Senior Subordinated Notes due _____ (the "New Senior Subordinated Notes") plus $115.40 in accrued interest for each $1,000 in principal amount of 13% Notes exchanged, 50 percent of which was paid in cash and 50 percent of which was paid in additional New Senior Subordinated Notes. The exchange of 14% Notes for New Senior Notes and the exchange of 13% Notes for New Senior Subordinated Notes described above are collectively referred to herein as the "Exchange Offers." Thus, $22,496,000 in aggregate principal of New Senior Notes and $13,431,700 in aggregate principal amount of New Senior Subordinated Notes were issued and approximately $3,030,300 of cash representing accrued interest was paid as part of the Exchange Offers.

$11,259,000 in principal amount of the 14% Notes (approximately 33 percent) was not tendered pursuant to the Exchange Offers. Since the 14% Notes were due and payable on _____, approximately $12,701,000 was paid in the aggregate to the holders thereof representing all principal and accrued and unpaid interest due on such untendered 14% Notes.

$3,445,000 in principal amount of the 13% Notes (approximately 21 percent) was not tendered pursuant to the Exchange Offers and approximately $235,000 was paid in the aggregate to the holders thereof representing accrued and unpaid interest due on such untendered 13% Notes.

Consummation of Consent Solicitation

Concurrently with the Exchange Offers, ABC solicited the consents (the "Consent Solicitation") of holders of the 13% Notes to certain amendments to the indenture governing the 13% Notes (the "Amendments"). As of _____, $11,605,000 in principal amount of 13% Notes owned by persons other than ABC and its affiliates (77 percent) consented to the Amendments and the Amendments were approved. An amendment and restatement of the Indenture dated as of _____ between ABC and John Doe Bank & Trust Company, as trustee, governing ABC's 13% Notes, as amended by the First Supplemental Indenture dated as of _____ between ABC and John Doe Bank & Trust Company, as trustee (the "Amended 13% Note Indenture"), was entered into as of _____ and the Amendments became effective

_____. The Amendments are binding upon all holders retaining 13% Notes, whether or not such holders consented to adoption of the Amendments. Holders of 13% Notes who consented to the Amendments also waived certain events of default under the indenture governing the 13% Notes (the "13% Note Indenture") and eliminated substantially all the restrictive covenants and certain default provisions in the 13% Note Indenture.

Purchases of New Preferred and 5% Notes for Cash

Pursuant to the terms of a Securities Purchase Agreement dated _____ (the "Securities Purchase Agreement"), _____, _____, and _____ purchased from ABC 40,000, 12,500, and 30,000 shares of Series A Convertible Preferred Stock, a newly designated series of ABC's Series Preferred Stock ("New Preferred"), respectively, in exchange for $40,000,000, $12,500,000 and $30,000,000, respectively. Pursuant to the Securities Purchase Agreement, _____ also purchased from ABC $30,000,000 in aggregate principal amount of 5% Payment-in-Kind Convertible Subordinated Notes due 2002 (the "5% Notes").

Satisfaction of Strategic Investor Loan

Pursuant to the terms of a Contribution and Exchange Agreement dated as of _____ (the "Contribution and Exchange Agreement"), in satisfaction of approximately $17,686,000 of a $32,200,000 loan plus accrued interest (the "Strategic Investor Loan") previously extended to ABC by _____, _____, and _____ (collectively, the "Strategic Investors"), ABC transferred to the Investors 3,885,223, 1,180,030, and 1,180,030 shares of the common stock of XYZ, respectively, representing all the shares of XYZ common stock held by ABC. Pursuant to the Contribution and Exchange Agreement, the remaining portion of the Strategic Investor Loan was satisfied by the issuance to the Strategic Investors of 8,586,543, 3,051,660, and 3,253,337 shares of ABC's common stock, $.01 par value per share (the "Common Stock"), respectively.

Exchange of Existing 10% Debentures and Series D Preferred

8,000 shares of ABC's Series D Convertible Exchangeable Preferred Stock, $1 par value per share (the "Series D Preferred"), representing all of ABC's out-

standing Series D Preferred (other than 300,000 shares held by _____),
were exchanged for 600,000 shares of ABC's Common Stock. The holder of Series D Preferred also received $20,000 in cash representing a portion of ac-
crued but unpaid dividends thereon. In addition, $14,600,000 in face amount
of ABC's 10% Convertible Subordinated Debentures due 2006 ("Existing 10%
Debentures"), representing all of ABC's outstanding Existing 10% Debentures (other than $35,000,000 in aggregate face amount held by two of the Stra-
tegic Investors), was exchanged for 21,900,000 shares of ABC's Common
Stock.

Exchange of Certain of the Strategic Investor's Securities for Common Stock

Pursuant to the Contribution and Exchange Agreement, each of the Strategic
Investors exchanged a portion of ABC's outstanding preferred stock and Ex-
isting 10% Debentures held by it for an aggregate of 72,000,000 shares of
ABC's Common Stock. Specifically, _____ received 37,824,031 shares of
Common Stock, _____ received 22,950,471 shares of Common Stock, and
_____ received 11,225,498 shares of Common Stock.

Contribution of Certain of the Strategic Investors' Securities to the Company

In addition, pursuant to the terms of the Contribution and Exchange Agreement, each of the Strategic Investors transferred to ABC, as a capital contribution, ABC's remaining outstanding preferred stock, certain related options
and warrants, and any Existing 10% Debentures held by it after the exchanges
described above and all accrued but unpaid dividends and interest thereon
and on the securities exchanged and certain other obligations. As a result of
the various exchanges and contributions, all of ABC's Existing 10% Debentures, Series B Convertible Preferred Stock, Series C Convertible Exchangeable Preferred Stock, Series D Preferred, and Series E Convertible Preferred
Stock ceased to be outstanding.

Standby Purchase and Investment Agreement

ABC, _____ (New Investors), and the Strategic Investors entered into a
standby purchase and investment agreement (the "Standby Agreement")
pursuant to which the Strategic Investors have committed to purchase up to

$27,500,000 principal amount of ABC's new 7% Convertible Subordinated Notes due 2006 (the "7% Notes") on the later of _____ or the date upon which certain conditions are met, and the New Investors have committed to invest up to $27,500,000 in coproductions of ABC's product, commencing upon the satisfaction of certain conditions, but in no event earlier than _____ (the "Coproduction Investments"). The total amount invested pursuant to the Standby Agreement will not exceed $47,500,000.

The Standby Agreement provides that the Strategic Investors have committed to purchase $7,500,000, $10,000,000, and $2,500,000 in principal amount of 7% Notes, respectively, which amounts are subject to adjustment. Also, under the Standby Agreement, the New Investors have committed to make $17,500,000 and $10,000,000, respectively, of Coproduction Investments, which amounts will be subject to adjustment. One of the New Investors is entitled to reduce its obligation to make Coproduction Investments by up to $7,500,000 if its subsidiary commits to purchase additional 7% Notes in the amount of such reduction.

The amount of each investor's commitment to make Coproduction Investments will be in the nature of a revolving commitment in that the commitment will be reduced by the amount of funds actually contributed by such investor and will be increased by the amount of previous contributions recovered by such investor. Subject to certain limited exceptions, the commitment to make Coproduction Investments will terminate on _____.

Other Agreements

ABC also entered into certain agreements with respect to potential equity investments in ABC by one of the Strategic Investors. ABC, the Strategic Investors, and MGM Holdings also entered into a Registration Rights Agreement dated as of _____, pursuant to which ABC granted certain registration rights covering the New Preferred, the 5% Notes, and the Common Stock issuable to Strategic Investors and MGM Holdings in connection with the Restructuring and Common Stock issuable upon conversion of the New Preferred, 5% Notes, and 7% Notes and certain other Common Stock held by the other Strategic Investors.

ACQUISITION OF V COMPANY

In conjunction with the Restructuring, ABC acquired all of the outstanding shares of common stock (the "V Common Stock") of the V Organization, Ltd., a Delaware corporation ("V"), other than shares owned by ABC, together with all of the ABC Series A Common Stock Put Rights associated therewith and represented thereby (the "Series A Puts") in a two-step transaction consisting of a tender offer and a subsequent merger. As a result thereof, $19,181,800 in principal amount of New Senior Notes was issued and cash of $1,961,000 in interest was paid in exchange for 17,765,093 shares of V Common Stock and associated Series A Puts. In addition, approximately $3,465,000 in cash was paid to the holders of V Common Stock and associated Series A Puts (other than ABC or its affiliates), in exchange for 4,618,016 shares of V Common Stock and associated Series A Puts. As a result of these transactions, V became a wholly owned subsidiary of ABC.

Additional information regarding the Restructuring and the actions taken in conjunction therewith, including certain management agreements, is contained in ABC's Current Report on Form 8-K dated _____(the "Form 8-K").

REVOLVING CREDIT

ABC anticipates that by _____ it will be expanding and will look for funding for such future endeavors through borrowings under a new revolving bank credit facility, the terms of which are currently being negotiated through proceeds of the 7% Notes and possibly through additional capital-raising efforts. There can be no assurance, however, that all of such proposed production financing will be available when needed or that such production goals will be met.

E N D N O T E S

1. "Borrowers Get Smart on Interest Rates," *The Wall Street Journal*, February 20, 1998, pp. A-1ff.
2. "Dizzying New Ways to Dice Up Debt," *Business Week*, July 21, 1997, pp. 102ff.
3. The "good bank, bad bank" strategy can be abused, and regulators watch it carefully (Edward D. Herlihy and Craig M. Wasserman, "Harnessing the Good Bank, Bad Bank Strategy," *American Banker*, April 1, 1992). Securitization came under scrutiny in early 1992, when William Smithe, director of the Securities Valuation Office of the National Association of Insurance Regulators, criticized it in a letter to state commissioners. Stocking of mutual banks can also lead to problems when depositors who are supposed to get a first buying opportunity buy on behalf of third parties. Hearing such a scheme, in October 1992, U.S. marshals for the Federal Bureau of Investigation seized 278,000 newly issued First Rock Bancorp Inc. shares issued as part of an initial public offering. The Office of Thrift Supervision conducted a separate inquiry in the matter.

4. Restructuring this debt may not seem to conform to our definition of refinancing as a change in the terms of an agreement, or an action triggered by terms in such an agreement. In fact, however, it fits the definition, because every form of financing is based on an agreement, whether or not in writing. For more on this concept, see the conclusion to this book.

5. This statement is based on years of reports appearing in *Bank Loan Report,* a newsletter of Securities Data Publishing. As mentioned in Chapter 1, this newsletter used to publish a chart showing what percentage of bank loans (for the current year and preceding four years) went for what purpose. For more details, see Chapter 1.

6. As an aside, we would note that it may seem difficult to refinance with three banks, but consider Valuejet, which in 1997 had to do a refinancing with *seven* banks.

7. Gordon McLaughlin, "1989: He Shopped 'Til He Dropped: Campeau's Refusal to Let Federated Escape Left Trouble in Store," *The Financial Post,* February 2, 1998.

8. As an example, consider the experience of Erwin Schultze, chairman and CEO of Ceco Corporation, who testified in defense of LBOs and asset sales before the House Ways and Means Committee on February 2, 1989, during the famed "LBO hearings" on Capitol Hill. By that time, Ceco was able to retire $100 million of the $165 million it borrowed to take Ceco private three years earlier. Ceco used a combination of cash from operations and proceeds from the sale of noncore company divisions to repay the debt. "Prior to the transaction, we had initiated plans to sell some small, regional businesses that did not fit with our core construction-related businesses, much as major conglomerates were selling off divisions that did not fit into their core strategies .... [T]his points to another issue often raised about LBOs and leveraged acquisitions—the evil asset sale. There is a view around that an asset sale is the same as a liquidation. In most cases, it is not. We sold our divisions to people who were more intent on building them than we. The jobs were 'lost' at Ceco but 'created' elsewhere. As of last week, the units we sold employed more people now than when they were under our control. In other words, employment at Ceco 'declined' to 5,834 workers from about 7,300. But the 1,400 'lost' employees are still working for the divisions we sold—and their jobs are probably more secure than before."

9. "Johnson Controls' Container Business Will Be Sold to Unit of Germany's Viag," *The Wall Street Journal,* December 10, 1996, p. C2.

10. For example, Al Checchi, who borrowed $3.1 billion to do a $3.65 billion buyout of Northwest Airlines in 1989, raised $300 million in cash in 1991 by doing a sale/leaseback of Northwest Aircraft. As mentioned earlier in this book, Northwest Airlines today is a public company again—Northwest Airlines Corporation, a $10 billion Nasdaq company.

11. When buying back debt from holders at a discount, managements must be sure to disclose all material information about company prospects, especially favorable developments.

12. Consider, for example, the 1994 Blockbuster-Viacom issuance that was retired
    in 1996. When Blockbuster acquired Viacom in 1994, shareholders received
    Viacom stock and a new security called variable common rights (VCR) stock.
    Blockbuster shareholders were promised that they could exchange these shares
    for Viacom shares two years later at an exchange rate to be determined by the
    price of Viacom stock at the time. In September 1996, Viacom issued 6.4 million
    common shares of its widely traded Class B common stock to holders of its spe-
    cial VCR stock. The 6.4 million was considered a low number, happily for
    Viacom. A few months before, when Viacom stock was selling poorly, the com-
    pany faced the prospect of issuing 39 million new common shares to retire the
    VCR issue. See "Viacom Needs to Issue Far Fewer Shares Than Thought to Re-
    tire Special Securities," *The Wall Street Journal*, September 29, 1996, p. B3.

13. As mentioned in Chapter 9, July 1998, Accel Partners, a venture capital firm
    that specializes in the Internet and communications industries, acquired 15 per-
    cent of HireSystems, a subsidiary of Kaplan Educational Centers, which in turn
    is a subsidiary of the Washington Post Company, a publishing company listed
    on the New York Stock Exchange.

14. "Reverse LBOs," *Mergers & Acquisitions*, November/December 1998, pp. 46ff.

15. A reporter from *Bank Loan Report* recently asked two lenders (neither of them
    involved in junk bonds) what they thought of a recent rise in junk bond activ-
    ity. "The volume we lose by virtue of assets flowing into the high-yield market
    is more than made up by the business LBO loan sponsors can now generate,"
    said Bruce Ling, managing director of Credit Suisse First Boston. "Net net, I
    think it's an overall positive statement, because we'll have more transaction
    volume," said Mike Mauer, managing director of J. P. Morgan. See "Junk Bond
    Revival to Boost LBO Syndications," *Bank Loan Report*, November 30, 1998, p. 1.

16. The definitive work on this topic is Dennis J. Block, Nancy E. Barton, and Ste-
    phen A. Radin, *The Business Judgment Rule: Fiduciary Duties of Corporate Direc-
    tors*, 5th ed. (New York: Aspen Law and Business, 1998). This ever-expanding
    work now has 2,496 pages—an indication of the reach and complexity of the
    business judgment rule concept.

PART FIVE

Global Issues: Macro/Micro/Tax

Most deal makers will agree that money (along with other vital elements) makes the world go 'round. But how many realize that the *world* makes *money* go 'round? That is, just as economic systems influence global events, so too do global events impact economic systems. We are not the first to make these twin observations, but we may well be the first to apply them to M&A financing. This section of our book explores this interplay of life and money.

In Chapter 13, we take a macroeconomic view, exploring world financing systems and the flow of currency. In Chapter 14, we bring this down to the nitty-gritty level of the deal, using leveraged buyouts as an example. And in Chapter 15 we focus on often overlooked elements of international deal taxation, both inbound and outbound.

In all this, we have tried to remain rooted in practical reality—the real goals of real people in real time. When we discuss derivative instruments, for example, we not only make the abstract point that their purpose is to hedge risk, but we report on what can happen (and has happened) when such instruments are used for gambling.

As Alex Sheshunoff notes in his Foreword to this book, financial ideas can have great power—but this power must be harnessed for the public good. This point is especially true in the heady world of international finance, where the magnitude and rapidity of change tempt us to lose our bearings in the simpler truths of finance.

This, indeed, is a key message in what may be the world's most famous novel about money, *Les Faux-monnayeurs,* written by André Gide, son of the famed economist Charles Gide. In this novel, published just three years before the world-shaking U.S. stock market crash of 1929, the main character tries to write a novel about people, but keeps getting swept away by ideas.

> *Son cerveau, s'il l'abandonnait à sa pente, chavirait dans l'abstrait, ou il se vautrait toute à l'aise. Les idées de change, de valorisation, d'inflation, peu à peu envahissaient son livre . . . ou elles usurpaient la place de personnages.* *

> His mind, if he let it wander, capsized in a sea of abstractions, where it weltered at complete ease. Ideas about currency exchange, revaluation, and inflation little by little invaded his book . . . where they usurped the place of characters.

Let Gide's words be a warning to us. The technicalities of finance, while important, should never take the place of what really matters: people working together to create valuable new combinations of companies. We hope that the details in this final section support, rather than undermine, that ultimate goal for international M&A financing and refinancing.**

---

* André Gide, *Les Faux-monnayeurs* (Paris: Editions Gallimard, 1925), p. 188, translated by Alexandra R. Lajoux.
**The authors are thankful to investment banker and author John F. Childs for his observations on the importance of the global economy.

Macroeconomic Aspects of Global M&A Financing

I drink some coffee/read a paper read by millions
all the misery/all the destruction in the world
herded into headlines and catch phrases
the only part I trust/is the financial page
a completely blank space governed/
by the mechanics of capital and pure speculation

Riuichi Tamura, *Every Morning After Killing Thousands of Angels,* 1987

INTRODUCTION

As a new millennium begins to dawn, financiers around the world see both threats and opportunities on the horizon.

In the fall of 1998, following negative economic developments in every continent, public officials in various countries made grave pronouncements on the state of global capital markets. William McDonough, president of the New York Federal Reserve Bank, spoke for many when he said, in a speech to global bankers in Washington, D.C., "I believe that we are in the most serious financial crisis since World War II—and one that has a propensity to get worse rather than better."[1]

In some markets, McDonough's words still ring true. In Asia, for example, some currencies continue to be low against key benchmarks such as the U.S. dollar, and important financial institutions (such as some leading Japanese banks) have failed or are struggling. And no one can ignore the lasting impact that Year 2000 (Y2K) computer problems may have on global financial markets as we actually enter the new millennium.

Yet as we go to press in early 1999, these current and potential problems have been upstaged by rebounding stock markets, and the early success of the *euro*—Europe's grand experiment in a shared currency. The overall mood of the M&A community is optimistic. Despite warnings of global economic turmoil ahead, mainstream thinking says that we will see a continued rise in the amount of money crossing borders to fund M&A activity, both domestic and international.[2]

As nondomestic funding and deal making increase, so too does the need for M&A deal makers to understand the macroeconomic picture in M&A financing, the subject of this chapter. But even setting aside cross-border M&A transactions and financing, *all* business buyers and sellers today need to understand the global financial system, because they operate in a truly global economy. All aspects of M&A—from planning, to valuation, to financing, to structuring, to due diligence—may have international aspects in a major transaction today. The "purely" domestic deal—involving two companies located entirely in the same country and financed entirely by local sources—is becoming an anachronism in a world that sets no firm national boundaries for corporate and financial growth.

In these multinational times, institutions and individuals are more willing than ever before to invest their funds overseas. U.S. direct investment abroad currently stands at nearly $861 billion, significantly up from previous years. Conversely, foreign investors are placing more of their money here; direct investment in the United States is just under $682 billion, also up from the recent past. Adding the two flows together, we see that the total volume of cross-border investment is now over $1.5 trillion—an all-time record.[3]

Moreover, a significant portion of this international flow of capital involves actual purchases of controlling interests in companies, not merely purchases of shares. In 1998, U.S. companies closed 2,223 cross-border deals valued at $5 million or more, either as buyer or seller for a total dollar amount of $333 billion. By deal volume, this was 24 percent of all deals; by dollar volume it was 25 percent. In absolute numbers, this cross-border merger movement is one of the largest ever recorded—and it represents a particularly dynamic rebound from the low activity recorded in the early 1990s.[4]

As noted earlier in this book, 1998 was the year of the megamerger: Eight of the 10 biggest deals of all time happened in 1998.[5] All these megamergers—including those involving U.S.-based companies—were "international" in the sense that they involved truly multinational companies. Two of these top eight mergers were "international" in an even more compelling sense, because they involved national icons headquartered in different countries. What could be more British than British Petroleum, or more German than Daimler-Benz? What could be more American than Amoco or Chrysler? Yet the BP/Amoco and Daimler/Chrysler mergers have proceeded without national outcry, providing further evidence of our global economy.

WORLD FINANCIAL SYSTEMS: THE BIG PICTURE

When people talk about reforming the global financial system, what do they mean? Is there really such a thing?

There is no global financial system per se. Instead, there are a myriad of contracts drawn up between individuals and/or entities, and there are a myriad of markets in which these contracts flourish. These contracts and these markets are driven by unseen laws that economists attempt to understand. National and regional regulators, and international groups may set and enforce policies that influence economic contracts and markets, but they cannot ultimately control them. Even tightly "controlled" economies have a way of asserting their own dynamics—generally through a parallel illegal market called a "black" market.

What are some of the actions that regional and international bodies have taken to influence the global economy?

Watershed events in the evolution of our global economy include the following:

- The 1944 Bretton Woods Conference establishing the International Monetary Fund to maintain monetary stability worldwide—first through fixed exchange rates, and later through floating ones[6]
- The 1985 "Plaza Hotel" meeting of Group of Seven or G-7 nations[7] (Canada, France, Germany, Japan, Italy, the United Kingdom, and the United States) to set up a system of coordinated intervention in world currency markets
- The 1986 founding in Caux, Switzerland, of the Caux Business Round Table—a group of senior business leaders from Europe, Japan, and the United States—to articulate ethical principles for multinational corporations
- The 1992 signing of the North American Free Trade Agreement (NAFTA) involving Canada, Mexico, and the United States
- The 1993 signing of the General Agreement on Tariffs and Trade (GATT) among 117 nations
- The 1998 formation of the Group of 22—G-7 nations plus 15 emerging-market governments—to strengthen the world economy in the new millennium[8]
- The 1999 debut of the euro as a standard currency for the 11 members of the European Monetary Union

Meanwhile, recent development of global standards for accounting, governance, and labor have all increased the willingness of capital sources to move beyond national boundaries. In December 1998 the London-based International Accounting Standards Committee released draft recommendations that urged adoption of a single accounting treatment for business combinations—namely, purchase rather than pooling. (For more details, see the end of Chapter 15.) Also in 1998, the Paris-based Organization for Economic Cooperation and Development published global guidelines for corporate governance,[9] and the Council on Economic Priorities Accreditation Agency released standards on workplace values.[10]

None of these proclamations have the force of law, but all promise to be influential on the behavior of companies doing international business. And all will eventually influence cross-border lending and investment decisions in the global capital markets.

What exactly are capital markets what do they mean? How are capital markets different from money markets?

Different segments of the financial market are characterized by different maturities. When the financial claims and obligations bought and sold in a market have maturities of more than one year, the markets are referred to as *capital markets*. If they have maturities of less than one year, the transactions constitute *money markets*.

Beyond time frame, what is the broad definition of *capital* and *capital markets*?

Real capital in an economy is represented by real resources—things such as plants, machinery, and equipment. There is even a considerable body of economic literature pointing to the existence of "human capital."[11] In finance, the term *capital* refers to the owner's share in a business, plus whatever operating profit can fund its long-term growth. Different industries have different capital requirements. For example, banks in the United States have a very stringent requirements for capital adequacy—capital (such as stock) in relation to assets.

Long-term financial instruments represent claims against the financial and real capital of organizations. For that reason, as mentioned, the markets in which these instruments are traded—generally as stocks and bonds—are referred to as *capital markets*.

What is the technical definition of *money* and *money markets*?

According to one definition accepted by a broad range of banking and financial authorities, *money* is anything commonly accepted for payment of debts—otherwise known as legal tender.[12] In the United States, legal tender is all forms of circulating paper money (mostly Federal Reserve notes) and coins. The term *legal tender* means that money offered or "tendered" as a payment to a creditor must be accepted, unless another method of payment is specified in the contract signed by the creditor and the borrower.

A *money market* is a market in which short-term debt securities are issued and traded. The money market is an information network of dealers and institutional investors, rather than an organized market like a national stock exchange. Participants include government securities dealers, managers of money market funds, and financial institutions such as banks.

What are *M1*, *M2*, and *M3*?

These are terms used by economists to analyze the supply of money in a country, a region, or the world.

M1 includes currency held by the public, plus travelers checks and money held in checkable deposits. A checkable deposit is any deposit account that may be drawn against by writing checks or drafts. One common type of checkable deposit is an ordinary checking account (known technically as a demand deposit), from which the depositor can draw funds without giving any notice. Federal and state banking laws define a demand deposit as any deposit payable within 30 days. (See, for example, Article 3 of the Uniform Commercial Code.) Other checkable deposits include any negotiable payment order, such as a negotiable order of withdrawal (NOW) account.

M2 includes M1 plus savings, small-denomination time deposits, money market accounts, and shares in money market mutual funds held by individual investors. A time deposit pays interest for a fixed term, with the understanding that the money cannot be withdrawn before maturity without giving advanced notice. A money market account is a high-yield savings account that pays a market rate of interest. A money market mutual fund is a mutual fund that invests in short-term debt instruments.

M3 includes M2, plus large time deposits, large-denomination repurchase agreements, and shares in money market mutual funds held by institutional investors.

Why do economists want to know about the supply of money in a country?

If there is too much money in circulation relative to goods and services, there will be an economic condition called *inflation*—a rapid rise in wages and prices. Inflation can discourage savings, because businesses and consumers want to pay for things now rather than later, when they will be more expensive. When savings are low, banks have less money (M2) to lend. Also, if inflation reaches very high levels, called *hyperinflation*, organizations cannot repay their debt to banks. Hyperinflation occurs when consumer prices rise at a rate of over 50 percent per month.

You have mentioned capital markets and money markets. What other types of economic markets are there?

Capital markets and money markets are not the only types of markets. In fact, any system of exchange can be called a market. International markets that affect the value of national currencies include the foreign exchange market (establishing current currency values), the foreign exchange forward market (hedging against future currency values), and the currency futures market (a similar instrument structured in a different way).

CURRENCY EXCHANGE

How are the exchange values of currencies established?

There are basically three ways to establish currency values.

First, they may be "floating"—that is, established by the market itself.

Second, they may be pegged to a currency basket—that is, a currency unit consisting of specific amounts of currencies from several nations. Nominal values of currency baskets vary with the fluctuation of the currencies they contain. Examples of currency baskets include the Asian Currency Unit (ACU), and the Special Drawing Rights (SDRs) of the International Monetary Fund.

Third, they may be pegged to a particular currency. For example, many Southeast Asian economies have been pegged to the dollar. Such pegging can increase the appeal of a country to foreign investors. On the other hand, it can leave a country more vulnerable to a currency crisis.

What causes currency crises? Could you give an example of how a currency crisis might develop?

Let's take, for example, the currency crisis that hit Southeast Asia in the mid-1990s.[13] To lower inflation and to keep it low, Indonesia, Malaysia, and the Philippines (among other countries) pegged their exchange rates at a fixed value to that of the dollar or a basket of currencies, with the idea of achieving an inflation rate comparable to these instruments.

In today's world of highly mobile capital and deep capital markets, a pegged exchange rate signifying a low inflation policy attracts large capital inflows from abroad. This is what happened to the Southeast Asian economies.

At first, the exchange rate peg and the declining inflation gave the investment climate enormous drawing power. But while the pegged nominal exchange rate was fixed, the real exchange rate appreciated with growing capital inflows. Widening of the current account deficit (i.e., an increase in imports versus exports) typically accompanied an appreciation of the real exchange rate. This made imports cheap and exports expensive. As the current account deficit mounted as a percentage of the gross domestic product (GDP), confidence in the economy deteriorated. Moreover, if the capital that was attracted from abroad was not used productively, the inflow became the basis for nonperforming loans by domestic banks, some of which were state owned.

Local lenders began doubting the future value of the domestic currency, and so put a risk premium on domestic securities. Therefore, the governments of these countries, as well as nonfinancial firms, were tempted to issue lower-interest-bearing debt denominated in foreign currencies. In each country, companies borrowed in dollars but earned revenue in local currencies—making it harder for them to repay their foreign indebtedness.

What is the difference between a currency crisis and a financial crisis?

Currency crises occur when internal economic conditions are incompatible with the external conditions set for the currency. *Financial crises* occur when there are unsound fundamentals in the national economy—flaws in market discipline, regulation, and oversight. Sometimes a currency crisis can reveal a financial crisis, but is not usually the underlying cause of that crisis.

Can currency crises be contagious?

Yes, they can, but only if they involve currencies that are pegged to a specific currency or to a basket of currencies. This linkage can cause what economists call "international transmission" or, more colloquially, the "tequila effect." Free-floating exchange rates are unlikely to bring about such an effect. By its very freedom, a floating currency will reflect the economy it represents, and will not be vulnerable to crises involving other currencies.

How can currency exchange rates affect M&A financing and refinancing?

Currency exchange rates can affect M&A financing first and foremost by affecting the value of the money received or paid back in the financing. Whether the financing comes through borrowing, the sale of stock, or some combination of the two, the money must be denominated in at least one currency. In any financing that is paid over time—for example, a bank loan that is paid back in installments, or buyer payments to a seller in an installment sale—the value of that currency may change. If the entities providing and receiving financing are from two countries that use two different currencies,[14] and if only one currency is involved in the deal,[15] then one of the entities will be receiving or paying a foreign currency. The value of that currency, measured against the entity's domestic currency, could rise or fall, changing the economics of the situation, and impacting accounting treatment as well.

On the economic front, there are two basic risks:

- A deteriorating U.S. dollar exchange rate may require U.S. parent companies to pay more for foreign denominated obligations than was originally anticipated when the obligation was approved.
- A relative increase in the value of a foreign currency may cause U.S. creditors to be repaid a lesser amount in satisfaction of U.S. denominated obligations to them.

On the accounting front, there is the risk that the balance sheet, which must express the value of assets and liabilities denominated in a U.S. currency at the exchange rate in place on the balance sheet date, will lose value in the translation from the local currency to U.S. dollars.[16]

Assuming that at least one party in a transaction is receiving a foreign currency, how can it decrease the impact of currency volatility?

In order to alleviate the risk of economic losses due to exchange rate volatility, borrowers can use currency swaps such as the forward purchase contract and the forward sales contract, or they can use currency options.

How do the forward purchase and forward sales contracts work?

They are respectively a "put" and a "call." Like all derivative instruments, they can be risky if used for speculative purposes, rather than for prudent hedging of risk.[17]

Forward purchase contracts are used to protect a U.S. debtor that is obligated to repay a certain amount in a foreign currency at a future date. When the value of the foreign currency rises relative to the U.S. dollar, the debtor will have to spend more dollars to obtain the necessary amount of foreign currency to repay its debt. The forward purchase contract locks up the price at which the debtor may acquire the needed amount of currency at the necessary time for a fixed price determined at the time the forward purchase contract is entered into. It is, in effect, a "call" on foreign currency.

Similarly, a U.S. creditor that is afraid rising exchange rates may cause it to lose the value of its foreign-denominated receivables may hedge against such loss through a *forward sales contract*. In this case, the creditor contracts to sell the foreign currency to be received at a future date for U.S. dollars at a fixed rate determined at the time the forward contract is entered into. This is a "put" equivalent. Both kinds of swaps are discussed in more detail in Chapter 14, which focuses on the microeconomics of international M&A financing.

How do currency options work?

Currency options are basically bets on the future prices of particular currencies. Offered on many securities exchanges worldwide, they offer the purchaser the option to buy particular currencies at a set future price. Currency options are listed on the exchanges at a particular fixed price (the "strike price") in accordance with the length of the option period, which is generally 30, 60, or 90 days. The hedging party pays a premium for the ability to purchase the optioned currency at the relevant strike price at any time up to the termination date of the option. If the actual price for one unit of foreign currency exceeds the strike price, the hedging party can exercise its option and receive the currency at a cheaper price per unit. If the actual price never exceeds the strike price for the currency during the option period, the hedging party loses its premium paid for the option but is not required to take delivery of (or pay for) the actual currency.

How can a borrower choose among these different instruments?

The degree of certainty of a hedger's need for a specific amount of foreign currency, plus the difference in the fixed price per unit of foreign currency between forward contracts and options at any given time, will dictate which form of hedging technique is used.

Besides these various derivative instruments, what are some other ways to reduce the risk of exchange rate volatility?

U.S. companies can consider shifting production and/or fulfillment to countries where currencies are weakening in relation to the dollar. This strategy was used during the European currency crisis of 1993.[18]

This alternative, like the hedging activities, adds to the cost of the overseas investment. It also may complicate issues with respect to foreign exchange control laws. Both legal and accounting experts should be consulted with respect to the tax and financial reporting consequences of any method chosen.

FOREIGN EXCHANGE CONTROL LAWS

What are foreign exchange control laws, and how can they affect postacquisition operations?

Foreign exchange control laws restrict the amount of a country's local currency that can be converted into foreign currencies. These laws can operate either to completely restrict, or partially limit, the ability of a foreign acquirer to remove funds from an acquired company's country to the foreign investor's home country ("repatriation") or, if the acquirer can remove funds, to force it to take those funds in the local currency.

Do foreign exchange control laws include restrictions on repayments of loans to nonlocal parent companies?

Yes, in some cases. Some countries' foreign exchange control laws apply to loans above a certain amount. Above this threshold, the loan transaction will require prior government approval. In some countries, if a subsidiary needs to obtain foreign currency to repay a loan from its foreign parent, the loan agreement itself must be submitted for approval to that country's central bank, and only then may the foreign currency be bought. Yet other regulations require approval from the exchange control authorities prior to each advance by a foreign company to its subsidiary or, conversely, for any setoff or voluntary prepayment of such loan by the subsidiary.

These are just a few examples of the way foreign exchange laws can affect M&A financing. Participants in M&A transactions should consult their accountants and attorneys to determine the applicable regulations in the particular countries involved.

After a foreign acquisition, can the investor repatriate profits or investment capital from its business interests located in a foreign country without limitations or restrictions?

Not in all cases. Most developing and newly industrialized countries have some form of repatriation restrictions, and some other nations that impose exchange controls also regulate repatriation. Repatriation restrictions or requirements are usually imposed for the same purposes as exchange controls—that is, to acquire or retain foreign currency in a country, to monitor foreign investment, and to police potential tax evasion. Many countries regulating repatriations also provide tax incentives for investors to reinvest profits.

Repatriation restrictions are generally accompanied by some form of additional restriction or reporting requirements, such as registration of foreign capital (with corresponding restrictions on withdrawal of capital from the host country) and notification of amounts of foreign capital invested in the host country.

Could you give an example of a currency exchange control law that includes repatriation restrictions?

In February 1998, the Russian Federation announced new restrictions on the use of foreign currency or foreign securities in that country. The new currency law specified two categories into which all foreign currency transactions are classified: "current currency operations" and "currency operations associated with the movement of capital."

Current currency operations include:

- Foreign currency settlements associated with the export and import of goods, work, and services
- Short-term loans (less than 180 days)
- Settlements of interest, dividends, and similar income operations not associated with the movement of capital

Currency operations associated with the movement of capital include all currency operations that are not current, and specifically include direct investment. This is defined as:

- Investments in the charter capital of a Russian enterprise
- Portfolio investments (defined as the purchase of securities)
- Transfers in payment of the rights to immovable property (defined as ownership of buildings, installations, and other assets, including land and subsurface resources, and other rights to immovable property)
- A deferral, for a period in excess of 180 days, of payment with respect to the export and import of goods, work, and services
- Granting or obtaining loans for a period in excess of 180 days

The currency law generally provides that all settlements between residents must be carried out in rubles. Regarding foreign currency transactions, residents may carry out current currency operations without restriction. Currency operations associated with the movement of capital, however, require the resident enterprise that is a party to the transaction to obtain permission (i.e., a license) from the Central Bank of the Russian Federation.[19]

CONCLUDING COMMENTS

The much-touted "global economy," then, is more than a cliché; it is a reality. In our lifetimes, representatives of national governments have hammered out numerous landmark agreements to encourage and strengthen the flow of capital and goods across national boundaries, and representatives from the private sector have achieved consensus on important values for accounting, business, governance, and work life, among other areas.

All these developments have encouraged a growth in cross-border M&A financing. To be sure, this new game is played within stringent rules—rules that are not always fair, or evenly applied. National laws continue to control currency exchange and related factors. These offsetting trends should not discourage the M&A deal maker. Rather, they should motivate deal makers to learn all they can about the evolving global economy and to retain professionals who can advise them in this area. Only the players who understand how the global economy works will have a chance to become a part of it—and to improve it in the new millennium.

E N D N O T E S

1. William McDonough made this statement in an October 1998 speech before the Institute of International Bankers in Washington, D.C. He was quoted in "Global Fragility Prompted the Fed to Cut Rates," *The Wall Street Journal,* October 6, 1998, p. A2.

2. A recent cover story on mergers cited the theory of Charles P. Kindleberger, who identified the following cycle: mania (e.g., merger mania), monetary expansion, swindles, international propagation, and crash. But the *Fortune* article ends on an optimistic note: "Of course, those who expect a crash have been expecting it for ages, and it keeps not happening. Things are different this time, says the opposing school, and things *are* different. Dozens of industries still carry heavy overcapacity; stocks are still strong; capital is still abundant and cheap. So don't think we're through the great merger wave. Maybe we haven't seen the half of it. The mind reels, that's something we're getting used to." "The Year of the Megamerger," *Fortune,* January 11, 1999, p. 64.

3. *The World Almanac and Book of Facts 1999* (Mahwah, NJ: World Almanac Books, 1998), p. 125.

4. *Mergers & Acquisitions,* March–April 1999, pp. 42ff.

5. The top eight for 1998 (and for history to date) were Exxon and Mobil ($86 billion), Travelers Group and Citicorp ($73 billion), SBC Communications and Ameritech ($72 billion), Bell Atlantic and GTE ($71 billion), AT&T and Tele-Communications ($70 billion), NationsBank and BankAmerica ($62 billion), British Petroleum and Amoco ($55 billion), and Daimler-Benz and Chrysler ($40 billion). Ranking ninth and tenth for 1998 were Norwest and Wells Fargo ($34 billion) and Banc One and First Chicago NBD ($30 billion).

6. The IMF has 146 members, including the United States. It works closely with the International Bank for Reconstruction and Development, known as the World Bank.

7. The G-7 is an international group comprised of the finance ministers of the seven leading industrial democracies who meet to coordinate their respective economic and monetary policies.

8. In addition to G-7 and G-22, other influential international economic groups include the Group of 10, also called the Paris Club, which is composed of 10 members of the International Monetary Fund (plus one associate member) that coordinate monetary and fiscal policies through general agreements to borrow; the Group of Four-plus-One (G4+1), comprised of representatives of national accounting standard setting bodies from Australia, Canada, New Zealand, the United Kingdom, and the United States, together with representatives of International Accounting Standards Committee of London (see Chapter 15); the Group of 24 (another name for the Organization for Economic Cooperation and Development, which has two dozen member nations that coordinate economic and social policy and help developing nations); and the Group of 30, an international group of commercial and investment banks that sets policies and procedures for the operation of financial services firms. As we go to press, a new global group is forming, the Group of Six, or G-6, which will be the Asian counterpart to G-7.

9. The OECD, a 29-member organization, released its guidelines in April 1998. The report, from the OECD's Business Sector Advisory Group on Corporate Governance, was entitled *Corporate Governance: Improving Competitiveness and Access to Capital in Global Markets.* The 107-page report emphasized the importance of flexibility in governance, but did advocate a number of universal goals, including maximizing shareholder value, increasing transparency (disclosure), independence of directors, and the adoption of minimum standards in business.

10. The key document, Social Accountability 8000, or SA 8000, sets forth guidelines on compensation, health and safety, and working hours, among other items. For more details, see "SA 8000: Workplace Value," *Director's Monthly*, October 1998, p. 13.

11. For a summary of economic literature on human capital, see Brian Friedman, James Hatch, and David M. Walker, *Delivering on the Promise: How to Attract, Manage, and Retain Human Capital* (New York: Simon & Schuster, 1999), pp. 202ff.

12. This definition is based on one appearing in Thomas P. Fitch, *Dictionary of Banking Terms*, 3rd ed. (New York: Barrons' Educational Series, 1997). Fitch consulted with a variety of organizations to derive the definitions in this dictionary, including American Bankers Assocation, the Office of the Comptroller of the Currency, the Federal Reserve Bank of New York, and the Federal Reserve Board of Governors, as well as numerous banks and other financial institutions. Other answers in this chapter are based on Fitch, including definitions of M1, M2, and M3.

13. This answer is adapted from a presentation entitled "How to Avoid International Financial Crises," by Anna J. Schwartz of the National Bureau of Economic Research, presented October 14, 1997, at the Cato Institute's Fifteenth Annual Monetary Conference. Dr. Schwartz is a member of the research staff at the National Bureau of Economic Research, a Distinguished Fellow of the American Economics Association, and a past president of the Western Economic Association.

14. We add this qualification because, in some cases, two countries might have the same currency. For example, as of January 1, 1999, the 11 members of the European Monetary Union may now use the euro as a medium of exchange.

15. Some transactions are denominated in multiple currencies. For example, when the Banque Nationale de Paris and Deutsche Bank arranged financing in 1998 (prior to the advent of the euro) for Louis Vuitton Moet Hennessy, they structured it as a "multicurrency revolver"—that is, a revolving line of credit payable in both French francs and Deutschmarks. *Bank Loan Report,* November 30, 1998, p. 8.

16. To a large extent, the accounting risk was reduced in 1981 by Statement No. 52 issued by the Financial Accounting Standards Board (FASB), which altered the rule that foreign currency translation gains and losses had to be immediately reported as income. Under Statement No. 52, such gains or losses resulting from the translation of foreign-denominated income statements are now reflected only as an adjustment to stockholder equity. This change allows a company's lenders or investors to analyze its income statements much more consistently, without worrying as much about the impact of a volatile currency exchange.

17. Derivative instruments can be very risky. In 1993, several major companies—including Procter and Gamble in the United States, Metallgesellschaft in Germany, and Allied Lyons in the United Kingdom—endured heavy losses from trading in derivatives, prompting regulatory scrutiny in all three countries. In the following six years, fewer derivatives-based failures have occurred, because of improved controls in this area. Some of these controls have come from new disclosure requirements from governments. Others have been voluntary. For example, the aforementioned Group of 30 has published 20 recommendations for banks to use as guidelines in managing and disclosing investments in domestic and international "derivatives" based on such instruments as forward contracts and options. Risk management firms have also provided guidance.

18. "U.S. Companies Move to Limit Currency Risk," *The Wall Street Journal,* August 3, 1993.

19. William R. Henry and Vladimir Zheltonogov, "Russian Federation Currency Policy Changes Create Foreign Currency Payment Problems," *East/West Executive Guide,* February 1998. *East/West Executive Guide* is published by World Trade Executive, Concord, Massachusetts.

Microeconomic Aspects of Global M&A Financing

Si fueris Romae, Romano vivito more; si fueris alabi, vivito sicut ibi.

Attributed to St. Ambrose (c. 339–397 A.D.)

INTRODUCTION

"When in Rome, live as the Romans do," says a proverb as old as that civilization. In fact, as St. Ambrose advised St. Augustine in the fourth century, *wherever* you are, live like everyone there does.

No advice could be more sage when it comes to obtaining M&A financing from foreign sources. Whether the financing sought is in the form of debt, equity, or a hybrid instrument, and whether the source is a lender, bondholder, shareholder, or backer, or an angel, it is important to master the customs, language, and laws of the foreign host. Conversely, suppliers of capital must know how to walk in their customers' shoes—every small step of the way.

Understanding global finance does not just mean understanding the big picture of capital flows and the like, as important as this may be. It also means mastering the minute mechanics of the deal in specific jurisdictions. The following chapter delves into this literally mundane material (*mundane,* derived from the Latin root *mundis,* means worldly) from a global M&A perspective.

GLOBAL FINANCING: LEGAL BASICS

Must foreign investors be concerned about specific state regulations as well as U.S. federal law when acquiring or investing in a U.S. business interest?

In general, states do not restrict foreign investment, except with respect to specific industries, such as banking and insurance. Most states (over 40 as of mid-1998) have passed antitakeover laws, but these apply equally to U.S. and foreign acquirers. Some states, such as California, Iowa, New Mexico, and Pennsylvania, restrict land ownership with respect to certain types of property, and the exploitation or development of natural resources by foreign investors. A foreign person desiring to acquire a business interest in the United States should seek legal counsel to ensure that there are no special restrictions imposed by the state in which the business is domiciled, as well as under the federal law.[1]

Do any of the foregoing restrictions apply to U.S. businesses in which foreign persons hold debt rather than equity?

No. In the United States, the percentage of equity owned is the exclusive means of measuring the extent of a foreign investor's control of a U.S. corporation. Debt holdings are not considered.

Does federal or state law limit the ability of a U.S. company to guarantee the indebtedness of a foreign affiliate?

There are no federal limitations on the ability of a U.S. company to guarantee foreign indebtedness. Any state limitations on a corporation's ability to guarantee indebtedness would be set forth in the state's corporation statutes, but such limitations are relatively rare. When limitations do exist under state law, they apply regardless of the nationality of the person on whose behalf the guarantee is given.

Are there legal limitations under U.S. law on the ability of a U.S. company to pledge its assets to a foreign lender?

The power of a corporation to acquire, manage, and dispose of assets arises from state corporation statutes and is not dependent upon the identity of other parties to the transaction. For example, Section 122 of the Delaware General Corporation Law empowers any Delaware corporation to "sell, convey, lease, exchange, transfer, or otherwise dispose of, or mortgage or pledge, all or any of its property and assets, or any interest therein, wherever situated." U.S. federal law imposes no restriction on the pledge of assets by U.S. individuals or entities.

Does the United States impose any restrictions on the amount of dollars that can be paid by a U.S. business to a foreign investor?

There is no limit, under current U.S. law, to the amount of money that can be taken out of the United States by either U.S. or foreign investors. In fact, it is the lack of such restrictions that has led to the rapid development of large offshore currency markets.

Can a foreign company lists its shares on U.S. stock markets, and if so, how?

Non-U.S. companies can list their shares on U.S. stock markets by using American Depository Receipts (ADRs). ADRs are negotiable certificates issued by a U.S. bank for shares of stock issued by a foreign corporation. The shares are held in a custodial account, either at the issuing bank or at an agent of the bank, such as a custodian. ADRs are priced in dollars and traded on stock exchanges and over-the-counter markets, as are other U.S. securities. Like any security, they must be registered with the Securities and Exchange Commission (SEC). Some 1,600 non-U.S. companies have obtained U.S. equity capital in this manner.

What exactly is a *custodian*—and what is a global custodian?

The custody business began as a simple matter of settling and safeguarding securities. Today, *custodians* offer additional services, such as cash management, investment accounting, securities lending, and treasury management services. This quiet force in international markets holds some $40 trillion in assets worldwide. Many custodians hold securities from multiple countries. Such global custodians include Bank of New York, Chase, Citigroup, and State Street.[2]

What regulations beyond national securities commissions govern international equity investment?

The central organization for equity involvement regulation is the International Organization of Securities Commissions (IOSCO). Headquartered in Montreal, it is composed of 80 regulatory agencies from around the world. Although stock market rules vary considerably from country to country,[3] the very existence of IOSCO points to a core of values. Moreover, the group and its individual members could gain more importance with the growth of major transborder deals such as the one creating DaimlerChrysler.

As the private sector collaborates, so too does the public sector. For example, securities commissions are working together more often. In October 1991, regulators in the United States and the United Kingdom approved the first single-offer document for a takeover affecting investors in both countries. To do so, the securities commissions had to agree to compromise on a number of regulatory points. At around the same time, the SEC relaxed requirements for foreign companies' repository securities in the United States.

It is also worth noting that many countries have laws to curb takeover activity. In 1996, the European Commission (EC) issued a new policy with five guiding principles:

- All securities holders should be treated equally.
- All those to whom an offer is addressed must have enough time and receive enough information to make a properly informed decision.
- The board of an offeree company must act in the best interests of the company as a whole.
- An offer must not create false markets in the securities of the offeree company, the offeror company, or any other company concerned by the offer.
- The business of an offeree company should not be hindered beyond a reasonable time by an offer for its securities.[4]

Furthermore, the EC has liberalized its stock market rules through a new rule called the Investment Services Directive (ISD). Ever since January 1996, all member states of the European Union (EU) have been required to offer open access to their domestic securities markets for regulated firms from other states. The ISD also set up groundrules for "remote members," allowing a firm in one country to transact business on an exchange elsewhere. This new rule, combined with the advent of the euro, has broadened the EC's capital reach.

AVAILABILITY OF GLOBAL M&A FINANCING

How easy is it to get financing for an international deal? Don't most domestic lenders shy away from this type of transaction?

For the most part, the methods of financing an international acquisition will not be very different from those used in a purely domestic deal. Various types of debt, ranging from standard commercial bank debt to subordinated debt (junior/senior/mezzanine), to debt secured by a variety of assets, can be used in the international context.

For example, as U.S. companies become more familiar with European financial markets, and as European companies become more familiar with U.S. high-risk bond markets, a European junk bond market is emerging. In the first six months of 1998, there were 20 high-yield offerings in euro currencies worth $3.2 billion. This is far more than the 13 offerings there were in all of 1997. Analyst Brian Bollen has predicted that demand for mezzanine financing could grow in Europe. As companies move beyond early stage financing, they might turn to junk bonds to "optimize" leverage in their operations. For now, however, says Bollen, "equity remains the financing vehicle of choice" for European companies, at least in the high-tech field.[5]

This debt financing can be obtained from both public and private sources. Equity financing through the sale and issuance of new securities is also possible in the global deal. But whatever sources of financing an acquirer uses, they will have a global dimension.

In considering an international transaction, the potential acquirer may find it necessary to call on a variety of different currencies and to operate within several international jurisdictions. The acquirer must learn how such financial transactions can be affected by regulations imposed by its own government, as well as the governments of the acquired company, the countries in which investors and lenders reside, and the countries in which banks and securities exchanges may be located. Areas of concern will include tax consequences, the ability of investors to repatriate profits, perfecting lenders' security interests, and the like. Similarly, the rules of certain supranational or regional institutions, such as the United Nations, the EU, and the Organization of American States (OAS) may apply. Also to be considered are agreements, such as the General Agreement on Tariffs and Trade (GATT) and the North American Free Trade Agreement (NAFTA), mentioned in Chapter 13.

What special public sources of financing are available to the transnational acquirer?

Many countries have government-backed loan programs for businesses that wish to expand into overseas markets. Although most of these programs focus on export, they are not limited to this realm. In the United States, the Overseas Private Investment Corp. (OPIC) provides hundreds of millions of dollars in yearly loans and loan guarantees to companies—including small companies—that do business abroad, sometimes by acquiring foreign companies. In some cases, the borrowers have used these public funds to invest in foreign concerns.

Even without government encouragement, commercial banks and other financial institutions are willing to loan money to companies acquiring abroad. Although we have no hard numbers on this amount, we estimate that it is approximately $50 billion. In 1997, for example, we know that U.S. financial institutions formed syndicates to loan $195 billion for the financing of 301 acquisitions, mostly large ones—an average of $648 million per acquisition.[6] (This number includes both loans to domestic and to international transactions, including some not involving U.S. companies.) We also know that historically, about one quarter of all transactions involving U.S. companies are transborder deals, either outbound or inbound. And we can assume that a similar percentage applies to non-U.S. companies that received M&A financing in 1997, since they, too, operate in a global economy. Therefore, we can assume that about one fourth of U.S. syndicated loan money goes to support cross-border acquisitions—or about $49 billion in all.

Suppose a seller demands to be paid in a currency that is different from the operating currency of the entity making the payments. How can the acquirer accomplish this?

The incompatibility of differing currencies has always ranked high among the challenges that buyers and sellers face when structuring an international transaction. Fortunately, solutions abound. The following brief history will explain how these solutions arose.

At the end of World War II, many American corporations decided to apply some of their newfound wealth to direct investment in foreign companies, particularly in Europe. To finance these investments, the acquiring companies found it necessary to come up with large amounts of the functional currency used by the company being acquired. To do this, the acquirers either had to borrow from unfamiliar banking institutions in the seller's home country, which did not always have sufficient funds to meet the purchase price, or had to go through the cumbersome process of obtaining the necessary funds in U.S. dollars and converting them into the needed currency, incurring the added expense of an intermediary broker.

Since the downfall of the Bretton Woods system in 1971, when the U.S. dollar was taken off the gold standard, potential acquirers have inherited the further difficulty of predicting the rise and fall of fluctuating exchange rates of individual currencies.

It is within this framework that large offshore international banking markets—called *Eurocurrency* markets—have developed as an alternative to currency conversion.

An example of such a system is the *Eurodollar* market—that is, the deposit or redeposit of U.S. dollars into a large pool on foreign territory without conversion of the funds into local currency. The transaction is recorded by book entry, and there is no physical importation of the dollars into the foreign country. The pooling entity into which dollars are deposited may be either a foreign branch of a U.S. banking institution or an independent foreign bank, both of which have become known as *Eurobanks*.

Because offshore banking in different currencies has not been heavily regulated by any jurisdiction (e.g., Eurobanks are not subject to the same reserve requirements as domestic banks), offshore banks are able to have a much higher percentage of bank funds committed to corporate and other loans.

The Eurobanks can make short-, medium-, or long-term loans for acquisitions or working capital and participate in a wide variety of interbank lending activities. Eurobank deposits also exist for offshore deposits of Japanese yen, British sterling, and many other currencies, including the new currency, effective since January 1999, used by members of the European Monetary Union. This new currency, called the *euro,* is not to be confused with the generic Euro prefix used in the global financial instruments and institutions described elsewhere in this chapter.

The euro supersedes the European currency unit (ECU) previously used to facilitate trade and commerce within Europe. Interestingly, there has been talk about a similar future development in Asia, which already has Asian currency units (ACUs) and may eventually develop a currency for use within Asia. This is not beyond possibility, since an infrastructure, called the Asian international currency market, already exists. Certain banks (i.e., those authorized by the government of Singapore to handle ACUs) accept deposits in all foreign currencies to accommodate corporate financing throughout the Pacific Rim. Just as the successful use of ECUs in Europe led to the euro, so the use of ACUs in Asia may eventually lead to the development of a pan-Asian currency. Meanwhile, offshore markets for currency continue to be viable around the world.

How are interest rates on funds borrowed in these offshore markets calculated?

Generally, interest in the Eurocurrency market is tied to the London Interbank Offered Rate (LIBOR), and ACUs are tied to the Singapore Interbank Offered Rate (SIBOR). The interbank offered rate is the interest charged by an offshore depository of a particular currency for funds lent in that currency to another offshore banking facility. This rate is used in international finance in the same way the prime rate is used in the United States—that is, as a reference rate from which the individual interest rate of a particular loan is created. LIBOR, SIBOR, and other interbank rates are listed in many of the world's financial newspapers.

What happens when one bank, whether an onshore or an offshore institution, does not have adequate funds to meet an acquirer's lending needs?

This is the function of the international syndicated loan market, which is particularly useful for onshore banks that must maintain a high ratio of capital reserves to borrowed funds, or banks that do not want to bear the entire risk of a large international loan by themselves.

How do international syndicated loans work?

The principles behind international syndication are generally the same as in a purely domestic syndicated loan, with the added considerations of differing currencies, interest and exchange rates, tax and other government regulatory schemes, supranational currency controls, and the like.

In an international syndication, a group of lenders will pool its funds via a network of selling participations and other agreements until the required borrowing amount is obtained. There is only one loan agreement between the borrower and the syndication, which is negotiated among the parties to fit the particular needs of the transaction. Funds can flow from either onshore or offshore currency markets.

Typically, the funds borrowed under an international syndicated loan agreement will be subject to five charges to the borrower: (1) interest (which can be tied to an international reference rate such as LIBOR or SIBOR, plus a spread); (2) a management fee, which is paid to the lead bank for arranging and managing the syndication; (3) a commitment fee; (4) an agent's fee, which is usually paid to the lead bank for negotiating the loan and acting as agent on behalf of the other members of the syndicate; and (5) any expenses associated with putting together the loan, which can include legal and accounting fees, travel costs, and the like.

There are generally two forms of international syndication. In one, the lenders that are party to the loan agreement commit to lend a stated amount directly to the borrower. The lenders are severally, but not jointly, liable on their lending obligations. Every member of the syndication receives a pro rata portion of the overall receipts from the loan on the basis of its individual commitment of funds.

In the other form of syndication, the lead bank is the only bank bound by a loan agreement to the borrower, and it is solely responsible for the commitment to fund the loan. The lead bank then signs participation or subscription agreements with other lenders that want to participate in the loan as it was negotiated by the lead bank. (In some cases, however, it may be necessary for the lead bank to come back to the borrower and ask for amendments that will facilitate the lead bank's finding willing participants.) Again, the lead bank will pay the participants their pro rata share of the loan receipts, after deducting whatever management, agent, or subscription fees it may have negotiated.

A very typical situation is where a U.S. company wants to finance the acquisition of another U.S. company that has significant overseas operations. In this case, the lead bank will usually be the primary domestic lender, which may use syndication as a means of bringing in foreign lenders familiar with the business and economic climates of the countries where the acquired company's overseas operations are concentrated. Such syndication will reduce the risk of a U.S. lender that otherwise may be reluctant to lend overseas, but lenders will need to work out a variety of intercreditor issues, including the priority of assets securing the acquisition funding.

You mentioned interest charges to the borrower, but isn't it true that some syndicated loans do not include an interest component—namely, those that involve Islamic participants?

Yes, this is true. Islamic banks can neither charge nor pay interest, because exacting (or, conversely, promising) a guaranteed return on money loaned or invested is considered exploitative according to the Koran. As an alternative, Islamic banks have partnership contracts with their depositors. The depositors are guaranteed a specific portion of any profits made with the money.

An Islamic bank can assume a number of roles, including providing investment funds for a project, acting as a middleman (buying goods, marking them up, and reselling them), or providing lease/purchase arrangements. Islamic banks are also permitted under Koranic law to make advance payments for a project with an outcome, repaying themselves by selling the outcome.

A relatively new phenomenon (the first bank partnership was formed as a cooperative in 1964), Islamic banks have kept up with the times. Faysal Islamic Bank has developed an Islamic banking software to analyze and, if possible, restructure the interest component in derivative instruments and loan syndications. When complex questions arise, transactions may go not only before the bank's statutory board but also before its religious supervisory, or Sharia, board.[7]

Are banks the only institutions that can participate in an international loan syndication?

No. Recently, international syndications have included large-scale investors willing to take the risk of lending for corporate acquisitions or refinancings. Such investors may be insurance companies, pension funds, government-sponsored investment pools, mutual funds, or large corporations. Whether or not a particular entity can participate in a syndicated loan may be governed by national regulations in force in the country where the potential participant is domiciled.

What types of requirements will the syndicating lenders generally request from the borrower?

The covenants and representations required by the lenders in an international syndication today are generally not much different from a domestic U.S. syndicator's requirements, although historically international loans have tended to be unsecured. Today, more and more foreign lenders are looking to corporate fixed assets, inventories, and accounts receivable as security for international syndicated loans. Most syndication agreements include, at minimum, a negative pledge clause (where the borrower promises not to encumber any future assets) and a *pari passu* clause, stating that the priority of the lending banks' rights will be equivalent compared with any other creditor of the same class. The loan agreement may also contain financial covenants and other restrictions upon the borrower typically found in domestic loans.

Are traditional loans the only kind of financing that can be syndicated?

No. Lenders may also wish to use syndication to spread the risk of bridge loans, large letters of credit or guarantees backed by offshore currency deposits, or international commercial paper programs such as certificates of deposit—Euro-CDs or Asian Dollar-CDs.

What exactly is a letter of credit?

A letter of credit, mentioned briefly in earlier chapters, is a credit instrument issued by a bank that guaranties payments of behalf of its customer to a beneficiary, normally a third part but sometimes to the bank's customer. As such, it is a type of bank guarantee. (For more on letters of credit and bank guarantees, see Chapter 12.)

A letter of credit substitutes the bank's credit for the credit of another party, typically an exporter or importer, who is authorized to write drafts up to a specified amount. A *draft* is a payment order in writing that directs a second party, the drawee, to pay a specified sum to a third party. This term is often used interchangeably with *bill of exchange,* but there is a difference: A draft is by definition negotiable and transferable, whereas a bill of exchange may be nonnegotiable and nontransferable.

There are different kinds of drafts. A *bank draft* is drawn on a bank; a *trade draft* is drawn on an entity other than a bank. A *time draft* may be paid in the future, and a *sight draft* must be paid upon presentation. A negotiable bank time draft involving two parties is known as a *banker's acceptance* or a *two-name paper.*

These terms relate mainly to international trade financing, rather than M&A financing, but they are relevant to M&A financing for two reasons. First, financial gains and commercial relationships built through trading can lead to alliance or merger. Second, some of the instruments used in trade finance may be adapted to M&A financing. For example, as mentioned in Chapter 12, senior revolving credit acquisition lenders often providea letters of credit after the acquisition and may well insist upon doing this as part of the deal.

Can an acquirer's international merger and acquisition activities be funded by issuing private or public debt securities?

Yes. Private or public placements of debt can be effectively utilized when issuers feel they can attract investors at lower rates than the interbank offered rates, or when they desire long-term, fixed-interest debt.

The offshore currency markets have funded individual corporate debt issues in a multitude of currencies, facilitating investment in corporations located all over the world. The most overwhelming example is the Eurobond market, which has been expanding at an astounding rate. The volume of new Eurobond issues has risen dramatically in the past 15 years.

What exactly is a Eurobond?

A *Eurobond* is a corporate or government bond denominated in a currency other than the national (or, in the case of the euro, regional) currency of the issuer. The bonds are ordinarily issued in bearer form by international syndicates of commercial banks and investment banks that bid on securities offered for sale through a *tender panel*—a group of commercial and investment banks authorized by a borrower to solicit bids on a project or deal on a best efforts basis.

Eurobonds can be denominated in any currency but are issued offshore and are usually structured to be sold outside the jurisdiction of the nation whose currency is used or where the issuer resides. In the United States, for example, the present policy seems to be that unregistered debt securities may be issued overseas by U.S. issuers but must not be sold or offered for sale to any U.S. person, or anywhere within the United States, until the passage of a 90-day "rest abroad" period. The SEC imposes certain requirements on U.S. issuers designed to ensure that no such sales are made during the rest abroad period, including the placement of a restrictive legend on the bond itself.

Offshore corporate bonds are generally issued in bearer form, and many have provisions that exclude the interest paid via withholding taxes imposed by countries where the bonds are distributed. They may be privately or publicly traded and often appear on the stock exchanges of the major financial centers from London to Tokyo. International syndicates of underwriters and lending institutions are often instrumental in issuing offshore corporate bonds.

What other types of debt financing besides bonds are available?

The list is long, thanks to two factors: borrowers' and lenders' needs for greater liquidity. These twin needs have led to the development of a whole spectrum of international negotiable instruments, the utility of which depends upon the needs and repayment abilities of borrowers.

Negotiable medium-term or long-term fixed rate notes (FRNs) are bearer notes evidencing the obligation of the maker of the notes to pay a stated principal amount upon maturity, with periodic payments of interest at a fixed rate. This type of note may be more convenient than conventional bank notes, which usually require the principal to be amortized over the life of the note, rather than deferring payment until maturity. Sale of the FRNs is accomplished through subscription agreements, which provide for investors to buy a note or notes worth a certain stated amount upon fulfillment of various conditions or the making of certain representations and warranties by the issuer. Terms and conditions appear on the reverse of the notes.

Another innovation in the Eurocurrency market is the *Euronote,* a short-term bearer note evidencing the obligation of the maker to pay the stated principal amount at maturity (from one week to one year, but generally one month to six months). Because of the short term of the notes, Euronote makers can take advantage of lower interest rates in the Eurocurrency markets. The terms and conditions of short-term notes will generally be much less rigorous than those found on FRNs or in bond underwriting agreements.

Suppose a non-U.S. company lends for a merger involving a U.S. company. What U.S. taxes will be levied on the interest stream?

It depends on how the deal is structured, but it is relatively easy to structure a debt to allow a foreign investor to receive interest free of U.S. tax. If the debt is recharacterized, however, a payment of purported interest may be treated as a dividend. Dividends received by foreign taxpayers are subject to U.S. tax at either the prevailing withholding rate or at a lower withholding rate provided for in a treaty. Where a foreign investor asks for and obtains an indemnification from U.S. taxes, the tax obligation will fall on the issuer and, indirectly, its shareholders.

On another topic, suppose an acquirer encounters a group of multinational investors, all of which want to lend, and be repaid, in their own currencies rather than in offshore funds?

One fairly recent innovation in promissory notes is the medium-term note (MTN), in which the maker offers a program of notes through one or more agents that place the notes for a commission on a best-efforts basis. Initial hold-

ers can negotiate the terms of their individual notes to suit such holders' specific repayment requirements with respect to currencies, payment structures, or rates of interest. Therefore, a maker using an MTN program may have a series of notes outstanding, each one with a different currency, interest rate calculation, or term. This kind of note program allows an issuer to attract a larger pool of investors by catering to their specific needs at a cost that is often less than a comparable underwriter's fee would be for an underwritten offering.

INSTRUMENTS IN GLOBAL M&A FINANCING

How can an acquirer obtain the different currencies it needs to meet its obligations to its investors?

It could simply convert the currency generated by the acquired company through a foreign exchange broker for a fee, or it could obtain the desired currency through some form of swap, such as a currency swap.

What is a swap and what different kinds of swaps may be used in international M&A?

A *swap* is a forward-contract type of derivative instrument. Swaps may be used to exchange currencies or to exchange interest rates, or they may combine the two. A *currency swap* agreement is a contract calling for the parties to supply each other with a stated amount of currency at specific intervals. For example, one party might agree to pay the other in euros in exchange for an equivalent amount of yen.

In such a case, an *interest rate swap* agreement is negotiated. An interest rate swap is very much like a short-term interest rate futures contract and is often used as an alternative to futures. The interest rate swap market has been a rapidly growing sector in the international capital markets in recent years, growing to hundreds of billions of dollars in value per year.

How can a currency swap and an interest rate swap agreement work together?

In such a combined swap, the borrower corporation and another party with access to various currencies, perhaps through its own subsidiaries, agree to pay each other a sum equal to the interest that would have accrued on a specific amount over a specific period of time at the desired rate.

The exchanging party may be a bank or a large corporation with access to various currencies, perhaps through its own subsidiaries. This corporation may have a Eurobond issue outstanding on which it is obligated to pay a fixed rate of interest. In this case, an interest rate swap agreement may be in order, in which the corporation and another party agree to pay to each other a sum equal to the interest that would have accrued on a specific amount over a specific period of time at a negotiated rate. Often a bank acts as an intermediary for the transaction, carrying the risk of nonperformance of the swap contract by either firm.

Swap agreements should generally be for short terms to protect against significant fluctuations in interest rates or currency exchange rates, which can throw off the economics of a merger transaction, with periodic rollover provisions allowing for the continuation of the agreement on the same or renegotiated terms of exchange. From a legal point of view, swap agreements are nothing more than international contracts that will be governed under the contract law of whichever country the parties choose to govern interpretation of contract terms. Swaps are complicated, and, some might argue, risky, but as international currency markets have grown, swaps—along with other derivative instruments such as options, futures, and forwards—have become more and more important in structuring transnational deals.[8]

Could you give some generic examples of how a complex swap like this might work?

As a simple example, take a company with outstanding loans bearing interest at LIBOR plus 0.25 percent, payable to one investor in euros and to another investor in yen, and another company that pays interest in U.S. dollars at a fixed rate (say, 8.5 percent) to its Eurobondholders. A swap could be structured so that the first company receives a payment from the second company in euros and yen equal to the interest it must pay its investors, in exchange for Eurodollar payments to the second company of the interest that would accrue on the same principal amount at the fixed rate of 8.5 percent. This is a combined interest rate and currency swap, which meets the first company's requirements for repayment to its investors. So long as the floating rate does not fall significantly below the fixed rate, the foregoing is a good business transaction for the first company.

As a more complex example, consider a company (AAA) that has a loan portfolio that earns the six-month LIBOR plus 2 percent. Its current financing is with a fixed rate Eurobond at 10.5 percent. It could also borrow at a floating LIBOR plus 0.5 percent. Another company (BBB) has a portfolio of fixed-rate

mortgages earning 13 percent. It is currently borrowing at the floating rate
LIBOR plus 1 percent. It could borrow at a fixed rate of 12 percent. The *quality
spread differential* (QSD) can be exploited to the benefit of each. AAA can obtain
floating rate funds at 50 basis points less than BBB and can obtain fixed rates at
a savings of 150 basis points. AAA's advantage in fixed rate funds less its advantage in floating rate funds is the QSD of 100 basis points.

In such a case, an interest rate swap can provide benefits to each. AAA
lends to BBB at a fixed rate of 11.5 percent. BBB lends to AAA at the LIBOR
rate. AAA company locks in a 200 basis point spread between the earnings of
its loan portfolio and what it is paying to BBB. The BBB company has locked in
a 150 basis point spread by borrowing from AAA at the fixed 11.5 interest rate.

Another well-known type of swap is a debt-for-equity conversion. How does this work, and when is it used?

Debt-for-equity conversions evolved as one solution to the paucity of hard currency foreign exchange available to a debtor country for external debt payments. The conversion allows the debtor country to discharge foreign hard
currency denominated debt through payments in soft local currency. Some
countries that have such formal debt-for-equity conversion programs are Ar-
gentina, Brazil, Chile, Costa Rica, Ecuador, Mexico, and the Philippines. There
are commercial firms that specialize in arranging such swap programs, which
tend to get rather complicated. Further, more and more negotiated and even
some limited auction markets are opening up for the purchase and sale of debt
instruments payable in many different currencies but taking advantage of the
growth and sophistication of the currency swap markets.

The basic steps in a debt-for-equity swap are as follows:

- The foreign commercial bank creditor decides either to invest in a
  local business located in the debtor country or to sell its loan asset to
  a third-party investor at a discount.
- The bank or the investor then redeems the credit for its designated
  value in the debtor's local currency.
- The bank or the investor subsequently invests the proceeds in a local enterprise.

The investor generally has one of two reasons for engaging in a
debt-for-equity swap transaction: the desire to make a new investment in the
debtor country, or the desire to recapitalize an existing subsidiary or affiliate
in the debtor country. In both cases, the highly favorable discount rate will

substantially reduce the cost of equity to the investor. As for the debtor country, it can reduce its external debt, creating value for itself if it can retire its debt at a price below its face value. The debtor country can also use debt-for-equity swaps to encourage investment interest in its economy. Indeed, preferential consideration is given to certain types of investments, such as those that bring new technology into the country, finance industry expansion or new product development, or increase exports of the debtor country.

In this chapter and the previous one, you have mentioned the riskiness of derivative instruments such as swaps and futures. Could you give an example?

The best and most current example is the near-collapse in late 1998 of the Meriwether Long-Term Capital Management Company (LTCM)—a private investment company specializing in hedging transactions, often through the purchase of derivative instruments.

As every deal maker knows, Meriwether—named after cofounder John W. Meriwether, a former star of the bond trading operations of Salomon Brothers—began life in a blaze of glory. The company had capital from 80 investors, each at a minimum of $10 million. Investors included top managers of Bear Stearns and Merrill Lynch, and partners included a former vice chairman of the Federal Reserve Board plus Nobel Prize-winning economists. Meriwether began betting on a variety of phenomena, including American stocks, British interest rates, Danish mortgages, and Russian bonds.

What happened? "In a nutshell," writes business journalist Heather Chaplin in an irreverant and insightful essay, "he lost too many bets."[9] The general consensus, notes Chaplin, is that the fund was risking *too much money* in areas where it had *too little expertise*. "It got hit by the emerging market meltdown, Russian troubles, the U.S. stock market decline, and a merger it was betting heavily on that didn't pan out." LTCM bought 2 million shares in Ciena, expecting it to be acquired by TelLabs. Ciena shares went from a high of $92 in July 1998 to $13 the day the deal was scrapped.[10] The fund was saved in the end. A group of 14 investors, lenders, and trading partners (including Goldman, Sachs & Co., Merrill Lynch, UBS of Switzerland, and J. P. Morgan) met with the Federal Reserve Bank of New York. Each of the 14 agreed to pay between $100 million and $350 million to infuse LTCM with cash. The total bailout has been estimated at $3.7 billion. In April 1999, a U.S. White House task force chaired by Treasury Secretary Robert E. Rubin announced recommendations for hedge fund reforms.

But in considering the Meriwether saga, we should note two things. First, there is a big difference between, on the one hand, a private investment firm that devotes *all* its capital to *bet* on phenomena and, on the other hand, an operating company that uses *part* of its capital to (most typically) *hedge* against risks incurred in the course of ordinary business.

Second, if two firms combine, and one of them experiences losses from derivative investments (whether made as bets or as hedges), the merger in fact may mute the impact of the losses. For example, shortly after Nationsbank and BankAmerica merged in 1998, the newly combined company sustained losses from BankAmerica's previous derivatives investments. Although the discovery had a negative impact on year-end results, the results were hardly catastrophic. Thanks in part to Nationsbank economics, most of the "bets" of the combined entities—using this term broadly to include traditional loans and investments—were collateralized with brick and mortar, rather than merely brains and math!

SECURITY INTERESTS IN FOREIGN ASSETS

Can acquirers obtain security interests on the assets of foreign companies to finance acquisitions?

Yes. Today, most foreign countries have the same or analogous concepts to those of the United States regarding security interests in assets to serve as collateral for borrowing.

There are many differences, however, in the types of assets that can be secured, the methods of accomplishing such a transaction, the type of notice required, if any, and to whom notice must be given. Thus, it is imperative that local counsel be enlisted to complete these transactions. In the United Kingdom, the method of securitization is similar to that employed in the United States. A fixed charge (or mortgage interest) is granted over specific real or leasehold property interests, fixed assets, and goodwill, and a floating charge (or after-acquired property security interest) is granted on accounts receivable and inventory.

France is an example of a country in which securitization becomes more problematic. A *contract hypothecaire* is used to grant a mortgage on real property, whereas a *nantissement de fonds de commerce* is the French document granting a security interest in tangible or intangible fixed assets. It becomes effective upon the occurrence of a default by the borrower. The *nantissement de fonds de commerce*, however, does not include accounts receivable or inventory, and, although it may be legally possible to include such assets in the agreement, perfecting it may not be a practical expedient. In the case of accounts receivable, perfection requires that notice of the security interest be sent to each account party by a French process server upon establishment of the account. In the case of inventory, the only method of perfecting such an interest is by possession—that is, a field warehousing arrangement whereby a third party is hired to keep custody of the inventory on behalf of the secured party.

In Japan, civil liens (*sakidori tokken*) and possessory liens (*riyachiken*) are given only by law and cannot be established by contract or by judicial decree. A Japanese entity may assign rights it has in real property or movable chattels (including inventory) by contract, but in the case of chattels, in order for such an assignment to be valid against third parties, the secured party must be in possession, and the consent of the assignor must be certified by a notary public or post office. Accounts receivable may be pledged as security in Japan, provided that there is nothing to the contrary contained in the agreement between the original parties establishing the account.

What happens if a country does not permit a floating security interest on after-acquired property?

As previously discussed, in contrast to the customary U.S. practice of obtaining "floating" liens on assets not as yet acquired, many countries do not permit this type of security interest. To include new assets as collateral, the parties must enter into additional security agreements and comply with all formalities imposed by the governing law of the country every time a newly acquired asset is to be included in the lender's security.

INTERNATIONAL LBOs

Can the concept of a leveraged buyout be applied in the international context?

Yes. The leveraged management buyout has become an accepted acquisition structure in several European nations, particularly the United Kingdom, France, and Germany. It is a useful tool for large family-owned enterprises established after World War II by owners now reaching retirement age, and for large state-owned conglomerates now in the process of privatizing. In the latter case, new owners are selling off unrelated businesses, a practice not permitted under state ownership.

What would the structure of a leveraged buyout look like, for example, in a management LBO in France?

The structure employed in France would not be vastly different from the structure used in the United States, with certain exceptions resulting from the corporate and business laws of France.

The financing will usually entail a tripartite structure comprising:

- Senior debt from a traditional lending institution, which may or may not be collateralized
- Middle-tier financing, including subordinated or convertible debt at a higher fixed rate of interest
- Straight equity investment by the managers and other investors

Applicable laws in France and other EC countries are, for the most part, sufficiently nonrestrictive to allow creativity in structuring an LBO.

Other than the perfection of security interests, which has already been discussed, are there any other problems a senior lender seeking security might face?

If shares of the foreign parent company's stock are pledged to a French lender, the lender may not be able to foreclose upon such shares in the event of a default without the prior approval of the French government. In practice, this risk has not been an impediment to accepting such pledges of foreign stock.

Can the acquired company in France guarantee the debt of the foreign parent for acquisition funding?

This sort of upstream guarantee is a problem, because French corporate law prohibits a French corporation from advancing moneys, making loans, or facilitating security interests with the intent of aiding a third party to purchase a French corporation's own stock. There is an exemption, however, for loans to employees of the French company. This problem goes away if the LBO is structured as an asset deal, but there are significant tax consequences in the event of an asset transaction, so the potential investor should be very careful in analyzing which structure to use.

In the case of an international LBO, as with all international transactions, it is wise to consult with local counsel in the country where the buyout candidate is located.

CONCLUDING COMMENTS

Mastering the mechanics of international transactions is not easy, especially if the deals draw on foreign capital. Financing customs and rules change often, and the further away one is from the scene of change, the more difficult it is to predict. In this chapter, we have tried to provide guidance and examples relating to current techniques and rules for M&A financing, but we have only scratched a part of the surface in this vast and deep arena. We urge continuing education in this area, and the use of qualified professionals. The same message applies to our next and final chapter, on international taxation.

E N D N O T E S

1. Ownership of a U.S. corporation by a foreign citizen, that is, a "controlled foreign corporation," should not be confused with the term *foreign corporation,* which has a narrower meaning. Unlike many countries, the United States has allocated to its 50 states the act of incorporation. For instance, a Delaware corporation—that is, a company incorporated in the State of Delaware—doing business in Virginia is known in Virginia as a foreign corporation.

2. These companies frequently appear in global custody lists published periodically by the *Financial Times* and *Pensions & Investments.*

3. For example, in 20 major equity markets around the world, the stake of equity ownership that must be disclosed ranges from 2 percent (in Italy) to 25 percent (in Germany). For a complete guide to international stock exchange requirements, see *International Securities Laws Handbook* (New York: Bowne Publishing Division, 1998).

4. For background on this directive, which is still under consideration by member states, see Alistair Bird and Penny Bryce, "The Proposed European Directive on Takeovers," *Corporate Governance Advisor,* November/December 1996, pp. 18ff.

5. "High-Tech Comes to Europe," *Euromoney,* June 1998, pp. 209ff., summarized in *Bowne Review for CFOs and Investment Bankers,* July/August 1998, p. 1.

6. Carrie Smith of Securities Data Publishing, Newark, New Jersey, in a fax to the authors dated December 2, 1998. For more statistics, see Chapter 1.

7. "Islam Rising: How Banks Do Business Charging No Interest," *The Philadelphia Inquirer,* February 25, 1996, pp. D1ff.

8. "U.S. Firms Abroad Ride Shifting Waves of Currency: Antidotes to Monetary Turmoil Include Hedging, Shortening Payment Terms," *The Wall Street Journal,* August 6, 1993. Kenneth R. Kapner and John F. Marshall, *The Swaps Handbook: Swaps and Related Risk Management Instruments* (New York: New York Institute of Finance, 1990).

9. This summary is based on several sources, including, notably, articles in *The Washington Post* and *The Wall Street Journal*. Heather Chaplin is quoted from an online magazine called *Salon* (accessible at SalonMagazine.com) in her October 9, 1998, issue.

10. "Lessons of Long, Hot Summer," *New York Times*, December 6, 1998, Section 3, pp. 1ff.

CHAPTER 15

International Financing: Tax Fine Points

Life seems to me to be like a Japanese picture which our imagination does not allow to end at the margin.

Oliver Wendell Holmes, Jr., Message to the Federal Bar Association, 1932

INTRODUCTION

"But in this world," wrote Benjamin Franklin, "nothing is certain but death and taxes." This statement has the ring of truth, like all of Franklin's sayings, but are taxes really so certain when it comes to international transactions? Yes and no. Yes because taxes, as a narrow area of law, do have an edge of certainty.

As Oliver Wendell Holmes, Jr., wrote in *The Path of the Law*, "Certainty *generally* is an illusion" (emphasis added). In other words, some things are certain. One can be certain, for example, that any business will be taxed in some way, shape, or form, by the government of the country in which it is doing business. Furthermore, within the codes imposing this taxation there will always be some provisions that are plainly expressed, never to be amended by legislators or subject to new interpretation in court. This, alas, is the exception to the rule. Taxes, particularly international taxes, are a morass of incertitude—ever changing, and complex to the point of being almost unintelligible to the average person.

How, then, do we dare to end this book on the arcane subject of international taxes? The answer is, because this area matters. In deals as in life, one must "render unto Caesar." This aspect of deal making need not be in the center of the picture, but it should be somewhere on a periphery—a necessary dimension to any transnational deal.

Let us then visit this important arena, beginning with the seemingly peripheral but always important subject of entity classification.

FUNDAMENTALS OF ENTITY CLASSIFICATION IN THE GLOBAL DEAL

In structuring an international merger transaction, which is best to use as the buying vehicle—a pass-through entity or a partnership corporation?

The question of whether a particular entity should be classified as a corporation or a pass-through entity (such as a partnership or trust) for U.S. income tax purposes matters greatly in any deal, but its importance is even greater in the international context.[1]

Let's start with inbound transactions (non-U.S. buying U.S). In these, if the foreign buyer is operating as a pass-through entity (operating a U.S. business), the foreign owner will be subject to regular U.S. income tax at graduated rates. In contrast, if the entity is classified as a corporation, the foreign owner will be subject to a withholding tax on dividend income at a flat rate (30 percent or reduced treaty rate). Depending upon the application of the branch profits tax, to be discussed later, the overall treatment in these two cases may be quite different. In outbound transactions, if a foreign entity is characterized as a corporation, its U.S. owners may be able to avoid being taxed currently on the income being earned abroad. If, instead, the entity is a pass-through entity, the U.S. owners will be taxed currently under any circumstances. In addition to the above, there are numerous other consequences of the classification of domestic and foreign entities as corporations, trusts, or partnerships.

How does the United States classify an entity that is formed under foreign law?

The Internal Revenue Service (IRS) has published a list of certain foreign entities and their classification for U.S. tax purposes. With respect to entities not named on this list, the proper classification of a foreign enterprise under U.S. law may occasionally be a difficult task because foreign countries have forms of business entities that do not have U.S. equivalents.

The U.S. classification principles applicable to foreign entities provide that, as a starting point, local law (that is, foreign law) will determine the legal relationships among the entity and its members, and among the entity, its members, and the public at large. When these legal relationships are ascertained, U.S. tax principles will classify an entity as a corporation, a partnership, or a trust. It is generally perceived that the IRS does not apply classification principles to foreign entities in the same manner as it does to U.S. entities. Therefore, caution must be used before assuming that the foreign entity would be treated for U.S. tax purposes in a similar manner to its foreign treatment. In addition, one should consider whether a tax treaty prohibits the United States from reclassifying the entity for federal tax purposes because of a specific definition in the treaty.

For classification purposes, when is a person considered foreign?

A U.S. person is an individual who is either a citizen or resident of the United States, a domestic corporation, a domestic partnership, or a domestic trust or estate. A foreign person is a person who is not a U.S. person. Under the above definition, a resident alien individual can be a U.S. person. Tax treaties may provide different rules.

When does an alien individual become a U.S. resident?

An alien individual is treated as a resident of the United States for a calendar year if such individual satisfies either of the following two tests:

- The alien is a lawful permanent resident of the United States.
- Subject to certain exceptions, the alien is physically present in the United States for a specified period of time (as of this writing, under U.S immigration law, 183 days or more during the calendar year).

An individual who is a U.S. resident is taxed on his or her worldwide income regardless of its source and is entitled to claim deductions and credits against that worldwide income. Resident aliens subject to foreign taxes on their foreign source income will be able to claim a *foreign tax credit* or deduction against U.S. tax liability. Tax treaties may provide "tie breaker" rules in situations in which an individual is treated as a resident by more than one country. Both resident aliens and U.S. citizens may receive a foreign tax credit deduction, which can be carried back or forward for use in previous or future tax years.[2]

What is a U.S., or domestic, corporation?

Under U.S. principles, all organizations incorporated under the laws of the United States or of any state (including the District of Columbia) are treated as domestic corporations for federal tax purposes. For certain purposes, corporations organized in or under the laws of Guam, American Samoa, Northern Mariana Islands, or the Virgin Islands will not be treated as foreign corporations.[3]

What is a dual resident company?

As far as the United States is concerned, a corporation incorporated in the United States is a U.S. corporation. This corporation, however, could at the same time be treated by country X as a country X corporation, if country X employes different criteria to determine whether corporations are resident for its tax purposes. In particular, some countries, including the United Kingdom and Australia, treat corporations as domestic corporations if they are managed and controlled therein. Thus, a U.S. corporation that is managed and controlled in one of these jurisdictions can also be a resident of the United Kingdom or Australia under their respective rules. Such companies are referred to as "dual resident companies." Although at one time there could be certain tax advantages in using such dual resident companies in lieu of corporations subject to "domestic" tax in only one country (such as the deduction of financing costs on the same loan in two jurisdictions), these advantages were substantially eliminated in 1986.

Can a foreign corporation be treated as a domestic corporation for U.S. tax purposes?

Yes. Section 269B of the Internal Revenue Code (the Code) provides that if a domestic corporation and a foreign corporation are "stapled entities," the foreign corporation will be treated as a domestic corporation. The term *stapled entities* applies if more than 50 percent in value of the beneficial ownership in each of two or more entities consists of stapled interests. (That is, if by reason of form of ownership, restrictions on transfer, or other terms or conditions in connection with the transfer of one of such interests, the other such interests are also transferred or required to be transferred.)

   More important, sometimes an election may be made to treat a foreign corporation as if it were a domestic corporation. For example, under the Foreign Investment in Real Property Tax Act (FIRPTA), a foreign corporation holding a U.S. real property interest may elect to be treated as a domestic corporation.

What is FIRPTA?

FIRPTA was enacted in 1980 to close a number of perceived loopholes that enabled foreign investors to own and dispose of U.S. real properties without incurring U.S. tax on the appreciation of the property, or on the cash flow from the property. Since 1985, FIRPTA has overridden all income tax treaties.

FIRPTA applies to dispositions of U.S. real property interests (USRPIs). A USRPI generally includes (1) an interest in real estate located in the United States or the United States Virgin Islands, or (2) any interest (other than an interest solely as a creditor) in a domestic corporation, unless it can be established that such corporation was at no time a U.S. real property holding corporation (USRPHC).

A domestic corporation is a USRPHC if the fair market value of its USRPIs equals or exceeds 50 percent of its worldwide real estate plus any other trade or business assets. Thus, if the assets disposed of are clearly not USRPIs or interests in certain pass-through entities that own USRPIs, neither the seller nor the buyer of the assets ought to be concerned about FIRPTA. FIRPTA regulations provide elaborate rules concerning the definition of a USRPI. Because many U.S. corporations own significant amounts of real estate, it will often be difficult to conclude at an early planning stage that a given company is not a USRPHC.

What are the general rules regarding FIRPTA, and how are they enforced?

FIRPTA provides that gain or loss of a nonresident alien individual or a foreign corporation from the disposition of a USRPI will be treated as if the gain or loss was effectively connected with a U.S. trade or business of such person. As such, the gain will be taxed at the regular rates applicable to U.S. citizens and residents, or domestic corporations, as the case may be. Unlike the case with other passive investments, gain recognized in a transaction subject to FIRPTA ought to be reported on a U.S. income tax return. Nonresident alien individuals are also subject to FIRPTA's minimum tax.

FIRPTA compliance is enforced through a withholding system. The Code generally provides that a transferee of a USRPI is required to withhold and pay over to the IRS 10 percent of the amount realized (i.e., the consideration) on the disposition by the foreign transferor. Partnerships and trusts disposing of real estate are required to withhold 34 percent of the amount allocable to their foreign partners or foreign beneficiaries. There are several exceptions to the withholding rules, but these are beyond the scope of this discussion.

FIRPTA applies to dispositions of interests in partnerships holding real estate and to dispositions of USRPIs by partnerships held by foreigners. Moreover, FIRPTA applies to distributions of USRPIs by foreign corporations to their shareholders, and to capital contributions to foreign corporations. In addition, FIRPTA provisions can override the nonrecognition treatment provided by various other sections of the Code, where necessary to ensure that the gain subject to taxation under FIRPTA is not diminished through transactions such as reorganizations and tax-free liquidations.

Who should be concerned about FIRPTA?

Although the FIRPTA provisions may seem to be of little importance in a merger or acquisition that does not involve real estate holding corporations or direct acquisitions of real estate assets, its application is far-reaching. First, as mentioned earlier, the definition of a USRPHC is broad enough to include even a manufacturing company that owns a large plant. A foreign acquirer should take future FIRPTA taxes into account in evaluating a potential acquisition. A domestic as well as a foreign acquirer from a foreign holder is liable as transferee-payor to withhold tax on the consideration paid for the stock if the corporation is a USRPHC and the payee is subject to FIRPTA. Failure to withhold may result in civil and criminal penalties. On the other hand, the foreign transferor (seller) is required to file a U.S. tax return to report his or her gain from the sale. Finally, if a public offering to refinance a portion of the acquisition indebtedness is contemplated, certain foreign holders (5 percent or more) will be subject to U.S. tax on the disposition of their holdings if the corporation is a USRPHC; under certain circumstances, the buyer of publicly traded stock from a 5 percent or more shareholder will be required to withhold FIRPTA tax.

Consequently, in any stock acquisition, consideration should be given to the value of the U.S. realty owned by the acquired entity, vis-a-vis its other assets, and to the tax status of the seller. If the seller provides a certificate that it is not a foreign person, no withholding will be required. In addition, no withholding is required if a domestic corporation furnishes to the transferee an affidavit stating that it is not and has not been a USRPHC during a certain test period.

Are U.S. persons and foreign persons treated alike under U.S. tax rules?

U.S. taxation of U.S. persons and foreign persons differs in a number of significant ways. The most noticeable difference concerns the scope of taxation: Whereas a U.S. person is subject to U.S. taxation on its worldwide income regardless of where it was derived (or sourced) and the class of income, a foreign person is subject to tax only on the income that has a substantial nexus to the United States. The nexus is generally defined with reference to a U.S. source or business. Often, the United States will not exercise its taxing jurisdiction over certain kinds of U.S.-related income that are generated by foreign persons, because of administrative difficulties concerning collection of the tax from foreign investors.

Would U.S. acquirers of foreign companies be indifferent as to whether they receive foreign or domestic source income?

Source of income (and loss), whether U.S. or foreign, can be a critical factor in determining the U.S. income tax liability of both U.S. and foreign persons. In the case of U.S. taxpayers, foreign source income is often desirable because it increases their ability to offset foreign taxes against U.S. taxes under the foreign tax credit mechanism. As mentioned earlier, foreign tax credits may be obtained by both resident aliens in the U.S. and by United States citizens.

On the other hand, if a loss can be sourced in the United States, the U.S. tax liability on domestic source income can be reduced and more foreign tax credits can be claimed against U.S. tax liability on foreign sources. In the case of a foreign taxpayer over which the United States asserts only a limited taxing authority, foreign source income would likely escape U.S. taxation altogether. Accordingly, in general, there is a strong incentive to convert U.S. source income into foreign source income.

How is the source of most investment income determined?

Generally, interest or dividends paid by a U.S. person will be *U.S. source income* and, therefore, subject to the current rate (or any lower treaty rate) of withholding tax. Exceptions are provided when the U.S. payor meets certain foreign income tests. Rentals or royalties are generally sourced in the United States if they are paid for the use of tangible or intangible property that is located in the United States.

Note that U.S. source interest income of a foreign person is not subject to a U.S. withholding tax if it qualifies as *portfolio interest*. Generally, among the other requirements for interest to qualify as portfolio interest, the foreign lender must be neither a bank extending an ordinary loan nor a party that is related to the U.S. borrower.

How do you determine the source of gain derived from the sale of stock of a foreign or a U.S. entity?

Income derived by a U.S. resident from the sale of personal property, tangible or intangible, is generally sourced in the United States. Similarly, income derived by a nonresident from the sale of personal property, tangible or intangible, is generally treated as foreign source income. This is called the *residence of the seller rule*.

Under the residence of the seller rule, when a nonresident individual who does not have a U.S. office to which the sale is attributed disposes of stock of a domestic corporation, the sale will generate foreign source income, gain, or loss. Similarly, when a U.S. resident individual sells stock in a foreign corporation and the sale is not attributable to a foreign office of the seller, the income, gain, or loss generated by the sale will be U.S. sourced.[4]

Note that for individuals, the definition of the term *U.S. resident* for sourcing purposes does not equal the definition of a U.S. resident for other tax purposes. The Code contains an antiabuse rule that is intended to prevent a U.S. person from claiming to be a nonresident of the United States for income that is sourced in a tax haven country. A *tax haven* is a sovereign tax jurisdiction that generally imposes only minimal or no tax on income, capital, or estates of nonresidents of such jurisdiction (e.g., the Cayman Islands, the Bahamas, and the Channel Islands). Note also that investment of $1 million or more in a business employing 10 people or more qualifies foreigners for permanent residency ("green card") status in the United States, and eventual citizenship.

TAX CONSIDERATIONS IN INBOUND ACQUISITIONS

What exactly is an inbound acquisition?

An inbound acquisition is an acquisition of a U.S. enterprise by a non-U.S. person. This acquisition may involve financing through loans made by financial institutions that are either resident in the acquirer's own country or third-country residents or by U.S. financial institutions, or a possible joint venture with U.S. or foreign equity partners. In debt-financed acquisitions, revenues received from the U.S. enterprise will likely be used to pay off acquisition indebtedness. The acquirers may wish at some point in the future to dispose of the entity or parts thereof in a transaction that will generate a profit over the acquisition price. For these and other reasons, U.S. tax considerations may be important in every stage of the acquisition and disposition process.

This section of our closing chapter discusses the basic U.S. tax consequences applicable to a foreign corporation or a nonresident alien engaged in M&A activities in the United States; particular attention will be given to financing the acquisition and planning for eventual disposition.

What are the basic U.S. income tax principles that determine the overall tax burden on U.S. income and repatriated funds of a foreign investor?

A foreign corporation not engaged in a U.S. trade or business is taxable at the going corporate income tax rate (or reduced treaty rate), collected by withholding at source, on its U.S. source passive income (such as interest, rents, royalties, dividends, and premiums). A foreign corporation engaged in a U.S. trade or business, even if it does not maintain an office within the United States, is subject to a U.S. net income tax at graduated rates on its U.S. source income that is effectively connected with its conduct of the trade or business in the United States. The latter tax may be referred to as the *regular income tax.*

In addition, a foreign corporation is subject to the branch profits tax rules on its "effectively connected earnings and profits," allowing for certain adjustments. If a foreign corporation owns an interest in a partnership (domestic or foreign) engaged in a trade or business in the United States, withholding under the Code may be required on distributions to the corporation. Capital gains, whether short term or long term, are not subject to U.S. tax if the foreign corporation is not engaged in a U.S. trade or business, or if the interest disposed of is not a real estate asset subject to FIRPTA.

A nonresident alien individual, who is not engaged in a U.S. trade or business, will also be subject to U.S. tax at the going flat rate (or reduced treaty rate) on his or her U.S. source passive income and will pay the going rate on net capital gains derived from U.S. sources provided that the individual spent 183 days or more in the United States within the taxable year of sale. In addition, if a nonresident alien is engaged in a U.S. trade or business within a taxable year but does not maintain an office in the United States, then any U.S. source income effectively connected with that trade or business will be subject to U.S. tax at graduated rates. Withholding rules may apply to distributions with respect to partnership interests held by such individual. Like a foreign corporation, if the nonresident alien is careful enough not to fall within the above restrictions, no U.S. tax will be imposed on his or her U.S. source capital gains.

If a nonresident alien or a foreign corporation engaged in a U.S. trade or business maintains an office in the United States, specified categories of such person's foreign source income are also treated as income effectively connected with a U.S. trade or business.

Tax treaties generally modify the rules described above as they apply to treaty country residents. In particular, tax treaties reduce withholding tax rates and limit taxation of business income to income attributable to a permanent establishment.

Thus, in summary, income from operations of the acquired U.S. company will ordinarily be subject to U.S. taxation, even if carried on directly by the foreign acquirer. On the other hand, with proper planning of their U.S. activities, foreign investors may find it relatively easy to avoid U.S. tax on capital gains (other than from the disposition of U.S. real property interests) derived from the sale of their interest in the U.S. activity.

When is a foreign person treated as engaged in a U.S. trade or business?

Neither the Code nor the regulations thereunder define when a foreign person is engaged in a U.S. trade or business. The determination is generally based on the facts and circumstances of each case and, in particular, on the level of the taxpayer's activities in the United States. If the U.S. activities of the foreign person are not considerable, continuous, and regular, the person will probably be considered as not engaged in a U.S. trade or business. Business activities of an agent in the United States will be attributed to its principal. U.S. real estate gains received by a foreign person will be deemed to be income effectively connected with a U.S. trade or business. Gains from U.S. securities trading activities for the taxpayer's own account are generally not trade or business income.

What issues should an investor consider when undertaking foreign debt financing to acquire a U.S. business?

Foreign financing to acquire U.S. business operations can take many forms. It may take the form of an investment of equity or debt, and it may involve only one foreign lender in a single-lender transaction or many lenders in an offshore public debt offering. Single-lender loans can be made from foreign banks acting in the ordinary course of their business or from foreign nonbanking institutions. In addition, loans can be made by foreign shareholders of the corporation. Publicly offered debt obligations may be in bearer form to protect investor anonymity but can also take place in registered form. Among these alternatives are various forms of syndicated loans and private debt placements to various investors. In addition, foreign financing may be in the form of short-term obligations, such as Eurocommercial paper, or long-term debt. Finally, the debt issued may be in the form of straight debt, convertible debt, or debt with equity features.

An entire book could be written on the tax treatment of transnational financing. Very broadly, when a foreign acquirer wishes to raise debt capital outside the United States, it should consider the following issues:

- Whether the acquisition indebtedness should be incurred by the acquired U.S. corporation or by the foreign acquirer. In this regard, the acquirer should weigh the relative values of the interest deductions in the United States and in the foreign jurisdiction.

- Whether the interest paid to the foreign lender will be free of U.S. withholding tax by virtue of a treaty exemption or a statutory provision (such as the portfolio interest exemption), or whether it will be subject to a reduced withholding rate. Note that investors in the Eurobond market generally require that interest payments be free of U.S. withholding tax. Furthermore, consideration should be given to the risk of change of law or treaty termination with respect to U.S. withholding tax liability.

- Whether a back-to-back loan structure to a U.S. corporation to take advantage of a tax treaty or statutory tax exemption will be respected by the IRS.

- Whether debt with equity features will be respected as debt for U.S. tax purposes.

Is it better to hold an acquired U.S. business through a U.S. or a foreign corporation?

The issue of whether to hold the acquired U.S. business through a U.S. or foreign corporation is often a major consideration in the acquisition process. If a U.S. business is held through a foreign corporation, the foreign corporation may be subject to a second layer of tax in the form of a branch profits tax, as mentioned earlier. If the U.S. business is held through a U.S. corporation, the tax cost may in certain circumstances be substantially reduced.

How does the branch profits tax fit in?

The *branch profits tax* (BPT) imposes a second layer of tax on profits of U.S. branches or other U.S. operations of a foreign corporation. The BPT was introduced in 1986 principally to duplicate, in the case of U.S. branches of foreign corporations, the second level of tax on dividends and interest paid by U.S. subsidiaries of foreign corporations.

To determine whether the BPT applies to certain U.S. operations, focus on these two rules: First, the BPT does not apply to foreign individuals engaged directly or indirectly through foreign partnerships in a trade or business in the United States; second, foreign corporations whose U.S. investments or contacts do not amount to a trade or business (or, in the case of a treaty-protected corporation, to a U.S. permanent establishment) are not subject to the BPT. Nonetheless, the BPT provisions contain certain antitreaty shopping rules that will affect even foreign corporations that are not engaged in a trade or business in the United States to the extent that they receive dividends or interest from a foreign corporation that is engaged in a trade or business in the United States. Thus, if an entity is neither a foreign corporation nor engaged (or deemed to be engaged) in a U.S. trade or business, and it does not receive dividends or interest from the U.S. operations of such a corporation, the following discussion will not pertain to its operations.

On the other hand, if one's U.S. operations might be subject to the BPT, the next two questions will provide a short road map on the effects of the BPT on the regular operations of a U.S. branch of a foreign corporation and on the financing of a branch of a foreign corporation.

What are the BPT rules concerning the U.S. operations of a foreign corporation?

Whenever a foreign corporation operates or acquires an unincorporated business (including a partnership interest) in the United States, consideration should be given to the BPT consequences of such operation. Remember that under the regular rules, the foreign corporation pays one income tax on its "effectively connected" U.S. trade or business income. The BPT is an additional tax equal to 30 percent (or a reduced treaty rate) of any foreign corporation's "dividend equivalent amount" for any taxable year in which such corporation is engaged, or deemed to be engaged, in a trade or business in the United States.

The dividend equivalent amount includes the "effectively connected earnings and profits" (E&P) of such corporation for the taxable year, as adjusted downward or upward to reflect certain increases or decreases in the

"U.S. net equity" for the year. In effect, the statute treats a decrease in U.S. net equity as a withdrawal of earnings by the foreign parent, and an increase in U.S. net equity as a contribution of capital to the U.S. branch. The use of the E&P account as the tax base was designed to approximate dividend treatment.

"U.S. net equity" is any money and the aggregate adjusted bases of the foreign corporation's property treated as connected with the conduct of a trade or business in the United States, less the foreign corporation's liabilities connected with such operation. Investments in business assets will increase the net equity amount and repatriations will decrease such amount, but only to include previous increases of net equity that reduced earnings and profits.

For the BPT to apply to a particular branch of a foreign corporation, such branch must generate "effectively connected" income. Generally, income will be treated as effectively connected if the corporation is engaged in an active business, if the corporation is a partner in a partnership engaged in a U.S. trade or business, or if the corporation invests in U.S. real property with respect to which the foreign corporation has elected under Section 897(d) to be taxed on a net basis, or with respect to a gain from a disposition of a U.S. real property interest (other than interest in a U.S. real property holding corporation). E&P includes certain items not subject to the regular corporate tax, such as tax-exempt income. Distributions by the foreign corporation within the taxable year will not reduce E&P for the purposes of the BPT.

If a treaty country corporation earns effectively connected income that is exempt from U.S. tax because such foreign corporation does not maintain a permanent establishment in the United States, such earnings will not be subject to the BPT, provided that the foreign corporation is a "qualified resident" of the treaty country, as defined above. In addition, BPT rules may be modified in other ways by an applicable tax treaty (see the discussion above).

How do the BPT rules affect the financing for a U.S. branch of a foreign corporation?

Generally, if a U.S. branch of a foreign corporation borrows money from a foreign lender, the branch (but in practice, the foreign corporation) will be required to withhold 30 percent (or reduced treaty rate) of the gross interest paid to the foreign lender. Certain Code provisions, such as the portfolio interest exemption and the bank deposit exemption, may apply to eliminate the withholding requirement. The tax treaties that will determine the lower rate of withholding on interest paid by the U.S. branch will be the treaty between the United States and the country of the foreign lender and the treaty between the United States and the country of the foreign corporation that maintains the

U.S. branch. Section 884, however, curtails treaty benefits to discourage treaty shopping. The effect of the withholding requirement can be to increase the cost of borrowing from foreign lenders that do not qualify for an exemption from U.S. taxation and cannot obtain complete foreign tax credit benefits in their own country.

Interest expense incurred by the foreign corporation on its worldwide borrowings may be allocated, under a formula, to the U.S. branch beyond the amount of interest actually paid or accrued directly by the branch ("excess interest"). Such excess interest will be deductible by the foreign corporation in computing its U.S. net taxable income for the U.S. branch but will be treated as paid by the U.S. branch to the foreign owner as if it were a separate lender. As such, unless a specific Code exemption applies, the excess interest will be subject to a withholding tax at the going 30 percent rate or any lower treaty rate imposed on the foreign corporation.

In determining the applicability of a treaty, the excess interest is deemed paid by the branch to the foreign corporation as lender. If the foreign corporation is a *qualified resident* of the treaty country, the excess amount may be subject to lower treaty rates. It is noteworthy that the tax imposed on excess interest allocable to the U.S. branch is levied regardless of whether the excess interest actually resulted in a tax benefit to the U.S. branch. Thus, it is possible that the tax on excess interest will exceed the foreign corporation's U.S. tax benefit from the deduction of excess interest, for instance, in situations where the U.S. branch has net operating losses. The BPT does not apply where its application would be inconsistent with an existing U.S. income tax treaty obligation, unless there is "treaty shopping." When treaty shopping is involved, treaty benefits are generally overridden. For instance, unless the actual or deemed creditor or dividend recipient, as the case may be, is a qualified resident of a treaty country, the creditor or the dividend recipient cannot claim treaty benefits to reduce the 30 percent withholding obligation.

It is noteworthy that U.S. shareholders of a treaty-shopping corporation or of a nontreaty country corporation may be subject to triple taxation.

How can a taxpayer determine whether the foreign corporation in which it holds stock will be treated as engaging in treaty shopping?

A foreign corporation will not be considered to be treaty shopping if it is a "qualified resident" of the treaty country at issue. A foreign corporation that is resident in a foreign country will be a qualified resident, unless either (1) more than 50 percent in value of the foreign corporation's stock is owned by individuals who are neither residents of such country (regardless of whether they are bona fide residents of another treaty country) nor U.S. citizens or resident aliens, or (2) 50 percent or more of the foreign corporation's gross income is used (directly or indirectly) to meet liabilities to persons who are neither residents of that country nor residents of the United States. Note that these rules still allow treaty benefits to inure to nontreaty country shareholders, as long as they hold less than 50 percent of the corporation's stock.

If the foreign corporation fails to qualify under these tests, it will nevertheless be treated as a "qualified resident" if either (1) the foreign corporation's stock is primarily and regularly traded on an established securities exchange in the country in question, or (2) the foreign corporation is wholly owned (either directly or indirectly) by another corporation organized in the country in which such stock is traded. This may provide an advantage to foreign shareholders of publicly traded treaty country corporations over shareholders of nontreaty or U.S. publicly traded corporations.

What is the best way to avoid the BPT?

Nontreaty investors and often residents in certain treaty countries will find that operating in the United States through a U.S. corporation is the most attractive way to avoid the BPT. In other words, in an asset acquisition, a foreign corporation will avoid the BPT if it incorporates the branch into a U.S. corporation. The rate of tax on dividends and interest required to be withheld at source by a U.S. subsidiary may be reduced if a treaty country parent corporation is used. If dividends are to be distributed, at least a 5 percent treaty rate withholding tax will apply. In addition, if the investor is a treaty country resident, he or she can capitalize the U.S. corporation with indebtedness and receive interest income, sometimes free of U.S. tax, contemporaneously with interest deductions at the corporate level.

TAX CONSIDERATIONS IN OUTBOUND ACQUISITIONS

What exactly is an outbound acquisition?

An outbound acquisition is an acquisition of a non-U.S. enterprise by a U.S. person. As with inbound acquisitions, this transaction may involve financing through loans made by financial institutions that are either resident in the acquirer's own country or third-country residents or by U.S. financial institutions, or a possible joint venture with U.S. or foreign equity partners. In debt-financed acquisitions, revenues received from the operation or sale of the non-U.S. enterprises may well be used to pay off acquisition indebtedness. For these and other reasons, to echo our earlier point about inbound deals, non-U.S. tax considerations may be important in every stage of the acquisition and disposition process.

In this section, we will outline the most prominent features of U.S. taxation of the foreign activities of U.S. persons. As explained earlier in this chapter, the United States asserts taxing jurisdiction over the worldwide income of its citizens, residents, and corporations. As a rule, the United States taxes only income received or accrued by U.S. taxpayers. In the domestic context, with the exception of a group filing a consolidated return or a subchapter S corporation, income earned by a U.S. taxpayer from a controlled corporation is not taxed to the U.S. owner except and to the extent that such earnings are actually distributed to the owner. As we will soon see, the exceptions to the above rules in the international context are so voluminous and complex in U.S. tax law as to suggest that the general rules do not apply at all. As a result of longstanding concerns about the avoidance of U.S. taxes through the expatriation of assets and earnings, there is now an extensive patchwork of rules under which the United States seeks to tax, or at least take into account, income generated in foreign subsidiaries of U.S. persons.

Needless to say, in any transaction involving an acquisition of a foreign business, the primary focus of the tax planner's attention must be the tax laws of the country or countries in which the acquired company does business and holds assets and the country or countries in which its shareholders are located. This is all the more true at a time when income tax rates of most industrialized countries significantly exceed those in the United States. There may in fact be significant opportunities to reduce the impact of foreign taxes through tax treaties and the U.S. foreign tax credit system. These mechanisms are inherently imperfect, however, and a great deal of attention must be paid to the rules of U.S. taxation of the international activities of its taxpayers in order to minimize the overall tax costs of U.S. persons engaging in a variety of multinational operations.

Today, when an auction process is commonly used to obtain the highest bid for a group of corporations that is for sale, the buyer cannot ignore the planned sale's tax consequences to the seller. To obtain a competitive edge over other bidders, the buyer should strive to maximize its own tax benefits without raising the seller's tax costs above its expectations. Alternatively, without sacrificing the purchaser's own goals, it may be possible to structure the offer in a way that reduces the seller's tax costs.

When planning an outbound acquisition, what information should the purchaser and its financing sources solicit from the seller in order to minimize foreign and domestic tax liabilities?

The purchaser should solicit from the seller the following information:

- A precise organization chart. The chart should describe the holding company (assuming that the company being acquired is a parent of a group of corporations) and the stock ownership in all the various tiers of the domestic corporations, if any, and of the foreign corporations or entities (the "group").

- The estimated U.S. and foreign tax bases as of the projected acquisition date that the holding company is expected to have in the various domestic and foreign corporations.

- To the extent feasible, a description of the overall income tax position of the company being acquired and the entity selling it (if different).

For each of the foreign companies, the following information should be solicited:

- The taxable year for both foreign and U.S. income tax purposes

- The actual and projected earnings and profits by taxable period of such corporation as of the acquisition date computed by the rules set forth in Sections 902 and 964 of the Code

- The creditable foreign income taxes paid or accrued during each taxable period ending on or before the acquisition date

- The earnings and profits and creditable foreign taxes set forth in subparagraphs B and C accumulated prior to the seller's ownership of the company

- The estimated net book value, or pro forma balance sheet, of each foreign company as of the acquisition date

- A listing of the intercompany receivables and payables, if any

- All other information—foreign currency gains and losses, distributions, utilization of foreign tax credits, tax accounting elections, and so on—necessary to determine the tax consequences of a later sale of each corporation

What is the value of an organization chart of the structure of the company being acquired?

An organization chart will describe the precise ownership of the group and of the different tax jurisdictions (and income tax treaties) that may affect the acquisition process and the subsequent disposition of the group or several of its members. A purchaser may be aiming to buy a Greek company but may find out that the Greek company is owned by a Spanish holding company, which is in turn owned by a U.S. subsidiary of the holding company. Therefore, in this scenario the prospective buyer will be required to evaluate the possible tax consequences of the acquisition in Greece, Spain, and the United States. The organization chart will also provide information as to whether any of the foreign subsidiaries is, or would be in the purchaser's hands, a *controlled foreign corporation* (CFC). As will be explained shortly, CFC status may have significant U.S. tax consequences to a U.S. shareholder.

What is a CFC?

A controlled foreign corporation, or CFC, is any foreign corporation of which more than 50 percent of the total combined voting power, or the total value of its stock, is owned directly or indirectly by "United States shareholders" on any day during the taxable year of the foreign corporation. A U.S. shareholder, in turn, is a U.S. person who owns, or is considered to own under attribution rules, 10 percent or more of the foreign corporation's voting power. Note that in the definition of U.S. shareholder, voting power and not stock value is the sole criterion.

In considering the application of Subpart F, it is important to keep in mind the separate status and consequences of the CFC and the U.S. shareholder. For example, because of the 10 percent voting power test, it is possible to have U.S. persons owning stock in a CFC who are not "United States shareholders" and, thus, not subject to Subpart F. In addition, there is much room for structuring flexibility so as to have substantial U.S. ownership of a foreign corporation without causing it to be characterized as a CFC. One thing to bear in mind in this area is that there may be circumstances in which it will be beneficial for a foreign subsidiary of a U.S. parent to be characterized as a CFC.

What is Subpart F of the Code?

Subpart F (Sections 951–964 of the Code) requires U.S. shareholders of a CFC to include in their U.S. gross income as *constructive dividends* certain amounts earned by the CFC, regardless of whether such earnings were actually repatriated to the U.S. shareholder. In addition to the CFC and U.S. shareholder requirements, Subpart F treatment will generally apply only to certain types of income earned by the CFC, which may be broadly termed Subpart F income. Note that a U.S. tax is not imposed on the CFC itself; in fact, if the foreign corporation were itself subject to U.S. taxation, an entirely different set of rules would apply.

How does Subpart F operate?

Subpart F provides that a U.S. shareholder must include in gross income certain classes of the CFC's income as a constructive dividend. Following such an imputation, the basis of the U.S. shareholder's stock in the CFC is increased in order to avoid double taxation when the U.S. shareholder later disposes of the stock of the CFC. An actual distribution of the CFC's earnings subsequent to Subpart F treatment will not be taxable to the U.S. shareholder if it pertains to the previously taxed earnings and profits, and a corresponding reduction in the basis of the stock will take place. Under certain circumstances, the U.S. shareholder may be eligible for the foreign tax credit with respect to foreign taxes paid by the CFC.

As explained in greater detail below, a U.S. shareholder of a CFC is also required to include in gross income its pro rata share of the foreign corporation's increase in earnings invested in certain U.S. properties.

What classes of CFC income are subject to Subpart F?

Subpart F income includes *insurance income, foreign base company income,* and certain other classes of income subject to specific limited rules (such as international boycott-related income, and illegal bribes). If more than 70 percent of the CFC's gross income is Subpart F income, the full amount of the CFC's gross income will be treated as Subpart F income.[5]

What is insurance income?

Insurance income is income attributable to the issuance of any insurance, reinsurance, or annuity contract in connection with property in, liability arising out of activity in, or in connection with the lives or health of residents of a country other than the country under the laws of which the CFC is created or organized.

What is foreign base company income?

Foreign base company income includes "foreign personal holding company income," "foreign base company sales income," "foreign base company services income," "foreign base company shipping income," and "foreign base company oil-related income" for the taxable year.

- Foreign personal holding company income consists of interest, dividends, rents, royalties, and other kinds of passive income.
- Foreign base company sales income generally includes various forms of income derived by the CFC in connection with the sale or purchase of property involving a related party, where the property originated in a country other than that of the CFC and is sold or purchased for use or disposition outside of the country of the CFC.
- Foreign base company services income generally includes income derived in connection with the performance of various services on behalf of a related person where the services are performed outside the country of the CFC.
- Foreign base company shipping income includes income from a variety of activities involving the use of aircraft or vessels in foreign commerce.
- Foreign base company oil-related income generally includes income from oil and gas products except where the income is derived in the country from which the oil or gas product was extracted.

What are the rules concerning a CFC's increase in earnings invested in U.S. property?

As a rule, each U.S. shareholder is required to take into gross income his or her pro rata share of the CFC's increase in earnings invested in U.S. property for the taxable year. This rule is applicable to all CFCs whether or not they have earned Subpart F income, but to avoid double counting this rule applies only after Subpart F income, if any, has been imputed to the shareholder.

To prevent certain abuses, indirect investments in U.S. property will also be subject to these rules. Under Treasury regulations, any obligation of a U.S. person for which a CFC is a pledgor or guarantor will be considered U.S. property held by such CFC. If the assets of a CFC serve at any time, even though indirectly, as a security for the performance of an obligation of a U.S. person, then the CFC will be considered a pledgor or guarantor of that obligation.

Consequently, if an acquirer plans to use the stock or assets of foreign subsidiaries as collateral for acquisition indebtedness, it may risk receiving a deemed distribution from the CFC to the extent of the earnings and profits of the foreign subsidiaries that are used as collateral.

When a foreign subsidiary of a U.S. company pledges stock or guarantees debt, is this considered a constructive dividend under Subpart F of the Code, and if so, what can be done about it?

Yes, there is a risk that the pledge or guarantee will be considered and taxed as a constructive dividend.[6] When one company is borrowing money to acquire another company's stock or assets, the acquirer's lenders may require the acquirer to do one of two things.

First, the lenders may require the acquirer to cause its subsidiaries to guarantee directly, assume, or pledge their assets to secure the acquirer's acquisition debt. Alternatively, the lender may require the acquirer to pledge the stock of its subsidiaries. In either case, the acquirer will be treated as having received a constructive dividend from the foreign subsidiary.

Why would such pledge or guarantee be considered a constructive dividend?

Code Section 956 provides that where a foreign subsidiary is a "pledgor or guarantor" of an obligation to a U.S. parent, the foreign subsidiary's interest in the obligation will be treated as an *investment in U.S. property* (under Code 956(c)(1)(C), as amended by 1993 tax law).

Under this Code and related Code sections,[7] any increase in the subsidiary's earnings invested in U.S. property is treated as a constructive dividend to the parent to the extent of the subsidiary's earnings and profits, except to the extent that these earnings and profits were previously taxed to the parent. Similarly, the subsidiary's assumption of its parent's debt will be treated as a constructive dividend to the parent for U.S. tax purposes. In addition, regulations under Code Section 956 provide that the U.S. parent's pledge of the subsidiary's stock as security for a parent debt will be treated as an indirect pledge of the subsidiary's assets, if the parent pledges two thirds or more of the subsidiary's voting stock and enters into one or more negative convenants that effectively restrict the subsidiary's ability to dispose of its assets or incur debt outside the ordinary course of business.

How can the acquirer avoid constructive dividend income from its foreign subsidiaries?

If the acquirer wishes to avoid such income, it must not allow the subsidiaries to guarantee directly, assume, or pledge their assets to secure any of the parent's debt. In addition, any pledges of the stock of a foreign subsidiary to secure the parent's debt should either involve less than two thirds of the subsidiary's voting stock or not contain any negative covenants such as the kind described above.

What is the foreign tax credit?

A common theme throughout the tax system is that a person should be relieved of the burden resulting from the imposition of tax by more than one jurisdiction on the same income. One example of this principle is the deduction for income taxes paid to states, localities, and foreign governments contained in Section 164 of the Code. In the case of income taxes paid to foreign governments, the Internal Revenue Code provides an alternative to the deduction of the foreign tax from gross income by way of a unilateral tax credit against U.S. tax for the foreign taxes.

When the credit works properly, it generally provides a more complete relief from double taxation of income than the deduction. The goal of the foreign tax credit system is to limit the overall rate of tax on foreign source income to the greater of the foreign rate or the U.S. rate. The foreign tax credit is elected by a taxpayer on an annual basis and is not binding for future years. Because of the various limitations under the foreign tax credit rules, in certain circumstances it may, in fact, be more advantageous for a taxpayer to claim the deduction instead of the credit.

How is the amount of allowable foreign tax credit determined?

The amount of foreign tax credit that may be claimed as a direct credit against U.S. income tax liability is generally determined by applying a fraction to the tentative U.S. tax liability for the year. The numerator of the fraction is the taxable income from foreign sources, and the denominator is worldwide taxable income. Foreign income and related foreign taxes are divided into several new categories, or "baskets," described in Section 904d of the Code. These are passive income, shipping income, high withholding tax interest, dividends from certain noncontrolled foreign corporations, financial services income, certain dividends from domestic international sales corporations (DISCs), certain distributions from present or former foreign sales corporations (FSCs), and certain taxable income attributable to foreign trade income.

Can a U.S. person obtain a foreign tax credit for foreign taxes paid by a foreign subsidiary?

Under Section 902 of the Code, a U.S. corporation owning 10 percent or more of the voting stock of a foreign corporation may be entitled to a "deemed paid credit," or indirect credit, for foreign taxes paid by the subsidiary. The deemed paid credit is available only against dividend income received (or deemed received under Subpart F or other provisions) from the foreign subsidiary. The principle underlying this indirect credit is that a U.S. corporation receiving a dividend from a foreign corporation is deemed to have paid the foreign taxes paid or accrued by the foreign corporation on the earnings from which the dividend is distributed.

The deemed paid credit generally works as follows. First, under Section 78 of the Code, a domestic corporation must include in income not only the amount of dividends actually or constructively received, but also an amount equal to the foreign taxes attributable to such dividend income. This is the so-called gross-up provision. Under Section 902, the U.S. corporation is deemed to have paid the same proportion of the income taxes paid by the subsidiary as the dividends received bear to the foreign subsidiary's total earnings. In addition, if the foreign corporation owns 10 percent or more of the voting stock of a second foreign corporation, it is deemed to have paid foreign taxes of the subsidiary on the same basis. The same rule goes for a third tier of subsidiary as well.

Under Section 960 of the Code, similar rules are provided for an indirect foreign tax credit with respect to deemed dividend income from the foreign corporation to the domestic corporate shareholder as a result of Subpart F. Under Section 962, an individual may take advantage of this indirect foreign tax credit by electing to be taxed on Subpart F income as if he or she were a domestic corporation.

How is a U.S. person treated upon the sale of stock in a foreign corporation?

For the application of Section 1248 of the Code, a U.S. person will generally recognize capital gain or loss on the sale of stock in a foreign corporation just as it would on the sale of stock in a domestic corporation. Recognizing that this provided an opportunity for the repatriation of foreign earnings at favorable capital gains rates, the United States enacted Section 1248 of the Code in 1962. The main purpose and effect of Section 1248 is to recharacterize the gain realized on the sale of stock in the foreign corporation from capital gain to ordinary dividend income to the extent of the selling stockholder's ratable share of the earnings of the foreign corporation accumulated during the period that the stock was owned by the U.S. person. If the selling shareholder is a domestic corporation, then it may claim the benefit of the indirect foreign tax credit with respect to the deemed dividends under Section 902. If the selling shareholder is an individual, Section 1248 includes a mechanism that indirectly reduces his or her U.S. tax liability on account of foreign taxes paid by the foreign corporation.

In the checklist above, you mentioned tax accounting elections. What are these, and what is their significance in an international deal?

A tax accounting election is the choice of the tax status of a transaction. For example, in a transaction involving a U.S. company, some transactions may qualify to be treated as poolings. As explained in Chapter 3, the treatment of a transaction as a pooling will ensure tax-free status, and may offer certain benefits—including stronger reported income, easier determination of price, and greater comparability with past periods.

Tax accounting elections can be complicated in an international transaction, because those structuring the deal must conform to the accounting laws in whatever country their securities are registered. If securities are registered in the United States, the accounting must conform to generally accepted accounting principles (GAAP), which means a purchase versus pooling election. Other countries, however, do not have pooling, and for this reason, both the Financial Accounting Standards Board in the United States and the International Accounting Standards Committee (IASC) in London have considered eliminating pooling as an option.

What does the IASC say about merger accounting?

The IASC has already proposed some 30 international accounting standards, many of which are relevant to mergers, especially (IAS 22) on accounting for business combinations. In its most recent communiqué, the IASC strongly hints that it may recommend the abolition of pooling, depending on the results of public comment in 1999.[8]

It all started on December 29, 1998, when the IASC published a discussion paper inviting comment on the "Convergence of the Methods of Accounting for Business Combinations." The paper presented the views of the Group of Four plus One standard setters (the G4+1). The G4+1 comprises representatives of national standard setting bodies from Australia, Canada, New Zealand, the United Kingdom, and the United States together with representatives of IASC.[9]

"International practice on accounting for business combinations is diverse, " noted the paper, adding that "achieving convergence on the method of accounting for business combinations would eliminate the cause of one of the most significant reconciling items." The paper concludes, therefore, that "the international debate on the methods of accounting for business combinations is highly relevant to the goal of IASC in promoting the harmonisation of accounting standards."

The position paper considers the following issues:

- Whether a single method of accounting for business combinations is preferable to two (or more) methods
- If so, which method of accounting should be applied to all business combinations
- If not, which methods should be applied and to which combinations they should be applied

The G4+1 position paper concludes that the use of a single method of accounting is preferable, and that the purchase method is the appropriate method. If this view prompts the FASB to ban pooling, significant changes will be in store for U.S. companies, their subsidiaries, and their suppliers—including suppliers of M&A financing.

CONCLUDING COMMENTS

In this closing chapter, we have ventured beyond the normal confines of deal making to consider some broader issues in the taxation of international deals. Now, in ending this chapter, we urge our readers to return to core issues, the subject of our Conclusion.

E N D N O T E S

1. This section and much of this chapter has been adapted from Stanley Foster Reed and Alexandra Reed Lajoux, *The Art of M&A: A Merger/Acquisition/Buyout Guide*, 3rd ed. (New York: McGraw-Hill, 1999).
2. Any excess foreign tax credit of a taxpayer, that is, the amount by which certain taxes paid or deemed paid to a foreign country for a taxable year exceed the

U.S. taxes against which such foreign taxes are currently credited, generally may be carried back two years and carried forward five years, under Code Section 904(c). Source: Martin D. Ginsberg and Jack S. Levin, *Mergers, Acquisitions, and Buyouts: A Transactional Analysis of the Governing Tax, Legal, and Accounting Considerations* (New York: Aspen Business Publishing, October 1998), ch. 12, p. 101.

3. Puerto Rico has its own tax law. For Puerto Rican residents, the U.S. income tax law is applied to income only from sources within Puerto Rico.

4. A sale by a U.S. corporation of stock in a foreign-owned subsidiary that is engaged in are active trade or business whose conduct takes place in the foreign country from which the affiliate has derived more than a certain percentage of its gross income for its last three taxable years will be sourced in that foreign country. The practical result of this exception to the residence of seller rule is that in such case, the income will be treated for U.S. tax purposes as foreign source income, and the seller will be able to credit foreign taxes against his or her U.S. tax liability. If this income were treated as U.S. source income, foreign taxes could not be credited against the U.S. tax liability.

5. Note that Rev. Rul. 97-48, 1997-49 I.R.B.5 of the IRS, released November 18, 1997, and published December 8, 1997, changed an important provision in Section 954 regarding foreign base company sales income (26 CFR 1.954-3). This ruling revokes Rev. Rul. 75-7, 1975-1 C.B. 244, and holds that the activities of a contract manufacturer cannot be attributed to a controlled foreign corporation.

6. This discussion of constructive dividend risk is based on Ginsburg and Levin, op. cit. (note 2), ch. 13, pp. 22ff.

7. That is, under Code Section 951(a)(1)(B).

8. Copies of the discussion paper, "G4+1 Position Paper: Recommendations for Achieving Convergence on the Methods of Accounting for Business Combinations," may be obtained directly from the IASC, at 166 Fleet Street, London EC4A 2DY, United Kingdom; telephone: +44 (171) 427-5927; fax: +44 (171) 353-0562; publications@iasc.org.uk; www.iasc.org.uk.

9. The following disclaimer appeared in an IASC press release (dated December 29, 1998) about the paper: "The Position Paper has not been considered by the Board of the International Accounting Standards Committee and does not necessarily represent the views of the Board. The Staff of the IASC is issuing the Discussion Paper to enable participation of the IASC constituency in the international debate on the methods of accounting for business combinations . . . . The G4+1 Position Paper is solely concerned with the topic of convergence on the methods of accounting for business combinations and does not address detailed points of application of those methods."

M&A Financing and Refinancing: Instruments for Successful Growth

What would we really know the meaning of?

Ralph Waldo Emerson, *The American Scholar,* Introduction, 1837

BACK TO THE BASICS

In this book, we have covered a broad range of M&A financing topics. We had no other choice, for the world of M&A finance is vast indeed. To seek, find, and use the proper type of financing, deal makers must be familiar with many subjects. They must know all the basic types of financing instruments, and they must know how to work with financing sources. Furthermore, deal makers must understand the key accounting, legal, and tax issues that can be triggered under various financing conditions. In addition, deal makers need to appreciate all the tactics they can include in their contracts, such as contingent payments, earnouts, and equity kickers.

Many of these topics are complex and technical. Our aim has been to provide a reference handbook that our entrepreneurial readers can consult to refresh themselves on the nuts and bolts of M&A financing.

But the key to successful M&A financing is starting with the foundation of a sound business and economic concept. Let us review some of the steps that may be helpful in developing a sound M&A plan. These steps are not just common sense, though they may seem like it. Rather, they are closely based on the overwhelming verdict of decades of empirical research on the economic value of mergers.[1]

Identify Your Core Capabilities. What kinds of skills and knowledge are required for your present operations? If you have these core capabilities, be sure that you are using them efficiently. If you are not doing well with your present capabilities and products with which you have experience, how can your firm possibly do well in unfamiliar areas?

Look for Your Gaps. Your firm may be in the right products and markets but lack some critical capabilities. If this is the case, you have a guideline for your M&A plan. You need to fill the gaps due to missing capabilities. Your plan must be to acquire people or form alliances or obtain companies to round out the critical capabilities for success in your present product-market areas.

Check Your Location. If your firm is not living up to its full potential, it needs to ask whether it is in the right industry or product markets. The first two guidelines are: (1) if you have the right capabilities, use them efficiently, and (2) if your firm lacks the critical capabilities, develop a plan for acquiring them. But if your firm is in the wrong product-market areas, then you must take the third, bold step of moving into more attractive growth opportunities. Here the basic idea is, try to move into areas where your firm's past experience and current capabilities can be applied and extended. Related diversification has been shown to offer higher probabilities of success than going into new areas where your firm lacks experience. Some product-market areas appear to offer great opportunities for growth. But the risks of mistakes and failure are high unless the firm can function efficiently in the new areas.

Vow to Lose (Dead) Weight. Sometimes the problem with an industry is that there is excess capacity in relation to sales opportunities. This is where consolidating mergers can be successful. A merger with another company in the same industry, followed by the sale or elimination of redundant or inefficient operations, can restore growth in profitability.

Break Out of Your Industry Mold. Successful M&A plans may involve changing the organization structure of an industry. Such a transformation has occurred through the roll-up phenomenon in industries characterized by a large number of individual operations that combined could yield significant savings.

Stay Ahead of the Technology Curve. Sometimes the technology of an industry changes so that new capabilities are required. Clearly, combining with the requisite new and related capabilities is a way to catch up.

Think Big. In some industries the nature of operations has changed so that operations on a larger scale are required. An example is the pharmaceuticals industry, which requires larger firms to be able to achieve the critical mass requirements for large-scale research and development endeavors. The global scale and risks of the petroleum industry have also stimulated M&As to meet these new challenges.

The largest merger of all times, the recent $86 billion deal between Exxon and Mobil, exemplifies this last point, but the principles we have set forth here apply at all levels of firm size. They are important for the small operation at its very beginning. They impact even the largest firms as they seek to meet the new challenges of their changing environments. These principles apply at all stages in the life of strategic visions—from the gleam in the eye to the 100-page business plan.

Our point here is that if a firm has a sound M&A plan, the likelihood of sound M&A financing and refinancing will be increased. A strong and compelling strategic vision, coupled with strong commitments, will receive backers. An experienced executive who has quit a $200,000 sure-thing job with a fire in his guts to follow his strategic vision will find financing and achieve profitable alliances—if he follows the principles set forth here. A bank loan officer who follows a hunch to lend to an upstart acquirer will reap long-term rewards—if he or she keeps these principles in mind when judging the deal from start to finish.

A FINAL WORD

The individuals and companies that extend capital to M&A entrepreneurs large and small provide a great service, not only to the companies, but to economic growth and well-being.

First and foremost, we believe that *the ability of one company to acquire another is a necessary part of any free economy.* If companies had to grow only on the basis of their own internal operations, or on temporary alliances with other companies, the lives of more companies would be, in the words of Thomas Hobbes, "nasty, brutish, and short." The ability to acquire has helped many a "weak" company become strong. Yes, synergy is real. One company, added to another, can increase the value of both incrementally. Given sound strategy, pricing, financing, and postmerger management, the combination of two companies can yield a value greater than the value of the two companies standing alone. This value extends not only to the shareholders and bondholders who receive the earliest returns on this incremental value, but also to the other stakeholders in the company, including employees, customers, suppliers, and the community at large.

Second, we affirm that *external financing is a necessary part of all company growth*, including growth through acquisitions. Just as companies cannot rely on their own internal operations to supply all the markets they merit, so they cannot rely on internal funding alone to achieve all the growth they deserve. To be sure, many companies have erred by asking for too much financing or too little, whether in the debt or equity mode, and this has caused turmoil to the organizations. The fault, however, lies in the structuring of the external financing, not in the financing process itself. External financing, far from being a problem, is a solution of great strength and resilience.

Third, and most fundamentally, we see *the process of financing and refinancing as a vital part of free enterprise itself.* If the firm is, as one school of economic thought says, a bundle of contracts, then an economy is a network of contracts. In a very real sense, the viability of our economic world can be traced to the quality of the contracts drawn up between consenting parties, combined with the integrity of the legal systems standing there to inform and enforce them.

As Alex Sheshunoff declares in the Foreword to this book, M&A financing has been a key driver of the financial services revolution. We wholeheartedly agree. And we would add another point. In addition to its "revolutionary" power, M&A financing has an *evolutionary* power—the power to sustain economic prosperity one deal at a time: "fragment by fragment, on a small scale, but in successive developments, cellularly, like a laborious mosaic," in the words of philosopher Anaïs Nin.[2]

We touched on this point in Chapter 13, when we noted that whenever there is economic failure in a country, our first impulse as human beings is to look for grandiose solutions from above. We look to the Federal Reserve Board in Washington, D.C., to the European Economic Commission in Brussels, Belgium, or to the Ministry of Finance in Tokyo, Japan. Or we hope for new policies from the Group of Seven or the International Monetary Fund. These broadly influential organizations can offer valuable "turning points" for our national and international economies, but—as we have reasoned earlier in this book—they cannot solve all our problems.

In the world of finance, unlike the worlds enacted in a Greek acropolis thousands of years ago, there can be no *deus ex machina;* neither a god nor a committee of sages will descend in a chariot to solve our problems. The solutions lie with us, men and women of business. And so, to paraphrase the old song, "Let it begin with us."

The key to sustained prosperity surely lies in the promises inherent in all the *handshakes*—expressed more fully in pieces of paper—that each of us makes in a free economy. Among these handshakes is the very important

M&A financing handshake. This says, in essence, "We give you these funds in the belief that in financing this transaction for you, we will get back more than we are giving"—and, conversely, "We receive these funds in the belief that our future work with this new company will increase its value, so that we can bring you back more than you are giving." To make it all work through effective implementation is the key to successful mergers.[3]

Isn't this, in the end, what economic activity is all about? Nor merely sustaining our status quo but striving for something better—*a better life* for ourselves, our families, and our neighbors—here and in the next nation and the next generation? How can we deliver this improvement—this return on investment?

Certainly we can help shape and then abide by the policies of the many national and international organizations that work to preserve and improve our economic system. But the heart of improvement lies in a more immediate plane. Improvement can come best in the crafting of our business plans and business promises—including, importantly, our carefully considered agreements for M&A financing and refinancing.

E N D N O T E S

1. The authors offer this guidance on the basis of empirical research. Weston, as a veteran scholar in finance, is culling these ideas from his close reading of literally hundreds of empirical research papers over the past four decades, as well as from his own research in this field. Both authors believe that this short list summarizes the most important lessons of merger experience in this century. For a recent example of the research supporting this list, see the authors' article entitled "Do Deals Deliver on Postmerger Performance?" *Mergers & Acquisitions,* September/October 1998, pp. 34ff.

2. From *The Diary of Anaïs Nin,* Vol. 1, Fall, 1943.

3. Claudia H. Deutsch, "The Deal is Done, the Work Begins," *The New York Times,* April 4, 1999, pp. 1ff. For a comprehensive treatment of merger integration, see Alexandra R. Lajoux, *The Art of M&A Integration: A Guide to Merging Resources, Processes, and Responsibilities* (New York: McGraw-Hill, 1998).

Typical Subordination Provisions
of Publicly Issued Notes

Section 1.1. Agreement to Subordinate. The Company agrees, and the holders of the Subordinated Notes by accepting the Subordinated Notes agree, that the Indebtedness evidenced by the Subordinated Notes is subordinated in right of payment, to the extent and in the manner provided in this Article, to the prior payment in full of all Senior Debt of the Company and that the subordination is for the benefit of the holders of Senior Debt of the Company, but the Subordinated Notes shall in all respects rank *pari passu* with all other Subordinated Debt of the Company.

Section 1.2. Default on Senior Debt of the Company. No direct or indirect payment by the Company of principal of or interest on the Subordinated Notes whether pursuant to the terms of the Subordinated Notes or upon acceleration or otherwise shall be made if, at the time of such payment, there exists a default in the payment of all or any portion of principal of or interest on any Senior Debt of the Company (and the Trustee has received written notice thereof), and such default shall not have been cured or waived. In addition, during the continuance of any other event of default with respect to such Senior Debt pursuant to which the maturity thereof may be accelerated, upon the receipt by the Trustee of written notice from the holders of Senior Debt, no such payment may be made by the Company upon or in respect of the Subordinated Notes for a period of [180] days from the date of receipt of such notice; provided, however, that the holders of Senior Debt may give only [one] such notice in any 360-day period, and provided, further, that this provision shall not prevent the payment of an installment of principal of or interest on the Subordinated Notes for more than [180] days.

Section 1.3. Liquidation, Dissolution, Bankruptcy. Upon any distribution of the assets of the Company in any dissolution, winding up, liquidation, or reorganization of the Company (whether voluntary or involuntary and whether in bankruptcy, insolvency, or receivership proceeding or upon an assignment for the benefit of creditors or any marshaling of the assets and liabilities of the Company or otherwise):

421

1. Holders of Senior Debt of the Company shall be entitled to receive payment in full on the Senior Debt of the Company before the holders of the Subordinated Notes shall be entitled to receive any payment of principal of, or premium, if any, or interest on the Subordinated Notes; and

2. Until the Senior Debt of the Company is paid in full, any distribution to which the holders of the Subordinated Notes would be entitled but for this Article shall be made to holders of Senior Debt of the Company as their interests may appear. Consolidation or merger of the Company with the sale, conveyance, or lease of all or substantially all of its property to another corporation upon the terms and conditions otherwise permitted in this Agreement shall not be deemed a dissolution, winding up, liquidation, or reorganization for purposes of this Article.

Section 1.4. When Distribution Must Be Paid Over. If distributions are made to the holders of the Subordinated Notes that because of this Article should not have been made, the holders of the Subordinated Notes who received the distribution shall hold it in trust for the benefit of the holders of Senior Debt of the Company and pay it over to them as their interests may appear.

Section 1.5. Subrogation. After all Senior Debt of the Company is paid in full and until the Subordinated Notes are paid in full, the holders of the Subordinated Notes shall be subrogated to the rights of holders of Senior Debt of the Company to receive distributions applicable to Senior Debt of the Company. A distribution made under this Article to holders of Senior Debt of the Company that otherwise would have been made to the holders of the Subordinated Notes is not, as between the Company and the holder of the Subordinated Notes, a payment by the Company on Senior Debt of the Company.

Section 1.6. Relative Rights. This Article defines the relative rights of the holders of the Subordinated Notes and holders of Senior Debt of the Company. Nothing in this Agreement shall:

1. Impair, as between the Company and the holders of the Subordinated Notes, the obligation of the Company, which is absolute and unconditional, to pay principal of, premium, if any, and interest on the Subordinated Notes in accordance with their terms; or

2. Prevent the holders of the Subordinated Note from exercising their available remedies upon a Default, subject to the rights of holders of Senior Debt of the Company to receive any distribution otherwise payable to the holder of the Subordinated Notes.

Section 1.7. Subordination May Not Be Impaired by Company. No right of any holder of Senior Debt of the Company to enforce the subordination of the Subordinated Notes shall be impaired by any act or failure to act on the part of the Company or its failure to comply with this Agreement.

Section 1.8. Modification of Terms of Senior Debt. Any renewal or extension of the time of payment of any Senior Debt or the exercise by the holders of Senior Debt of any of their rights under any instrument creating or evidencing Senior Debt, including without limitation the waiver of any default thereunder, may be made or done without notice to or assent from the holders of Subordinated Notes or the Trustee.

No compromise, alteration, amendment, modification, extension, renewal, or other change of, or waiver, consent, or other action in respect of, any liability or obligation under or in respect of any Senior Debt or of any of the terms, covenants, or conditions of any indenture or other instrument under which any Senior Debt is outstanding, shall in any way alter or affect any of the provisions of this Article or of the Subordinated Notes relating to the subordination thereof.

Section 1.9. Reliance by Holders of Senior Debt on Subordination Provisions. The holders of the Subordinated Notes by accepting the Subordinated Notes acknowledge and agree that the foregoing subordination provisions are, and are intended to be, an inducement and a consideration to each holder of any Senior Debt, whether such Senior Debt was created or acquired before or after the issuance of the Subordinated Notes, to acquire and continue to hold, or to continue to hold, such Senior Debt and such holder of Senior Debt shall be deemed conclusively to have relied on such subordination provisions in acquiring and continuing to hold, or in continuing to hold, such Senior Debt.

Section 1.10. This Article Not to Prevent Events of Default. The failure to make a payment pursuant to the Subordinated Notes by reason of any provision in this Article shall not be construed as preventing the occurrence of a Default or an Event of Default. Nothing in this Article shall have any effect on the right of the holders of the Subordinated Notes to accelerate the maturity of the Subordinated Notes.

Section 1.11. Definition of Senior Debt. "Senior Debt" means the principal of, premium, if any, and interest on (1) all indebtedness incurred, assumed, or guaranteed by the Company, either before or after the date hereof, which is evidenced by an instrument of indebtedness or reflected on the accounting records of the Company as a payable (excluding any debt that by the terms of the instrument creating or evidencing the same is not superior in right of payment to the Subordinated Notes) including as Senior Debt (a) any amount payable with respect to any lease, conditional sale, or installment sale agreement or other financing instrument, or agreement that in accordance with generally accepted accounting principles is, at the date hereof or at the time the lease, conditional sale, or installment sale agreement, or other financing instrument or agreement is entered into, assumed, or guaranteed by the Company, required to be reflected as a liability on the face of the balance sheet of the Company; (b) all borrowings under any lines of credit, revolving credit agreements, or promissory notes from a bank or other financial renewals or extensions of any of the foregoing; (c) any amounts payable in respect of any interest rate exchange agreement, currency exchange agreement, or similar agreement; and (d) any subordinated indebtedness of a corporation merged with or into or acquired by the Company and (2) any renewals or extensions or refunding of any such Senior Debt or evidences of indebtedness issued in exchange for such Senior Debt.

Typical Subordination Provisions of Privately Placed Institutional Notes

Section 1.1. Agreement to Subordinate. The Subordinated Notes shall be subordinated to Senior Debt to the extent set forth in this Article, and the Subordinated Notes shall not be subordinated to any debt of the Company other than Senior Debt.

Section 1.2. Default on Senior Debt of the Company. In the event of a default in any payment of interest or principal in respect of any Senior Debt, whether at the stated maturity, by acceleration or otherwise, then no payment shall be made on account of principal of or interest or premium, if any, on the Subordinated Notes until such default shall have been cured or waived.

Section 1.3. Liquidation, Dissolution, Bankruptcy. In the event of (i) any insolvency, bankruptcy, liquidation, reorganization, or other similar proceedings or any receivership proceedings in connection therewith, relative to the Company or its assets, or (ii) any proceedings for voluntary liquidation, dissolution, or other winding up of the Company, whether or not involving insolvency or bankruptcy proceedings, then all principal of and interest (including postpetition interest), fees (commitment or other), expenses, and premium, if any, then due and payable on all Senior Debt shall first be paid in full, or such payment shall have been duly provided for in the manner set forth in the proviso to the next sentence, before any further payment on account of principal or interest, or premium, if any, is made upon the Subordinated Notes. In any of the proceedings referred to above, any payment or distribution of any kind or character, whether in cash, property, stock, or obligations, which may be payable or deliverable in respect of the Subordinated Notes shall be paid or delivered directly to the holders of the Senior Debt (or to a banking institution selected by the court or Person making the payment or delivery as designated by any holder of Senior Debt) for application in payment thereof, unless and until all Senior Debt shall have been paid in full, provided, however, that in the event that payment or delivery of such cash, property, stock, or obligations to the holders of the Subordinated Notes is authorized by a final non-appealable order or decree which takes into account the subordination of the Subordinated Notes to Senior Debt, and made by a court of competent jurisdiction in a reorganization proceedings under any applicable bankruptcy or reorganization law, no payment or delivery of such cash, property, stock, or obligations payable or deliverable with respect to the Subordinated Notes shall be made to the holders of Senior Debt. Anything in this Article to the contrary notwithstanding, no payment or delivery shall be made to holders of stock or obligations which are issued pursuant to reorganization, dissolution, or liquidation proceedings, or upon any merger, consolidation, sale, lease, transfer, or other disposal not prohibited by the provisions of this Agreement, by the Company, as reorganized, or by the corporation succeeding to the Company or acquiring its property and assets, if such stock or obligations are subordinate and junior at least to the extent provided in this Article to the payment of all Senior Debt then outstanding and to payment of any stock or obligations which are issued in exchange or substitution for any Senior Debt then outstanding.

Section 1.4. When Distribution Must Be Paid Over. In the event that the holder of any Subordinated Note shall receive any payment, property, stock, or obligations in respect of such Subordinated Note which such holder is not entitled to receive under the provisions of this Article, such holder will hold any amount so received in trust for the holders of Senior Debt and will forthwith turn over such payment to the holders of Senior Debt in the form received to be applied on Senior Debt. In the event of any liquidation, dissolution, or other winding up of the Company, or in the event of any receivership, insolvency, bankruptcy, assignment for the benefit of creditors, reorganization or arrangement with creditors, whether or not pursuant to bankruptcy laws, sale of all or substantially all of the assets, or any other marshaling of the assets and liabilities of the Company, holders of Subordinated Notes will at the request of holders of Senior Debt file any claim or other instrument of similar character necessary to enforce the obligations of the Company in respect of the Subordinated Notes.

Section 1.5. Subrogation. Upon payment in full of all Senior Debt the holders of the Subordinated Notes shall be subrogated to the rights of the holders of Senior Debt to receive payments of distributions of assets of the Company applicable to Senior Debt until the principal of the premium, if any, and interest on the Subordinated Notes shall have been paid in full, and, for the purposes of such subrogation, no payments to the holders of Senior Debt of any cash, property, stock, or obligations which the holders of Subordinated Debt would be entitled to receive except for the provisions of this Article shall, as between the Company and its creditors (other than the holders of Senior Debt) and the holders of the Subordinated Notes, be deemed to be a payment by the Company to or on account of Senior Debt.

Section 1.6. Relative Rights. The provisions of this Article are for the purpose of defining the relative rights of the holders of Senior Debt on the one hand, and the holders of the Subordinated Notes on the other hand, against the Company and its property; and nothing herein shall impair, as between the Company and the holders of the Subordinated Notes, the obligation of the Company, which is unconditional and absolute, to pay to the holders thereof the full amount of the principal thereof, and premium, if any, and interest thereon, in accordance with the terms thereof and the provisions hereof, and to comply with all of its covenants and agreements contained herein; nor shall anything herein prevent the holder of any Subordinated Notes from exercising all remedies otherwise permitted by applicable law or hereunder upon Default hereunder or under any Subordinated Note, subject to the rights, if any, under this Article of holders of Senior Debt to receive cash, property, stock, or obligations otherwise payable or deliverable to the holders of the Subordinated Notes and subject to the limitations on remedies contained in sections 1.5 and 1.9.

Section 1.7. Subordination May Not Be Impaired by the Company. No present or future holder of any Senior Debt shall be prejudiced in the right to enforce the subordination of the Subordinated Notes by any act or failure to act on the part of the Company.

Section 1.8. Modification of Terms of Senior Debt. Each holder of Subordinated Notes consents that, without the necessity of any reservation of rights against such holder of Subordinated Notes, and without notice to or further assent by such holder of Subordinated Notes, (a) any demand for payment of any Senior Debt may be rescinded in whole or in part and any Senior Debt may be continued, and the Senior Debt, or the liability of the Company or any other Person upon or for any part thereof, or any collateral security or guaranty therefor or right of offset with respect thereto, and any Senior Debt, may, from time to time, in whole or in part, be renewed, extended, modified, accelerated, compromised, waived, surrendered, or released and (b) any document or instrument evidencing or governing the terms of any Senior Debt or any collateral security documents or guaranties or documents in connection therewith may be amended, modified, supplemented, or terminated, in whole or part, as the holders of Senior Debt may deem advisable from time to time, and any collateral security at any time held by such holder or any collateral agent for the benefit of such holders for the payment of any of the Senior Debt may be sold, exchanged, waived, surrendered, or released, in each case all without notice to or further assent by the holders of Subordinated Notes which will remain bound under this Agreement, and all without impairing, abridging, releasing, or affecting the subordination provided for herein, notwithstanding any such renewal, extension, modification, acceleration, compromise, amendment, supplement, termination, sale, exchange, waiver, surrender, or release. Each holder of Subordinated Notes waives any and all notice of the creating, renewal, extension, or accrual of any of the Senior Debt and notice of or proof of reliance by any holders of Senior Debt upon this Agreement, and the Senior Debt shall conclusively be deemed to have been created, contracted, or incurred in reliance upon this Agreement, and all dealings between the Company and the holders of Senior Debt shall be deemed to have been consummated in reliance upon this Agreement. Each holder of Subordinated Notes acknowledges and agrees that the lenders in any refinancing have relied upon the subordination provided for herein in entering into such refinancing and in making funds available to the Company thereunder. Each holder of Subordinated Notes waives notice of or proof of reliance on this Agreement and protest, demand for payment, and notice of default.

Section 1.9. Limitations on Rights of Subordinated Noteholders to Accelerate. The right of the holders of Subordinated Notes to declare the Subordinated Notes to be immediately due and payable pursuant to this Agreement upon the occurrence and continuance of an Event of Default under this Agreement shall be subject to the following:

1. If such Event of Default shall arise solely out of a default in specified financial covenants, then such holders may only so declare the Subordinated Notes due and payable if the holder of any Senior Debt shall have declared to be due and payable any obligations of the Company in respect of Senior Debt by reason of a default in respect thereof;

2. If such Event of Default shall arise out of a failure to make payments on the senior debt then such holder may not so declare the Subordinated Notes due and payable until the earliest to occur of (a) the continuance of such Event of Default for 180 consecutive days, (b) the day upon which the next payment is actually made of principal of or interest on any Senior Debt, or (c) the day upon which holders of Senior Debt declare to be due and payable before its normal maturity any obligations of the Company in respect of Senior Debt.

Section 1.10. Definition of Senior Debt. "Senior Debt" means Debt which is not by its terms expressly subordinated in right of payment to other Debt.

"Debt" of any Person means (i) all indebtedness of such Person for borrowed money or for the deferred purchase price of property, (ii) all obligations under leases which shall have been or should be, in accordance with generally accepted accounting principles (GAAP, as defined herein), recorded as capital leases in respect of which such Person is liable as lessee, (iii) all indebtedness referred to in clause (i) or (ii) above secured by (or for which the holder of such indebtedness has an existing right, contingent or otherwise, to be secured by) any lien, security interest or other charge or encumbrance upon or in property (including, without limitation, accounts and contract rights) owned by such Person, (iv) all indebtedness referred to in clause (i) or (ii) above guaranteed directly or indirectly in any manner by such Person, or in effect guaranteed directly or indirectly by such Person through an agreement to pay or purchase such indebtedness or to advance or supply funds for the payment or purchase of such indebtedness, or to otherwise assure a creditor against loss, and (v) liabilities in respect of unfunded vested benefits under Plans and withdrawal liability incurred under ERISA by such Person or by such Person as a member of the Controlled Group to any Multiemployer Plan, provided that Debt shall not include trade and other accounts payable in the ordinary course of business in accordance with customary trade terms and which are not overdue for a period of more than 60 days, or, if overdue for a period of more than 60 days, as to which a dispute exists and adequate reserves in accordance with GAAP have been established on the books of such Person.

Typical Subordination Provisions of Seller Notes

Section 1.1. Agreement to Subordinate.   The obligations of the Company in respect of the principal of and interest on the Subordinated Notes shall be subordinate and junior in right of payment, to the extent and in the manner set forth in this Article, to any indebtedness of the Company in respect of Senior Debt.

Section 1.2. Default on Senior Debt of the Company.   No payment of principal of or interest or distribution of any kind on the Subordinated Notes shall be made at any time when a default has occurred and is continuing under any Senior Debt, and, if any such payment or distribution is made, then the holder of the Subordinated Notes will hold the same in trust and pay it over to the holders of the Senior Debt.

Section 1.3. Liquidation, Dissolution, Bankruptcy.   (a) In the event of any insolvency or bankruptcy proceedings, and any receivership, liquidation, reorganization, arrangement, readjustment, composition, or other similar proceedings in connection therewith, relative to the Company or to its creditors, as such, or to its property, or in the event of any proceedings for voluntary liquidation, dissolution, or other winding up of the Company, whether or not involving insolvency or bankruptcy, or in the event of any assignment by the Company for the benefit of creditors or in the event of any other marshaling of the assets of the Company, then the holders of Senior Debt shall be entitled to receive payment in full of all principal, premium, interest, fees, and charges on all Senior Debt (including interest thereon accruing after the commencement of any such proceedings) before the holder of the Subordinated Notes is entitled to receive any payment on account of principal or interest upon the Subordinated Notes, and to that end the holders of Senior Debt shall be entitled to receive for application in payment thereof any payment or distribution of any kind or character, whether in cash or property or securities, which may be payable or deliverable in any such proceedings in respect of the Subordinated Notes.

(b) In the event that the Subordinated Notes are declared due and payable before their expressed maturity because of the occurrence of an Event of Default (under circumstances when the provisions of the foregoing clause (a) shall not be applicable), the holders of the Senior Debt outstanding at the time the Subordinated Notes so become due and payable because of such occurrence of such Event of Default shall be entitled to receive payment in full of all principal of, and premium, interest, fees, and charges on, all Senior Debt before the holder of the Subordinated Notes is entitled to receive any payment on account of the principal of, or the interest on, the Subordinated Notes.

Section 1.4. Relative Rights and Subrogation.   The provisions of this Article shall not alter or affect, as between the Company and the holder of the Subordinated Notes, the obligations of the Company to pay in full the principal of and interest on the Subordinated Notes, which obligations are absolute and unconditional. In the event that by virtue of this Article any amounts paid or payable to the holder of the Subordinated Notes in respect of the Subordinated Notes shall instead be paid to the holders of Senior Debt, the holder of the Subordinated Notes shall to this extent be subrogated to the rights of such holders; provided, however, that no such rights of subrogation shall be asserted against the Company until the Senior Debt has been paid in full.

Section 1.5. Subordination May Not Be Impaired by the Company.   No present or future holder of Senior Debt shall be prejudiced in his right to enforce the subordination of the Subordinated Notes by any act or failure to act on the part of the Company. This subordination of the Subordinated Notes, and the rights of the holders of Senior Debt with respect thereto, shall not be affected by any amendment or other modification of any Senior Debt or any exercise or nonexercise of any right, power, or remedy with respect thereto.

Section 1.6. Modification of Terms of Senior Debt.   The holders of Senior Debt may, at any time, in their discretion, renew or extend the time of payment of Senior Debt so held or exercise any of their rights under the Senior Debt including, without limitation, the waiver of defaults thereunder and the amendment of any of the terms or provisions thereof (or any notice evidencing or creating the same), all without notice to or assent from the holder of the Subordinated Notes. No compromise, alteration, amendment, modification, extension, renewal, or other change of, or waiver, consent, or other action in respect of any liability or obligation under or in respect of, any terms, covenants, or conditions of the Senior Debt (or any instrument evidencing or creating the same) and no release of property subject to the lien of the Senior Debt (or any instrument evidencing or creating the same), whether or not such release is in accordance with the provisions of the Senior Debt (or any instrument evidencing or creating the same), shall in any way alter or affect any of the provisions of the Subordinated Notes.

Section 1.7. Restrictions on Holders of Subordinated Notes. (a) The terms of the Subordinated Notes shall not be modified without the prior written consent of the holders of the Senior Debt.

(b) The holder of the Subordinated Notes shall not take any action against the Company with respect to any Event of Default until and unless (i) any event described in Section 1.3(a) has occurred, or (ii) a holder of Senior Debt shall have accelerated payment of any Senior Debt obligation of the Company, or (iii) the Senior Debt shall have been paid in full.

(c) The holder of the Subordinated Notes shall provide to the Company, at any time and from time to time, at the Company's request and at no expense to the holder of the Subordinated Notes, a written acknowledgment by the holder of the Subordinated Notes addressed to any holder of Senior Debt to the effect that such holder is a holder of Senior Debt, provided that prior to furnishing such acknowledgment, the holder of the Subordinated Notes shall have received from the Company such information as the holder of the Subordinated Notes shall reasonably request demonstrating to the holder of Subordinated Notes reasonable satisfaction that such holder is a holder of Senior Debt.

Section 1.8. Definition of Senior Debt. "Senior Debt" means (i) any indebtedness of the Company in respect of a certain Revolving Credit and Security Agreement between the Company and [the specific Lender], including any advances or readvances under refunding or refinancings with the same or other lenders of the aforementioned loan agreement, (ii) [specific existing long-term indebtedness of the Company], and (iii) all trade debt of the Company.

INDEX

A reorganization, 87n4
AA (Arthur Anderson Enterprise Group), 11
Accel Partners, 250, 328
Accounting considerations:
    charges and fees, 223, 272–273
    International Accounting Standards
      Committee (IASC) on, 354, 412–413
    pooling of interests method, 68, 69–74, 82,
      83–84
    purchase method, 68, 74–77, **78,** 79–80, 82
    pushdown accounting, 85–86
    sale/leaseback, 112
    tax accounting elections, 412
Accounting Principles Board Opinions:
    No. 16 (APB 16) business combinations,
      68–69, 76, 82
    No. 17 (APB 17) goodwill amortization, 67
Accounts receivable, collateral for, 177
Accredited investor, Regulation D, 130
ACG (Association for Corporate Growth), 12
Acquisitions:
    cost determination, 24–25
    exit strategies by backers, 248–249
    holding foreign or U.S. corporation, 399
    M&A financing and refinancing, 5–6
ACU (Asian Currency Unit), 356, 373–374
Adjustments, 34, 48, 84
Administrative costs, 25
ADRs (American Depository Receipts), 369
Advance rate, borrowing base, 182
Advisory services, 216, 220, 241–244
"Affiliated group" for tax purposes, 53
Aftermarket trading, 221
Agency basis, underwriters, 221
AHP (American Home Products
    Corporation), 250
AICPA (American Institute of Certified Public
    Accountants), 185, 337
Alchemy Partners, 186
Aliens, immigration, 391, 397
Allied Stores, 50–51
Allocation period, 79
Alphabet stock, 143
Amazon.com, 141, 217

AMBI Inc., 250
Amendments, intercreditor agreements, 313
America Online, 217
American Depository Receipts (ADRs), 369
American Express, 228
American Home Products Corporation
    (AHP), 250
American Institute of Certified Public
    Accountants (AICPA), 185, 337
American Research and Development
    Corporation, 244
The American Scholar (Emerson), 415
Amortization, as stepped-up asset basis, 67
Angel Capital Electronic Network web site,
    248
Angel Investors Institute, 248
Angels, 235, 251
Announcement of start-up private equity
    fund, sample, 253–254
Antitakeover laws, 129–130
Arkebauer, James B., 223
Armenia Hotel, 96
Arthur Anderson Enterprise Group (AA), 11
Asian Currency Unit (ACU), 356, 373–374
Aspect Resources, 137
Aspect Telecommunications Corporation,
    272–273
Assessment of financing needs:
    basic principles, 17–21
    danger zones, 21–24
    estimation of value, 26–34
    selection of debt *vs.* equity, 35–40
    targeting amount, 24–25
Assets:
    asset basis and stepped-up deductibility,
      67
    asset-backed securities, 148
    asset-based financing and lenders, 10, 11,
      101, 170
    bond covenant restriction against sales of,
      207
    as collateral, 177
    costs allocated and purchase method,
      76–77, **78**

Note: Numbers in **bold** indicate additional display material; n indicates note.

Alexandra Reed Lajoux is president of Alexis & Company, a research and communications firm in Arlington, Virginia, and editor-in-chief of *Director's Monthly*, the official newsletter of the National Association of Corporate Directors in Washington, D.C. Dr. Lajoux is the author of *The Art of M&A Integration* and coauthor of *The Art of M&A: A Merger/Acquisition/Buyout Guide*, both published by McGraw-Hill. Her work has appeared in *International Business*, *Los Angeles Times*, *M&A Today*, *Mergers & Acquisitions*, *Trustee*, and numerous other publications. The former editor of *Mergers & Acquisitions*, Dr. Lajoux has two decades of experience speaking and writing about M&A. A graduate of Bennington College, she holds an M.B.A. from Loyola College and a Ph.D. in Comparative Literature from Princeton University.

J. Fred Weston is Professor Emeritus Recalled of Managerial Economics and Finance at the John E. Anderson Graduate School of Management at the University of California-Los Angeles. Since 1968 he has been Director of the UCLA Research Program on Takeovers and Restructuring. Dr. Weston has served as President of the American Finance Association, President of the Western Economic Association, and President of the Financial Management Association. He has also served as a member of the American Economic Association U.S. Census Advisory Committee. A Fellow of the National Association of Business Economists, he has been a consultant to business firms and governments on financial and economic policies since the early 1950s.

Dr. Weston is the author or coauthor of 29 books, including *Takeovers, Restructuring, and Corporate Governance,* Second Edition, Prentice Hall, 1998; *Managerial Finance,* Ninth Edition, Academic Publishing, 1998; and *Financial Theory and Corporate Policy,* Third Edition, Addison Wesley, 1988. He has published 145 articles in scholarly journals, including most recently *Business Economics, Financial Management,* and *Journal of Energy Finance and Development.* Dr. Weston holds an A.B., an M.B.A., and a Ph.D. in Finance from the University of Chicago.

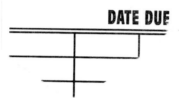

DATE DUE